W9-BSZ-126

Dedication

To my parents, Herbert and Margaret.
A.J.F.

Dedicated to the memories of my grandfather, Russell Dewey
Wiles, for those early investment lessons; my grandmother Mabel
Kappes, for her many positive examples; and my mother-in-law
Marjorie Yuskaitis, for her warmth and encouragement.

R.W.

How
MUTUAL
FUNDS
WORK

SECOND EDITION

Albert J. Fredman and Russ Wiles

Foreword by A. MICHAEL LIPPER
Lipper Analytical Services

NEW YORK INSTITUTE OF FINANCE

NEW YORK • TORONTO • SYDNEY • TOKYO • SINGAPORE

Library of Congress Cataloging in Publication Data

Fredman, Albert J.
    How mutual funds work / Albert J. Fredman and Russ Wiles.—2nd ed.
        p. cm.
    Includes index.
    ISBN 0-13-839721-X (paper)
    1. Mutual funds. 2. Investments. I. Wiles, Russ. II. Title.
HG4530.F73 1997
332.63'27—dc21   97-19142
                                                               CIP

© 1998 by Prentice Hall, Inc.

All rights reserved. No part of this book may be reproduced in any form or by any means, without permission in writing from the publisher.

This publication is designed to provide accurate and authoritative information in regard to the subject matter covered. It is sold with the understanding that the publisher is not engaged in rendering legal, accounting, or other professional service. If legal advice or other expert assistance is required, the services of a competent professional person should be sought.

From a Declaration of Principles Jointly Adapted by a committe of the American Bar Association and a Committee of Publishers and Associations.

Printed in the United States of America

10 9 8 7 6 5 4 3 2

ISBN 0-13-839721-X

ATTENTION: CORPORATIONS AND SCHOOLS
Prentice Hall books are available at quantity discounts with bulk purchase for educational, business, or sales promotional use. For information, please write to: Prentice Hall Special Sales, 240 Frisch Court, Paramus, New Jersey 07652. Please supply: title of book, ISBN, quantity, how the book will be used, date needed.

 NEW YORK INSTITUTE OF FINANCE
Paramus, NJ 07652

A Simon & Schuster Company

On the World Wide Web at http://www.phdirect.com

Prentice Hall International (UK) Limited, *London*
Prentice Hall of Australia Pty. Limited, *Sydney*
Prentice Hall Canada, Inc., *Toronto*
Prentice Hall Hispanoamericana, S.A., *Mexico*
Prentice Hall of India Private Limited, *New Delhi*
Prentice Hall of Japan, Inc., *Tokyo*
Simon & Schuster Asia Pte. Ltd., *Singapore*
Editora Prentice Hall do Brasil, Ltda., *Rio de Janeiro*

Foreword

How Mutual Funds Work is an excellent guide for those who are about to embark on what I hope will be a lifetime course of investing in mutual funds. For those who have already started, this book will highlight certain key areas that many investors have been overlooking. The best part of this work is that the information is presented clearly through words, not buried in an overwhelming display of numbers. It is written for people who think in words, not numbers. With that in mind, allow me to paint a word picture.

All of the great investors I've had the privilege to know view investing as an art form where the artist (investor) sees something that others do not see and has the vision and passion to commit to an uncertain future. Great artists do not paint by the numbers. If you will grant that investing is an art form, then a fund is like an art gallery, a collection of investments that are tied together by some overall feeling or attribute. As at an art gallery, different pieces of art (securities) will be sold at different times—hopefully at optimum prices.

What Al Fredman and Russ Wiles and I advocate is owning a portfolio of funds. This portfolio can be viewed as an art museum in that there are a number of different galleries within the museum, representing different approaches and probably created in different time frames. Fredman and Wiles are excellent museum guides who walk you through each of the galleries at your own pace. They start by helping you determine where you are by the use of a questionnaire. (I only wish some of the museum guides I have trailed behind had done the same.)

Most guide books, even museum guide books, are really sales documents and rarely give the reader a balanced view. This is not the case here as the authors discuss both the advantages and the disadvantages of mutual funds. They also provide you with some of the key tools of the trade used by fund analysts so that you will be able to assemble your own mix of funds. Perhaps their most important contribution to the fund investor is their recognition that risks are plural. There are many definitions of risk, but Fredman and Wiles quite properly focus on the key motivators that generate risks: fear and greed. This is the heart of their common-sense approach to fund investing, which they expand to both closed-end funds and variable annuities.

Just as good museum guides will go back and review what you have learned tromping through the many galleries, Fredman and Wiles give us one final Question-and-Answer section that brings together and amplifies many of the thoughts found throughout the book. In summary, this book equips you to get more value out of your multiple visits to the museum of fund investing. It does not—and cannot—guarantee your success, just a deeper understanding.

A. Michael Lipper, CFA
President
Lipper Analytical Services, Inc.

Introduction

Saying that mutual funds are in vogue is an understatement. Whether you're a Generation Xer, baby boomer or retiree, these investments can play a major role in your quest for a financially fit future. How you manage your nest egg now can mean the difference between comfort and security or barely scraping by. The investment-company industry has done a laudable job of creating a far-ranging assortment of fund flavors and offers a superb menu of shareholder services.

Now the crucial question is: What kinds of funds do you need and in what proportions? Mutual funds were designed to simplify investing but they've grown increasingly complex. There are more than 6,000 funds to choose from, in dozens of categories. You can find "growth" funds and "value" funds. There are passive as well as managed portfolios and a whole world of foreign-stock choices, including some that trade on exchanges. Funds can generate tax-free or taxable income. There are variable annuities for those who want more tax-deferred growth than traditional retirement plans can offer. Then there are closed-end funds that sometimes sell at compelling markdowns if you like to bargain hunt. The list of choices goes on and on.

You also have several ways to acquire funds. You can buy direct through a family, shop in a discount brokerage's "supermarket," or do both. You can create your own mix of funds or invest in an all-in-one portfolio. Perhaps you prefer a mutual-fund wrap account. If you need advice, you can deal through a full-service broker or financial planner. Of course, you could do it all on your own.

Individuals are taking greater responsibility for building their retirement nest eggs using IRAs, 401(k)s, and similar "defined-contribution" programs. Consequently, most people need to have a basic knowledge of how mutual funds work so they can use them to their best advantage. Unfortunately, too many people are their own worst enemies when it comes to investing. They often don't understand what they're buying—or even what they're paying. With so many choices, people risk making the wrong decisions. In addition to investing in inappropriate and high-cost portfolios, people sometimes buy duds. There's no shortage of laggards.

WHAT IT TAKES TO SUCCEED

What separates the winners from the losers? For starters, successful investors have three essential qualities: Emotional discipline, patience, and understanding. Most important, they know what not to do. They don't let fear and greed get the best of them, and they steer clear of investment rip-offs. They don't play it so conservatively that they lose money after taxes and inflation take their toll. They know how to manage risks and what perils to avoid. Successful people realize that there are no shortcuts—investing takes homework, and wealth-building needs time.

The first step is to take a close look at yourself because funds that are highly appropriate for one person may be totally unacceptable for another. We help you get started in Chapter 1 with a detailed questionnaire. You will become familiar with the different kinds of stock and bond market dangers and learn how to deal with them. Unfortunately, risk-free investments don't exist. Even seemingly safe harbors such as passbook savings accounts, certificates of deposit, and money-market mutual funds can be dangerous if you have too much of your nest egg anchored there.

ABOUT THIS BOOK

As authors, we approach our topic from two separate yet complementary perspectives. One of us is a professor of finance and the other a financial journalist. This combination enables us to bring you the most comprehensive, up-to-date, and readable book possible. Many mutual-fund books are superficial in their coverage and focus on a more limited range of topics, based on the writer's personal biases. We simply tell it like it is because we have no ax to grind, and no newsletter or service to sell.

How Mutual Funds Work is appropriate for a wide audience. Although geared primarily to the do-it-yourself investor who buys no-commission or low-load products, the information also is applicable for people who work with a broker or financial planner. These investors require an understanding of mutual funds to be sure their adviser is doing the best possible job.

In addition to its thorough treatment of mutual funds, *How Mutual Funds Work* includes detailed coverage of the stock and bond markets because understanding them is essential for investing successfully. For instance, our discussion of stock-market efficiency will help you evaluate the wisdom of keeping a portion of your nest egg in index funds, or unmanaged portfolios. As you'll see, most managed funds underperform their market benchmarks.

Unlike some other mutual-fund books, our objective is not to profile individual portfolios and tell you what to buy. No one knows which funds are going to perform best in the future. The financial world is simply too unpredictable. Rather, we provide you the background and tools to help you make better choices on an ongoing basis, which should lead to improved results.

Following in the footsteps of our popular first edition, we have prepared a thoroughly revised and expanded second edition of *How Mutual Funds Work* containing 26 information-packed chapters. Plenty of insightful illustrations can be found throughout the book, and each chapter contains one or two boxed-off discussions of high-interest topics. We have also compiled a comprehensive glossary and five helpful appendices.

Investment Trends

Since our first edition was published in 1993 a number of trends have become more pronounced. The following four are particularly noteworthy:

1. One-stop shopping in mutual-fund "supermarkets" has become highly popular. These superstores allow individuals to buy and sell funds from many families in a single brokerage account.

2. More investment tools have become available to individuals who use the computer and the Internet. Many mutual-fund companies now offer Web sites.

3. New products have appeared in the foreign-stock fund arena. These include exchange-traded, single-country index funds and portfolios that focus on emerging-stock markets.

4. The great bull market in U.S. stocks has continued to roar ahead, confounding many observers. In fact, 1995 and 1996 were the two best back-to-back years stocks have seen since the mid-1950s.

The generous returns earned since the bull market began in 1982 will probably diminish because extended periods of stellar performance are eventually followed by times of below-average results. Returns in the mid-teens are not sustainable decade after decade. Stocks have averaged about 10 percent a year over the long haul, and there's no reason for that number to change much. With the possibility of lower returns on the horizon, it's even more important to pay attention to fund costs, which reduce returns. Although industry assets have escalated, expenses have drifted upward. As in our first edition, we cover fund costs thoroughly, including transaction expenses associated with portfolio turnover.

New Chapters

The following are new chapters in our second edition:

- *Chapter 5:* "Getting Familiar with Market Indicators." Stock indexes are explained, their history is traced, and readers learn how indicators can be used to evaluate fund performance.

- *Chapter 9:* "Shopping for Discounts." Closed-end funds are more complicated than mutual funds, but these inefficiently priced investment vehicles can offer unique opportunities for bargain hunters.

- *Chapter 16:* "All About Money Market Funds." These popular products are covered in depth, including a thorough discussion of the different types of securities they hold, and tips on how to select the best money funds.

- *Chapter 19:* "Allocating Your Assets." You'll learn how to determine appropriate asset-class weights by considering factors such as your age, time horizon, and risk tolerance. Other topics include portfolio rebalancing, college planning, and investing in retirement.

- *Chapter 21:* "Fund 'Supermarkets' and Investment Advisers." All the essentials of buying mutual funds through discount brokerages are covered. For those who need an adviser, this chapter offers guidance in choosing one.

- *Chapter 23:* "Tax Considerations." Mutual-fund investing can get complicated at tax time. This chapter goes a long way toward clearing up the confusion.

- *Chapter 24:* "Using Your Computer." We explore such topics as computerized spreadsheets, fund databases, fund-company Web sites, and online investing.

- *Chapter 25:* "The Mutual-Fund Phenomenon." This chapter provides a short history of the mutual-fund industry and its growth. It concludes with two dozen steps for making the mutual fund phenomenon work for you.

Because of the growing importance of international investing, we have expanded our coverage in this edition from one to two chapters. After all, about 60% of the total value of the world's stock markets exists outside the United States. For reasons relating to diversification and growth, you should consider allocating a portion of your assets to foreign-stock funds. This is particularly prudent considering the prospects for somewhat lower returns on domestic equities.

The growth and maturation of the mutual-fund industry is the greatest investment success story of the 20th century. Of course, each person's experience with mutual funds will be different. As authors, our goal is to convey knowledge and understanding. But only you can supply the emotional discipline and patience so essential for successfully building wealth. We wish you well!

Acknowledgments

The authors thank Ellen Schneid Coleman, executive editor at Prentice Hall, for helping make a second edition of *How Mutual Funds Work* a reality. Barry Richardson and Zsuzsa Neff, also at Prentice Hall, were very helpful as well. We also are indebted to A. Michael Lipper, president of Lipper Analytical Services, Inc. for providing much of the mutual-fund data found in this book. The Investment Company Institute has provided considerable data and assistance. Analysts at Morningstar helped during our research. Individuals at many mutual-fund companies provided data and answered our countless questions. We are particularly indebted to the media representatives at Vanguard, T. Rowe Price, and Scudder. George Cole Scott, president of Closed-End Fund Advisors, offered valuable insights.

Al Fredman thanks Maria Crawford Scott, the editor of his quarterly mutual-fund column at the *AAII Journal*, for her continuing support. He also thanks Dennis J. O'Connor, Chair of the Finance Department at Cal State Fullerton, for support and encouragement. Donald B. Crane, also at Cal State Fullerton, provided useful comments.

Last but not least, we thank all those who purchased and read our first edition. The tremendous response we have received has motivated us to prepare this thoroughly revised and expanded second edition.

Contents

Foreword by A. Michael Lipper. . . . . *v*

Introduction . . . . *vii*

Acknowledgments . . . . *xii*

Chapter 1
Patience and Discipline Pay   1

Three Great Bull Markets 3
Dealing with Emotions 4
The Power of Compounding 6
Characteristics of a Disciplined Investor. 7
Knowing Yourself 9
Investor Questionnaire 9
How Much Should You Invest in Stocks? 14

Chapter 2
Understanding Mutual Funds 16

Mutual-Fund Characteristics 17
The Prospectus 21
A Fund's Objectives 22
Mutual-Fund Categories 22
Diversified or Not? 23
Open-End Funds That Close 24
Mutual-Fund Sales Charges 25
Voting on Fund Matters 26
Other Pooled Investments 27
Advantages of Mutual Funds 28
Mutual-Fund Drawbacks 30

Chapter 3
Blending Styles 32

Sorting by Size 33
Valuing Stocks 34
Growth, Value, or GARP? 34
Identifying Styles 36
Small-Stock Funds 38
Getting International Exposure 40
Indexing Pays 41

Chapter 4
Analyzing a Fund 42

Shareholder Distributions 42
Total Returns 44
Tracking Expenses 45
The Standard Fee Table 48
The Income Ratio 48
Portfolio-Turnover Rate 49
Published Performance Data 51
Considering Portfolio Size 52
Sizing Up Cash Flow 53
Analyzing Management 54
Don't Overrate Performance Ratings 55

Chapter 5
Getting Familiar with Market Indicators 57

How Indexes Work 58
A Short History of the "Dow" 60
Other Indicators 61
Market Indexes and Mutual Funds 65
Comparing Apples to Apples 66

Chapter 6
Living with Risk 67

Market Risk 69
Sector Risk 71
Inflation Risk 71
Asset-Class Risk 73
Simple Ways to Gauge Risk 73
Volatility Gauges 76
Why Standard Deviation 78
Gauging the Downside 79
Risk Pointers 79

Chapter 7
Profiting from Volatility 81

Greed and Fear 82
Market Timing 83
Asset Allocation 86
Dollar-Cost Averaging 86
Averaging through Thick and Thin 87
Value Averaging 89
Investing Large Lump Sums 91
Keeping Tabs on Your Manager 92
Set Your Sights on the Long Term 93

Chapter 8
The Virtues of Indexing 95

Regression to the Mean 96
Most Funds Lag 97

No Free Lunch 98
The Birth of Index Funds 99
Passive Resistance 100
How Efficient Is the Market? 101
Market Anomalies 101
What's Available 102
Building Your Portfolio 104
"Spiders" with 500 Legs 105
A Checklist for Index Investing 106

Chapter 9
Shopping for Discounts   108

The Roaring '20s. 109
Part Fund, Part Stock. 109
Many Choices 112
Closed-End Versus Open-End Funds 113
Why Invest in Closed-End Funds?. 114
Analyzing Discounts and Premiums 115
Market Price Versus NAV Returns. 120
Rights Offerings 121
Mergers, Open-Endings, and Liquidations. 122
Ten Classic Blunders 122

Chapter 10
Global Investing   124

Mutual Funds: Your Ticket Overseas. 125
Promising Opportunities. 125
Opportunities in Emerging Markets 128
Special Risk Considerations 131
Understanding Currencies 132

Chapter 11
Sizing Up World-Stock Portfolios   136

Broad-Based Packages. 137
More Specialized Choices 138

Narrowing Your Geographic Focus........................139
Country-Specific Index Funds 142
Do's and Don'ts for Global Investors 145

Chapter 12
Hybrid and Specialized Products   148

Hybrid Funds...148
Specialized Products 153
Socially Responsible Investing 160

Chapter 13
How Fixed-Income Securities Work   162

Money and Capital Markets.............................163
Why Invest in Fixed-Income Securities?..................163
Bond Characteristics 164
The Yield Curve 166
Primary Risk Factors 167
More on Interest-Rate Risk 168
Inflation Risk and Real Returns 170
Credit Risk 171
A Bondholder's Total Return 172
Interest-Rate Forecasts.................................173
"Fed Watching" 173
Yield Spreads 175
Bond Funds Versus Individual Bonds....................176

Chapter 14
Taxable Bond Funds   180

Grouping by Maturity..................................182
U.S. Government Bond Funds 182
Target-Maturity Funds 184
Mortgage-Backed Bonds...............................185
Corporate Bond Funds 186
High-Yield Bond Funds................................186
Foreign-Bond Funds 191

Flexible-Bond Funds 192
Tracking Expense Ratios 192
What the Management Fee Covers 193
Understanding Yields 194
A Word on Derivatives 196

Chapter 15
Shopping for Tax-Free Income   198

Tax Considerations 199
Characteristics of Munis 202
Risk Factors. 203
Classifying Muni-Bond Funds 204
Closed-End Portfolios 207
Unit Investment Trusts (UITs) 208
Selecting a Muni-Bond Fund 210

Chapter 16
All About Money-Market Funds   212

Money-Fund Applications 214
Portfolio Building Blocks 215
Money-Fund Choices 217
Risk and Return 218
Tax-Free Products. 221
Checking Expenses 222

Chapter 17
Mapping Out Your Retirement Strategy   225

Accounting for Inflation 226
Retirement Planning 101 226
Voluntary Retirement Plans 229
Managing Your Nest Egg 232
Tax-Deferred Compounding. 232
The Advantage of Starting Early 234
Increasing Your Purchasing Power 234
Moving Retirement Assets Around 237
Divvying Up Your Nest Egg. 238

Chapter 18
Sizing Up Variable Annuities 240

How Annuities Work. 241
Accumulation and Distribution 243
Sorting Out the Costs 246
Weighing the Criticisms 248
Getting Information. 251
Caveat Emptor 251

Chapter 19
Allocating Your Assets 253

An "All-Seasons" Mix 254
Questions to Ponder 255
A Life-Cycle Approach 257
Rebalancing to Your Targets 260
How Much Flexibility? 262
Avoiding Bonds 263
A College Portfolio. 264
Managing Your Nest Egg in Retirement 265

Chapter 20
Dealing with Your Fund Family 267

Getting Started 268
Shareholder Services 271

Chapter 21
Fund "Supermarkets" and Investment Advisers 279

The Supermarket Concept 280
The Perils of Margin 283
Dealing in Exchange-Traded Funds. 285
Do You Need Advice? 285

Chapter 22
When and How to Sell 293

Should You Bail Out?. 293
Withdrawing Gradually 296

Chapter 23
Tax Considerations 302

Sorting out Distributions. 303
Selling Shares 305
Dealing with the "Kiddie Tax" 309
Tax Efficiency 310

Chapter 24
Using Your Computer 313

Saving for Retirement 314
Screening for Winners. 316
Going Online 319
Tracking Your Holdings 322

Chapter 25
The Mutual-Fund Phenomenon 325

Why the Love Affair? 326
Observations and Cautions. 326
Making Mutual Funds Work 328

Chapter 26
Mutual Fund Q & A 334

Getting the Facts 334
Sizing Up a Fund. 336
Understanding the Market. 338
Stock Funds 339
Foreign-Stock Funds 340
Exchange-Traded Funds 342
Bond and Money-Market Funds 344
Managing Your Mutual-Fund Portfolio. 345
Tax Considerations 346
Behind the Scenes 347
Computerized Investing. 350
Fund Supermarkets 351

Glossary 353

Appendix 1
Resources for Mutual-Fund Investors 372

Appendix 2
Mutual-Fund Telephone Directories 376

Appendix 3
Total Return with Reinvestment 379

Appendix 4
Finding the Geometric Average Total Return 381

Appendix 5
Total Returns Can Be Shown in Three Different Ways 383

Index 385

CHAPTER 1

Patience and Discipline Pay

It was the age of jazz, silent movies, flappers, Babe Ruth, and the Model T Ford. But what most investors visualize when they think back to the Roaring Twenties was a four-week market panic in the fall of 1929 that sliced off one-third of the value of stock prices.

That trauma, and the ensuing decline that continued into the 1930s, turned off an entire generation to the idea of stock investing. These people focused their attention on bonds and bank accounts which, commencing in 1934, began to pay government-insured yields. The crash of 1929, in other words, scared millions of people out of the stock market.

Too bad.

The simple truth is that stock investments have greatly outpaced bonds and savings accounts throughout the 20th century, notwithstanding the calamity of 1929 and the early 1930s. Well-managed, diversified common-stock portfolios rank as one of the best means to accumulate wealth over the years. The fact that stocks are risky creates an opportunity for superior returns.

1

Table 1-1   Long-Term Performance of Stock Versus Bond Funds

	30 Years	25 Years	20 Years
Stock funds	10.9%	11.6%	14.3
Bond funds	8.1	8.4	9.2

Compound average annual total returns, assuming all dividends have been reinvested. Periods end 12/31/96.
Source: Lipper Analytical Services Inc.

Mutual funds have emerged as one of the most popular ways to invest in stocks, along with bonds and other securities. Americans have socked away roughly $4 trillion into more than 6,000 stock, bond, and money funds. Two of every five households owns at least one portfolio, with roughly 40 million individual shareholders. About half of the $4 trillion committed to mutual funds has been placed in stock portfolios.

How Mutual Funds Work provides thorough coverage of the most interesting and promising galaxy of the mutual-fund universe—the stock portfolios. Just look in Table 1-1 at the investment results for the past 30, 25, and 20 years, as calculated by Lipper Analytical Services Inc., a company that monitors fund performance. The past three decades, over which stocks returned an average of 10.9 percent a year, contained major bull and bear markets along with periods of economic and political trauma. Yet from this it's clear that stock funds fare better over long periods than do bond or "fixed-income" portfolios. And although the stock market can be highly erratic over short intervals, the results tend to smooth out over time.

For most people, well-managed stock or "equity" funds offer the best chance for a successful, long-term experience. Stock investments are especially suitable for younger people, who have many more years to compound wealth and can afford to accept greater risks. But this does not mean novices should make costly, rash mistakes by being overly aggressive. All they need to do is take moderate risks and let time work for them.

Equity investing also is important for many older individuals. People are living longer than ever before, and they need protection against inflation. Stock funds provide a dependable, long-term inflation hedge in the sense that they can be expected to appreciate faster than inflation is eroding your purchasing power. For example, over the recent three-decade period when stock funds returned a generous 10.9 percent a year, the consumer price index rose at about a 5 percent annual rate. Less volatile, dividend-oriented stock funds often work well for retired people, especially when combined with some bond and cash holdings.

Though we're clearly biased in favor of stock funds, we offer complete coverage of bond and money-market funds—including their risks—in Chapters 13, 14, 15, and 16. Fixed-income investments can play an essential role in a diversified portfolio even if the lion's share of your wealth is in equities.

Though stock investments offer excellent potential, they also come with many pitfalls, as most investors know. People may end up doing far worse with poorly selected equity instruments than they would by simply keeping their money in a passbook savings account. Stocks have a habit of badly misbehaving. They don't always do what their owners want.

Even stocks or stock funds that merely break even over time are really losers, because there is an "opportunity cost" to having an investment rise and fall and wind up where it started. You have to move ahead in the investment world just to stay even with inflation.

THREE GREAT BULL MARKETS

The 20th century has witnessed three major periods of rising or "bullish" stock prices. These intervals offer important lessons for today's investors.

- *The Roaring Twenties:* From 1921 to 1929, the Dow Jones Industrial Average rose nearly 600 percent.

- *The Post-War Golden Era:* From 1949 to 1966, the Dow advanced more than 600 percent.

- *The Roaring Eighties and Nineties:* From August 1982 through mid-1997, the Dow had ascended about 900 percent.

Bull markets make investors of all stripes look smart, but the good times do not last forever. The rising prices of the 1920s ended in a massive collapse that saw stocks plunge more than 80 percent by the time they hit bottom in 1932. Of course, things were a lot different then. People used borrowed money to buy stocks to a much greater extent than is possible today. Also, we didn't have the Securities and Exchange Commission or the important investor-protection laws that we have today.

In more recent times, investors suffered through the 1973-1974 bear market that saw the Dow decline about 45 percent. This was the stock market's worst setback since the Depression. The 1970s proved to be an even worse decade for stocks than the 1930s, on an inflation-adjusted basis. The 1980s witnessed a brief but painful crash on October 19, 1987, when prices plunged about 23 percent—the largest single-day drop ever.

Do Bear Markets Spook Investors?

The simple answer, of course, is yes. People grow fearful when their investments keep dropping, and for good reason. But research from the Investment Company Institute, the national fund-industry trade association, suggests that people are more disciplined and patient than you might think. The ICI looked at cash outflows from mutual funds between 1945 and 1995 and found that investors generally do not panic. The largest outflow within the half-century span of the study amounted to a mere 4.5 percent of stock-fund assets, during the 1987 tumble. Fund shareholders are experienced and have a long time horizon, the study concluded.

Why do we recount these dark moments of the stock market's past? So we can point out that periods of extraordinarily high returns are often followed by months or years of stagnation and despair. These, in turn, represent the best bargain-hunting times of all, because bear markets lay the seeds for the periods of rising prices that invariably follow.

DEALING WITH EMOTIONS

Many investors simply have not been able to harness the amazing long-term growth of the stock market for their own gain. They earn lower returns than they should, given the risks they assume. Incomplete investment knowledge may contribute to their problems, but for many people a lack of emotional discipline weighs more heavily. Controlling your emotions is one of the biggest hurdles you face as a long-term wealth builder.

You have probably heard the gibe, "If you're so smart, how come you're not rich?" Bright, knowledgeable individuals often make dumb investment decisions. People don't always act rationally, according to those who study a discipline known as "behavioral finance." People often act emotionally when making a money decision.

Investing Versus Speculation

The first step to winning is simply not losing. Betting big time on a few individual stocks is an easy way to get wiped out. Building wealth takes understanding, time, and patience.

It's important to distinguish between "investing" and "speculating." *Investors* hope to increase their purchasing power over time using diversified portfolios that match their personal objectives. They don't look to their portfolios for quick profits or excitement, though they are willing to accept calculated risks—such as periodic bear markets—as facts of life along their wealth-building journey. Investors have discipline and patience. They aim to accumulate assets gradually and as predictably as possible.

Conversely, *speculators* lay their money on the line in the hopes of making a quick buck. Wall Street has developed many products to satisfy their quest for fast profits, including penny stocks, options, futures, and speculative new stocks known as "initial public offerings," or IPOs. Speculators may strike it big once in a while, but their many losses typically outweigh the occasional large gains. Unreasonable expectations of making large profits can lead to their financial downfall. People who try to get rich quickly often experience the pain of becoming poor quickly.

Gambling

Gambling differs from speculating in that the odds for making money are far worse. In fact, the odds greatly favor the "house," whether it's a casino or state-lottery commission. The expected payoff from state lotteries and Las Vegas-style casino games is negative from the public's perspective. State lotteries on average return less than half of what they rake in. It's not misleading to say that a gambler accepts risk primarily for the thrill. A speculator at least perceives a favorable risk/reward tradeoff.

Another difference is that gamblers know the outcome of their wagers almost immediately—with, say, the roll of the dice—whereas speculators might have to wait weeks or even months to find out. Most people who gamble are seeking entertainment, not a means of earning a living or building a retirement nest egg. The risks that exist in gambling are created by the casino solely for purposes of the game. These are greatly different from the usual risks that exist in a business setting.

Spotting a Gambling Addiction

Some stock-market junkies embrace fast action, and relish risk. Their frenzied trading is actually a form of addictive behavior, like gambling. Some people are so impulsive that they can't take the time to properly research a stock or fund before jumping in—they're afraid of missing the boat! At-risk individuals are those who get out on a limb, sustain big losses, lie to conceal them, then keep bouncing back for more action. Some psychologists even specialize in treating these cases.

This book is designed for investors, not gamblers or speculators. By using mutual funds and following a sensible long-term buy-and-hold policy, people are less likely to trigger any latent speculative or gambling tendencies than they would by dabbling in penny stocks, options, and the like.

Playing It Too Safe

At the other extreme, you can find plenty of individuals who focus too heavily on guarding against losses. They find short-term declines so painful that it prevents them from trying for any gains. Many people fall in the trap of extrapolating temporary losses into the future, assuming they will continue indefinitely. They might respond by earmarking or "allocating" too large a slice of their assets to the most conservative investments such as money-market funds and certificates of deposit, practically ensuring long-term underperformance. With a better understanding of how mutual funds and the stock market work, these people could learn to live with a greater exposure to riskier investments and their heightened potential.

THE POWER OF COMPOUNDING

The first step in successful investing requires that you focus your attention on how money grows.

A key lesson involves compound interest. Time is extremely powerful in the financial world. Wealth builds up steadily, bit by bit. Table 1-2 shows the effect of compounding $1 at various rates of return over differing time horizons. Note that a single dollar invested at 10 percent for 40 years produces $45.26. The 10-percent rate is significant because this is roughly what stock funds have made over the long haul.

It's fine to invest money in a single lump sum, but you also can fare well by following a regular savings program. Depositing modest amounts monthly, quarterly, or yearly into a mutual fund can work big wonders, and you probably won't miss the money as much since it's put away gradually. Table 1-3 shows the impact of investing $1 annually at the same rates and over the same periods as in Table 1-2.

Table 1-2   The Power of Compounding a $1 Initial Investment

Rate of Return	Investment Time Horizon (Years)			
	5	10	20	40
4%	$1.22	$1.48	$2.19	$4.80
6	1.34	1.79	3.21	10.29
8	1.47	2.16	4.66	21.72
10	1.61	2.59	6.73	45.26
12	1.76	3.11	9.65	93.05

Table 1-3   The Power of Compounding a $1 Annual Investment

Rate of Return	Investment Time Horizon (Years)			
	5	10	20	40
4%	$5.42	$12.01	$29.78	$95.03
6	5.64	13.18	36.79	154.76
8	5.87	14.49	45.76	259.06
10	6.11	15.94	57.27	442.59
12	6.35	17.55	72.05	767.09

For example, an investment of $1 a year for 40 years at 10 percent pro-duces $442.59. Socking away $1,000 annually for 40 years at the same rate would produce $442,590.

The power of compound interest should not be taken lightly, especially by people trying to save for retirement, which is the top investment goal for many mutual-fund investors. By earning higher rates of return—and giving your money more years to work—you will build a larger nest egg.

Suppose Beth, a 25-year-old accountant, invests $2,000 at the start of each of the next 30 years. Further imagine she puts her money into a stock fund that earns 10 percent annually on average. Also assume that Beth uses a tax-sheltered retirement plan such as an Individual Retirement Account so her savings compound tax-deferred. Using a finance calculator, we find that she would have a $361,887 nest egg at the end of 30 years.

Consider the following three facts about compound interest:

1. A few extra years can make a huge difference in your final accumu-lation. Adding just seven years to Beth's 30-year investment period *doubles* her nest egg to $726,087.

2. A seemingly small increase in yield also can work wonders. Raising Beth's return from 10 percent to 12 percent would boost her account from $361,887 to $540,585, nearly a 50-percent gain.

3. Taken together, the seven extra years and the 2-percentage-point increase in return result in a $1,217,661 nest egg for Beth. That's more than three times the $361,887 accumulated under our original assumptions.

CHARACTERISTICS OF A DISCIPLINED INVESTOR

The ability to stick with a good plan might be the single most important quality of successful investors. As evident from our compounding example, your best shot at building up wealth is to put time on your side. You also want to avoid the temptation to stray from a chosen path. Do you have what it takes to be a disciplined investor? The following eight characteristics are vital:

1. *Careful planning.* Investing requires a certain amount of preparation. You should think through your next moves like a chess player, never buying or selling on the spur of the moment.

2. *A willingness to maintain some cash in reserve.* If you don't get in over your head, you're less likely to slip into a desperate situation where you're forced to sell at inopportune times. Paper losses aren't a real problem unless you lock them in. Keep savings for emergencies and planned expenditures separate from your long-term portfolio. Cash reserves also can be used to shop for bargains during corrections or bear markets.

3. *A willingness to stick to a regular savings plan.* Set aside as much money as you can each month. The surest way to build wealth is to invest more. A $50 monthly investment earning 10 percent yearly compounds to $316,204 after 40 years. If you can double the sum to $100, you would double your portfolio to $632,408.

4. *Patience.* Financial moves rarely pan out immediately. You need to stick with a buy-and-hold strategy through all seasons. Good times eventually follow the bad. Recent research suggests that mutual-fund shareholders tend to unload their investments too soon.

5. *Understanding.* It's essential to have a good knowledge of mutual funds and of the stock and bond markets. Of course, not all investments are easy to comprehend, nor are they worth learning about. It's a wise rule to invest only in what you can understand.

6. *Independence.* Successful investors like Warren Buffett, Peter Lynch, and Michael Price think for themselves—they don't let well-meaning relatives or friends mislead them. You need a certain amount of conviction, for which understanding is essential.

7. *Humility.* Disciplined investors don't set their sights on unrealistic payoffs. Rather, they aim to get rich slowly, but surely. Overly aggressive individuals are really speculating, or gambling, if they exaggerate the profit potential or underestimate the risks.

8. *A willingness to learn from mistakes.* Even the most successful market participants make mistakes. By examining your track record, you can see where you went wrong. Learn from past errors so you won't repeat them.

KNOWING YOURSELF

Not all investments make sense for everybody. Nor would a certain financial plan be suitable for every investor. You need to define your financial goals and estimate your time horizon. You also should develop a sense about your "risk tolerance"—your ability to live with temporary portfolio losses. In short, you need to get to know yourself so you can select the most appropriate investment mix to match your goals, within any self-imposed limits or constraints.

Three factors interact to determine your risk tolerance.

1. *Your age and time horizon.* Younger investors can accept more short-term volatility because they have more time to make up for losses, and because they may not have to dip into their nest eggs for decades. But even they will have to plan for certain inevitable expenditures and potential emergencies.

2. *Your assets and earning potential.* Like time, sufficient income can make up for investment setbacks. If you have a secure, high-paying job, and a sizable financial cushion, you can afford to be more aggressive. But if your job is "iffy" and you don't have much of a margin of error, you can't afford volatile investments even if you are young.

3. *Your emotional composition.* Some people are just plain nervous about money. They may not be able to live comfortably with a volatile portfolio even if they have other things going for them. If the prospect of loss keeps you awake at night, you might want to stay conservative. Just recognize that there are certain other perils that can result from maintaining too large a stake in money-market funds, certificates of deposit, and the like.

Finally, recognize that your risk tolerance may change with the seasons. Many people can accept more volatility in a long, rewarding bull market than they could in a nasty bear rout. Also, they might find that they're becoming more bold as their income rises, or more conservative as they age. For these reasons, a person's risk tolerance can be difficult to pinpoint.

INVESTOR QUESTIONNAIRE

To help determine your investment profile and risk tolerance, answer the following questions. Circle what seems to be the most appropriate response for each question. In most cases, there are no right or wrong answers.

1. **In which age group do you fall?**
   A) 30 or under

B) 31 to 44
C) 45 to 54
D) 55 to 64
E) 65 or over

2. **What is your investment time horizon—for how long can you let your money grow?**
   A) More than 20 years
   B) 15 to 20 years
   C) 10 to 14 years
   D) 5 to 9 years
   E) Under 5 years

3. **For how long have you been investing in mutual funds or directly in stocks or bonds?**
   A) More than 10 years
   B) 5 to 10 years
   C) 3 or 4 years
   D) 1 or 2 years
   E) Less than a year

4. **In which range does your household salary fall?**
   A) More than $100,000
   B) $75,000 to $100,000
   C) $50,000 to $75,000
   D) $25,000 to $50,000
   E) Less than $25,000

5. **How many dependents do you have, including grown children and elderly parents who depend on your financial assistance?**
   A) None
   B) 1
   C) 2
   D) 3 or 4
   E) 5 or more

6. **How do you expect your employment income will change over the next several years?**
   A) I anticipate a steadily growing income.
   B) I expect a fairly level income.
   C) I think it will fluctuate widely.
   D) I anticipate my income will probably trend downward.
   E) I fear I might lose my job or I plan to retire.

7. **Which statement best describes how you plan to add or subtract money from your investment portfolio in the near future?**
   A) I expect to add a significant amount of cash regularly to my portfolio.
   B) I think I can add only modest amounts of cash, on an infrequent basis.

C) I do not plan to funnel any more money to my portfolio, but I don't anticipate making any withdrawals either.

D) I will withdraw modest sums from my portfolio on a regular basis to help meet living expenses.

E) I must take out sizable amounts of money from my portfolio regularly to meet living expenses.

8. **How would you describe your financial "cushion" to meet unexpected emergencies such as the replacement of a stolen vehicle and major planned expenditures such as a down payment on a home?**

A) *More than adequate.* I have more than enough cash in a money-market fund and other short-term investments to meet my needs. I may even carry more insurance than I require.

B) *Adequate.* I have ample liquid assets. I have enough insurance and my monthly obligations are manageable.

C) *Borderline.* I have a modest amount of cash and some insurance. But I may need to dip into my investments or borrow in an emergency.

D) *Inadequate.* My reserves are insufficient at the present time.

9. **How important is a regular stream of investment income to you?**

A) *Unimportant.* My goal is to build up a nest egg over the long haul.

B) *Somewhat important for peace of mind.* I prefer a modest amount of income from my portfolio even though I don't really need it. I simply feel more comfortable holding investments that generate cash.

C) *Important.* Investment income helps make ends meet, but I'm not totally dependent on it.

D) *Highly important.* Investment income provides for the majority of my needs. I want investments that produce cash on a highly predictable basis.

10. **What's your attitude toward insurance?**

A) I don't believe in having any more insurance than is absolutely necessary.

B) I have adequate coverage, but I buy policies with high deductibles to lower my premiums.

C) I have adequate insurance and my deductibles are low.

D) I stay well-insured because I'm highly adverse to suffering large losses. I spend more for policies with low deductibles because I want maximum coverage.

11. **Which statement best describes your knowledge about investing?**

A) *Highly knowledgeable.* I have a very good understanding about how the stock and bond markets work, and I spend considerable time keeping up with financial happenings.

B) *Somewhat knowledgeable.* I have a fair comprehension of investing, but I'd like to know more.

C) *Minimal knowledge.* I don't know much about the financial world.

D) *Neophyte.* I know virtually nothing about investing and don't find the subject that interesting.

12. **Which of the following statements best describes your investment experience?**

    A) *Extensive.* I have invested in a variety of vehicles including stocks, bonds, and mutual funds. I'm a do-it-yourself investor. I have experienced a bear market or two.

    B) *Average.* I have some experience in mutual funds and stocks. I do my own research but sometimes use the advice of others.

    C) *Limited.* I have invested in mutual funds and a few stocks, but my expertise is limited and I rely on a financial professional to guide me.

    D) *Slight.* I mostly stick with savings vehicles such as certificates of deposit, although recently I have begun to participate in a tax-deferred retirement plan through work.

    E) *Virtually none.* I'm new to the area of investing.

13. **How would you react if your portfolio of stocks or stock funds plunged 30 percent in a bear market?**

    A) I wouldn't be upset because I have a long time horizon and could use this as an opportunity to invest more at bargain prices.

    B) I would be somewhat concerned because a 30-percent paper loss is substantial. I wouldn't throw in the towel and sell, though.

    C) I wouldn't feel comfortable in this situation. I'm not sure what I would do.

    D) I probably would sell before I lost even more money.

    E) I would not have invested in stocks in the first place because I can't tolerate the risks.

14. **Suppose you can invest $10,000 in one of five portfolios with preset payoffs but you won't know your outcome until five years from now. The two payoffs are equally likely. Which pair do you prefer?**

    A) Payoff of $50,000 or $5,000

    B) Payoff of $30,000 or $10,000

    C) Payoff of $25,000 or $12,000

    D) Payoff of $20,000 or $15,000

    E) Payoff of $18,000 or $17,000

15. **Which of the following statements best describes your investment philosophy?**

    A) I like to keep up with fast-moving investments day-to-day. These include options, futures, initial public offerings, and volatile mutual funds, and I like to invest using borrowed money.

    B) I expect my investments to "beat the market." Good fund managers should have no trouble outperforming market benchmarks such as the

Dow Jones Industrial Average, and I think I can do the same buying individual stocks.

C) I recognize that it's very difficult to beat a broad market indicator such as the Standard & Poor's 500 index. I would be happy if my stock investments just matched the market over the long pull.

D) My philosophy is to "play it safe" with money-market funds, high-quality bond funds, certificates of deposit, and individual bonds. Stocks are not for me.

Now total your points based on the values in the score key.

Risk Tolerance Score Key

Question	A	B	C	D	E
1	10	8	6	3	1
2	10	7	5	3	1
3	7	5	3	1	0
4	8	6	4	2	1
5	7	5	3	2	0
6	6	4	3	2	0
7	6	4	2	1	0
8	6	4	2	0	na
9	6	4	2	1	na
10	5	4	3	1	na
11	4	3	2	0	na
12	5	3	2	1	0
13	6	4	2	1	0
14	8	6	4	2	1
15	6	4	2	0	na

TOTAL = ___ POINTS

Your score can be interpreted as follows:

71 - 100 *Above-Average Risk Tolerance* Individuals scoring in the upper end of this range have significantly greater tolerance than those at the lower end, but people in both situations should put stocks and stock funds at the core of their portfolios.

46 - 70 *Average Risk Tolerance* Again, there is a large difference between those at the extreme ends of the range, but all investors in this second category should make at least some use of stocks or stock funds.

21 - 45   *Low Risk Tolerance*   Many in this range are older individuals who perhaps lack adequate financial resources or investment experience. If possible, they should maintain a small footing in stock investments in an attempt to stay ahead of inflation.

20 or less   *Extremely Intolerant of Risk*   People scoring this low are probably too conservative to enter the stock market.

HOW MUCH SHOULD YOU INVEST IN STOCKS?

The percentage of your investment pie that you place in the stock market is the most crucial dimension of your asset allocation. Equities are more volatile than bonds, which also can decline in price. In the mutual-fund world, money-market portfolios offer the ultimate in stability because their prices stay at $1 a share, while their yields change. However, bonds and, especially, money-market funds may not offer sufficient returns to offset the corrosive impact of inflation, particularly over several decades. Even at 3 percent a year or so, inflation can be a problem.

Your age is often the single most important determinant of your asset allocation, so consider the following age-specific guidelines as rough rules of thumb:

- Conservative investors with a fairly low risk tolerance should consider a stock allocation percentage equal to 100 minus their age. These people might split the balance—equal to their age—between cash and bonds. A conservative 30-year-old would have 70 percent in stocks and 30 percent in bond and money-market funds.

- Moderate investors might boost their stock allocation to 110 minus their age. A moderate 40-year-old would have a 70/30 split in favor of stocks and stock funds.

- Aggressive investors with a high risk tolerance could use 120 minus their age as a target. A bold 50-year-old would have 70 percent in the stock market.

Of course, the above percentages are not cast in stone. They're simply a starting point. In addition to figuring your stock-bond-cash split, you also need to determine how to divvy up your allocation among different subcategories, such as among large-stock, small-company, and international funds within the equity classification. Chapter 19 covers asset allocation in detail.

AT THE CLOSE

Stock investments have an exaggerated reputation for risk and an underappreciated profile for reward. In spite of major bear markets such as the crash of 1929, stocks have generated returns that greatly exceed those on competing investments, especially bonds and cash instruments.

One key to investing involves staying put for many years, thereby giving your stocks or stock mutual funds ample time to perform. Investing thus makes little sense for gamblers seeking quick thrills with their money. Disciplined investors are patient, knowledgeable, careful, and willing to stick to a savings plan. They also understand how much risk they can emotionally handle.

CHAPTER 2

Understanding Mutual Funds

An investor walked into a stock-brokerage office recently and was surprised to learn that the company preferred to sell mutual funds, not individual stocks, to new clients. Mutual funds, the woman was told, offer more diversification for less money, especially for people just getting started with only a few thousand dollars. "Besides," the broker said, "You don't want to be holding an individual stock on a day when the company reports lower profits—things can get nasty really fast."

Mutual funds increasingly are becoming the investments of choice for middle America. Funds have become so popular that they now outnumber companies on the New York and American stock exchanges combined. You can find portfolios that fit nearly every investment style, approach, and focus. So where should you begin?

People learn about funds in many ways. You might see their ads or articles about them in newspapers, magazines, investment newsletters, and electronic sources such as the Internet. Publications with ongoing coverage range from *The Arizona Republic* and *Investor's Business Daily* to *Mutual Funds Magazine* and the American Association of Individual Investors' *AAII Journal*.

They could be mentioned, or their managers interviewed, on television programs such as *"Wall Street Week."* Or your friends could be talking about them around the water cooler at work or at the kids' soccer match. But how should you check out a mutual fund? And how can you find the best ones?

A good place to start would be the library. Check your local newspaper and major national publications such as *The Wall Street Journal*, *Forbes*, *Barron's*, and *Money*. Look at one or more of the mutual-fund guidebooks for an overview. The major guidebooks are identified and briefly described in Appendix 1.

Two sources of information on every mutual fund are the shareholder report and the prospectus. To get these documents, you need a fund company's phone number or its Internet address. Most have toll-free 800 numbers, and many have Web sites. Appendix 2 lists phone numbers. The *Directory of Mutual Funds and Other Investment Companies* published annually by the Investment Company Institute (the national industry association) provides phone numbers, addresses, and a few other basic facts about more than 6,000 funds. The *Investor's Guide to Low-Cost Mutual Funds* from the Mutual Fund Education Alliance offers more in-depth coverage for no-load portfolios. See Appendix 1 for more details on these low-cost publications.

The Securities and Exchange Commission requires fund companies to prepare and issue both an annual and a semiannual shareholder report. The former provides the most detail and must contain a statement by independent auditors. Most fund groups also issue briefer quarterly reports. Among other things, the various shareholder reports list the investments within a portfolio.

In general, however, it makes little sense for shareholders to spend much time analyzing the stocks in a fund's portfolio for their investment potential. In fact, the most current report already may be out of date, especially if the manager trades a lot. But by reviewing the major holdings, you can at least determine whether management is on target. For example, if a small-stock fund holds lots of medium-sized companies and some blue chips, this might not be the kind of portfolio that's advertised. The shareholder reports also feature a summary of recent results, as well as comments by management about the future.

MUTUAL-FUND CHARACTERISTICS

A mutual fund is a diversified portfolio of stocks, bonds, or other investments run by a professional money manager or, in some cases, a management team. Funds must register with the Securities and Exchange Commission and meet specific requirements, such as those contained in the Investment Company Act of 1940. These regulations don't guarantee a fund will be profitable, but they do provide certain safeguards.

Understanding "NAV"

Mutual funds also are known as open-end funds because they stand ready to issue new shares to incoming investors at the current price or "net asset value" (NAV), plus any front-end "load" or sales charge. They also must stand ready to repurchase or "redeem" shares from investors exiting the fund at NAV, minus any back-end load or redemption charge. The NAV is calculated once a day based on closing market prices. The management company tallies each stock's price and multiplies these by the number of shares held by the fund. The NAV computation for a hypothetical fund is illustrated in Table 2-1.

NAV fluctuates from day to day based on changes in the values of the portfolio holdings. You can look up the prices or NAVs for individual funds by checking the daily mutual-fund tables in newspapers, or by calling the company directly. Not all portfolios appear in newspaper tables. Fund groups supply their prices daily to the National Association of Securities Dealers for distribution to wire services and then to the press. But a portfolio must have either $25 million in assets or 1,000 shareholders to gain entry to the NASD's automated quote service. Many newspapers prune the list even further because space is a costly commodity.

By calculating daily percentage changes in NAV, you can get a good idea about how volatile a particular portfolio is relative to other funds and market indexes, such as the Standard & Poor's 500. But long-term changes in NAV do not have the same significance as multiyear variations in a stock's price. For this reason, a fund's NAV isn't exactly like a stock's price, though there are similarities.

Think of it this way: If an equity fund never sold any of its holdings, changes in NAV over the years would closely mirror the performance of the stocks held. However, funds sell stocks and lock in or "realize" gains and losses. When they do, net capital gains must be distributed periodically to shareholders in accordance with IRS guidelines. When gains are paid, the NAV falls by the same per-share amount.

Table 2-1   Computation of Fund A's NAV

Cash and equivalent holdings	$200,000
Plus today's total market value of all stocks held	1,500,000
Equals total assets	$1,700,000
Less current liabilities (including accrued expenses)	100,000
Equals total net assets	$1,600,000
Divided by today's fund shares outstanding	100,000
Equals net asset value (NAV) per share	**$16.00**

Thus, because of these distributions, you can't track changes in a fund's NAV over the years the way you might monitor movement in a stock's price. To see how the fund did, you have to analyze it in terms of its "compound annual total return," which is easy enough to do. Chapter 4 explains this process.

Mutual-Fund Families

There are about 400 fund groups or "families." Most offer at least a few types of investment products, to give shareholders some choices. Money-market funds, which were popularized in the mid-1970s, served as the catalyst for the growth of families by providing a safe place for investors to park cash during rough periods in the stock or bond markets. The smallest groups generally consist of a money fund and a couple of additional choices, such as at least one stock and one bond portfolio. Most families are larger and some are huge. Families grow as they try to keep up with rivals, introducing new types of products so as not to be left behind in the competition for investor dollars.

Large well-known fund complexes include AIM, Alliance, American Century, American Funds, Dreyfus, Fidelity, Franklin/Templeton, Merrill Lynch, T. Rowe Price, Putnam, Scudder, Smith Barney, and Vanguard. Bigger families offer periodic newsletters, investment software, and other educational material to shareholders. In some groups, all the funds adhere to a particular philosophy such as "growth" or "value" investing. The former approach focuses on stocks with rapidly expanding earnings, whereas the latter targets unpopular companies selling at depressed prices.

Families may also have other distinguishing characteristics. For example, Vanguard prides itself on its rock-bottom expenses and an array of passive portfolios indexed to market benchmarks such as the S&P 500. T. Rowe Price, Scudder, and Templeton are noted for their expertise in international investing. Fidelity, the largest group, has more than 250 funds in its stable, including three dozen specialized "sector" or industry-specific portfolios. We could go on and on because there are many other excellent families with special qualities.

Investment Minimums

Virtually all fund companies set minimums for initial and subsequent investments. Most firms allow prospective shareholders to buy in with $1,000 to $3,000, although lower thresholds still can be found. The trend has been away from low minimums, however, because it's costly for a fund group to handle lots of small accounts. Minimums of $10,000 or more are found at a minority of funds. For instance, a few fixed-income portfolios impose higher minimums to hold down shareholder-servicing costs. The Fidelity Spartan, T. Rowe Price Summit, and Vanguard Admiral products are examples. So-called "institutional" funds, which are marketed to big investors such as pension funds and endowments, may require $1 million or more.

Most groups allow lower subsequent investments of perhaps $100 or less. Some fund groups will even waive their customary minimum if you agree to sign up for an automatic investment plan, whereby cash is shuttled regularly from your checking or savings account to the fund company. In addition, minimums are often lower for Individual Retirement Accounts—a maximum of $2,000 a year.

Structural Safeguards

It's important to emphasize that each mutual fund, whether it stands by itself or belongs to a family, is a separate company. Occasionally, you will see individual portfolios switch their allegiances. This is one of several inherent safeguards for investors made possible by the basic mutual-fund structure created by federal legislation. These safeguards are outlined below.

Shareholder ownership. A mutual fund is a corporation or trust owned by its hundreds or thousands of individual shareholders. It's the shareholders, not the management company, who bear the fund's investment risk.

Board of directors. Elected by shareholders, the board members are responsible for overall fund management and must keep a watchful eye on the management company. It's up to them to renew or reject the firm's contract each year. The SEC requires that boards include some independent, or outside, members.

Management company. This company handles daily administration and is usually the same firm that organized the fund. The management company also typically serves as the fund's "investment adviser," buying and selling stocks for the portfolio.

Investment adviser. This party runs the portfolio in accordance with the objectives spelled out in the "prospectus," or shareholder contract. The adviser earns a fee that it deducts directly from the portfolio in small amounts over the course of the year. This management fee, not the sales load, is what keeps the fund company in business. It typically runs between 0.5 percent and 1 percent a year. Most of the sales load goes to the broker selling the fund and his or her firm.

Independent custodian. The fund's assets—stocks, bonds, and cash—are kept by an independent third party, typically a bank or trust company. This arrangement protects shareholders against theft by management. The custodian also handles payments and receipts for the fund's investment transactions. The adviser merely buys and sells stocks or bonds on behalf of shareholders.

Transfer agent. This party handles sales and redemptions of fund shares, maintains shareholder records, computes NAV daily, and pays out dividends and capital gains. The transfer agent is usually a bank or trust company. Some fund families serve as their own transfer agents.

Principal underwriter (or fund distributor). Usually a management-company affiliate, the underwriter helps to sell fund shares to the public. The underwriter may act as a wholesaler, selling shares to brokerages which then sell to investors, or it might deal directly with the public.

THE PROSPECTUS

This legal document discloses certain key, standardized information about mutual funds. If you know what to look for, it can answer most of your investment questions. The federal Securities Act of 1933 requires fund distributors and dealers to provide potential investors with a current prospectus. The document must be updated at least annually. The SEC has simplified prospectus requirements in recent years, but in many cases the documents still can be tedious to wade through. Anyone wanting more details can request the fund's "Statement of Additional Information," also known as Part B of the prospectus. Conversely, "profile" or summary prospectuses also are becoming available. These shortened documents list key information at a glance.

Here's what to look for in a standard prospectus:

1. An explanation of the fund's goals or objectives.

2. A description of the strategy or the kinds of investments the fund focuses on.

3. The types of risk facing shareholders.

4. A table displaying the sales charges, if any, and operating expenses.

5. The fund's financial history, based on data in the financial-highlights table.

6. Annual returns for the past 10 years, or for the life of the fund, if shorter, contained in the financial-highlights table.

7. Information on the fund's investment adviser and advisory fees.

8. An explanation of how to purchase and redeem shares, including initial and subsequent investment minimums.

9. Descriptions of services offered, such as telephone-exchange privileges, automatic share-purchase plans, withdrawal plans, and tax-sheltered retirement programs.

10. Information on when and how shareholder distributions are paid.

Before anything else, seek out funds with the kinds of objectives you are looking for, as discussed below. Next, select the best portfolios you can find within a given category. You will need to consider several criteria, the most important of which are performance and costs. Chapter 4 shows how to pick the best funds.

A FUND'S OBJECTIVES

All mutual funds share the common goal of making money for shareholders. Otherwise, the primary objectives of any fund fit into one of three broad categories:

1. *Income.* The emphasis here is on producing a steady flow of dividend payments.

2. *Capital gains.* The manager concentrates on increasing the value of your investment through appreciation of the stocks and even bonds held.

3. *Income and capital gains.* A combination of the two.

Many funds also list "stability" or "capital preservation" as an ancillary goal.

Naturally, each objective has its drawbacks, and investors face certain tradeoffs. It would be virtually impossible to find a stock fund that simultaneously offers both generous income and exceptional capital gains. If you want maximum appreciation potential, you have to forego income. As another example, the most stable portfolio would be one invested exclusively in Treasury bills. But it would offer no growth potential and less in the way of dividends compared to funds that hold bonds.

There is, of course, much more to selecting a fund than merely finding one with the right objectives. You also must decide how you want the manager to reach these goals. For example, a growth fund could invest in domestic or foreign equities, or some combination. It might or might not use derivatives. It could be actively managed or follow a passive indexing strategy.

MUTUAL-FUND CATEGORIES

The simplest way to classify funds is to group them as stock, bond, or money-market portfolios. Then, you would want to fit them into various subclassifications. The distinction between different groupings isn't always clear-cut. Many funds fit easily into two or three. To be really sure about how to label a fund, you have to examine its underlying portfolio. For our purposes, stock and hybrid funds are grouped into the broad categories highlighted in Figure 2-1. Broadly speaking, bond portfolios are labeled as either taxable or tax-free. Chapter 14 provides a table that sorts out the fixed-income subclassifications.

DIVERSIFIED OR NOT?

One additional classification reflects the degree to which a portfolio spreads its investments around. Most funds are categorized as "diversified,"

Figure 2-1   Stock-Fund Categories and Their Objectives

DOMESTIC EQUITY

Capital appreciation	Maximum capital gains. May employ speculative strategies. Also labeled "aggressive growth."
Small company	Appreciation from companies with relatively low market capitalizations.
Micro cap	Appreciation from the tiniest firms.
Growth	Appreciation from larger, established, growing firms.
Growth and income	Appreciation and income from larger, established companies.
Equity income	Income and moderate growth from stocks paying above-average dividends.

FOREIGN EQUITY

Global	Growth from both foreign and domestic firms, emphasizing the former.
International	Growth from non-U.S. stocks spread around the world.
Emerging market	Growth from companies in developing countries.
Regional	Growth from companies in either Europe, Latin America, or Asia.
Single country	Growth from stocks in a specific nation.

OTHER EQUITY-ORIENTED PORTFOLIOS

Index	Appreciation and possible income from a portfolio that replicates a specific market index such as the S&P 500 or the Wilshire 5000.
Sector	Appreciation and perhaps income from firms in a particular industry.
Balanced	Income and growth from a fairly stable mix of stocks and bonds.
Asset allocation or flexible	Income and growth from a varying mix of stocks, bonds, and cash.

which means more than merely holding numerous stocks or bonds. In the fund business, this is a precise definition that signifies the following:

1. They invest no more than 5 percent of their assets in any single company. If a stock position should appreciate to more than 5 percent of assets, however, the excess need not be sold.

2. They own no more than 10 percent of the voting stock of any company.

Funds that don't follow these two guidelines for 75 percent of their assets are "nondiversified" and tend to be more volatile. The statement of objectives in the prospectus will reveal this information. However, to qualify for various tax treatments, all funds—nondiversified or not—must follow the above two guidelines for at least 50 percent of their assets. Only a small number of portfolios have chosen not to be diversified.

Why would a fund not want to be diversified? Some capital-appreciation portfolios find it easier to achieve their objectives by holding a smaller number of stocks, which lets them take bigger positions in a handful of companies. So too with many "sector" funds, which focus on stocks in a particular industry. In addition, a few funds that target big blue-chip stocks appear to be following billionaire Warren Buffett's highly successful approach of concentrating on a limited list of big companies. These funds may own two dozen or fewer stocks. The concentrated approach is a lot safer with well-established blue chips than with fledgling small stocks.

OPEN-END FUNDS THAT CLOSE

Certain mutual funds stop accepting new money when management believes assets have swelled to the point where additional cash could hurt performance. These are often highly successful small-stock funds that have been flooded with new money from investors eagerly stampeding to get on board. PBHG Limited stopped accepting cash after a single day in 1996, when assets topped $100 million. When a portfolio shuts its doors, it's said to be "closed." However, the situation is rarely permanent as closed funds can and often do reopen.

Too many assets within a fund can hurt performance. Most managers have a relatively small group of favorite stocks that they know well and have high hopes for. That list might number five, ten, or perhaps as many as two dozen. Most funds hold more than two dozen companies, of course. As a portfolio grows beyond the manager's top picks, he or she has no alternative but to start buying secondary choices. The bigger a fund gets, the more performance can be diluted by including additional second- and third-tier stocks. So even though diversification is good, too much can dampen the sizzle, especially of a small-stock fund.

MUTUAL-FUND SALES CHARGES

In earlier decades, there was a clear distinction between load and no-load funds. The former frequently levied an 8.5 percent up-front commission on both initial and subsequent purchases. The latter charged nothing. But the introduction of "12b-1" fees by the Securities and Exchange Commission in 1980 changed things. The two types of products started to blur. Whereas investors formerly had just chocolate and vanilla, they now face a confusing assortment of different flavors, or pricing structures, to choose from. Here are the key ingredients:

- *Front-end loads.* These up-front charges range from 3 to 6 percent or so. With larger purchases, the charge generally declines as specified discounts or "breakpoints" are reached. But to reach the first discount level, you might need to invest $50,000 or $100,000.

- *Ongoing 12b-1 fees.* These fees, named after a section of the SEC rule-book, allow funds to charge an annual levy for distribution costs, including commissions, advertising, and marketing. Such fees commonly range from 0.25 percent to a maximum of 1 percent a year. A fund with a front-end load might also carry a modest 12b-1 fee. Table 2-2 shows the amount of 12b-1 fees charged by mutual funds.

- *Contingent deferred sales charges (CDSCs).* Also known as "back-end loads," these charges often accompany a relatively large 12b-1 fee. The CDSC applies only if investors sell or redeem shares during the first several years after purchase. It may begin at 5 percent for redemptions during the first year, and decline by one percentage point each year thereafter until it phases out entirely.

You can buy mutual funds from investment companies directly and from brokerages, banks, insurers, and financial planners. You also can purchase them through your employer in a 401(k) or other tax-sheltered retirement plan. Where you buy determines what, if any, sales charge you pay.

Table 2-2   Rule 12b-1 Funds

Maximum Fee Range	Percent of All Funds
0.01% to 0.25%	22%
0.26% to 0.50%	10%
0.51% to 0.75%	8%
0.76% and up	20%
Non-12b-1 funds	40%

Source: Lipper Analytical Services Inc.

You often can choose how to pay your fees. Many funds offered through brokers or other salespeople provide A, B, and C shares as alternatives. "A" shares have a front-end load and usually a modest 12b-1 fee. "B" shares have no front-end load but levy a higher 12b-1 fee coupled with a contingent deferred sales charge. Typically, B shares automatically convert to A after 6 or 7 years. Finally, "C" shares have no front-end load or CDSC. Rather, they impose a relatively hefty "level" or ongoing load of perhaps 1 percent a year, coupled with a modest redemption charge of 1 percent or so if you sell within a certain period. The share-class nomenclature can differ somewhat among fund families, and additional classes are sometimes offered. For example, a special class may exist for institutional investors and another for fund-company employees; these usually represent the best deals! Load funds may offer a commission-free share class for regular investors but those shares can only be acquired through financial advisers who charge you a fee for their services.

Funds that sell direct to the public usually charge little or no commission. They are known as "no-loads." Some such portfolios might impose a modest 12b-1 fee of, say, 0.25 percent, or a redemption charge, so it's essential to study the fee table in the prospectus carefully.

There has been a trend in recent years toward purchasing more no-load funds. Investors have become increasingly sophisticated and realize that with a little study they can make their own choices. Funds with sales charges perform no better or worse than those without. Just because you're paying a sales charge does not imply you're getting something superior. Many studies have confirmed this fact.

That said, there are two reasons to consider buying a load fund. First, you might need someone to help you select funds and to monitor your portfolio. Second, you might favor a particular manager who only runs a load fund. Otherwise, you should lean to no-commission products.

VOTING ON FUND MATTERS

Unlike AT&T, General Motors, and other public companies, mutual funds do not hold regular shareholder meetings. They do, however, ask investors to vote on important proposals such as fundamental changes in investment policies. If some such major issue comes up, your fund must hold a shareholder meeting and issue a "proxy statement" discussing the agenda and seeking shareholder approval. You also will receive a "proxy card" in the packet, on which you should voice your opinion.

Shareholders receive one vote for each share they own, so if you hold 5,000 shares you are entitled to 5,000 votes. Although many investors routinely decline to participate, it's important to read the proxy material, vote, and then mail in your proxy card. Voting allows you to voice your approval or disapproval of the measures under consideration. It also helps to hold down the fund's expenses. Sending out proxy materials is costly. If a vote is postponed owing to insufficient response, the fund company must go to the expense of sending out additional proxies in a second attempt to garner sufficient votes. It's best for everyone concerned for shareholders to voice their opinions.

What sort of things might you be asked to vote on? Here are some examples:

1. *Changes in sales charges.* Your fund might want to switch from a load to a no-load format, or vice versa; or, management may hope to institute a 12b-1 fee.

2. *Changes in advisory fees.* Management might want to change from a "flat" management fee to an "incentive-fee" arrangement, which allows the firm to charge more when it delivers superior returns but requires it to reduce fees when performance lags. Or perhaps the company simply desires higher fees.

3. *Changes in investment policy.* Perhaps management wants more flexibility in selecting stocks or bonds. For example, a fund that focuses on Japanese securities may now wish to invest in other Pacific rim countries.

4. *Name changes.* The fund may propose to alter its name to one that's more descriptive of what it actually does. ABC Small-Cap might want to change its moniker to ABC Mid-Cap.

5. *Mergers and structural changes.* A fund may want to merge into another portfolio, or one family may seek a marriage with another. Perhaps a "closed-end" fund (which is explained next) might seek shareholder approval to convert to the open-end format.

OTHER POOLED INVESTMENTS

Mutual funds aren't the only form of investment in which shareholder dollars are pooled by a money-management firm. However, they are much more popular than the rival products described below.

Closed-End Funds

These diversified, professionally managed portfolios trade like regular stocks, usually on an exchange. Like mutual funds, they have an NAV. But they also have a separate market price, and the two can vary widely. In contrast to open-end funds, their closed-end relatives do not stand ready either to issue new shares or to redeem them. Chapter 9 tells how to spot bargains in this inefficient corner of the stock market.

Unit Investment Trusts (UITs)

These are unmanaged portfolios of stocks or bonds. A money-management firm puts together a portfolio that's designed to endure for a specified number of years. Once chosen, the mix of securities does not normally change. Although the number of unit trusts exceeds that of mutual funds, the dollar amount invested in them is much less. Most UITs invest in municipal bonds.

When a UIT is established, a sponsor such as Merrill Lynch or Nuveen assembles a portfolio of bonds or stocks. A trustee, typically a bank, holds the securities for safekeeping, collects income and principal payments, and remits them to unit holders. Bonds usually are held to maturity, but may be called by the issuer or sold when there's a danger of default or if money is needed to meet investor redemptions. New bonds cannot be acquired once a trust is assembled. Most UITs are broker-sold, and carry front-end loads ranging up to about 5.5 percent.

A trust normally isn't liquidated until the last of the bonds has matured, but it typically loses assets in the meantime. Principal flows back to investors from bonds that are called, sold prematurely, or mature. You can reinvest your interest and principal distributions back into a mutual fund, but not into a UIT. For this reason, trusts are most suitable for people seeking income.

Hedge Funds

These are private limited partnerships available only to very wealthy individuals or institutions. In contrast to mutual funds, they are relatively unregulated, cannot advertise, and have high minimum investments of $1 million or more. These funds often try to excel in both bull and bear markets, a goal that's nearly impossible to achieve. Hedge-fund managers have considerably more liberty than their mutual-fund counterparts and often engage in nontraditional tactics, such as betting a stock will drop in price by selling it short. Many of these portfolios are global in nature and bet huge sums on currencies as well as on different bond and stock markets in their quest for fast profits.

ADVANTAGES OF MUTUAL FUNDS

People with the time and skill to analyze companies can do well by picking individual stocks, but for most investors mutual funds are probably a better way to go. Funds offer several important advantages over direct ownership.

1. *Diversification.* This is the idea of spreading your eggs around into more than one basket. By holding at least 12 stocks, you avoid the

---

Selected Facts About Mutual Funds

- Mutual funds do not dominate the U.S. stock market. Mutual funds held about 15 percent of the $10.1 trillion total value of domestic shares at year-end 1996, according to figures from the Federal Reserve Bank.

- No mutual funds have collapsed or gone bankrupt since the Investment Company Act of 1940 was passed.

- Unlike most business corporations, a mutual fund's income is only taxed once—when received by the shareholders.

- Most mutual funds underperform market benchmarks such as the Standard & Poor's 500 index.

- It's virtually impossible to find a stock fund that will deliver exceptional returns in both up and down markets.

- A fund's costs and "volatility," or risk, are easier to predict than its returns. By sticking with low-cost funds, you improve your odds for success.

---

danger that one bad apple will turn your whole portfolio to mush. Funds own anywhere from two dozen or so stocks to several hundred. A diversified portfolio generally holds up well even if a few stocks get wiped out. Other stocks will do much better than expected, offsetting losses on the "dogs."

2. *Continuous professional management.* Mutual funds are run by skilled pros who are judged by the returns they generate. Those who don't produce lose their jobs. A number of managers, and management teams, have excellent track records.

3. *Economies of scale.* Mutual funds incur proportionately lower trading commissions than do individuals, even those who deal with the cheapest discount brokers. A fund might pay only a few cents a share on a very large stock transaction, whereas an individual might shell out 50 cents a share or more for that same stock. Lower transaction costs can translate into significantly better investment performance.

4. *Shareholder services.* Fund families offer automatic investment plans, retirement plans, recordkeeping for tax purposes, and systematic withdrawal plans, and they allow investors to make exchanges or switches between funds over the telephone. One of the most impor-

tant services is the automatic reinvestment of income dividends and capital gains distributions into additional shares. This is a good way to build your wealth more quickly.

5. *Liquidity.* This refers partly to the speed and ease with which an asset—such as a stock, bond, or mutual fund—may be purchased or sold. Highly liquid investments also can be traded with no significant negative price impact. Mutual funds typically offer more liquidity than individual stocks, bonds, or closed-end portfolios. Tens of thousands of dollars can be invested or redeemed at the fund's NAV for the day, plus or minus any load or redemption fee. And money can be switched between funds at little or no cost.

6. *Safety from loss due to unethical practices.* You can certainly lose money if your fund declines in price. But the probability of loss stemming from fraud, scandal, or bankruptcy involving the management company is very small. Since they transfer investment risk to shareholders, mutual-fund companies are not likely to go belly up themselves. Thus, they sidestep the problems that have afflicted certain thrifts, banks, and insurance companies. The legal structure and stringent regulation of mutual funds offer major safeguards.

MUTUAL-FUND DRAWBACKS

Critics argue that funds are boring because shareholders don't have any say as to which stocks are selected. You don't enjoy the same opportunities, as you do with individual stocks, of finding Wall Street's future darlings. That's a valid argument. Some people have been able to strike it rich with the right stock. But, there's also a danger of getting carried away and ending up with a big stake in a promising company that suddenly runs into deep trouble, plunges in value, and takes your life savings down with it. There's virtually no chance of that happening with stock funds because they are so widely diversified.

Mutual funds subject you to "management risk," or the danger that your investment pro will fizzle. Most funds do underperform the broad market benchmarks. And even though a fund has beaten the market in the past, there are no guarantees it will continue to do so. A star manager may leave or lose his or her touch. Individuals who stick with poorly run funds risk substantial underperformance, which can compound over time. However, it's not difficult to identify and avoid perennial losers. Chapter 4 shows how to select funds that offer a better than average chance for good future performance. In fact, investors in index mutual funds avoid management risk altogether. Chapter 8 covers these products.

Another potential drawback of mutual funds is that they must pay out a portion of their capital gains to shareholders each year, subjecting investors to ongoing taxes if the portfolio is held in a taxable account. By contrast, you could hold a stock for many years, deferring the realization of capital gains indefinitely. The same could be true of a bond that gains in value until the issue matures. Yet capital gains are not a problem if your fund is held in a tax-deferred retirement account such as an IRA or 401(k) plan. And there are other ways to deal with the tax issue. For example, Chapter 18 covers variable annuities, which offer tax deferral for investors with long time horizons.

AT THE CLOSE

The unique structure of mutual funds explains much of their heightened popularity. Fund companies pass investment risk to shareholders, thereby insulating a portfolio itself from bankruptcy dangers. Also, funds feature an unusual set of checks and balances that include independent directors and third-party custodians. These safeguards minimize the risk of loss from foul play.

Other fund advantages include affordable diversification, a wide selection of investments, and plentiful information. Shareholders can track prices daily in the newspaper and research detailed portfolio characteristics by checking the prospectus and related reports. Perhaps the major stumbling blocks are the high and sometimes-confusing fees that certain funds charge. But these annoyances can be minimized with commission-free products.

CHAPTER 3

Blending Styles

A woman came up to a well-known financial commentator following a speech he delivered to ask what he thought of a certain technology fund. The woman already owned a diversified stock fund and wanted to expand her stake in the technology arena. The commentator asked which fund she currently owned and recognized it as one that had taken nearly a 50-percent stake in the high-flying tech sector. He raised this word of caution and steered her into something else.

The anecdote illustrates an important lesson in the investment world: It's important to mix mutual funds to get broad diversification, and doing it right requires that you incorporate distinctly different types of funds, not just a larger number of them. Stock funds, in particular, offer a colorful assortment of choices. There are at least four different ways you can divvy up your equity allocation:

1. *By company size.* Just like clothing, stocks come in large, medium, small, and petite. Smaller firms offer more growth potential, but if

income and capital preservation are your top priorities, you should favor funds that target bigger, established outfits.

2. *By stock-picking style.* Not all fund managers share the same philosophy. "Growth" managers seek out firms with rapidly expanding earnings whereas "value" buffs want only the screaming bargains that have been passed over by others. Still other stock-pickers blend these two styles.

3. *By national orientation.* The world is getting smaller, and fund investors today have ample choices among both U.S. and foreign stock markets. For your non-U.S. allocation, you need to select among markets in developed countries as well as those in emerging nations. While riskier, the latter can offer greater growth potential.

4. *By the degree of management activity.* Most stock-fund managers actively seek out attractive issues, but some take the passive approach of merely buying the same companies as those included in popular market benchmarks such as the S&P 500. Your allocation between active and passive funds may depend on whether or not you think your fund manager can beat the market.

SORTING BY SIZE

To understand equity funds and their investment styles, you have to start at the beginning—with the stocks themselves. The most basic way of screening companies is by size. A stock's size, market value, or capitalization (or "cap") is simply the company's price per share times the number of outstanding shares. For example, if Emerging Growth Corp. trades at $15 and has 10 million shares outstanding, its capitalization is $150 million. Four different market-cap ranges exist, in roughly the following dollar amounts:

Micro cap	$10 million to $300 million
Small cap	$300 million to $1 billion
Mid cap	$1 billion to $5 billion
Large cap	More than $5 billion

These boundaries are not cast in stone. They vary according to different financial professionals. We provide them merely to give you a feel for the different size classifications. Keep in mind that smaller firms are normally subject to greater business and financial risks than their well-established big brothers. The trade-off is that they also might deliver larger profits if you have the time to be patient. We will return to size later in this chapter.

VALUING STOCKS

Size is not the only way to classify stocks. Over the years, investors have come up with numerous other approaches to evaluate companies. Four of the most common and widely used yardsticks are the following:

1. *Price-earnings ratio.* The P/E ratio is an indicator of a stock's popularity, where higher numbers reflect greater investor interest. A stock trading at $25 that earned $1.25 a share in profits over the past four quarters has a P/E of 20 ($25/$1.25). This, more precisely, is known as the "trailing" P/E. Analysts also use "forward" or expected earnings for the upcoming four quarters, especially when dealing with growth stocks. Average P/E ratios can be calculated for mutual funds too, reflecting cumulative numbers for stocks in a portfolio.

2. *Price-to-book-value ratio.* Another yardstick used by analysts measures the per-share price divided by the firm's "book value," or stockholders' equity, per share. Like P/E figures, this ratio reflects a stock's popularity. Many high-flying issues sell at lofty multiples of book, while others occasionally drop below one times book, especially if the firm is burdened with serious problems. In addition to average portfolio P/Es, *Morningstar Mutual Funds* and *The Value Line Mutual Fund Survey* report price-book ratios for the funds they cover.

3. *Dividend yield.* This measures the annual dividend divided by the stock's price. If a utility's dividend is $3.50 and its stock sells for $50 a share, the yield would be 7 percent. When P/Es and price-book ratios in general are high, yields will be low.

4. *The expected growth rate.* The projected appreciation of a company's revenues and earnings per share is a crucial variable in stock valuation. Higher anticipated growth rates are generally associated with higher P/Es but they also entail greater risk because the expected profits might not materialize.

GROWTH, VALUE, OR GARP?

Profits are what ultimately drive stock prices, but not all investors view profits in the same light. Growth managers seek companies promising dramatic increases in revenue and earnings. They typically search for smaller or medium-sized firms that they expect will expand significantly faster than the economy as a whole—generally at rates of 15 to 20 percent yearly. Unlike cyclical issues, genuine growth stocks should be able to post steadily improving profits regardless of natural fluctuations in the economy. For the most part, growth managers don't mind paying high prices to get the right stocks. The P/Es of favored firms could reach 40, 60, 80, or even higher. Thus, growth-oriented funds typically sport higher average P/E and price-book ratios than their value cousins.

Conversely, value investors search for firms that can be bought cheaply because the market is ignoring them. These outfits may sell at low ratios of price-to-earnings or book value, or they may have high dividend yields or "hidden" assets. Some managers will even buy bankrupt companies when they feel there's good potential for a turnaround. Value investors pinpoint why the stock is inexpensive, then look for a catalyst such as a change in management that hopefully can turn things around. Cheap stocks that stay cheap are obviously no bargain.

As contrarians, value managers are more patient, longer-term buyers than growth investors, who quickly head for cover when dark clouds appear. It often takes time for the market to recognize the intrinsic worth of a particular company. Thus, a value portfolio would tend to have lower turnover and assume less risk than a growth fund. Value stocks often are found in cyclical industries such as the automobile, chemical, construction, or financial-services businesses.

As with clothing styles, one investment approach could be hot for several years while another runs cold. Value managers tend to do best coming

---

Labeling Stocks

Wall Street professionals use terms such as "blue chip," "growth," "income," "cyclical," "defensive," and "special situation" to describe stocks. A company might simultaneously fit into two or more of these loose classifications. "Blue chips" are large, established, high-quality enterprises, such as those represented in the Dow Jones Industrial Average. In poker, blue chips are the most valuable.

"Growth stocks" tend to be small or medium-sized companies that are expected to enjoy substantially above-average earnings advances. They typically pay little or no dividends. "Income stocks," such as utilities and real estate investment trusts (or REITs), offer generous dividend yields. "Cyclical companies," such as automakers, see their profits fluctuate sharply over the business cycle. "Defensive stocks," such as supermarket and telephone companies, tend to resist profit declines during recessions. "Special situations" describe undervalued stocks that could suddenly appreciate if some favorable development occurs, such as the successful launch of a revolutionary new product or a badly needed change in management.

out of an economic slump as their teetering companies begin to recover. Growth seekers fare better during the advanced stages of a bull market, when investors turn more aggressive. A slowing economy hurts cyclical value issues. You can't predict the future, but you can smooth out the ups and downs by diversifying into both the growth and value camps. They tend to do well at different times.

Many managers stick to one investment style at all times, but others might modify their orientation with changing market conditions. In addition, some investors blend these styles, perhaps screening for companies they expect to grow at a rate at least equal to the stock's P/E. Wall Street uses the term "growth at a reasonable price," or GARP, to describe this approach. Investors may overreact to negative news or a disappointing quarter, sending a growth stock tumbling and putting it temporarily in the value camp. These kinds of companies offer the chance for a "double play"—accelerating earnings coupled with a rebounding P/E. The GARP strategy is a variant of the low-P/E approach, which can lead to superior long-run returns, according to many academic studies.

IDENTIFYING STYLES

Figure 3-1 lists 12 stock-fund styles. Equity funds vary in terms of both median market capitalization (or the size of companies in the portfolio) as well as the emphasis on growth or value. Morningstar includes a nine-category style box with profiles of individual stock funds so you can easily find out what approach your managers follow. Rival Value Line offers its own chart.

Small companies are more volatile than their larger relatives, and growth stocks shoulder more risk than value stocks. Thus, the ride gets wilder with small- and micro-cap growth funds, and it's most tranquil with the big-cap value outfits.

This underscores why it's important to include small, mid-sized, and large stocks in your allocation if you're investing primarily for appreciation and working with a fairly long time horizon. In addition, you can split your

Figure 3-1   Twelve Stock-Fund Styles

Value	Blend	Growth
Large-cap value	Large-cap blend	Large-cap growth
Mid-cap value	Mid-cap blend	Mid-cap growth
Small-cap value	Small-cap blend	Small-cap growth
Micro-cap value	Micro-cap blend	Micro-cap growth

cash between managers who follow the growth and value styles. Because the two approaches tend to do well at different times, it pays to have both.

Unfortunately, many managers don't cling steadfastly to their styles at all times. Some helmsmen modify their approach with changing markets, going with what currently appears to offer the greatest potential. This phenomenon is referred to as "style drift." For example, a small-stock manager might decide to shift a good chunk of the portfolio's assets to foreign companies, or a growth manager may decide to dabble in value shares. Check the Morningstar or Value Line style boxes if you have access to these publications, and check for style drift.

Getting Income from Mature Firms

So-called "equity-income" funds pursue a special kind of value investing. Managers of these portfolios focus primarily on dividend yields. They seek payouts significantly higher than that of the overall market. Their holdings include utility, financial, and natural-resource companies. Some of these funds hold modest amounts of convertible securities, bonds, and preferred stock. Many of their favored picks are companies that may be temporarily out of favor. Whole industries can be depressed at times, offering higher than normal yields.

Equity-income funds represent a relatively low-risk approach to investing in stocks. But by no means are they risk-free. High-yielding stocks tend to be especially sensitive to interest rates, as long-term bonds are. When rates rise, the prices of dividend stocks fall so that their yields can remain competitive with bonds.

While funds in the equity-income category tend to look more for dividends and less for appreciation than other stock portfolios, the distinction is not that clear cut. That's why you should study the prospectuses and top holdings of funds in this group to find the ones that do as they say.

Getting Growth from Mid-Sized Companies

Medium-sized stocks have produced better long-term returns than the big blue chips but are less volatile than small firms. Thus, they offer a compromise. Some well-known examples of second-tier corporations include Briggs & Stratton, Circuit City, Revco Drug Stores, Starbucks, and Wendy's International. The S&P 400 MidCap index has been tracking the performance of this group since 1991. The index contains both value and growth issues, with about a third of its components consisting of low-growth financial and utility equities. A number of mutual funds target this arena and some even have "mid-cap" in their names.

Why the growing interest in medium-sized stocks? It's because of the compromise factor. If you feel uneasy about venturing into the volatile small-stock arena, you may want to use a mid-cap offering instead. Medium-sized companies typically have surmounted the initial hurdles with which many smaller businesses are still struggling, but they also have a lot more growth potential than the big blue chips. If you really want more sizzle, however, you also need exposure to the truly small companies.

SMALL-STOCK FUNDS

This is one of our favorite groups, especially for younger investors. These funds share similarities with the capital-appreciation portfolios, and they sometimes get lumped together. But the latter are highly volatile and may use speculative strategies such as making big sector bets, "flipping"—moving quickly in and out of hot initial public offerings—and even selling stocks short. Many capital-appreciation managers concentrate on a fairly narrow list of holdings, including smaller, unfamiliar outfits.

Small-company funds are generally more conservative than those in the capital-appreciation group, so there is a distinction. Most have a growth orientation, but some search for value. The increased interest in foreign markets has resulted in global and international funds with a small-cap orientation. There also are some small-stock index portfolios.

Immature companies can grow at a faster rate than large firms because their expansion takes place on a smaller base of assets and revenues. It's much easier for a firm with revenues of $10 million to double its sales than it is for a firm with $10 billion to do so. Small corporations usually have a much narrower business focus than do large corporations—they typically make or market one or a few closely interrelated products or services. Their managers often have much more freedom and flexibility to be creative and to innovate. In fact, their owner-managers often hold a large slice of the firm's outstanding shares, providing them with a real incentive to do their best for all stockholders.

Small-stock funds generally operate in the Nasdaq stock market, a network of brokers and dealers linked by telephone and computer. The Washington-based National Association of Securities Dealers (NASD) oversees this market. Some managers might also shop for shares in the so-called "over-the-counter" or OTC market, an arena of tinier firms that also is regulated by the NASD but with less visibility than Nasdaq.

Small companies face plenty of risks, and many fledgling enterprises bite the dust. Obtaining financing is often a problem. The management team may be inexperienced or simply not trustworthy. And cut-throat competition from much larger firms could spell disaster. In addition, small stocks often are illiquid and thinly traded, which means their transaction costs are much greater. You need a skilled portfolio manager to succeed in this arena.

How Small Is "Small"?

The cutoff point for small stocks is not hard and fast. These companies typically range from $300 million in capitalization to around $1 billion. Some small-stock funds might hold even larger companies. A common reason for this is that a manager may have invested in a firm some time ago when it was a lot smaller. Known as "capitalization creep," this tendency becomes more apparent as a small-cap portfolio grows older and larger.

You can get a feel for the range of companies in a small-cap portfolio by examining the top holdings. The fewer names you recognize, the smaller the stocks. If possible, check the portfolio's median market cap, which both Morningstar and Value Line provide for the funds they track. This single number tells you a lot about the size of companies held.

The asset base of the fund itself is another factor to consider. Funds with assets of perhaps $400 million or less have an easier time investing in truly small stocks. There are two reasons for this. First, small companies tend to be illiquid. That means it's hard for a mutual fund to buy or sell a meaningful amount of shares without bumping up or undercutting the price in the process. Suppose an $80-million fund invests $2.4 million, or 3 percent of its assets, in a promising small firm. An $800-million fund would need to invest 10 times more, or $24 million, to give that same stock the identical 3-percent portfolio weighting. For a company with a limited number of shares available, this could drive the stock's price up by an intolerable amount.

Second, "diversified" funds are essentially limited by SEC regulations to owning no more than 10 percent of the outstanding shares of a given company. The 10-percent restriction is designed to protect investors, and to keep mutual funds from taking over control of companies in which they have large stakes. In part because of this regulation, larger small-cap funds may end up owning several hundred stocks. But too much diversification can be unfavorable in the small-company arena because it dilutes the impact of the most promising choices. It's best if managers can focus on a shorter list of issues about which they have particularly strong convictions. A manager's top 10 stock selections are bound to be better than picks 101 through 110. To reiterate, smaller portfolios are easier to operate.

Sizing Up the Relative P/E

Smaller companies normally trade at higher P/E ratios than mature, slow-growing firms because they offer more excitement and appreciation potential. Several fund families publish charts showing the historic P/E relationship between small and large stocks. For example, T. Rowe Price maintains such a chart using its own New Horizons Fund as a proxy for small companies. New Horizons has been investing in emerging-growth companies since it began in 1960.

Suppose New Horizons' P/E is 15 and the multiple for the S&P 500 is 10. That puts the relative P/E at 1.5, a historically normal reading. The relative P/E generally has varied between 1.0 to slightly above 2.0 since 1961. When the indicator gets close to 1.0, small stocks offer outstanding value. Conversely, as the barometer nears 2.0, small stocks can be viewed as especially pricey. The higher the relative P/E, the greater the risk of poor performance. But small caps can remain cheap or expensive for several years at a stretch. For this reason, mutual funds targeting those companies work best for investors with plenty of time to be patient.

Most small-stock managers emphasize growth, but an increasing number are focusing on value. The latter types of funds would tend to have a lower P/E than growth portfolios. To determine the P/E of a fund, you can call the company's phone reps. Or check figures provided by Morningstar or Value Line. P/Es for the S&P 500 are listed weekly in *Barron's*.

Investors who favor even smaller stocks can add a so-called "micro-cap" fund for good measure. These portfolios focus on the tiniest of companies, which have market values ranging up to about $300 million, depending on whom you ask. About 5,000 micro-cap stocks exist and most of them are neglected by Wall Street analysts, thereby providing opportunities for bargain hunters. Micro-cap enthusiasts believe these tiny companies can significantly outperform larger stocks over the long haul. But you have to be patient since young firms need lots of time to develop.

GETTING INTERNATIONAL EXPOSURE

About 60 percent of the value of the world's stocks exists outside the United States. Investing exclusively in American companies can be far too limiting. Many developing nations in Asia, Latin America, and other areas are growing at higher rates than the mature U.S. economy. Just as you may be able to get greater appreciation potential with smaller companies, you can also find more opportunities in countries that have not yet fully industrialized.

International diversification also can reduce volatility because stock markets in different countries generally don't move in lockstep—they can hit their peaks and valleys at different times. This has certainly been true of the U.S. and Japanese markets in recent years. It's also true with many emerging markets. Foreign nations usually carry greater economic, political, and stock-market risks, but these dangers can be minimized through diversification.

Investing in non-U.S. companies is an essential part of building a well-rounded portfolio. While many domestic-stock funds have stakes in foreign stocks and own large multinationals, you can improve your long-run performance by getting pure overseas exposure, both in emerging economies such as Brazil, China, and India as well as in larger developed nations such as

Japan, Canada, and Britain. Chapters 10 and 11 provide the background you need to internationalize your nest egg.

INDEXING PAYS

Still another way to mix your stock investments is to own both passively and actively managed funds. Index portfolios, which represent the passive approach, have experienced a surge in popularity in recent years, as investors have become more aware of how hard it is even for professional stock-pickers to beat the market.

Index funds have a lot going for them, and there are more portfolio choices than ever before. You can find index choices built around large, small, and medium-sized companies, as well as various foreign-stock choices. Low costs, the assurance of beating most active managers, and tax efficiency are big pluses, as we will demonstrate in Chapter 8.

The idea discussed in this chapter of mixing stock investments offers a great route to long-run growth. But it requires discipline and patience to set up a portfolio of diverse fund categories and styles, and then to stick with it.

AT THE CLOSE

Investors face no scarcity of choices when it comes to stock mutual funds. Portfolios distinguish themselves by the size of companies they hold, by investment style, by national orientation, and by the degree of management activity.

Growth funds, for instance, tend to be riskier and potentially more rewarding than their value counterparts. So, too, are products that target excitable small stocks. Before you sink money into any equity fund, you should look behind the label to make sure management does what the fund's name implies.

CHAPTER 4

Analyzing a Fund

At a financial conference, a stock-fund manager was stumped when a prospective shareholder asked what the fund's dollar investment minimum was and whether it was reduced for Individual Retirement Accounts. The manager had prepared to answer detailed questions about the portfolio holdings but was thrown for a loop by such simple shareholder-service queries. But he minimized any lingering embarrassment by reaching for the fund's prospectus and looking up the answers.

The prospectus is the key document for locating information about mutual funds. Think of it as the owners' manual for shareholders. It's a required disclosure pamphlet that all companies must distribute. Particularly useful is the financial-highlights table. It contains data about the past 10 years or the fund's life, whichever is shorter. You also can find this table in the annual and semiannual shareholder reports.

SHAREHOLDER DISTRIBUTIONS

This chapter discusses key elements of the financial-highlights table. Three years of information for a hypothetical fund appear in Table 4-1. Your first observation should be to note that mutual funds make two kinds of periodic payments to investors:

Table 4-1   Fund A's Financial-Highlights Table

	Year ended December 31		
SELECTED PER-SHARE DATA	**1997**	**1996**	**1995**
1. Net asset value, beginning of period	$8.20	$8.50	$8.00
Investment Operations			
2. Net investment income	0.10	0.08	0.05
3. Net realized and unrealized gain			
(loss) on investments	1.00	0.10	1.50
4. Total from investment operations	1.10	0.18	1.55
Less Distributions			
5. From net investment income	(0.10)	(0.08)	(0.05)
6. From net realized gain on			
investments	(0.70)	(0.40)	(1.00)
7. Total distributions	(0.80)	(0.48)	(1.05)
8. Net asset value, end of period	$8.50	$8.20	$8.50
9. Total return	+13.41%	+ 2.12%	+19.38%
RATIOS AND SUPPLEMENTAL DATA			
10. Net assets, end of period			
(000 omitted)	$335,750	$278,800	$272,000
11. Ratio of expenses to average			
net assets	1.20%	1.20%	1.09%
12. Ratio of net investment income			
to average net assets	1.20%	0.96%	0.61%
13. Portfolio turnover rate	61%	70%	55%
14. Average commission rate*	$0.0548	$0.0562	—

*Disclosure required by the SEC beginning 1996.

1. *Distributions from net investment income.* This consists of dividends and interest earned on the fund's portfolio, less expenses (line 2, Table 4-1). Mutual-fund dividends are then declared (line 5). Tax law requires funds to pay out at least 98 percent of their net investment income. The amounts in line 5 appear in parentheses because they are paid to shareholders.

2. *Distributions from net realized gain on investments.* Line 3 of the financial-highlights table reports the net realized and unrealized gain (loss) on investments. "Realized" refers to stock or bond positions that have been closed out at a profit or loss, whereas "unrealized"

refers to positions that are still open. At least 98 percent of any net realized gain must be distributed to shareholders (line 6). Like the income payment in line 5, these amounts are in parentheses. As evident in this illustration, there is no set percentage relationship between the numbers in lines 3 and 6.

Stock funds pay out income at least once a year, and many pay out quarterly. The frequency depends in part on the extent to which a portfolio focuses on income or on growth. Bond funds normally distribute income monthly. Current tax law requires capital-gains dividends to be declared prior to December 31 and distributed by January 31 of the following year. Capital-gains distributions are taxable to shareholders in the year declared. Either form of payment can be taken in cash or in additional shares. Figure 4-1 explains the key dates associated with shareholder distributions.

TOTAL RETURNS

The most important way to tell how well a fund performed is by checking its total return, which includes the impact of income and capital-gain payouts as well as changes in NAV. Yearly total returns for Fund A appear in line 9 (Table 4-1). Table 4-2 shows in detail how the result for 1997 was derived.

Figure 4-1   Dates Associated with Income or Capital-Gains Distributions

Record date	On this date the fund determines its "shareholders of record" who are entitled to the distribution.
Ex-dividend or ex-distribution date	Normally one business day after the record date. The fund's NAV falls by the amount of the distribution, although market movements that day may also affect NAV. Those who buy shares on or after the "ex" date don't get the payout.
Reinvestment date	Generally the same as the "ex" date. Distributions are reinvested at NAV in full and fractional shares for those who chose that option.
Payable date	Payment to those who did not elect reinvestment is made anywhere from a few days to several weeks following the record date.

Table 4-2   Computation of Fund A's 1997 Total Return

Change in Net Asset Value	
1. Net asset value at *end* of year	$8.50
2. *Less* net asset value at *beginning* of year	8.20
3. *Equals* increase in net asset value	$0.30
Total Dollar Return	
4. Distribution from net investment income	$0.10
5. *Plus* distribution from net realized gain on investments	0.70
6. *Plus* increase in net asset value	0.30
7. *Equals* total *dollar* return per share	$1.10
Total Rate of Return	**+13.41%**
(*Equals* line 7 *divided by* line 2)	

Total-return figures are net of expenses but do not normally show the impact of front-end loads or redemption fees. Total returns must be distinguished from the yield on an investment, which considers only income, not price changes.

The approach illustrated in Table 4-2 shows total return *without including the impact of reinvestment*. That is, it assumes all distributions are received at the end of the year in cash and not used to purchase additional shares. However, total returns are customarily calculated by fund families and tracking organizations assuming such payouts have been reinvested. Thus, the results will differ somewhat from those illustrated in Table 4-2, as explained in Appendix 3. It's worth noting that reinvesting dividends helps to build wealth faster.

The total returns appearing in the financial-highlights table normally track periods of one year. For longer time frames, fund companies and monitoring firms use a geometric (or compound) average annual return, which is calculated based on results in the individual years. This procedure, which is a bit more complicated, is explained and illustrated in Appendix 4.

Total return numbers for individual funds are commonly published in newspapers, magazines, and other sources. By themselves, the total returns say little. The numbers need to be analyzed on a comparative basis, as explained later in this chapter.

TRACKING EXPENSES

The expense ratio helps to shed light on a fund's efficiency and cost effectiveness. It is the ratio of total expenses to net assets (technically, average monthly net assets). Lower numbers are desirable because they translate into higher total returns. Past expense ratios can be found in the financial-high-lights table (line 11, Table 4-1).

The expense ratio includes the following kinds of costs:

1. *Administrative costs.* Included in this category are shareholder-servic-ing costs, custodian and transfer-agent fees, shareholder-report expenditures, legal fees, auditing fees, interest expense, and directors' fees.

2. *Management fees.* These fees are charged by the advisory firm for the investment-management functions it performs and generally range from 0.4 percent to more than 1.0 percent annually.

3. *12b-1 fees, if any.* These charges are used to pay a portion or all of the costs of marketing the fund's shares to investors. These fees com-monly range from 0.25 percent to a maximum of 1 percent yearly.

The management company subtracts the above costs from fund assets bit by bit rather than in one lump sum. They remain in force for as long as you own a fund. Some investors erroneously believe the expense ratio includes brokerage commissions the fund incurs to buy and sell stocks or bonds, but that's not so. We address commissions in the section on portfolio turnover later in this chapter.

Depending on the portfolio, expense ratios vary from well under 0.5 percent to more than 3 percent. The lowest numbers are found among plain-vanilla stock and bond index funds, which follow a passive strategy of buy-ing and holding the same issues included in popular averages such as the S&P 500. Small, sector-equity funds and focused foreign-stock portfolios run up some of the highest numbers. Table 4-3 contains median expense ratios for several objective groups as compiled by Lipper Analytical Services.

Table 4-3   Median Total Expense Ratios

Investment Objective	Expense Ratio
World equity	1.78%
Sector equity	1.51
World income	1.40
Balanced/mixed equity	1.32
General equity	1.30
Taxable fixed income	0.94
Municipal debt	0.89
Retail money market	0.67
S&P 500 index	0.37

Source: Lipper Analytical Services Inc.

In general, expense ratios below 1 percent are considered low for a stock fund. Sometimes you might have to accept a higher number if you want a particular type of portfolio. Here are some points to keep in mind:

- *Small funds tend to have higher expense ratios than large funds do.* The latter benefit from economies of scale because their legal fees, accounting costs, and even portfolio management costs—which are relatively fixed in nature—can be spread over a bigger asset base.

- *The management fee should decline as the fund grows.* The prospectus will tell you if the adviser plans to reduce the fee percentage as the portfolio's asset base swells. ABC Growth Fund may have a management fee of 0.7 percent for the first $100 million of assets, 0.6 percent for the next $400 million, and 0.5 percent for amounts above $500 million. Unfortunately, this practice of reducing fees is far from universal.

- *The expense ratio tends to be higher for funds that have smaller average account sizes.* These are often funds with lower minimum-investment thresholds of $1,000 or less. Smaller accounts lead to proportionately higher shareholder-servicing costs.

- *Funds that invest internationally tend to have significantly higher expense ratios than do domestic portfolios.* The former incur greater research and other costs associated with foreign stocks, including travel expenditures. But the important advantages of international diversification often outweigh the added cost, provided the portfolio is well managed.

- *Stock funds have higher expense ratios than do fixed-income portfolios.* It's important to recognize that low costs are particularly critical for bond-fund investors. That's because fixed-income portfolios generally produce skimpier long-run returns than stock products, making low costs even more critical.

- *"Funds of funds" often layer fees.* Some funds invest in other portfolios, rather than directly in individual securities. If there's a double layer of fees, that may put a big drag on performance. "All-in-the-family" products such as those offered by T. Rowe Price and Vanguard, which invest in selected funds within their own groups, do not layer fees.

When evaluating expense ratios, compare a given fund's current number with its past values to spot the trend. Also, compare the expense ratio with figures for other portfolios of about the same size. One thing to avoid for sure is a high 12b-1 fee, which can exert a huge drag on results if the investment is held for a long period.

Table 4-4   Comparing BBB Bond Fund's Assets and Expense Ratios

	Year					
	6	5	4	3	2	1
Net assets (in millions)	$700	$500	$325	$200	$145	$110
Expense ratio	1.50%	1.45%	1.25%	1.20%	1.19%	1.20%

In addition, watch out for portfolios that have been getting bigger over the years but hit up their shareholders with ever-expanding expense ratios. The hypothetical BBB Bond Fund in Table 4-4 shows an extreme case of what to avoid. Its expense ratio increases sharply as assets grow over the years. You want to see at least some modest benefits from economies of scale.

THE STANDARD FEE TABLE

The SEC requires all fees charged by funds to be summarized in a prominently displayed table in the prospectus. The fee table is one of the most important parts of this document and deserves careful consideration. It is divided into three sections:

1. A summary of shareholder transaction expenses.

2. A breakdown of the fund's operating expenses.

3. A standardized hypothetical example of the effect of fees over time.

The fee tables for two hypothetical funds are illustrated in Table 4-5. The funds are similar in most respects except that ABC features a 6-percent front-end load and no 12b-1 fee, whereas XYZ has no up-front charge but a 0.75-percent 12b-1 fee. The 12b-1 fee raises XYZ's annual expenses.

Note that these figures are cumulative. In other words, you would have paid $99 over three years by holding ABC Fund, not $99 in the third year alone. Watch out for funds that have temporarily capped their expenses at a certain level. This is often done for competitive purposes and is accomplished by waiving a portion of the advisory fee. A newer fund may promise to hold expenses to, say, 1.2 percent until December 31 of the following year. Examining a footnote in the prospectus reveals that, without the expense limitation, actual expenses would have been 1.6 percent instead of the capped 1.2 percent.

THE INCOME RATIO

Mutual funds also have an income ratio. It measures net investment income divided by average net assets. This statistic is akin to a dividend yield

Table 4-5   Sample Prospectus Fee Tables

Shareholder Transaction Expenses	ABC Fund	XYZ Fund
Maximum sales charge on purchases	6%	none
Maximum sales charge on reinvested dividends	none	none
Deferred sales charge on redemptions	none	none
Redemption fee	none	none
Exchange fee	none	none
Annual Fund Operating Expenses		
Management fee	0.80%	0.70%
12b-1 distribution fee	none	0.75
Other expenses	0.50	0.50
Total operating expenses	1.30%	1.95%

Hypothetical Example

You would pay the following expenses on a $1,000 investment in each fund assuming (1) a 5% annual return and (2) redemption at the end of each period.

	1 Year	3 Years	5 Years	10 Years
ABC Fund	$73	$99	$127	$208
XYZ Fund	20	62	106	229

on a stock. It's not as significant as total return since the latter is a complete measure of performance, while this ratio focuses just on the stock dividends or bond interest collected. The income ratio is found in the financial-highlights table (Table 4-1, line 12), and trends upward over the past three years for Fund A. For portfolios that concentrate solely on capital appreciation, this number would be very low, perhaps even negative if expenses top income. Conversely, for income-oriented equity funds and balanced portfolios, the ratio could be 4 to 5 percent or more.

PORTFOLIO-TURNOVER RATE

This gauge measures the amount of buying and selling done by management. It is defined as the lesser of assets purchased or sold divided by the fund's average net assets.

How do you interpret the numbers? A 100-percent turnover implies that management holds each stock or bond, on average, for one year. A 50-percent turnover says positions are retained for about two years, 200 percent for six months, and so on. The turnover for the average equity fund ranges from 75 to 85 percent, but you might see portfolios with ratios above 500 percent. At the other extreme, index funds might have minuscule turnovers of just 5 or 10 percent.

Turnover rates for stock funds generally fall into the following broad ranges:

Low turnover	Up to 30%
Average turnover	40% to 100%
High turnover	More than 120%

The portfolio turnover for past years is found in the fund's financial-highlights table. As with performance and expense numbers, compare turnover for similar types of funds and look at an average over several years. For example, Fund A's average over the three years reported was 62 percent (line 13, Table 4-1).

Turnover varies by type of fund and the investment philosophy of the manager. Some managers seek quick profits and tend to buy and sell aggressively. Others follow a long-term buy-and-hold strategy. Funds that rely on options, futures, and short-selling strategies can be expected to have higher turnovers and transaction costs. But unless this activity is accompanied by consistently good performance, look elsewhere. Other things being equal, high turnover is a drawback. Lean to stock funds with turnover ratios below 60 percent. A high number can mean excessive trading expenses.

A Few Words on Transaction Costs

You can spot the amount of brokerage commissions paid by a fund in its financial-highlights table. Line 14 in Table 4-1 provides an illustration. But there are other, more important cost components that are virtually impossible to document:

Dealer spreads. Every stock has both a bid and an asked (or offered) price. For example, ABC Corp. might be quoted at 20 bid, 20-1/4 asked. The fund manager, like other investors, would typically buy at the asked and sell at the bid. The 1/4-point difference is the dealer's spread. Funds typically pay only 2 to 8 cents a share in brokerage commissions, but they can't easily minimize the spread. Thus, it is generally a bigger cost component than are brokerage fees, especially if the manager deals in smaller, less liquid stocks.

Transaction-size effects. If the manager wants to buy or sell a lot of stock, he or she will face another pricing problem beyond the customary spread. A large purchase order, perhaps staggered over a period of days or weeks, exerts upward pressure on a stock's price. Big sell orders do the opposite. Suppose a helmsman wants to acquire 300,000 shares of a technology firm at a $25 target price. The shares may be driven up to $27 or $28 by the time the order is completed. The degree to which the quote changes would depend on three factors: the liquidity of the stock, the quantity of shares the manager wants to buy or sell, and how quickly he or she needs to make the trade. Transaction-size effects are particularly common among very large stock funds.

As noted, these factors do not show up in the prospectus, but they can impair performance nevertheless. This is why investors are often better off with funds that do little trading. It can be very costly.

PUBLISHED PERFORMANCE DATA

The most practical way to compare the results of different funds is to consult publications that regularly supply total-return numbers. *Barron's* quarterly report on mutual funds provides a comprehensive evaluation done by Lipper Analytical Services for the most recent quarter, year, three-year, five-year, and ten-year periods. *The Wall Street Journal* publishes a similar quarterly survey.

Investor's Business Daily gives a letter grade reflecting three-year performance for the funds it tracks. The paper supplies year-to-date results daily and the latest four-week results Tuesday through Thursday. Also included are the total assets managed by the fund companies, and their phone numbers. *The Wall Street Journal* supplies year-to-date performance and closing NAVs from Monday through Thursday, plus comprehensive mutual-fund results on Fridays that include year-to-date, four-week, and one-, three-, and five-year performance numbers based on Lipper Analytical data. Certain regional newspapers, such as *The Arizona Republic* in Phoenix, also supply rotating performance numbers and letter grades on different days of the week, plus phone numbers, sales charges, and other key information. Magazines such as *BusinessWeek, Forbes, Kiplinger's Personal Finance Magazine, Money,* and *Worth* also are good sources of fund performance data, though not on as timely a basis as newspapers.

For periods beyond one year, you may see fund performance listed as "cumulative" total returns. Or, you may see how $10,000 would have grown if it had been invested in the fund during various time frames. For the sake of both consistency and clarity, you may wish to convert these bigger numbers to a compound annual return, if this hasn't already been done. Appendix 5 explains how to make this conversion.

It is important to know how to study performance numbers once you've got them. Focus on results for the past 1, 3, and 5 years. Longer periods might be misleading, especially if there have been major changes in the fund or its management. Also, compare a fund's results with that of other portfolios having the same or similar objectives. It might be wrong to conclude that a small-stock fund has inferior management if the lackluster results came during a period when larger stocks sparkled. Gauge a small-stock fund against direct competitors and an appropriate index such as the Russell 2000.

Does Total Return Say It All?

Some mutual-fund experts will tell you to focus only on the bottom line. That is, study past total returns and their ups and downs, but ignore expense ratios and turnover numbers. This argument has some merit. The logic is that all costs—including management fees, administrative expenses, 12b-1 fees, plus turnover-related transaction costs—are automatically netted out when calculating per-share prices and thus total returns.

But this assumes that past performance is representative of the future. Our feeling is that expenses and turnovers are more predictable than total returns. Thus, if you start with a fund that has low expenses, low turnover, and good performance, your odds for success are a bit better.

As a footnote, front- and back-end loads generally are not netted out of published performance numbers the way ongoing expenses are. You would need to consult the fee table in the prospectus to get a realistic view of the impact of these sales charges.

What about funds with poor past performance? Generally, you should avoid those that have logged consistently subpar results over several years, unless the types of stocks that they target have done badly or their investment style has been out of favor. Studies have shown a tendency for long-term losers to continue doing poorly relative to others with the same objectives. This is particularly true for funds saddled with eye-popping expense ratios. Funds that underperform market benchmarks and their peers by even modest amounts can really lag over long periods.

CONSIDERING PORTFOLIO SIZE

A fund's asset base is another factor to consider. The financial-highlights table lists this information and shows how size has changed over time (Table 4-1, line 10). Mutual funds range from under $10 million to more than $10 billion. The largest, Fidelity Magellan, counts assets in excess of $50 billion. Most of the largest funds are stock portfolios.

Advantages of Small Portfolios

Size may affect performance for certain types of funds. In particular, small players have several distinct advantages.

- *Maneuverability.* Small funds are more nimble, in that it's simpler for their managers to reshuffle holdings. A $5-billion fund could not easily turn on a dime if it needed to eliminate certain big positions. Rather, a manager might have to feed unwanted stock back into the market gradually over a period of weeks or months, to minimize the price impact of selling large holdings.

- *Portfolio focus.* Small funds can target their holdings better, in that they can own fewer stocks. Small-company and capital-appreciation funds often can accomplish their objectives more easily by concentrating on a handful of favorite stocks, as explained in Chapters 2 and 3.

- *Relative performance.* It's hard for a large fund to beat the market. A giant portfolio will tend to perform like the market averages, or like an index fund, except that it's saddled with management and transaction costs. This cost disadvantage explains why large managed funds often trail market averages and index portfolios.

Advantages of Large Portfolios

But the size issue is not entirely one-sided. Despite the many factors favoring small funds, large ones often post better performance. They benefit from the following characteristics:

- *Lower expense ratios.* With more assets under management, large funds enjoy economies of scale. Other things being equal, lower costs lead to improved results.

- *Better talent.* The organizations that run large funds are the most prestigious and generally can pay top dollars to attract the best portfolio managers and analysts. They also have more people watching different areas of the market and therefore get broader coverage.

- *Trading edges.* Certain types of investments are well-suited to larger size. Money-market and bond portfolios are a case in point. Trades within these arenas tend to be very large, and better deals can be negotiated by managers swapping bigger blocks.

SIZING UP CASH FLOW

"Cash flow" refers to the net amount of new money invested in a mutual fund—the excess of purchases over redemptions. It should be expressed as a percentage of the portfolio's total assets to be meaningful. Suppose a capital-appreciation fund increased from $20 million to $40 million in a year. Assume further that $5 million of the advance was due to appreciation, and the other $15 million represented new shareholder money. The cash flow would therefore amount to 75 percent of the original $20 million.

During the late 1960s, fund analyst Alan Pope popularized the link between cash flow and performance. Pope observed that certain funds delivered stellar results for a few years, then faded noticeably. Did these managers suddenly lose their Midas touch? Pope concluded that performance did well when substantial sums of new money cascaded in, and then cooled off when the flow stopped.

Why might a large net cash inflow favorably affect performance? Consider the following three reasons:

1. *The manager can use the new money to add to existing positions.* This additional demand will normally raise the price of the stock; more so if the fund invests in smaller firms with fewer shares outstanding.

2. *The manager would not have to sell one stock to buy another.* The new money could be invested in the second company, allowing the first issue to remain in the portfolio with an additional chance to blossom.

3. *A large cash flow occurring as the market peaks could be retained as a cushion against an ensuing decline.* Thus, the manager would not be forced to sell existing holdings to meet shareholder redemptions, and could use the money later to pick up some bargains.

Experts disagree as to how important cash flow really is. Despite the intuitive appeal, it is only a minor factor in fund selection because future cash flows can be hard to predict. Also, a huge increase near a market peak could be a headache for a manager who tries to stay fully invested. The extra cash could force him or her to embark on a shopping spree at a time of high prices.

Cash Flow in Reverse Spells Trouble

Large, consistent net redemptions are a definite red flag. It means investors are bailing out because they are unhappy with the performance, the imposition of new fees, or some other negative development. This can force the managers to hold larger cash balances than they would like and to sell off stocks to meet redemptions. As the portfolio shrinks, the managers might lose enthusiasm and self-confidence, and the expense ratio could rise. A trend of declining net assets over the years signals a pattern of redemptions.

ANALYZING MANAGEMENT

A portfolio is only as good as the people who run it. But how do you evaluate them? It's easy. Most of what has been covered in this chapter reflects the quality of management.

Performance is the bottom line. Good managers don't let transaction costs get out of control by doing a lot of trading. Nor do they constantly alter the mix of companies in the portfolio. Rather, they take a longer-term viewpoint. Superior fund families don't get greedy with the advisory fee. They want to attract more investors and increase assets over the years. When it comes to analyzing management, consider the following questions:

- How long has the manager been running the fund? It's best to have the same person at the helm for five years or longer.

- What is the manager's background? If the person running the show has been at the fund for less than five years, look for related work experience and good education credentials. You should be able to get this information from the fund company or a research service like Morningstar or Value Line.

- Is the fund run by an individual or a team? Depending on how a team is organized, it may result in more stable performance. If the managers operate independently, as is the case at American Funds, a bad year for one person could be offset by better results from the others. The team approach also ensures management continuity. There's less disruption if only one of perhaps five or six managers leaves.

On the other hand, many observers feel that talented professionals work best by themselves. If they are forced to compromise with others in a group, they may not be as creative, or their results might be diluted. The majority of funds are managed by a single person rather than by committee.

DON'T OVERRATE PERFORMANCE RATINGS

Fund researchers such as Morningstar and Value Line offer mutual-fund ratings over various periods. The Morningstar and Value Line measures gauge "risk-adjusted performance" and rank funds on a five-point scale that considers their risk or volatility as well as their raw returns. Because rational investors like returns and dislike risk, the higher a portfolio's return relative to its volatility, the better its rating. Chapter 6 covers risk in depth.

A word to the wise: It's fine to use these ratings as one piece of information in your quest for the best funds, but don't place too much reliance on them. They reflect past results, which might not be repeated in the future. Ratings can serve as a good starting point when you're searching for top funds, but you'll have to do your homework and dig deeper.

AT THE CLOSE

Predicting future top funds remains more of an art than a science. Still, several factors can help foretell good or bad performance. In general, you should favor low-expense funds, portfolios that are growing moderately in size, and those with modest turnover ratios. Past performance results are tricky—they can be insightful, but might also be misleading.

Most of the information you need can be found in a fund's prospectus. You should be able to read and understand this report, especially the financial-highlights table that it contains.

CHAPTER 5

Getting Familiar with Market Indicators

People make comparisons all the time. We check out the neighbors' lawns. We evaluate how colleagues at work dress. We study the cars other people drive. In the investment arena, we gauge the performance of our stocks, bonds, or mutual funds against broad market indicators. Chances are, we first ask how the market did as a whole before we inquire about our particular holdings.

Market indexes have been designed entirely for this purpose, as measuring tools. They tell at a glance how a representative group of stocks, bonds, or funds has performed. Indexes play a vital role in mutual-fund investing for several reasons: They give you a feel for the market's behavior, they serve as a gauge of value, and they facilitate performance comparisons. The total return on a market index reflects the results obtained by following a buy-and-hold policy. Investors hope that their actively managed funds will do as well or better. Indexes also can be used to measure risk. Chapter 6 discusses the concept of "beta." This common risk measure expresses the volatility of a portfolio relative to the ups and downs of a particular index such as the Standard & Poor's 500 or the Wilshire 5000. And, of course, market indicators are the basis for index funds. These increasingly popular, common-sense vehicles are covered in Chapter 8. With a better understanding of the various indexes, you will have a better feel for the differences among competing index portfolios.

HOW INDEXES WORK

Today's market indicators are far more sophisticated than the original 12-stock average compiled by Charles Dow in 1884 for his *Customer's Afternoon Letter*—a gauge that preceded the famous Dow Jones Industrial Average. Modern indexes are more comprehensive and finely tuned. Today's yardsticks can be differentiated by the following factors:

1. *The size of the sample.* How many stocks are included and in what percentage of the total number? Larger samples are desirable but a small group of representative companies may be adequate.

2. *The kind of companies sampled.* Indicators can cover small, medium, or large stocks or the overall market. Some indexes are divided by investment style into growth or value components. Indexes also can focus on industry groups or individual foreign countries or regions. And there are many useful bond-market benchmarks.

3. *The method of calculation.* Indicators may be computed in different ways, depending on how the stocks are weighted and other factors.

Assigning Weights

Stocks can be ranked in importance within an index in a number of ways. The method of weighting can affect an index's behavior.

Price weighted. The venerable Dow Jones Industrial Average falls within this classification. Only the share prices of the Dow's 30 component stocks are used to derive its value. The Nikkei 225 Stock Average, the most widely quoted yardstick of the Tokyo market, also is price weighted. More expensive stocks, which are not necessarily the biggest companies, carry more weight than cheaper ones. For example, a 10-percent increase in a $150 stock will have 10 times more of an impact on a price-weighted indicator than a 10-percent rise in a $15 stock.

Value weighted. This type of index is far more common. The S&P 500 and Wilshire 5000 are prominent examples. In a value-weighted grouping, each component stock is weighted in proportion to its size, as reflected by a company's "capitalization," or price per share multiplied by the number of shares outstanding. For example, a $40 stock with 100 million shares would have a $4-billion market capitalization and would be five times bigger than an $80 stock with 10 million shares, worth $800 million. Thus, it would exert five times more of an impact in a cap-weighted index. Value-weighted indexes are generally thought to be more meaningful than their simpler price-weighted counterparts.

Equally weighted. A few benchmarks, such as the Value Line Composite, fall within this category. One way to visualize an equally weighted index is to assume that the same dollar amount is invested in each stock within the portfolio. That is, each stock exerts the same relative importance as any other, irrespective of share price or market cap. A 20-percent gain in the price of an $80-million company would have the same impact as a 20-percent increase in an $80-billion corporation. This greatly increases the importance of smaller companies compared to their role in a value-weighted yardstick.

An Index Illustration

Suppose just four stocks make up a hypothetical F&W 4 Index, as shown in Table 5-1. Stock B, with the highest market cap at $6 billion, carries the largest weight in the index at 50 percent, while Stock D has the lowest, 8.3 percent. The weights are found by dividing each stock's market cap by the $12-billion total for all the companies in the F&W 4. If the F&W were price weighted, each stock's importance could be calculated by taking its price and dividing by the sum of all prices, $290. Stock D, at $100, would make up a leading 34.5 percent of the index, despite its low capitalization.

Giant companies such as Exxon, General Electric, and Wal-Mart exert the largest influence on a cap-weighted index such as the S&P 500 or the NYSE Composite. For example, General Electric accounts for about 3 percent of the value of the S&P 500. If the index were equally weighted, General Electric, like any other stock, would account for only 0.2 percent, or 1/500th. In fact, the largest 50 companies in the S&P 500 represent around 50 percent

Table 5-1 The F&W 4 Cap Weighted Index

Stock	Share Price	Shares Outstanding (millions)	Total Capitalization (billions)	Weight in Index
A	$80	25	$2	16.7%
B	60	100	6	50.0
C	50	60	3	25.0
D	100	10	1	8.3

of the weighting, even though they comprise only 10 percent of the group numerically. The performance of those 50 largest stocks is, therefore, much more important than that of any other 50 companies in the index.

A SHORT HISTORY OF THE "DOW"

A staple part of the evening news, the Dow Jones Industrial Average is a household name that has served the test of time. This popular indicator reflects the average price of 30 United States blue-chip stocks. Figure 5-1 identifies these corporate titans. It is a yardstick by which the general public can keep track of what "the market" is doing throughout the day.

The average was preceded by Charles H. Dow's original market indicator, which debuted in 1884. Dow was co-founder with Edward Jones of Dow Jones & Co., publisher of *The Wall Street Journal* and *Barron's*. The earlier benchmark consisted of 11 stocks—nine railroads and two industrials—and was published from time to time in Dow's *Customer's Afternoon Letter*, which developed into *The Wall Street Journal* in 1889. The railroads, however, did not provide a complete representation of the market. It was vital, Dow felt, to have an indicator that was representative of industrial companies, a new and highly speculative group at that time. So Dow tinkered with the mix and introduced the Dow Jones Industrial Average in 1896.

The Dow yardstick, originally containing 12 industrial companies, was subsequently expanded and reached its present number of 30 in 1928. Firms such as American Cotton Oil, American Tobacco, Chicago Gas, and the Tennessee Coal, Iron & Railroad Co. were among the original dozen. Only General Electric remains part of the average today under its original name.

In the beginning, the closing prices of the 12 industrials were simply summed and divided by 12 to obtain the average. All you needed was a pen-

Figure 5-1
Companies Included in the Dow Jones Industrial Average Today

AlliedSignal	Eastman Kodak	Merck
Aluminum Co. of America	Exxon	Minnesota Mining
American Express	General Electric	J.P. Morgan
AT&T	General Motors	Philip Morris
Boeing	Goodyear	Procter & Gamble
Caterpillar	Hewlett-Packard	Sears Roebuck
Chevron	IBM	Travelers Group
Coca-Cola	International Paper	Union Carbide
Walt Disney	Johnson & Johnson	United Technologies
DuPont	McDonald's	Wal-Mart Stores

cil and paper. But the divisor of the Dow has been adjusted (usually downward) over the years to reflect the effects of share splits, the payment of large dividends in additional shares, or the occasional substitution of a new company. For example, a $200 stock would immediately fall to $100 after being split two-for-one. (Investors would receive two shares for each one they previously owned so the value of their positions would remain unchanged.) To avoid distortions, the divisor would need to be reduced by an appropriate amount.

Because the Dow is based on only 30 firms, care must be taken to ensure that they represent the broad economy. As a result, the Dow's composition has changed over time to reflect changes in the economy. In 1896, for instance, the companies reflected our agrarian economy. Since the mid-1950s, the substitutions have mirrored the growing importance of technology, service, and entertainment firms.

The Dow's divisor recently stood at about 0.3. That's why the average itself is much higher than the prices of any of the 30 component companies. If each Dow stock increased by a point, the average would jump by 100 points assuming a divisor of 0.3. As you can see, the divisor works like a multiplier.

Adjusting the divisor prevents distortions and therefore maintains consistency in the readings over time. The Dow has been criticized because it contains only 30 companies, but the firms have been carefully chosen to represent different sectors of the economy. While the sample may be small, it nicely reflects the market for large U.S. stocks.

Dow Jones & Co. also publishes a 20-stock Transportation Average of airline, trucking, and railroad stocks, a 15-stock Utility Average of electric and natural-gas companies, as well as a 65-stock composite of the three indicators. Although the Dow industrials are the best-known yardstick of stock prices, this is only one of the company's many indicators. For example, Dow Jones also compiles a variety of value-weighted global indexes that appear daily in the "World Stock Markets" column of *The Wall Street Journal*.

OTHER INDICATORS

Thanks to today's high-speed computers, rising industrialization around the globe, and the popularity of the capitalist system, stock-market indicators have proliferated in recent years. Leading benchmarks for foreign markets include the Hang Seng Index of the Hong Kong market, the Tokyo Stock Exchange Price Index, and the Financial Times Index of London stocks. Most of the newer benchmarks contain broad samples and typically are value-weighted as opposed to price-weighted.

Standard & Poor's indexes. Standard & Poor's Corp. introduced its first market indicator in 1923, the predecessor to today's popular S&P 500, which began in 1957. This gauge measures the price changes in 500 large firms that reflect about 70 percent of the value of the domestic market. Most index mutual funds are based on the S&P 500, as we explain in Chapter 8. The S&P 500 also is separated into growth and value groups based on the S&P/Barra Growth and Value indexes.

Standard & Poor's also publishes a 400-stock Industrial Index, a 20-stock Transportation Index, a 40-stock Utility Index, and a 40-stock Financial Index. The S&P 500 is a composite of the four benchmarks. In addition, there is an S&P 400 MidCap, an S&P 600 SmallCap, and an S&P 1500, which combines the S&P 500 with the medium- and small-stock indicators.

Wilshire 5000. With more than 7,000 U.S. companies, including all those from the New York and American Stock exchanges as well as actively traded Nasdaq firms, the Wilshire 5000 is the most comprehensive domestic index. Developed in 1974 by Wilshire Associates in Santa Monica, Calif., it is based on the capitalization of its component companies as of year-end 1980. This means changes in the indicator reflect approximate dollar changes in the U.S. equity market since then. The Wilshire 4500 represents the Wilshire 5000 minus the companies in the S&P 500. It provides a benchmark for the "extended" market of mid-cap and smaller companies and is the target for the Vanguard Index Trust Extended Market Portfolio. Wilshire also compiles growth and value subindices. As you can tell, the Wilshire indexes have not changed their names, even though the number of stocks they track has expanded.

The Value Line Composite Index is an equally weighted benchmark of some 1,700 companies from 95 industry groups. These corporations are tracked in the widely used *Value Line Investment Survey.* Essentially, Value Line calculates the percentage change in the price of each stock for a specific period such as a day. Then the percentage changes of the individual stocks are averaged.

Because the Value Line Index is equally weighted and thus reflects the overall market, it represents a useful benchmark for mutual-fund investors. As noted earlier, value-weighted indicators attach the greatest importance to the largest companies, as does the Dow, because it's based exclusively on corporate giants. However, fund managers often do not structure their portfolios that way.

Russell indicators. These indexes are compiled by Frank Russell Co. in Tacoma, Wash. The Russell 3000 represents the 3,000 largest U.S. corporations and accounts for about 98 percent of the value of the domestic market. It is a broad alternative to the Wilshire 5000. The Russell 1000 and 2000 are subsets covering the top 1,000 and next 2,000 biggest companies.

The Russell 2000 represents small firms worth between roughly $160 million and $1 billion each. With a median market cap of about $350 million, it is the most popular small-stock bogey and is used as the benchmark for various index funds including the Vanguard Small Capitalization Stock portfolio. The Russell 2000 makes a good benchmark for evaluating small-stock funds. Russell also publishes separate growth and value indexes for companies of various sizes.

Stock exchange indicators. The NYSE publishes a composite index of the more than 3,000 "Big Board" stocks, as well as subindices for industrial, utility, transportation, and finance companies. The fluctuations of the NYSE industrial index generally follow those of the S&P 500 and the Dow Jones Industrials. These indexes are useful to people investing primarily in large-stock mutual funds. The American Stock Exchange also publishes an index of its market.

Nasdaq indicators. The Nasdaq electronic market compiles a composite as well as various subindices of the more than 5,500 companies traded there. You also can find separate indexes for the National Market, which consists of the more popular, actively traded Nasdaq companies. Nasdaq, of course, is not a stock exchange but rather a computerized linkage of stock brokerages and dealers. Many Nasdaq companies are technology firms, which makes the indicator appropriate for both technology and small-stock mutual funds.

Morgan Stanley Capital International's EAFE. This foreign index represents nearly 1,100 companies in Europe, Australia, and the Far East, and is the most widely followed overseas benchmark. It's basically an index of non-American companies. Figure 5-2 lists the 20 countries with firms in the EAFE. Japan, the world's second-largest stock market, has a sizable impact. Morgan Stanley indexes also are available for individual countries within the EAFE. These provide the benchmarks for WEBS (or World Equity Benchmark Shares), discussed in Chapter 11. Morgan Stanley also compiles benchmarks for emerging stock markets such as Argentina, Greece, Israel, India, Poland, and Turkey.

Japan's OTC Market

Several funds focus on Japan's growing over-the-counter market, which is attracting more foreign investors. The closed-end Japan OTC Equity Fund has invested there since 1990. Fidelity and Warburg Pincus subsequently introduced open-end portfolios that target smaller Japanese companies. Special indicators track these volatile, illiquid issues, which took investors on a wild ride during Japan's lengthy bear market. The Nikkei Over-the-Counter index is a price-weighted benchmark, whereas the Jasdaq is a comprehensive capitalization-weighted indicator that includes about 900 smaller companies.

Figure 5-2   Countries in the Europe, Australia, and Far East (EAFE) Index

Australia	France	Japan	Singapore
Austria	Germany	Malaysia	Spain
Belgium	Hong Kong	Netherlands	Sweden
Denmark	Ireland	New Zealand	Switzerland
Finland	Italy	Norway	United Kingdom

The International Finance Corp.'s emerging-market indexes. In 1981, these became the first performance gauges of stock markets in developing countries. The Emerging Markets Data Base now covers 45 markets, and provides regular updates on more than 2,000 stocks. These capitalization-weighted indexes can be found in the IFC's annual *Emerging Stock Markets Factbook,* a useful publication for investors in single-country closed-end funds. You can obtain daily and weekly updates of the indexes at www.ifc.org on the World Wide Web.

Bond market indicators. Bond benchmarks are more difficult to compile than their stock counterparts. The bond universe is far broader than that of stocks and is continually changing because of new issues, maturing obligations, and bond calls. In addition, it's often more difficult to price corporate or municipal debt issues than stocks. Still, it's important to keep track of the bond market.

Several indicators measure the performances of various groups of bonds including high-yield, municipal, U.S. government, and foreign obligations. Merrill Lynch, Lehman Brothers, and Salomon Brothers all publish indexes. The Lehman Brothers Aggregate Bond Index is a primary indicator of market

---

Keep Tabs on Treasuries

Interest rates on long-term Treasury bonds are highly sensitive to changes in economic growth, inflation, the level of employment, and likely alterations in Federal Reserve monetary policy. Bond prices vary inversely with interest rates, so if rates are going up or are expected to rise, Treasury prices will fall. But stock prices also often head south when interest rates are rising or likely to increase. There are several reasons for this: Higher rates make bonds more attractive so investors shuttle money from stocks to bonds. Also, higher rates boost corporate borrowing costs, cutting into profits. And rising rates exacerbate consumer borrowing costs and act as a spending deterrent. Falling rates work in an opposite manner.

performance. Like stock-market indicators, these benchmarks can be found in *The Wall Street Journal, Barron's,* and other publications. Morningstar and Value Line both offer performance comparisons for bond funds and the relevant market benchmarks. Various index funds track selected bond-market indicators.

MARKET INDEXES AND MUTUAL FUNDS

Fund performance numbers are evaluated against stock-price indexes all the time. You'll see comparisons in prospectuses, shareholder reports, and research publications such as those from Morningstar and Value Line. The SEC requires mutual funds to list their performance numbers against a relevant market benchmark. However, there are several factors to be aware of when comparing fund performance with a market index.

Mutual funds hold cash. The average stock fund normally keeps 5 to 10 percent of its assets in cash to help meet redemptions and to provide buying power when bargains arise. Market timers, when fearful of a downturn, may sock away even more cash. This often reduces returns, however. Suppose the market advances 30 percent in a year when a bearish stock-fund manager has 20 percent of the portfolio in cash. Say the fund earns 5 percent on its cash holding and 30 percent on the 80 percent of assets in stocks. The overall return would be 25 percent, five percentage points below the market's. Of course, cash does cushion the blow in down markets. But when stocks tumble, funds face redemptions—so they can quickly lose this cushion if the decline is sudden and severe enough.

A cash position of up to 10 percent or so won't necessarily lower a portfolio's volatility all that much, especially if the manager tilts the fund toward more volatile stocks. This is evident from the fact that the total returns of many funds fluctuate up and down more than those of their market benchmarks, as evidenced by a comparison of betas and standard deviations. We expand on these risk measures in Chapter 6.

Mutual funds incur expenses and trading costs. Funds must shoulder the burdens of advisory fees, operating costs, distribution costs (including any 12b-1 fees), and transaction expenses. These outlays total at least two percentage points or so for the typical stock fund. If the average fund just matches the Wilshire 5000 before costs, it would still underperform by two percentage points. Its results could be nicked even further by cash holdings.

Differences in component stocks. The typical equity fund does not hold the exact same issues as a market index. For example, a growth portfolio might own many of the same companies as found in the S&P 500, along with significant stakes in mid-caps, small-caps, and even foreign firms. Furthermore, the fund's composition would change over time.

COMPARING APPLES TO APPLES

Don't be upset if your fund trails its relevant market benchmark by a modest amount from time to time. In fact, the average growth or growth-and-income portfolio should lag the S&P 500 by an amount equal to its expenses. It's highly commendable if your fund slightly outperforms the market over time. Mutual funds, after all, provide important services that a market benchmark can't. Nor could most people afford to buy all of the constituent stocks in an index.

It's often more revealing to see how a fund is doing relative to its peers. You can compare a fund's performance over various periods with several of its closest competitors, or you can check its progress against more comprehensive benchmarks. Lipper Analytical Services provides "equally weighted" indexes for numerous stock and bond fund categories. The equal-weighting feature ensures that each fund has the same impact on the index, so no single portfolio can dominate. These indexes provide a good way to gauge a fund's recent performance, and you can check them daily in the "Mutual Funds Quotations" section of *The Wall Street Journal*.

You wouldn't want to hang on to a fund that has been underperforming both its peers and a relevant index for several years. If you want performance that's predictably close to an indicator, consider holding index funds, which are discussed in Chapter 8. The law of averages says that there always will be a handful of funds that beat the market over long periods. The difficult part is predicting which portfolios will do so.

AT THE CLOSE

Stock and bond indexes help investors answer the key question, "How are my mutual funds doing?" Indexes give you a feel for market behavior at a glance, and facilitate comparisons of both risk and return.

To use this information, you need to know how a particular benchmark has been compiled. Indexes vary in terms of composition and weighting. Yet they all share a basic unmanaged, fully invested posture. These attributes, among other factors, give them a natural performance edge over mainstream mutual funds.

CHAPTER 6

Living with Risk

A California man we know faces danger every day. He rides a motorcycle to work, participates in a martial-arts club at night, and skydives on the weekends. Yet this person also worries about the stock market. Although he owns several equity funds through a retirement plan at work, the experience makes him a bit uneasy.

Risk is in the eye of the beholder. We all face perils on a daily basis that we usually take for granted—in the form of traffic, crime, pollution, and more. Yet when it comes to the stock market, many of us worry excessively about monetary loss, temporary though it may be. In many cases, it's an overblown fear.

Risk, in a generic sense, is the possibility of loss, damage, or harm. For investors, it is the chance that your actual return will be less than you expected. People sometimes think that a high return can be achieved with little or no risk. Unfortunately, that's impossible. To achieve your objectives, you need to assume certain perils and avoid others.

Investment risk is generally defined as variability, or period-by-period fluctuations (or "ups" and "downs") in total return. It often is expressed numerically, using a statistical measure such as "standard deviation." The more an investment's returns vary, the greater the risk or standard deviation. But there's more to risk than volatility, as we'll see. Most people would agree that high returns are good and risk is bad. The problem is that the two usually go hand in hand. To earn higher gains over the years, you must be willing to tolerate higher levels of volatility.

Risk is a complex, multidimensional concept that manifests itself in various ways including stock-market crashes, corporate bankruptcies, currency devaluations, unanticipated surges in inflation and interest rates, and even major changes in the tax code. And sophisticated risk measures, like beta and standard deviation, can be tricky and have limitations.

What causes volatility? For mutual funds, three factors affect the variability of investment performance.

1. *The kinds of stocks in the portfolio.* Small-growth companies are more volatile than large blue chips, and foreign stocks carry greater risks than domestic ones.

2. *The degree to which a fund diversifies.* A portfolio of only a dozen stocks would tend to have greater volatility than one holding 100 or more. In addition, a fund focusing on a single industry sector—particularly if it's a volatile one such as precious metals—would have greater fluctuations than a portfolio that spreads its assets widely.

3. *The extent, if any, to which the manager tries to "time the market" or "hedge."* A manager can smooth out volatility with shrewd use of options and futures or by raising the cash position in anticipation of a market decline. However, these strategies often backfire and managers who try to control short-term volatility often end up reducing long-run returns as a consequence.

Your ability to handle risk is closely related to your individual circumstances, including your age, time horizon, liquidity needs, portfolio size, income, investment knowledge, and attitude toward price fluctuations. What's highly risky to one person may be no problem to another. For an 85-year-old who's fearful of near-term losses, money-market and short-term bond funds would probably constitute low-risk choices, while growth funds would be aggressive ones. But, for a 30-year-old who's mainly concerned about loss of purchasing power, the opposite may be true. Short-term fluctuations are not that relevant for long-term investors who have the discipline, patience, and understanding to deal with them. Stock funds are actually less risky than money-market portfolios for people with long time horizons.

Well-informed investors are far less likely to let risk get the best of them. Those who understand the various dangers are better equipped to enjoy a profitable financial journey. Here are the major dangers confronting investors in domestic-stock funds. Chapters 10 and 13 contain a more focused coverage of risk for foreign-stock and fixed-income portfolios, respectively.

MARKET RISK

Market risk is really a double-edged sword. Most people regard it as the threat of declining prices on a wide scale. That's the most obvious danger; but it also involves the possibility of being on the sidelines during rallies. Many investors do not recognize this drawback and try to play it safe. But staying too conservative introduces a subtle danger: the purchasing-power threat that investors face in an inflationary world.

Market risk is sometimes called "nondiversifiable" risk because you can't avoid it no matter how many stocks are held in a portfolio. All sorts of political and economic problems in a country, from rising inflation to sky-rocketing interest rates, can send stock prices into a tailspin. Some managers try to "hedge," or offset market risk, with options or futures contracts that would appreciate during market drops. However, hedging has a cost, and these managers may be sacrificing return. Specifically, they could limit their funds' upside potential if prices instead go higher, as often happens.

Some stock funds get hit worse than others in bear routs. These are typically the more appreciation-oriented portfolios that hold mid-sized and smaller firms. Conversely, equity-income funds, which focus on larger corporations that pay good dividends, often hold up best. Table 6-1 shows the cumulative returns for each of Lipper Analytical Service's general equity-fund categories over four periods of declining stock prices—the most serious being

Table 6-1   Down-Market Performances of General Equity-Fund Categories

| Category | Cumulative Total Returns | | | |
	12/31/72 to 09/30/74	11/30/80 to 07/31/82	08/31/87 to 11/30/87	07/12/90 to 10/11/90
Capital Appreciation	-52.2%	-10.3%	-29.6%	-21.4%
Equity Income	-29.0	6.8	-21.5	-15.1
Growth	-48.0	-12.3	-29.0	-21.0
Growth & Income	-40.2	-7.2	-25.5	-17.2
Mid Cap	-55.3	-11.1	-33.1	-23.9
Micro Cap	na	na	-33.4	-27.6
Small Cap	-52.2	-19.3	-32.1	-27.7
S&P 500 Index	na	-17.0	-29.7	-18.3
Averages	**-45.3**	**-9.6**	**-28.2**	**-20.5**

Source: Lipper Analytical Services Inc.

the 1973-1974 bear market. It took investors more than five years on average to recover from that tumble. The 1980-1982 decline was relatively modest, and the 1987 crash steep but short-lived. The 1990 bear market also was brief.

To make money in the stock market, you have to go with the probabilities. That means hanging in there for the long term. One of the most important points to remember about stock risk is the following: ANY STOCK FUND CAN BE VERY RISKY AS A SHORT-TERM INVESTMENT.

What do we mean by short-term? Nobody can answer that precisely. It's possible, although not likely, for stocks to perform miserably for a whole decade. For instance, general-equity funds eked out a meager 1.6 percent a year over the decade ended December 1978, according to Lipper. Under such circumstances, you wouldn't want to put much money into equity portfolios if you think you will need to spend the cash in the next few years.

You can deal with market risk in several ways. The key is to remain a long-term investor and accept the fact that stocks will fluctuate, sometimes violently. But if you stick with good equity funds through thick and thin, you can assume they will eventually bounce back. The worst you can do is yank your money out of a fund at the bottom, just before the market turns around. Consider this as the flip side of market risk—the danger of missing out on rallies.

The Perils of Buying on Margin

Investors who buy mutual funds through brokerage firms can "margin" their purchases, or use borrowed money in the hopes of augmenting returns, just as those who buy stocks have been able to do for years. But think twice before you get out on a financial limb. Margin can easily magnify your losses when prices tumble. Plus, you must pay interest costs for the privilege of borrowing.

Suppose you invest $20,000 in a growth fund by using $10,000 of your own money and borrowing the other $10,000 from your broker. If the fund drops 20 percent, you would wind up losing 40 percent of your original

---

Does Time Reduce Risk?

Just as risk can be reduced by adding more stocks to a portfolio, so can market risk be lessened by adding more years to your holding period. Time diversification cuts the standard deviation of yearly returns. This means that your odds of earning a decent result improve the longer you remain invested. You stand a better chance of achieving the 10-percent average yearly return on stocks over a decade than in a single year.

$10,000 investment because the value of your $20,000 position would decline by 20 percent or $4,000. Margin is very effective at compounding losses during a downward spiral.

SECTOR RISK

The whole rationale behind mutual funds is the idea of diversification, or holding bunches of stocks. There's a good reason for this. Academic research has determined that with at least 12 and preferably 20 different stocks in a portfolio, investors can eliminate most "company-specific" risk. In other words, they can reduce the odds of being burned by just one or a few investments. The misfortunes that weigh heavily on some of the stocks—such as lawsuits, intense competition, or loss of key personnel—will be offset by the good fortunes of others.

Most mutual funds hold at least a few dozen stocks; some hold several hundred. Diversification doesn't depend just on owning a large number of stocks, however. They also have to be different types of stocks. Diversification is of limited value if all you have are banks, or airlines, or gold-mining companies.

Sector or industry risk reflects the reality that companies providing similar products or services are vulnerable to common dangers. Firms in a particular industry can go through extreme ups and downs together, and so can mutual funds focusing on them. Individuals who invest in such specialized portfolios must recognize their greater potential volatility. The prospectuses or disclosure brochures for these types of funds warn that they are risky and do not provide broad diversification. Industry risk also may be present in more diversified funds that make big sector bets, but the danger is almost never so acute.

INFLATION RISK

Consider the following statements:

- At 4-percent inflation, $1 would lose nearly one third of its value in 10 years.

- At 4-percent inflation, that same dollar would lose over half its purchasing power in 20 years.

- At 5-percent inflation, you would need $105,600 in 40 years to buy a Toyota that now costs $15,000.

The numbers in Table 6-2 show the purchasing-power erosion of $1 at different inflation rates for several periods. For example, at inflation of 4 percent annually, $1 today will depreciate to 21 cents 40 years from now. If inflation runs at 6 percent, the 21 cents becomes 10 cents. The higher the inflation and the longer the period, the greater the bite.

We've talked a lot about volatility. But there's more to risk than ups and downs. Even an investment with a locked-in return and no danger of default, such as a Treasury bill, can be risky. Although there may be virtually no threat of price declines, such investments can be disappointing in an inflationary sense.

Along with taxes, inflation threatens anyone wanting to build wealth over the long haul. Ways to ease the tax bite, such as tax-deferred retirement plans and variable annuities, are covered in Chapters 17 and 18, respectively. The only way to reduce the impact of inflation is to compound your investments at higher rates of return.

Short-term fixed-income vehicles—such as certificates of deposit, Treasury bills, and money-market funds—expose people to purchasing-power or inflation risk. They don't provide that much-needed inflation hedge. They're most appropriate as places to park idle cash for short periods or to keep money for possible emergencies.

These options can appear incredibly attractive at times, such as in the early 1980s, when short-term yields touched levels as high as 17 or 18 percent. But 18 percent rates can compress to 3 percent rates, as money-market investors have seen. In fact, over the long run, returns on Treasury bills have stayed only slightly ahead of the inflation rate.

As explained previously, stock investments offer the kind of growth potential that you may need to provide for a secure retirement, to educate your children, or to meet other major outlays. Along with good real estate, they provide the most effective inflation hedge. Unlike the fixed payments on a bond, a stock's dividends tend to grow over the years. And stock prices generally trend upward over time in tandem with the increasing levels of dividends and profits.

Table 6-2   Future Purchasing Power of $1

Inflation Rate	Years in Future			
	5	10	20	40
3%	$0.86	$0.74	$0.55	$0.31
4	0.82	0.68	0.46	0.21
5	0.78	0.61	0.38	0.14
6	0.75	0.56	0.31	0.10

ASSET-CLASS RISK

Stocks, bonds, and cash are the three major asset classes. If you allocate too much of your wealth to any one of them, you may be subjecting yourself to what's known as "asset-class risk." It's prudent to diversify across all three major categories even though you may want to emphasize one—namely, stocks. It's also important to spread your money around different stock sub-categories and various groupings of bonds.

Younger investors who might see little purpose in owning bonds should realize that they can add stability to a portfolio, while producing higher returns than money-market funds. As we saw in Table 6-1, stock funds could lose more than 40 percent in a severe bear market. However, bond funds are unlikely to slump even 10 percent, regardless of how bad things get because principal losses are cushioned by the periodic interest payments.

Older investors often favor bonds and bond funds for their comparative stability, yet these people should have at least a small stake in stocks. Most seniors require some long-term growth to reduce the likelihood of outliving their nest eggs. For these people, good choices include stock funds from the equity-income and growth-and-income categories.

Mixing dissimilar funds into a portfolio can lead to remarkably steady returns. Volatile funds may not be that risky when used sparingly as part of a well-diversified strategy. International funds, for instance, can help trim market risk a bit, even though they tend to be volatile in isolation. That's because while some markets might be flat or heading down, others could be charging ahead. Other aggressive diversifiers include high-yield or "junk" bond funds, growth-stock portfolios, and small-stock investments. A modest stake in a real-estate fund can add another dimension of diversification. Some advisers also recommend keeping 5 percent or so of your assets in a gold fund, but these investments have been poor long-haul performers.

With a judicious blend, you'll face less turbulence because not all of your holdings will be going up or down at once. Occasionally, nearly all types of stock and even bond funds may stumble together, but they won't all fall to the same degree. This makes it easier not to become frustrated by the biggest plungers but rather to assess the damage in terms of your overall portfolio. Viewed in this manner, the impact might not be so bad.

SIMPLE WAYS TO GAUGE RISK

You don't have to be a Ph.D. candidate to get a good handle on a mutual fund's risk. Several uncomplicated approaches can help you judge volatility. The first step is to read the prospectus, the closest thing to an owner's manual for a fund. It will spell out the portfolio's objectives and risk factors in detail. For example, a capital-appreciation fund may reveal that it concentrates on a small number of companies or invests in embryonic firms issuing shares through initial public offerings—two signs that it could be more volatile than normal. A sector fund that targets a specific industry, especially gold mining, also would likely experience wider price swings than a more conservative alternative.

Ups and Downs of Returns

A simple way to determine a fund's risk is to examine its returns over several years. You can quickly see how the portfolio fared in weak market years such as 1987, 1990, and 1994. You also can compare the results with those of similar types of funds and with a market index such as the S&P 500. The bar chart in Figure 6-1 illustrates the ups and downs of two small-company growth funds. It's pretty easy to see that A is more volatile.

Annual returns, however, can conceal a lot of volatility along the way. For this reason, you may want to analyze quarterly numbers. Past quarterly results for mutual funds are not as accessible as yearly numbers, but you can find them in publications such as *Morningstar Mutual Funds* and *The Value Line Mutual Fund Survey*. You also may be able to get these numbers from the fund company itself. It is useful to know how a portfolio held up in particularly bad stretches such as the fourth quarter of 1987 and the third quarter of 1990, but for most purposes, a study of past annual returns will suffice.

How Pricey is the P/E?

The price-earnings ratio, as explained in Chapter 3, can be a telling statistic of a fund manager's aggressiveness. The P/E for a portfolio is simply a weighted average of the P/Es of the stocks held. The higher the number, the wilder the ride.

Composite P/Es or "multiples" for individual funds can range from below 10 to 30 or more. Morningstar and Value Line include such figures in their stock-fund profiles, with each fund's multiple compared to that of the S&P 500. For example, if a portfolio's P/E is 30 when the S&P 500's is 20, its relative value would be 1.5. P/Es calculated by Lipper Analytical Services appear in *Barron's* quarterly mutual-funds report.

Be sure to compare fund P/Es with the multiples of similar portfolios and those of the market averages at roughly the same date. Statistics for a particular portfolio may be several months old because of reporting lags. If the P/E for the market is 20 or more and a fund's multiple is even higher, watch out for a sharp fall in the event of a major sell-off. Excessive P/Es spell substantial risk.

In addition to P/Es, Morningstar and Value Line also report a "price/ book value" ratio for individual funds relative to the S&P 500. As explained in Chapter 3, book value represents the common stockholders' equity in a

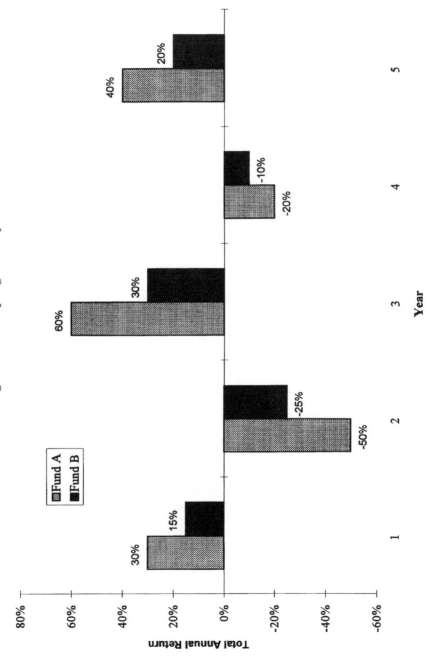

Figure 6-1   Analyzing Volatility

75

company. This is another useful gauge of a company's worth. Again, higher numbers reflect more risk.

VOLATILITY GAUGES

While the above statistics can prove helpful, there are more precise ways to measure a fund's up or down movements. These yardsticks typically are not mentioned in a fund's advertising or in its prospectus, so you might have to rely on research publications that monitor mutual funds.

Standard Deviation

This statistic reflects the degree to which returns fluctuate around their average. The higher the standard deviation, the greater the risk. The measure is typically an annualized value calculated using monthly returns over the past 36 months. A conservative domestic-equity fund might have a number below 8 percent, whereas a volatile Japanese-stock portfolio could have a value of 18 percent.

What do such numbers mean? You should realize that, by definition, a fund's actual yearly returns will range within plus or minus one standard deviation of its yearly average about two-thirds of the time. Also, by definition, its returns will vary within two standard deviations about 95 percent of the time. Suppose a fund has an average yearly return of 10 percent and a standard deviation of 15 percent. Based on the above definition, we can expect that its annual performance will fall within the –5 percent to +25 percent range about two-thirds of the time. And about 95 percent of the time, returns should lie within the bounds of –20 percent and +40 percent. This gives you an idea of the magnitude of loss you might expect in an unusually bad year.

Standard deviation can be used to gauge how much more risky one fund is versus another over a particular time frame. The measure helps to evaluate the riskiness of bond as well as stock portfolios. The standard deviation of a bond fund's returns would reflect price fluctuations resulting from such factors as changing interest rates or changes in the ratings of the bonds held.

Table 6-3 displays the standard deviations and risk rankings for the fund groups tracked by the American Association of Individual Investors (AAII). Notice that the bond categories have lower risk than the stock groups. The AAII also provides a useful "risk index" based on the standard deviation of a fund relative to its group average. A portfolio with a risk index of, say, 1.4 would be 40 percent more volatile than its peers.

Beta

Many investors measure market risk using what's known as the "beta coefficient." This relates the return on a stock or mutual fund to a market

Table 6-3   Standard Deviations and Risk Rankings of Fund Categories*

Category	Standard Deviation	Total Risk
Gold	27.7%	high
Aggressive Growth	14.8	high
Small-Capitalization Stock	11.1	above avg.
Domestic Equity	10.4	above avg.
Growth	10.0	above avg.
International Stock	9.4	avg.
Growth & Income	9.1	avg.
Balanced	6.4	below avg.
International Bond	5.4	below avg.
Tax-Exempt Bond	4.5	low
Corporate Bond	4.2	low
Corporate High-Yield Bond	3.8	low
Domestic Taxable Bond	3.7	low
Government Bond	3.7	low
Mortgage-Backed Bond	3.5	low
General Bond	3.4	low

* As of 3/31/97
Source: American Association of Individual Investors

index, commonly the Standard & Poor's 500. It's often done by taking returns for the past 36 months, and comparing them with the index's monthly results.

This statistic thus reflects the sensitivity of a fund's return to fluctuations in the market index. By definition, the beta for a well-diversified stock portfolio that seesaws in perfect sync with the market equals 1.0. Betas greater than 1.0 indicate above-average volatility—the higher the number, the greater the risk. For example, a fund with a beta of 1.5 would be expected to advance or decline 15 percent if the market rose or fell 10 percent.

Funds with betas below 1.0 bounce around less than the market. These include defensive portfolios that invest primarily in slow-moving stocks such as utilities or real-estate securities. Money-market funds have a beta that's close to zero because their returns are fairly independent of the stock market. Negative betas can exist but are rare.

Beta Shortcomings

Beta isn't perfect. Academics have criticized it on several grounds. For instance, the measure isn't necessarily a reliable indicator of future performance, especially over shorter periods. A high-beta fund might not advance or may even decline if the market rallies.

Also, beta's value depends on how it's calculated. For instance, a given mutual fund would have one beta based on data stretching back 36 months and another for 60 months. It also would vary depending on the market index that's being used as a benchmark—say, the S&P 500 versus the Russell 2000 or the much-broader Wilshire 5000.

Beta won't reveal much about funds with highly specialized holdings, such as those investing in particular industries or in precious metals. These portfolios can be plenty volatile, reflected in lofty standard deviations, but their betas might be below 1.0, even close to 0. This is because the returns of specialized portfolios do not correlate closely with the overall market. Also, betas often don't work for foreign-stock portfolios, since international equities do not move in lockstep with the U.S. market.

Checking the "R-Squared"

A measure known as "R-squared" can help spot questionable betas. This statistic indicates how much of a fund's fluctuations are attributable to movements in the overall market. R-squared readings range between 0 percent and 100 percent. The greater a fund's diversification, the higher the number. The Vanguard Index Trust 500 Portfolio, which replicates the S&P 500, has an R-squared of 100 percent. Large, well-diversified funds have R-squared values of 90 percent or higher. But other portfolios, especially those classified as "nondiversified," could have readings of 60 percent or less. A gold fund might have an R-squared of only 1 percent. Morningstar and Value Line report these numbers, along with betas and standard deviations.

The beta of a fund with a very low R-squared is generally not meaningful since that portfolio would have an extremely low correlation with the market index. For example, a gold fund may have a beta of only 0.1 yet a very high standard deviation. Think of the R-squared figure as a screening device to spot suspicious betas.

WHY STANDARD DEVIATION

This yardstick also has its shortcomings because it's based on past data that might not be repeated in the future. Nevertheless, it's the single best risk measure for mutual funds. Here's why:

1. Standard deviation is a broader measure than beta, as it gauges total risk, not just market-related volatility.

2. Standard deviation is a purer number. It doesn't depend on any relationship to an arbitrarily chosen market index.

3. It can measure the riskiness of specialized portfolios as well as broadly diversified ones.

4. It can be used to gauge the variability of both bond and stock investments.

GAUGING THE DOWNSIDE

Beta and standard deviation reflect potential ups as well as downs in NAV. But people fear only the declines. Nobody would mind owning volatile investments if they always moved higher. The ideal way to gauge downside risk would be to examine a fund's returns in down periods alone.

This concern has led to the development of some one-sided risk measures. For example, Morningstar tracks how often and to what extent a fund's monthly returns fall short of the returns on three-month T-bills. The more frequent and the greater a portfolio's shortfalls relative to its peers, the higher the Morningstar risk rating. Consistent underperformers would be rated as riskier than funds that incur big losses occasionally, but perform well for long stretches. So-called "management risk" is evident if a fund trails its peers over long periods. The returns may not even be volatile, just consistently inferior.

RISK POINTERS

Keep the following points in mind when evaluating the risk-reward characteristics of your funds.

- *There's no such thing as a "risk-free" investment.* All securities carry uncertainty, although the dangers differ.

- *Stable investments are vulnerable to inflation.* T-bills, certificates of deposit, and money-market funds are the most perilous in this regard over the long haul. Their low returns simply can't beat inflation by a meaningful amount.

- *Watch out for laggards.* Management risk is a subtle danger. The more years you remain with a subpar performer the greater the damage to your nest egg.

- *Market risk is a double-edged sword.* In addition to losing money when prices fall, investors face the danger of being on the sidelines during bullish stampedes.

- *There's no magic number.* Risk is too complex to be reduced to a single quantitative yardstick such as standard deviation or beta. Nevertheless, these measures provide historic insight and can be useful in fine-tuning a portfolio, in combination with other information.

- *Risk should be evaluated in terms of an overall portfolio.* It doesn't matter as much if certain investments stumble badly as long as others hang onto their values or head higher.

AT THE CLOSE

Daily living entails certain risks that most people take for granted. Some of the biggest perils a person faces are neither predictable nor controllable. Yet when it comes to the stock market, some investors exaggerate the dangers. Stocks and equity mutual funds certainly can lose money, but over many years they will likely rise in price to offset another important danger—decay of purchasing power. Viewed in light of the inflation threat, stock investments actually are less perilous than Treasury bills, CDs, and the like.

Investors can choose from several measures to evaluate the riskiness of their mutual funds. Although none is perfect, standard deviation is perhaps the best tool around.

CHAPTER 7

Profiting from Volatility

Change is a certainty in the stock market. Prices rise and fall. Nothing is guaranteed. Even the sharpest minds on Wall Street don't know for sure what will happen next. "The stock market will fluctuate," said turn-of-the-century financier J. Pierpont Morgan, when asked to make a prediction. Morgan's simple statement remains as descriptive as ever because it's the only forecast anyone can make with virtual certainty. The market does what it must to perplex the maximum number of people.

Stock prices do work their way upward gradually over the years, but they fluctuate dramatically around their long-term path, moving in cycles. So-called "bear" markets, generally defined as declines of 20 percent or more in stock prices from the most recent peak, are a fact of life in the investment world. So are less severe setbacks of 10 percent or more, known as "corrections." Bear markets vary in length and intensity, but they're usually of shorter duration than rising or "bull" markets. Stock prices are climbing, on average, about 70 percent of the time.

GREED AND FEAR

Disciplined investors understand the major factors that move stock prices. These include not just tangibles such as interest rates and corporate earnings but also crowd psychology and human emotions. For centuries, people have overreacted, buying too high and subsequently selling too low. Greed and fear drive prices to extremes of overvaluation and undervaluation. Academic research has shown that investors often overemphasize the significance of unexpectedly good or bad news by immediately bidding stock prices up too far or hammering them down excessively. Stated differently, price changes often overshoot any changes in value, because people respond emotionally.

When stocks are rallying, more people join the festivities. Stories of profits told by friends and acquaintances convince others that there is still a chance to make money. Greed predominates during speculative bubbles, just as it did during the infamous tulip-bulb craze in 17th century Holland when Dutchmen bid up prices for bulbs producing the choicest flowers, setting the stage for a prolonged depression in that country.

When prices eventually reverse course, fear enters the picture. Investors who lack discipline capitulate in trepidation, selling out and retreating to seemingly safe harbors such as money-market funds. As prices fall still further the selling intensifies, adding insult to injury. People find it difficult to go bargain hunting when they've seen 20, 30, or even 40 percent of their nest eggs evaporate!

But such periods of despair are typically the best times to go shopping. After a while, prices will stop falling and, ultimately, reverse direction. Diversified mutual-fund portfolios always head to higher ground once a decline has run its course.

Taking the Market's Temperature

To help spot times when greed and fear predominate, you practically need a thermometer and a stethoscope. At a minimum, it's useful to track the following valuation indicators:

The earnings multiple. The P/E or price/earnings ratio for the overall market is a popular sentiment gauge. The multiple for the S&P 500 is generally used, although others are available. This yardstick has ranged from less than 10 in depressed markets to more than 20 when stocks are pricey. It has averaged about 13.5.

The price-to-book ratio. This indicator tracks what investors are willing to pay for a company's net assets or "book value." The price/book ratio for the S&P 500 ranges from about 1.0 during bear market troughs to well above 4.0 when stocks are very pricey, with an average near 2.0. Extended bull markets generally start from low price/book ratios, as did the prolonged ascent that began in 1982 with a reading of less than 1.0.

The yield. This tracks the relationship of dividends paid to share prices. Some feel that this is the most telling valuation indicator because cash dividends can't be manipulated through accounting policies like earnings can. The S&P 500 yield has ranged from more than 6 percent at market troughs to below 2 percent at peaks, with the average running near 4.5 percent. The paltry yields of less than 2 percent observed in 1996 and 1997 were the lowest of the century, pointing to an extremely pricey market. But many investors feel that a lower range of yields may be normal now because corporations are generally plowing back more money into their businesses and, consequently, paying out less in dividends. In addition, more companies now use extra cash to repurchase their shares rather than pay dividends.

The P/E, market-to-book ratio, and dividend yield for the S&P 500 and other market indexes can be tracked weekly in *Barron's* "Market Laboratory." The dividend yield is especially revealing because it can help you estimate the probable long-run return on stocks.

Estimating Your Probable Return

A rough but nevertheless useful formula for gauging the likely long-run total return on the S&P 500 is to add the index's dividend yield and its historic yearly growth in dividends:

Expected return on S&P 500 = Dividend yield + growth

This formula is based on the well-known "dividend-discount model," which analysts use to value both dividend-paying stocks and the overall market. Suppose the S&P 500 currently yields a meager 2 percent in an overheated market. Using a long-run growth rate of 6 percent, which represents the average annual rate of increase of the S&P 500 dividend over the past several decades, you could anticipate earning about 8 percent over the long pull if you invest today in an S&P 500 index fund. A robust 6 -percent dividend yield in a depressed market would point to a 12-percent long-run return. Increasing your stock allocation would make good sense in this case. An average 4.5-percent dividend yield points to a 10.5-percent probable return, which is close to the historic average for equities.

MARKET TIMING

Market timers don't try to fight the trend or their emotions. They don't try to buy at the absolute low or sell at the very top either. Instead, they hope to participate in most of a rally while avoiding most of a decline. Even though market timing is an inexact science and has some serious pitfalls, it is, at least to a modest degree, practiced by most individual investors and portfolio managers.

There are many approaches to market timing. Some are highly intricate, requiring lots of work. Others are simple and maintenance-free. For example, dollar-cost averaging, one of the most basic of strategies, is actually an effective timing tool. Why? Because it gets you to buy more shares when prices are low and fewer when they are high. The more active trading strategies involve switching among funds within a family based on signals generated by market indicators. The larger the proportion of assets switched, the more aggressive the approach.

Needless to say, market timers are enthusiastic about their following. They employ many "technical," or numerical trading indicators, and sophisticated computer models to discern likely changes in the market's direction. Timers often claim they can beat the market averages by retreating to cash to preserve their gains when a decline is anticipated. It's not uncommon for hard-core timers to move between the extremes of 100 percent stocks during an up market and 100 percent cash when their indicators signal a major downturn. Market timing is especially easy to do with mutual funds. Virtually all funds offer telephone switching at little or no cost.

But does the approach work? To answer that, consider the following key arguments often made by market timers.

Market-Timing Argument #1: You can be reasonably successful at pinpointing times to exit and reenter the market.

OUR POSITION: Buying low and selling high is easier said than done. It's virtually impossible to be consistently right in timing both your exit and reentry points. The market's performance over the next few months or even the next few years is impossible to foretell with enough precision to offset taxes, trading costs, and the impact of losses. To do well as a hard-core timer, you've got to be right at least 70 percent of the time, according to academic research.

Market-Timing Argument #2: Market timing reduces risk.

OUR POSITION: True, market timing can reduce volatility because you're in cash part of the time. But it also increases the danger of missing out on short, sharp rallies. By reducing their returns, timers assume more inflation risk than buy-and-hold investors because they don't keep their money working around the clock.

Market-Timing Argument #3: A growing body of academic research indicates that investors can take advantage of market inefficiencies.

OUR POSITION: Maybe so, but the big question is how? If there were a timing system using mathematical models that consistently beat the market, it would self-destruct with widespread usage. And as noted, frequent trading increases taxes and transaction costs, offsetting some of the opportunities created by inefficiencies. Chapter 8 explores the controversial notion of market inefficiency in greater detail. Suffice to say that staunch believers in market efficiency hold that any timing system is futile.

Market-Timing Argument #4: Most individuals don't have the emotional discipline to follow a buy-and-hold strategy through the ups and downs of the market.

OUR POSITION: This may well be true. We don't have any evidence indicating it's not. But that doesn't mean you can't succeed with a buy-and-hold program, or that you will succeed with timing. It's highly unlikely that most investors have the courage to shift their cash around the instant a timing signal is flashed. In other words, it can be emotionally difficult to follow a timing strategy, too.

Market-Timing Argument #5: Avoiding the worst down months is more important than participating in the best up months.

OUR POSITION: To the contrary, participating in the best up months is the key to building wealth. Stocks have a bullish bias. Buy-and-hold investors have the odds on their side. As we said, stocks move up about 70 percent of the time, and the market gains a lot more in bullish phases than it loses on the downside. The really dramatic market surges are unpredictable, of short duration, and few and far between. Market timers risk being in cash at the wrong time.

Do you need more evidence? Table 7-1 contains a study conducted by Lipper Analytical Services over the 240-month period from December 1976 through December 1996. The results illustrate that missing out on a few big up months can make a sizable difference. If you bought and held the S&P 500, you would have earned 14.2 percent compounded annually over the entire 240 months. The more great months you missed, the worse the outcome.

Table 7-1   The Risk of Missing the Best Up Months

Time in Market	Return*
Entire 240 months	14.2%
Less the best month in the market	13.6
Less the 3 best months in the market	12.7
Less the 5 best months in the market	11.8
Less the 10 best months in the market	9.8

*Compound annual results based on S&P 500 returns from December 1976 to December 1996.
Source: Lipper Analytical Services Inc.

ASSET ALLOCATION

This approach avoids some of the pitfalls of aggressive timing but still demands patience and discipline. There are various offshoots, but they're all based on drawing up an optimal portfolio before you start to invest, then sticking with it, more or less.

As explained in Chapter 1, all investors should determine their optimum stock allocation based on their age, time horizon, risk tolerance, and other factors. As a starting point, you might invest a percentage of your nest egg equal to "100 minus your age" in stock funds; then place the remainder in bond and money-market holdings. More volatility-tolerant individuals might allocate 110 or even 120 minus their ages to stocks. Try not to trim back your targets even if the market seems pricey, unless you're going to tap into your nest egg sometime within the next five years. If stocks appear cheap, however, consider adding to your normal stock weighting.

Rather than using a fixed stock allocation as suggested above, you might prefer to operate within a target range of, say, 70 to 90 percent invested in equity funds. This approach, which is known as "tactical asset allocation," allows you the flexibility to lighten up when you perceive a cyclical peak, and perhaps switch from more aggressive holdings into income-oriented portfolios. Thus, it entails a limited amount of market timing. But you wouldn't want to make drastic shifts or your approach will soon resemble an aggressive market-timing strategy.

DOLLAR-COST AVERAGING

This approach combines simplicity, risk reduction, and affordability. It's an ideal way to space out your purchases to avoid paying too much. It takes the guesswork out of deciding when to buy. It also helps you diversify over time. You essentially buy more shares when prices are low, fewer when they are high. Dollar-cost averaging is a good discipline since it forces you to commit cash at market lows, when others are fearful. You may even be pleased when prices fall because your fixed-dollar outlays fetch more shares.

Investing $1,000 quarterly in a volatile fund might work out as illustrated in Table 7-2. Just after the July 1 purchase, you would have 305 shares worth $3,812.50. The cost per share would be $9.84. Note that the average of the three NAVs works out to $10.17, higher than the figure achieved with dollar-cost averaging. This would be the cost if you bought an equal number of shares each time.

For dollar-cost averaging to be a success, stock prices and your mutual fund must push higher over time. Fortunately, this describes the long-term trend. One of the problems encountered when applying an averaging strategy to individual stocks is that there's a much greater possibility that they may

Table 7-2   Dollar-Cost Averaging

Date	Amount Invested	NAV	Shares Bought	Shares Owned	Account Value
Jan. 1	$1,000.00	$10.00	100	100	$1,000.00
Apr. 1	1,000.00	8.00	125	225	1,800.00
July 1	1,000.00	12.50	80	305	3,812.50

Average cost per share under plan = $9.84 ($3,000/305)
Average of net asset values = $10.17 [(10.00 + 8.00 + 12.50)/3]

fall in price and never recover, especially if the company ends up in bankruptcy. Fund buyers do not have this worry since they own a diversified portfolio. Only a handful of funds have been long-term losers, and they are pretty easy to spot.

Dollar-cost averaging works even better if you have the discipline to increase your investments during down markets. That's when you can take advantage of rock-bottom prices, which will further reduce your average cost and increase your return. In the example shown in Table 7-2, suppose you doubled up by investing $2,000 instead of your usual $1,000 on April 1, when the fund had an $8 NAV. After your July 1 transaction, you would own 430 shares at an average cost of $9.30.

When establishing a program, you need to consider the frequency of your investments—monthly, quarterly, semiannually, or any regular interval. More frequent intervals increase your chances of buying shares when prices are especially low. On the other hand, this can lead to somewhat more complicated recordkeeping, especially if you must track your transactions for tax purposes.

Many people are already following a dollar-cost averaging strategy, even though they might not realize it. If you invest regularly in a 401(k) plan or in an IRA, you are diversifying your purchases. And if you're reinvesting distributions into additional fund shares, this too amounts to a form of dollar-cost averaging, though the cash amounts aren't equal.

AVERAGING THROUGH THICK AND THIN

Bear markets offer a nice bonus if you are dollar-cost averaging and have a long time horizon. You can actually do better over the long term when the market plunges and then recovers than if it climbs gradually upward. That's because you are able to accumulate more shares at low prices with your fixed-dollar investments.

Want some proof? The illustrations in both Tables 7-3 and 7-4 assume that $1,000 is invested quarterly over a five-year period. Table 7-3 has a built-

Table 7-3   Dollar-Cost Averaging Through a Down Market

Investment Amount	NAV	Shares Bought	Shares Owned	Account Value
$1,000	$40	25.00	25.00	$1,000
1,000	35	28.57	53.57	1,875
1,000	30	33.33	86.90	2,607
1,000	27	37.04	123.94	3,346
1,000	25	40.00	163.94	4,099
1,000	23	43.48	207.42	4,771
1,000	24	41.67	249.09	5,978
1,000	25	40.00	289.09	7,227
1,000	28	35.71	324.80	9,094
1,000	30	33.33	358.13	10,744
1,000	32	31.25	389.38	12,460
1,000	34	29.41	418.80	14,239
1,000	35	28.57	447.37	15,658
1,000	37	27.03	474.39	17,553
1,000	40	25.00	499.39	19,976
1,000	44	22.73	522.12	22,973
1,000	48	20.83	542.96	26,062
1,000	55	18.18	561.14	30,863
1,000	58	17.24	578.38	33,546
1,000	60	16.67	**595.05**	**35,703**

in bear market, whereas Table 7-4 assumes prices move upward, uninterrupted by setbacks. In both instances the initial purchase is made at $40 a share and the final investment five years later at $60. Thus, the important difference in these illustrations is what happens in the meantime. For simplicity we assume no distributions.

The results can be summarized as follows:

- In Table 7-3 the NAV plunges from an initial $40 to a low of $23 before beginning its climb to $60. In Table 7-4 the NAV moves gradually upward, with no setbacks, from $40 to $60.

- Despite the roller-coaster ride, our tenacious bear-market investor in Table 7-3 accumulates more shares after five years and enjoys an account value that's 42-percent greater. His compound yearly return is 22.9 percent, compared with 9.4 percent for the steadily rising market.

Table 7-4   *Dollar-Cost Averaging in a Steadily Rising Market*

Investment Amount	NAV	Shares Bought	Shares Owned	Account Value
$1,000	$40	25.00	25.00	$1,000
1,000	41	24.39	49.39	2,025
1,000	41	24.39	73.78	3,025
1,000	42	23.81	97.59	4,099
1,000	43	23.26	120.85	5,196
1,000	43	23.26	144.10	6,196
1,000	45	22.22	166.32	7,485
1,000	45	22.22	188.55	8,485
1,000	46	21.74	210.29	9,673
1,000	48	20.83	231.12	11,094
1,000	49	20.41	251.53	12,325
1,000	50	20.00	271.53	13,576
1,000	51	19.61	291.13	14,848
1,000	51	19.61	310.74	15,848
1,000	52	19.23	329.97	17,159
1,000	53	18.87	348.84	18,489
1,000	54	18.52	367.36	19,837
1,000	56	17.86	385.22	21,572
1,000	58	17.24	402.46	23,343
1,000	60	16.67	419.12	25,147

VALUE AVERAGING

You don't have to follow dollar-cost averaging strictly by the book. You can improve your results by investing more when prices are depressed and socking away less or perhaps even selling some shares when prices are very high. This describes another approach known as "value averaging."

Developed and popularized by finance professor Michael Edleson, value averaging requires that you increase the dollar amount of your holdings by a set figure each period. To do this, you need to put in more money when prices have dropped to offset losses on existing shares. After prices have risen, you would buy fewer shares, perhaps do nothing, or even unload some shares. Unlike dollar-cost averaging, this method has built-in sell rules. In addition, the system makes it easier to estimate how much money you will have by a specific future date. For instance, if you want $40,000 in 10 years, your account would need to grow by $1,000 each quarter.

Value averaging requires more work than dollar-cost averaging and is not as easy to implement because different amounts of cash must be invested each period. It also can complicate your recordkeeping for tax purposes when you sell shares. However, if you practice value averaging with an IRA or similar plan, you need not worry about this. If you hold a mutual fund in a taxable account, you can forego the option of selling shares when the NAV rises and still derive much of the benefit from the strategy. This is doubly desirable if selling would give rise to taxable capital gains.

Taking our initial dollar-cost averaging illustration in Table 7-2, and assuming you desire your account to grow by $1,000 quarterly, the value-averaging program would work out as detailed in Table 7-5. The columns are ordered differently here since the focus now is on account value. Notice that to determine the total shares needed on each purchase (or sale) date, you must divide the account value by the current NAV. The shares bought or sold would be the difference between the number previously held and the new number needed. For example, on April 1 the target account value is $2,000. With an NAV of $8, you require a total of 250 shares ($2,000/$8). Since you already hold 100, you must purchase 150 more.

After the July 1 transaction, your average cost works out to $8.65, well below the $9.84 obtained with dollar-cost averaging. The more volatile the portfolio's NAV, the greater this advantage. Since value averaging generally results in a lower average cost, it also generates a higher compound annual return.

Both value and dollar-cost averaging can sometimes pose problems for people trying to maintain specific weightings in each of several asset categories. Suppose you want to keep 60 percent in equity funds, 25 percent in bond portfolios, and 15 percent in money-market funds. With an averaging strategy, you will find that your asset proportions have changed after some time, requiring you to rebalance your holdings. This, in turn, may interfere with the results of your averaging program. While this might not be a serious problem, it is something of which you should be aware.

Table 7-5   Value Averaging

Date	Target Account Value	NAV	Shares Needed	Shares Bought (Sold)	Transaction Value
Jan. 1	$1,000.00	$10.00	100	100	$1,000.00
Apr. 1	2,000.00	8.00	250	150	1,200.00
July 1	3,000.00	12.50	240	(10)	(125.00)

Average cost per share:
Value averaging = $8.65 [(1,000 + 1,200 - 125)/240]
Dollar-cost averaging = $9.84 (Table 7-2)

INVESTING LARGE LUMP SUMS

The whole rationale behind averaging strategies is to avoid taking a big plunge into the stock market. Most people do invest gradually, following some sort of an averaging strategy because they typically receive money in small increments over time, such as from a weekly paycheck. But what if you suddenly find yourself with a large amount of cash, say, $500,000? Lump sums could come from an inheritance, proceeds from the sale of real estate, or a payout from a pension plan. Or perhaps the cash simply piled up over the years in a savings account or money-market fund.

Academic studies show that you're probably better off putting the amount you want to allocate to equities to work right away rather than averaging into the market. Why? Because stocks trend upward over time. In most years the return on equities exceeds the return on cash. This is particularly true if you have a long time horizon and won't need to tap into your nest egg for at least 10 years or so. Table 7-6 illustrates one of many possible mixes for a growth investor with a $500,000 lump sum.

If you've got a long time horizon, it may be best to divvy up a lump sum in accordance with your established portfolio weights as illustrated in Table 7-6. That way you don't risk dumping everything into just one investment or asset class.

Here are some other points to ponder:

1. *The level of interest rates.* Is it one of those rare periods when short-term rates are relatively high, perhaps even in the double digits? In this case the opportunity cost of staying on the sidelines is lower because you can earn generous returns in a money-market fund. Under such a scenario, it may make some sense to average into the stock market over at least several months. But don't wait too long because interest rates, especially on the short end, can quickly decline.

Table 7-6   Growth-Portfolio Allocation for $500,000 Lump Sum

Fund Category	Dollar Value	Percent of Portfolio
Large-stock fund	$150,000	30%
Small-stock fund	100,000	20
International-stock fund	100,000	20
Emerging-markets fund	50,000	10
Short-term bond fund	50,000	10
Money-market fund	50,000	10

2. *The valuation of the market.* If stocks are extremely pricey and speculation rampant, you might be able to make a good case for averaging into equity mutual funds, rather than committing cash in a lump sum, particularly if your time horizon is not especially long.

3. *Your age.* Older individuals may not be able to withstand the danger of investing at a market peak. They might not have enough time to recoup their losses if the market drops by, say, a third. The psychological stress could be unbearable even for investors who are well off and building up assets for heirs.

KEEPING TABS ON YOUR MANAGER

You might prefer to own a fund that always maintains a fully invested position so you can decide for yourself how much to allocate to stocks, bonds, and cash. Or you may want one that does some or a lot of market timing. Our preference is for managers who stick pretty closely to their primary objective and don't do a lot of tinkering. However, most managers do more timing than you might realize, including those who maintain a more or less fully invested posture. It's part of their job to keep abreast of changing investment conditions and to rotate their holdings accordingly. Portfolio managers can time the market in one or more of the following ways:

1. *Altering the cash position.* You can see to what extent a manager "times" by tracking the fund's cash position. If the proportion of cash equivalents jumps from, say, 5 to 20 percent or more, it's obvious that the manager doesn't always stay fully invested.

2. *Pursuing a value strategy.* Value investors look for stocks that are cheap when measured by earnings, cash flow, book value, and similar yardsticks. A manager might find a company that he thinks offers a dollar's worth of assets for 50 cents. When a manager loads up on defensive value stocks rather than high-flying growth issues, this approach might be thought of as a form of indirect market timing since these companies won't drop as much in a market downturn. Permanent value investors tend to be more heavily committed to stocks at market troughs but may hold large cash positions at peaks.

3. *Hedging with futures or options.* Managers who expect a significant decline in stock prices can use futures and options as defensive measures. Usually they don't hedge the full portfolio, just part of it. Futures and options can serve as an effective substitute for increasing the fund's cash position and thus can be viewed as market-timing tools.

4. *Rotating sectors.* This means the manager moves in and out of certain industries or other stock groups based on the investment outlook. For instance, if a downturn looms, he or she might underweight cyclical stocks such as automakers in favor of more defensive or recession-resistant groups such as pharmaceutical or food companies. Managers rotate among sectors based on their perceived growth potential as well as their current valuation.

5. *Rotating country holdings.* Global and international fund managers often move in and out of specific nations as a market-timing response. They favor countries and regions that offer good value and steer clear of those that appear expensive.

SET YOUR SIGHTS ON THE LONG TERM

If you have the time, try to focus on the long term and patiently ride with the market's ups and downs. Good years for stocks historically have out-

---

Tracking Mutual-Fund Cash Positions

The Investment Company Institute tabulates a composite cash ratio for equity funds. This closely watched gauge shows the percentage of cash-equivalent holdings by stock funds each month. Since the ICI began this tabulation in 1961, the yardstick has ranged between 4 and 13 percent of fund assets. Mutual funds account for a major percentage of the trading on the New York Stock Exchange, so what they do with their cash is pretty important.

Recent values for the cash statistic can be found on the Internet at http://www.ici.org, the ICI's Web site. By tracking the numbers monthly, you might get some feel for portfolio-manager sentiment. An increase generally signifies that managers are building up cash because their outlook is becoming less sanguine; a decrease may reflect optimism. The cash percentage draws greatest attention at extreme levels. But its interpretation is controversial and some even feel the number is irrelevant.

Should you worry if cash holdings are skimpy when stocks are at nosebleed heights? Many fund-watchers do. The theory is that if investors yank their money out when the market begins to tumble, managers will be forced to trim their holdings to meet redemptions, thereby accelerating a market slide. But no one indicator has predictive value. The financial world is just too complex.

weighed the bad, both in frequency and in magnitude. If you hang on to stock funds for many years, you can really expect to see your wealth rise. Bear markets should not be a time for panic or emotional depression. Rather, view them as opportunities to add to your stock portfolio at bargain prices, as illustrated in Table 7-3.

Probably the single most important strategy covered in this chapter was the simplest: dollar-cost averaging. This widely used approach has several important benefits:

- *It gets you to focus on building wealth slowly but surely over the long haul.* People who follow this disciplined program are less likely to yank their money out at the wrong time or jump in and out of different funds.

- *It eliminates the guesswork.* Aggressive market timing doesn't work. It's wiser to devote more effort to selecting solid mutual funds as long-term investments. At a minimum, dollar-cost averaging will spare you the expense of subscribing to a market-timing newsletter.

- *It's effective in reducing your average cost in volatile markets.* Stocks will fluctuate, as J. P. Morgan said. With an averaging strategy, the more movement the better from a pricing standpoint. Rather than worry about volatility, you can rest assured that it will work in your favor.

AT THE CLOSE

Stocks and stock funds will fluctuate over time—that's the only accurate prediction anyone can make with certainty. The market does what it can to perplex the greatest number of people. But successful investors know how to make volatility work in their favor while keeping fear and greed at bay.

Active market timers face an uphill battle. This includes mutual-fund managers who vary their positions frequently. People will fare better if they place as much money as they can into equities as soon as possible, then leave it alone for many years. But lump-sum investing can be hard to accomplish, for emotional and budgetary reasons. That's why an ongoing investment program utilizing dollar-cost averaging or value averaging often works best.

CHAPTER 8

The Virtues of Indexing

Whether it's due to exceptional skill, plain luck, or both, there always seems to be a small group of hot-handed money managers able to beat the market more or less consistently. But identifying these astute stock-pickers early enough to do some good isn't easy. Of the people running the more than 2,000 domestic stock funds in existence today, how can you tell in advance who the big winners will be? Who knew Peter Lynch would compile such a stunning record when he took the helm of Fidelity Magellan in 1977? In fact, how many people even knew who Lynch was back then? Certainly a lot fewer investors than when he retired in 1990.

If you are caught up in the quixotic quest for the next decade's celebrity managers and mutual funds, here's a word of caution: Don't bet too heavily on past performance. Take a close look at the data in Table 8-1 from Lipper Analytical Services. These numbers show how the two dozen top-ranked funds in the 1976-1986 period fared in the subsequent decade. All but one of the 24 top funds in that first decade achieved a lower ranking in the second—much lower in most cases. Similar shifts in rankings also are evident over shorter periods. The hot hands of all-star managers frequently turn to icy fingers when the music stops.

Table 8-1
*Subsequent Performances of 24 Top Equity Funds from 1976-1986**

Ranking 1976-1986	Ranking 1986-1996	Ranking 1976-1986	Ranking 1986-1996
1	42	13	426
2	184	14	12
3	295	15	188
4	345	16	61
5	281	17	337
6	356	18	235
7	360	19	414
8	79	20	233
9	129	21	140
10	97	22	258
11	25	23	226
12	70	24	56

*283 funds were ranked in the first decade; 655 in the second.
Both decades end 12/31.
Source: Lipper Analytical Services Inc.

REGRESSION TO THE MEAN

Why the dramatic shifts in ranking? Mutual funds with the best records have a definite tendency to gravitate gradually back down to mediocrity. The longer a fund has delivered a star-studded record, the more likely its margin of superiority will wear thin. This reflects a well-established financial principal called "regression to the mean." A common reason for slipping is that a portfolio may have grown too large to deliver the same eye-popping numbers it once did. Or perhaps the star manager responsible for the superior record has left the fund or turned his or her attention more to administrative chores.

Enter index funds. These portfolios essentially are unmanaged. They buy and hold the same stocks or bonds that are included in a popular benchmark, such as the Standard & Poor's 500 or Lehman Brothers Aggregate Bond Index. They appeal to investors seeking low costs and the assurance of very closely tracking the market's returns. They make sense for anyone pursuing a long-term buy-and-hold strategy because of their low expenses, relatively predictable returns, and tax efficiency.

In a pure, passive index fund, turnover and thus transaction costs are low. The management fee also tends to be minimal. The fund doesn't make bets on particular securities or sectors, and it remains fully invested, without attempting any market timing. Of course, not every index fund fits these descriptions precisely. Some quasi-index products follow different strategies such as trying to weed out an index's weakest stocks. And there are some active managers who are really "closet indexers" because they hold a broad group of "safe" companies—representative of the market as a whole. Investors in such funds have to live with the higher fees associated with active management and the real danger of mediocre performance.

MOST FUNDS LAG

Overall, the majority of actively managed stock funds fail to beat the market consistently. Table 8-2 shows the percentages that outperformed the S&P 500 over various periods. Over the full 35-year span, only 36 percent of the managed portfolios exceeded the S&P 500. And it's important to recognize that these results are tilted in favor of the managed funds because of "survivorship bias." Essentially, only those portfolios that fared well enough to remain in existence throughout each period are included.

Table 8-3 looks at the phenomenon of underperformance differently. It shows the total return of the broadly based Wilshire 5000 compared with that of the average stock fund. The return of the Wilshire 5000 has been reduced 0.3 percent each year, a reasonable approximation of index-fund costs. Of course, when the market heads south, index funds can be expected to decline a bit more than the typical managed stock fund, which likely will maintain some cash cushion.

Table 8-2   General Equity Funds Versus S&P 500

Past Period*	Percentage Beating Index	Number Beating Index	Total Funds
5 years	31%	230	754
10 years	18	69	388
25 years	41	82	198
35 years	36	34	95

*All periods end 12/31/96, including reinvested dividends.
Source: Lipper Analytical Services Inc.

Table 8-3   Total Returns: Active Versus Passive

	Ten Years Ended 12/31/96	
	Cumulative Return	Annualized Return
Wilshire 5000 Index*	356.52%	14.50%
Average General Equity Fund	314.36	13.09

*The returns of the index have been reduced by 0.3 percent per year to reflect approximate index-fund costs.
Source: Lipper Analytical Services Inc.

A Zero-Sum Game

Why do active managers underperform? To answer that, it helps to remember that all investors collectively form the market. So if one manager is beating a benchmark by, say, four percentage points, someone else must be underperforming by the same amount. Relative performance is, therefore, a zero-sum game, with outperformers offset by laggards.

Given this simple fact, managers face considerable difficulty in struggling to beat a market average because they shoulder the burdens of advisory fees, operating costs, distribution outlays (including any 12b-1 fees), and transaction costs. The latter include bid-asked spreads and any unfavorable price impacts of relatively large trades. It's safe to assume that all of these costs amount to at least 2 percentage points a year for the typical stock fund. That's a fairly steep price to pay given that the market has returned about 10 percent on average over the long run. So if you're hoping to exceed 10 percent for any lengthy stretch, you're betting on more good things than history suggests will happen. Also, keep in mind that actively managed funds commonly hold 5 to 10 percent of their assets in cash, and sometimes more. This represents another performance hurdle to overcome. Index funds stay fully invested. Their shareholders know that they will always more or less match the market's return and never drastically underperform it.

In short, the typical actively managed fund really must beat its benchmark by at least 2 percentage points yearly just to stay even. This is difficult in "efficient" markets, where finding bargains is like looking for the proverbial needle in a haystack.

NO FREE LUNCH

By "efficient," we mean markets where active management doesn't do much good. Plenty of academic research was done in the 1960s and 1970s that led to a theory called the "efficient-market hypothesis." According to this hypothesis, stocks virtually always sell for what they're worth at any given moment. There are no underpriced or overpriced issues and thus few opportunities for astute stock-pickers to nibble away at bargains. In other words, there's no "free lunch" on Wall Street.

Under this hypothesis, each stock hovers very closely around its true value. New information can and does cause the value of a company to change from time to time. Prices respond quickly to *unanticipated* news, moving up or down rapidly. News itself appears more or less randomly over time. The faster the stock's response to news, the more efficient the market.

Figure 8-1 illustrates graphically the concept of market efficiency for a company that has a significant favorable news release on day 0, the announcement date. The worth of the stock increases from $20 to $25 on that day. With

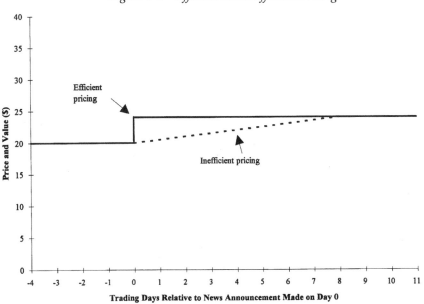

Figure 8-1   Efficient and Inefficient Pricing

perfect efficiency, price would always exactly equal the per-share value. The company's price in our example would immediately jump to $25. But when the market is inefficient, a lag occurs in the adjustment of a stock's price to the new information, as represented by the dashed line. So how do believers in the efficient-market hypothesis explain the fact that a handful of highly successful investors have been able to beat the market over long periods? It's simply a matter of luck, they say.

But other observers don't believe in market efficiency, at least completely. They see opportunities to outperform the market by making bets. A manager would buy when he or she thinks a stock's price is significantly below its true value and sell when it equals or exceeds this value. This approach is also known as value investing. If markets were completely efficient, prices and values would never diverge far enough for anyone to earn an extraordinary profit, especially after factoring in the high costs of frequent trading. But while not 100-percent efficient, the U.S. stock market and even several foreign ones have been shown to be efficient enough to make indexing a sound strategy.

THE BIRTH OF INDEX FUNDS

Indexing began to appeal to pension funds in the 1970s because of a growing acceptance of the efficient-market hypothesis and compelling evidence indicating that well over half of all portfolio managers underperform the popular averages. The thinking was that if you can't beat the market, you could at least perform closely in line with an appropriate index. This could be done by holding a large, well-diversified portfolio and trading as little as possible to minimize costs. The concept has proven popular. Indexed assets have grown to about 25 percent of the money in corporate pension plans and about 6 percent of 401(k) plans.

The first index mutual fund, the Vanguard Index Trust, was introduced in 1976 and has closely tracked the S&P 500 since then. At this writing, the Vanguard 500 portfolio had an average expense ratio of just 0.20 percent and yearly turnover of 5 percent. It stands as one example of a fund that has seen its per-share costs decline in recent years thanks to the efficiencies of larger size. The portfolio crossed the $40-billion asset mark in 1997, a nice testimony to its success. It has now become the second-largest portfolio in the mutual-fund industry, exceeded in size only by Fidelity Magellan.

A number of other index funds have been introduced in recent years, both by Vanguard and by other families. For instance, in 1996 USAA Investment Management unveiled an S&P 500 product with even lower annual expenses than Vanguard's flagship fund. Of course, expense ratios are subject to change.

An added plus of index funds, of which many people are unaware, is their tax efficiency. With portfolio turnover rates of just 5 percent or so, these investments do not realize and distribute much in the way of capital gains. Some index funds strive to be even more tax-efficient by offsetting realized gains with losses on other holdings. But a tax-managed fund probably would not track the performance of its market benchmark as closely as a pure index portfolio since some active decision making goes into the equation. Vanguard is among the firms offering tax-managed portfolios in addition to conventional index funds.

PASSIVE RESISTANCE

The indexing approach has gained rapid acceptance over the past couple of decades. Yet stock index funds still account for just 6 percent of all assets in the equity arena, according to Lipper. Clearly, not everyone has caught the passive-investing bug. Here are three reasons why not:

1. *The old college try.* Many investors feel that they can or should be able to identify top-performing mutual funds and, therefore, beat the market. Others think they can bypass funds entirely and pick their own winning stocks. It's simply human nature to let one's ego enter the picture. But many people fail to recognize that it's a lot harder to be a superb investor or to identify future fund superstars than it is to excel in school, sports, hobbies, work, or other activities.

2. *Indexing is boring.* Index funds commonly are viewed as mediocre if not outright boring, since they will never beat the market. But the investment arena isn't the place most people should look for fun and excitement. More aggressive financial products and strategies can be highly speculative. Some even verge on gambling.

3. *Passive portfolios are bought, not sold.* Low-cost index funds don't generate the kinds of profits for fund companies that their actively managed counterparts do, so there is less incentive to introduce and market them. The concept is especially ill-suited for the broker sales channel because a hefty load can offset much of the fee-cutting index advantage.

HOW EFFICIENT IS THE MARKET?

A better understanding of the reasons for market efficiency may help you decide whether to add an index component to your asset mix. An efficient market depends on the watchful eyes of many intelligent, highly trained analysts who respond instantly to any significant news item. The U.S. stock market is far more efficient today than it was in the 1930s, when security analysis was in its infancy and there were fewer skilled investors. These days, according to efficient-market advocates, it's practically impossible for individuals or fund managers to fare much better than average by quickly reacting to news. The competition is simply too keen.

Yet market efficiency, as noted, isn't perfect. The important question thus becomes: How efficient is it? While the market may be highly efficient for large, heavily researched, actively traded stocks, pockets of inefficiency do exist. Examples include many obscure, thinly traded micro-cap companies and shares traded in certain foreign bourses. In addition, investors tend to overreact to both good and bad news, which can create temporary mispricings. And there is a considerable amount of "noise" trading going on. Noise traders buy and sell in response to unsound information or emotional impulses. They could be reacting to rumors, tips, or their own superficial knowledge.

As you might expect, the efficient-market school has been a target of some strong criticism. In the 1980s, academics searched intensively for anomalies to the hypothesis and they found some. Now the pendulum has swung back somewhat from the view of pure efficiency to a position of compromise.

MARKET ANOMALIES

Stocks do not always sell exactly for what they are worth. As explained in Chapter 7, investors often overreact to both good and bad news. Hints of war, signs of inflation, or symptoms of other problems can send share prices stampeding over a cliff. If the situation is unexpectedly resolved, they often bounce back just as quickly. The same kind of overreaction occurs on a micro scale, in response to favorable and unfavorable news on individual companies. Consequently, prices usually fluctuate more widely than values. Times of panic often provide bargain hunters with great opportunities. And when investors become wildly optimistic, good money managers cut back on their equity positions. Periods of overvaluation and undervaluation can persist for some time on individual stocks or in the market as a whole.

In the 1980s, research turned up a number of anomalies to the efficient-market hypothesis. These exceptions indicate that there are a number of strategies that may allow you to beat the market, at least to a limited extent. For instance, low-P/E stocks have been shown to produce better performance than stocks with high or average earnings multiples. This implies that value investors should do better than their growth counterparts over lengthy spans. In addition, purchasing the shares of good closed-end funds trading at abnormally wide discounts can prove profitable. Chapter 9 takes a close look at these quirky portfolios.

Mutual-fund investors should pay some attention to market efficiency because they will want to know whether a highly skilled manager can continue to outperform. Efficient-market purists would argue that the handful of managers who have consistently delivered superior gains have simply had a run of good luck. This is debatable. Certain managers clearly are talented and capable of generating above-normal returns. The real issue is whether you can identify today those managers who will excel tomorrow. If not, then an index fund could be appropriate for at least a portion of your nest egg.

WHAT'S AVAILABLE

Index mutual funds offer a broad array of investment choices. Garden-variety portfolios track well-known indexes pegged to small stocks (such as the Russell 2000), mid-size companies (the S&P MidCap 400), both small and mid-size firms (the Wilshire 4500), larger companies (the S&P 500), or a sampling of the entire domestic market (Wilshire 5000). The most popular index vehicles are funds that track the S&P 500, which represents about 72 percent of the U.S. market. A Wilshire 5000 portfolio would be a good choice if you're looking for one-stop shopping or want a piece of virtually every domestic stock around. The Wilshire index, which has grown to include about 7,300 companies, is structured as follows: 70 percent large stocks, 20 percent medium, and 10 percent small. That's basically the same way the U.S. market breaks down.

Vanguard offers portfolios that separate the S&P 500 into growth and value groups. Each S&P 500 stock is classified on a semiannual basis as either "growth," showing high earnings gains, or as "value," with a low price-to-book ratio. The Value portfolio yields more in dividends than the S&P 500, and the Growth portfolio yields less. The returns of the two portfolios also typically diverge from the index itself.

Several broad international index funds offered by Vanguard and a handful of other firms invest in Europe, Asia, and an assortment of emerging stock markets. While efficiency typically is less in selected foreign nations, trading costs commonly are higher, which can give index products an edge. In addition to traditional index mutual funds, Chapter 11 introduces some relatively new single-country passive portfolios that trade on exchanges and share characteristics of both open- and closed-end vehicles. These interesting products mainly target stocks in the world's more developed markets. You can even find some highly specialized index funds targeting real-estate securities, gold stocks, or the natural-gas industry.

You also can make a good argument for holding bond-index portfolios, which tend to outperform well over half of their actively managed rivals. The bond choices break down into short-, intermediate-, and long-term portfolios. If you want both bonds and stocks in one package, a balanced index fund might be the answer. In the bond arena, low costs and thus passive investing can be especially important.

One caveat about index funds is that some carefully replicate an index while others try to outperform their benchmark through active management. If a portfolio uses options or futures heavily, has a high expense ratio, or has a relatively high turnover, it can't be a pure index fund. Be sure to read the prospectus carefully. There can be huge differences among funds tracking the same yardstick. Funds that do not follow a traditional, passive indexing strategy are not necessarily bad investments. But you need to compare the costs

---

Tracking Errors

It's wise to determine how well an index fund has mirrored its benchmark before you invest. Not all portfolios track their targets closely. The difference in performance depends partly on a fund's expense ratio. The greater the costs, the more a fund may trail its benchmark. Incidentally, the average S&P 500 index product runs up yearly expenses of about 0.4 percent, well under half that of the typical stock portfolio, according to Lipper Analytical Services. A second factor explaining performance divergence is that a fund may take an imperfect sampling of stocks from its target index, rather than investing in all of them. This is particularly likely with portfolios that invest in indexes containing thousands of companies such as the Russell 2000 or the Wilshire 5000.

with the expected benefits, and you shouldn't buy anything you don't understand. Index funds make most sense when they are truly passive and consist of big blue-chip stocks that tend to be efficiently priced.

In addition to Vanguard, which offers an extensive menu of index products, various other companies have at least one such fund. The list includes Dimensional, Dreyfus, Federated, Fidelity, Galaxy, Gateway, SEI, SSgA, Rushmore, Schwab, T. Rowe Price, and USAA.

BUILDING YOUR PORTFOLIO

Owing to their broadly diversified, low-cost nature, index funds typically make good portfolio anchors. Generally speaking, there are three alternative routes you can take: all passive, all active, or an indexed core.

1. *All passive.* It's not unthinkable to put all of your investment dollars into index funds. While you forego the opportunity to beat the market, you are assured of not being a laggard, either. Over time, you will probably fare better than most of your friends who own actively managed portfolios. However, your portfolio won't have much of a cash cushion if a global bear market develops. Table 8-4 shows one possible way for an appreciation-oriented investor to structure an all-passive mix.

2. *All active.* Conversely, perhaps you prefer to forego index products entirely. By definition, traditional index funds are not concerned with finding bargains. And since no markets are totally efficient, it still makes sense to look for value. Managed portfolios are most suitable for less-efficient pockets occupied by small stocks and "special situation" or turnaround companies. And they make good choices for foreign markets, many of which are relatively inefficient.

3. *An indexed core.* As a compromise, you might use index funds as core holdings amounting to anywhere from 25 to 50 percent of a portfolio.

Table 8-4   Sample Index-Fund Allocation for a Growth Investor

Fund Category	Percent of Portfolio
S&P 500 index	40%
Small-stock index	20
International index	20
Real-estate securities index	5
Bond index	15

Using this as a base, you can add actively managed products that you feel could beat the market, along with funds that target investment areas where there are few index choices.

While a total indexed portfolio may not appeal to most individuals, the core approach has wide applicability. It can help you resist the urge of jumping in and out of faddish actively managed funds, which can be damaging to long-run performance. And by indexing a portion of your portfolio, you can maintain a buy-and-hold strategy for at least some of your assets—a wise course. If you do invest in a mix of index and actively managed funds, it's generally best to place the former in your taxable accounts, and the latter in your retirement plans.

"SPIDERS" WITH 500 LEGS

"Spiders," or Standard & Poor's Depositary Receipts (SPDRs), bear no resemblance to their eight-legged namesakes. They are index portfolios that trade like stocks on the American Stock Exchange. Two versions are presently available: the original contract based on the S&P 500 and a newer product targeting the S&P MidCap 400. Trading symbols are SPY and MDY, respectively. Both are passive, low-cost, tax-efficient portfolios that compete directly with index mutual funds like the Vanguard 500 and the Dreyfus S&P MidCap Index Fund. In fact, the expense ratio for the S&P 500 Spider is even lower than those for other comparable portfolios.

How do Spiders work? Basically they represent ownership in the SPDR trust, a unit investment trust that holds the stocks in the underlying index. Spiders can be bought and sold at varying prices throughout the day. The S&P 500 Spider trades at about 1/10 the value of the S&P 500, MidCap Spiders at 1/5 of the S&P 400. You pay the usual stock brokerage commission when you buy or sell. Spiders are highly liquid and closely track their underlying benchmarks as they can be arbitraged by professional investors if their prices deviate from the index by more than 1/32nd or so.

What advantage, if any, do Spiders have over a passive mutual fund? Basically, they give you more control over your money and greater liquidity. Because Spiders fluctuate during the day, you can place a "limit order" to buy or sell at specified prices, as you would with any stock. Such an order gets executed only if you receive your stipulated price or better. The ability to get in and out at various prices during the day gives Spiders a trading edge over mutual funds, which can be bought or sold only at the day's closing mark. This can be advantageous in volatile, fast moving markets. But unlike trading with mutual funds, you face bid-asked spreads when you buy and sell Spiders. And, of course, you pay brokerage commissions.

Spiders are best used as a long-term investment, even though they can be traded frequently, bought on margin, and sold short. With the latter strategy, investors sell a security borrowed from their broker, which they hope to buy back later at a lower price. Short selling represents the reverse of the normal buy-now, sell-later procedure. But it's a risky strategy because a stock can theoretically rise a lot further than it can fall.

Spiders pay dividends quarterly. Dividend reinvestment is possible if your broker offers it, but you can only buy full shares, not fractional shares as with a mutual fund. In addition, your broker may charge a fee for this service, which is normally free with funds.

Because cash redemptions are not possible with Spiders, they are even more tax-efficient than garden-variety index funds. If the market tumbles, index funds may have to sell some shares and realize capital gains to meet investor redemptions. But this never happens with Spiders. The only time shares are bought and sold within the portfolio is if the composition of the underlying index changes. (Call 1-800-THE-AMEX for more information on Spiders.)

A CHECKLIST FOR INDEX INVESTING

Index funds have a lot going for them, with more portfolio choices than ever. Low costs, the assurance of beating most active managers, and tax efficiency are big pluses. Here are some points to keep in mind if you're shopping for such investments.

- *Be a penny pincher.* Favor domestic index funds that have expense ratios below 0.5 percent or slightly higher fees on international portfolios. Also, be aware of any account-maintenance fees. Some portfolios charge perhaps $10 a year to help defray shareholder-borne expenses. On a $3,000 investment, such a fee would add 0.33 percent in costs.

- *Take note of redemption fees and switching limitations.* Index portfolios commonly impose such hurdles to discourage frequent buying and selling by investors. But that's not necessarily bad, since index funds are not recommended for in-and-out traders.

- *Examine turnover.* True index funds replace just 5 to 10 percent of their holdings each year, or less. But higher readings might be justified if the composition of the benchmark changes frequently, as with certain bond indexes. Somewhat higher turnover rates also can be expected in funds that use a sample of stocks or follow a specialized strategy.

- *Favor index funds for taxable accounts.* The low turnovers of these investments make them decent tax shelters by themselves. Place less tax-efficient holdings in retirement accounts.

- *Avoid "closet indexing."* If you use actively managed funds, try not to own so many that you essentially get complete index-like diversification anyway. Why not? Because you would be paying the higher expenses typical of active management.

- *Beware of enhanced products.* If you see a portfolio that calls itself an index fund but lacks certain characteristics, it's not true-blue. Enhanced index funds commonly fail in their attempts to beat a particular index by trying to predict the best performers.

AT THE CLOSE

It's not easy to beat the market. Nor is it simple to select actively managed mutual funds that can do so. These arguments explain why index funds have become increasingly popular, especially as core holdings.

Index products have a natural cost advantage. Also, they tend to stay fully invested, which gives them a long-run advantage. Among the criticisms, index portfolios often are labeled as boring or dull. But usually they will rank in the top half when compared with their managed peer groups, if not higher.

Index funds vary in several respects, including the target benchmark, the degree of stock replication, and the level of expenses and other charges. Thus, it pays to shop around. So-called "Spiders" represent an alternative to mutual funds for investors seeking an indexed stake in U.S. stocks.

CHAPTER 9

Shopping for Discounts

A finance professor was walking down a busy street with a graduate student who spotted what looked like a $20 bill, stopped, and began to retrieve it. "Don't bother," said the professor. "If it was a real $20 bill, someone would already have grabbed it." He had a point: Good deals often don't exist for longer than the blink of an eye.

There are exceptions, however, as in the world of closed-end funds. These investments offer bargain potential. Often you can spot portfolios priced, say, 15 percent below the value of their underlying investments, allowing you to buy a dollar's worth of assets for 85 cents.

Closed-end funds have a long, colorful history, punctuated by episodes of speculative frenzy. They predated the first mutual fund by more than a century. In 1822, King William I of the Netherlands created the forerunner to today's modern vehicle. In the 1860s, closed-end companies were started in England and Scotland. These "investment trusts," as they are still called in Britain, played an important role in financing the development of the U.S. economy.

The World's Oldest Surviving Closed-End Fund

The Foreign & Colonial Investment Trust was formed in London in 1868 and pioneered the concept of international diversification. The trust originally specialized in overseas government bonds. In 1891, its scope was broadened to include railway and industrial debentures, or bonds. Still going strong today, Foreign & Colonial has set the pattern for the British and American closed-end fund industries. In 1961 it was one of the first United Kingdom investment companies to buy Japanese equities. In 1987 it became the first British trust to be listed on the Tokyo Stock Exchange. Its long-term performance record is impressive.

THE ROARING '20s

Closed-end funds traded actively during the 1920s bull market, when they far outnumbered their open-end relatives. The earliest such funds were conservatively structured, like their British counterparts. But as the decade wore on, speculative fever intensified and many highly leveraged portfolios were created to satisfy the public's ravenous appetite for fast profits. Besides issuing common shares, the funds also sold bonds and preferred stocks—which greatly enhanced their volatility and risk—because of the need to maintain yield payments. The high-flying funds were ultimately hit hard during the Crash of 1929 and the subsequent bear market, damaging their reputation with investors.

The closed-end format then remained something of an oddity. Mutual funds emerged as the vehicles of choice as investors gradually returned to equities. But the bull market of the 1980s brought forth a closed-end renaissance, with many new stock and bond portfolios going public. In contrast to their predecessors of the 1920s, today's closed-end funds are highly regulated.

PART FUND, PART STOCK

Simply put, a closed-end portfolio is a cross between a mutual fund and a stock. An open-end fund has an NAV, or per-share asset value, which always equals its price. Conversely, stocks have a share price, but not an NAV. Closed-end portfolios have both.

Discounts and Premiums

The NAV of a closed-end fund is the same as the NAV for a mutual fund. But the share price and NAV on the closed-end fund rarely are equal and, at

Table 9-1   Discounts and Premiums Illustrated

	First Fund	Second Fund
Stock price	$8	$11
NAV	10	10
Stock price *minus* NAV	-$2	+$1
Difference *divided by* NAV	-20%	+10%

times, vary widely. A "discount" exists when the share price is below the NAV; a "premium" prevails when price exceeds NAV. Discounts and premiums are computed as follows:

$$\frac{(\text{Stock price - NAV})}{\text{NAV}}$$

Suppose two funds have a $10 NAV. The first has a stock price of $8 and thus sells at a 20-percent markdown. The second sports a price of $11 and thus commands a 10-percent premium. Table 9-1 shows the discount and premium calculations.

Discounts and premiums are reported weekly in *Barron's, The Wall Street Journal,* and some other newspapers, along with the corresponding NAV. An increasing number of closed-end portfolios compute their NAVs daily, and you can get this information by calling them. Up-to-date valuations are useful when you are buying or selling in volatile markets.

The Initial Public Offering (IPO)

Although initial public offerings of closed-end funds are not common these days, that could change at any time. Thus, it's important to see how these deals are handled. Closed-end vehicles traditionally have been brought to market by Wall Street investment bankers when the perceived demand was strong. After an offering, the shares trade on the New York Stock Exchange or, less commonly, on the American Stock Exchange or even on Nasdaq.

A new stock fund might issue 10 million shares at $10 each, raising $100 million. The offering price typically has included an underwriting "spread" of about 7 percent, used to pay the various parties responsible for the marketing effort, including brokers. Assuming a 7-percent spread for our illustration, investors would receive about $9.30 a share in assets for their $10 investment. Thus, the shares essentially were offered at a 7.5-percent premium to their asset value ($0.70 divided by $9.30).

It's thus easy to see how investors who purchased a closed-end portfolio on the initial public offering got burned. It was common for funds to be

The Death of Closed-End Funds?

Closed-end IPOs virtually dried up in the mid-1990s, despite a roaring bull market in U.S. stocks. This prompted various investment periodicals to suggest that this corner of the fund industry may go the way of the dinosaurs. But closed-end portfolios have been written off several times before in their long history, only to bounce back. The format makes good sense as an alternative to stocks and straight mutual funds. The best time to buy is when sentiment is negative because that's when you'll often find the best values. An environment of fewer closed-end IPOs actually lays the seeds for better general performance down the road.

sold at a premium based on the usual 7-percent underwriting spread. Worse yet, closed-end vehicles typically were marketed when demand was peaking for the securities they focus on—not a great time to shop for bargains.

These two factors worked against the unsuspecting investor, inflicting losses and disenchantment. Prices often held steady for a few months, while the underwriting syndicate supported them by purchasing shares. But when this effort ended after several months, market prices typically slipped below NAV, perhaps even to a double-digit markdown.

Because of a growing awareness of the dangers of buying IPOs, it's doubtful that there will be many closed-end offerings in the future, unless the investment bankers come up with a method that won't inflict losses on initial buyers. The old adage "a fool and his money are soon parted" seems to be less true today than it once was. There are plenty of existing closed-end funds that offer better deals for investors to consider.

No Cash Inflows or Outflows

Because they raise money once, during a public offering, closed-end funds typically have relatively constant capitalizations. You normally don't buy shares directly from the management company as with mutual funds, which continuously stand ready to issue more shares to incoming investors. Also unlike open-end funds, closed-end portfolios do not redeem shares on an ongoing basis.

Then again, the huge inflows or outflows of cash can be problematic for mutual-fund managers, who may be forced to buy or sell investments at inopportune times. Closed-end managers need not worry about this, which allows them to be more concerned with long-term gains—a plus for shareholders.

Raising More Money

Closed-end portfolios do not enjoy a constant stream of new investor dollars, as regular mutual funds do. Still, they can increase their assets in three basic ways.

1. *Rights offerings* are a means to raise money from existing shareholders. As an incentive, the fund issues rights allowing investors to buy more shares at a modest discount to the market price. More on this later.

2. *"Leveraging,"* or borrowing, is a common strategy used by bond funds, especially those that target municipal bonds. The typical leveraged muni portfolio borrows about 50 cents for each dollar of investor capital to buy more bonds.

3. *Secondary stock offerings* are another possibility, but they have not been used much. Here the fund simply sells more shares to the public.

MANY CHOICES

Total closed-end assets represent only about 4 percent of the roughly $4 trillion invested in mutual funds. All told, more than 500 different funds exist. Despite the relatively modest size of the closed-end industry, a healthy array of categories exists, including municipal bond, taxable bond, domestic equity, sector, international, regional, and single country. The municipal-bond group enjoyed considerable popularity during the late 1980s and early 1990s and now comprises about 30 percent of all closed-end assets. Municipal and taxable bond funds together account for about 60 percent.

A handful of the domestic stock funds created in the late 1920s are still actively traded today. This group of stalwarts includes Adams Express, Central Securities, General American Investors, Petroleum & Resources, Salomon Brothers Fund, and Tri-Continental. As a whole, they offer some excellent choices.

Many other funds target foreign-stock markets. Regional portfolios focus on countries within a broad geographic area such as Europe or Latin America. Most of the numerous single-country funds specialize in emerging markets such as Brazil, China, the Czech Republic, India, Indonesia, Mexico, the Philippines, and Russia. A smaller number focus on developed markets including France, Germany, Japan, and Britain. Chapter 11 covers single-country and other foreign-stock funds.

CLOSED-END VERSUS OPEN-END FUNDS

These two types of investment portfolios have much in common. Both are diversified, professionally managed vehicles. In fact, some successful stock and bond pickers who run mutual funds also oversee closed-end portfolios.

In addition, closed-end portfolios are highly regulated in the same way as mutual funds. The most prominent law affecting both is the Investment Company Act of 1940, which sets forth detailed rules for diversification, dividend policy, financial reporting, and so on. It also requires extensive oversight of fund activities by the Securities and Exchange Commission. Like their open-end counterparts, closed-end funds have boards of directors charged with protecting shareholder interests. As conduits, both types of funds are required to distribute virtually all net investment income and realized capital gains to shareholders each year.

However, several key differences exist between closed-end funds and their open-end relatives:

Newspaper coverage. Unlike the daily mutual-fund table, there's no separate listing of closed-end prices. The funds appear daily in newspaper stock tables, alongside regular corporations such as Exxon and Walt Disney. This means you can find such information as a 52-week price range, daily trading volume, and the previous day's high, low, and closing prices. In some cases, a special closed-end box appears weekly with discounts, premiums, and market-price total returns for the past 52 weeks.

Buying and selling shares. Since closed-end funds trade like stocks, you normally must deal with a broker, paying the usual transaction costs for stock trades. Mutual-fund terms such as "load," "no-load," "low load," and "contingent deferred sales charge" don't apply to closed-end vehicles. Chapter 21 provides more details on how to buy and sell them.

Investment liquidity. Closed-end portfolios are less liquid than their open-end relatives. You can buy or sell indefinitely large dollar amounts of a mutual fund at NAV, without impacting the price. However, a large closed-end buy or sell order could easily bump the price up or down. That's because many of these investments are essentially small-capitalization stocks, held largely by individual investors. Chapter 21 explains how to deal with liquidity problems.

Shareholder services. Like open-end funds, most closed-end portfolios offer dividend reinvestment programs. Some even have optional cash-payment plans, where you can send additional money directly to the fund. Many companies also now offer toll-free 800 numbers and will respond to your inquiries, including NAV updates. Closed-end portfolios can be held in self-directed retirement accounts such as IRAs and SEP-IRAs. However, they don't provide telephone switching since they aren't structured like mutual-fund families.

Changes in fund size. Unlike mutual funds, which often experience dramatic inflows and outflows of money, closed-end vehicles typically have a fairly constant share base. Unless there is an additional offering of stock or an optional cash-payment plan exists, investors don't buy shares direct from the fund. In addition, they cannot normally redeem shares at NAV.

Cash holdings. Because closed-end funds need not maintain a cash buffer to meet shareholder redemptions, they can stay more fully invested. The liquidity for a closed-end fund is provided by the stock market. If shareholders want out, they simply sell to other investors. A mutual fund might need to keep 5 percent of its assets in cash, whereas a comparable closed-end vehicle maintains only 2 percent in cash.

Use of leverage. As a group, closed-end bond funds make more extensive use of borrowing than their mutual-fund counterparts. Most municipal-bond vehicles are leveraged with preferred stock. A portfolio with $200 million in assets provided by the common shareholders might add $100 million through a preferred stock issue, thereby leveraging the common. Leverage increases a fund's potential return but it also adds risk, as Chapter 15 explains.

Price volatility and performance measurement. The stock price of a closed-end fund is more volatile than its NAV. Fluctuating discounts and premiums add an additional dimension of risk and reward, and can provide trading opportunities. In a practical sense, this is the most important distinction between the two forms of investment company.

Shareholder reports. Mutual funds distribute prospectuses to interested investors. However, unless there is an initial public offering or a rights offering, you normally won't find a closed-end prospectus, because the portfolios are not continuously making new shares available. Like mutual funds, closed-end vehicles publish annual, semiannual, and even quarterly reports. The format of these reports is basically the same for both the open- and closed-end varieties.

WHY INVEST IN CLOSED-END FUNDS?

Perhaps the main reason to consider closed-end funds involves the large markdowns at which they sometimes sell. If you purchase shares at a wide discount and it narrows or turns to a premium, your return will be enhanced. Suppose a fund with an NAV of $10, trading at a 15-percent discount, enjoys a 25-percent increase in NAV. If the discount also disappears because of investor enthusiasm, the share price moves up 47 percent, as seen in Table 9-2. You can also make money if the discount doesn't narrow, as we'll explain.

Table 9-2   *Leveraging Up Your Returns*

	Original	Present	Change
Net asset value	$10.00	$12.50	+25%
Stock price	$8.50	$12.50	+47%
Discount	-15%	0%	

Taking Advantage of Shifts in Sentiment

A fund's share price often bobs up and down more than its NAV. This spells opportunity for vigilant investors who can take advantage of favorable price movements, particularly during times of fear and greed. With closed-end portfolios, you can track intraday prices and place "limit" orders to buy or sell at your price or better, perhaps using a discount brokerage. If you're patient and disciplined, you can be rewarded handsomely.

A Stable Pool of Assets Helps

Because closed-end managers don't face large inflows or outflows of shareholder money at inopportune times, they can invest more than equivalent mutual funds can in less liquid or more volatile securities, such as those traded in emerging foreign markets. In addition, managers can afford to be more long-term oriented. And because closed-end funds need not maintain a cash buffer to meet redemptions, they can be more fully invested. All of these factors provide advantages.

ANALYZING DISCOUNTS AND PREMIUMS

At any given time the markups and markdowns can vary widely among funds. For example, you might see one foreign-stock portfolio trading at a 20-percent premium, while another sells at a 25-percent haircut. In addition, the discounts or premiums on an individual fund can fluctuate widely over time. Figure 9-1 illustrates these facts.

Most closed-end vehicles trade at discounts most of the time; on rare occasions they sell at or slightly above NAV. This is as it should be since there are certain costs associated with buying and holding a fund. In addition, investors face the danger of a widening discount or a deflating premium.

Discounts are somewhat puzzling, since no completely satisfactory explanation has ever been offered for their existence, despite years of sophisticated research. However, a variety of reasons have been put forth that help account for these pricing peculiarities.

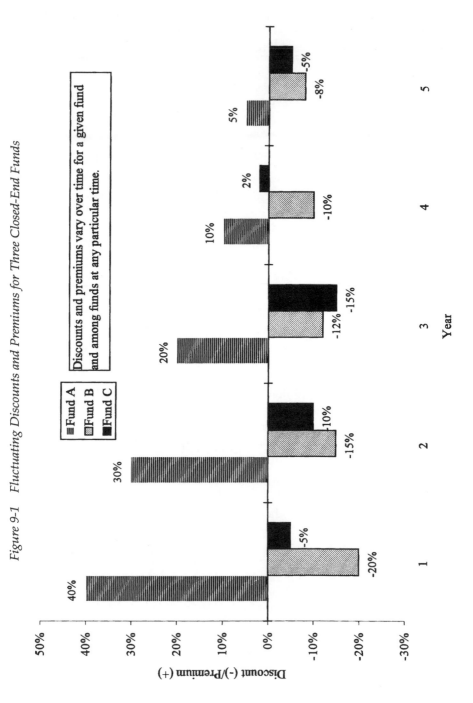

Figure 9-1   Fluctuating Discounts and Premiums for Three Closed-End Funds

Discounts and premiums vary over time for a given fund and among funds at any particular time.

In a simple sense, a closed-end fund's discount or premium reflects its popularity. In addition, prices are determined by the interaction of other factors, such as the following:

1. *Fear and greed.* Fear leads to deepening markdowns; greed results in narrower discounts or premiums. Investors often overreact to new developments. A prominent news story that affects a particular group of funds, such as those investing in India, can move prices up or down fast.

2. *Portfolio composition.* Stock funds tend to sell at deeper discounts than bond funds. Also, closed-end vehicles that own obscure securities may trade at wider discounts than those with more liquid holdings.

3. *Performance and management reputation.* Above-average returns lead to premiums or narrower discounts. A celebrity manager with an outstanding track record would likely command a premium.

4. *Expenses.* Higher shareholder-borne costs often result in steeper markdowns. That's why it's important to compare a fund's discount with its expense ratio. More on this later.

5. *Investment liquidity.* More actively traded closed-end funds—those featuring higher daily share volume—tend to sell at narrower discounts.

6. *Unrealized appreciation.* Large potential tax liabilities that could be realized by the sale of stocks in the future may lead to deeper discounts. This is often the case with older stock funds that have made major investments many years ago at much lower prices.

7. *Random factors.* Aspects such as the purchase or sale of a large block of its shares can impact a closed-end fund's discount or premium, especially if the fund is not liquid.

8. *Rights offerings.* The sale of new shares to investors can lead to steeper markdowns. More on this later.

A Three-Dimensional Approach

In addition to the investment objective and caliber of management, the discount is probably the single most important factor for investing in a closed-end fund in the first place, so it's important to make sure you really are getting good value. In doing your homework, examine a fund's discount relative to three factors:

1. The size of past discounts.

2. Discounts on competing portfolios.

3. The fund's expense ratio.

An ideal scenario would be a fund with a discount that's deep relative to its past values, deep compared to competing funds, and deep in relation to its expenses. Morningstar provides past discounts and premiums for the closed-end portfolios it tracks, allowing you to make historical evaluations easily.

An important link exists between a fund's discount and its expense ratio. Costs are more predictable than future returns and should not be taken lightly. They also eat into returns. An insightful analytic exercise is thus to divide a fund's discount by its expense ratio. If the resulting number is 10 or more, give the fund further consideration. Examples appear in Table 9-3, where Fund C is the clear winner even though it has the smallest discount.

Factoring in Liquidity

Closed-end funds are generally less liquid than their open-end relatives, whose prices are not affected by large shareholder orders. The simplest way to gauge any stock's liquidity is to examine its average daily volume. So too with closed-end products. A fund that trades 100,000 shares a day is far more liquid than one that averages only 10,000. Liquidity is a function of the size of your order relative to the stock or fund's daily volume. If you are investing $10,000 or more in a closed-end portfolio, you need to be concerned about its liquidity. Otherwise, you may have to accept poor transaction prices as a consequence.

Less-liquid funds tend to trade at deeper discounts. But if you try to invest a sizable amount in such a portfolio, you may see its discount quickly and temporarily narrow as the dealer raises the asked price. It's often wise to break a big order into smaller pieces, spacing your trades over several days or weeks. In addition, the use of "limit" orders may help you get a better price, if you're patient.

Table 9-3   Comparing Discounts with Expense Ratios

	Discount %	Expense Ratio %	Discount/ Expense Ratio
Fund A	28	3.0	9.3
Fund B	20	2.5	8.0
Fund C	12	0.4	30.0

Three Strategies for Playing the Discount

Closed-end funds tend to be overlooked by investors. This creates opportunities. Here are three strategies that can be profitably employed.

1. *Buying at "double discounts."* Contrarians search for good funds at attractive markdowns when investor sentiment sours during market setbacks. Cheap securities in general, plus a deeply discounted fund make a winning combination.

2. *Picking up year-end bargains.* Go shopping during November and December, when other investors are taking tax losses on funds that have not fared well recently. Tax-loss selling can temporarily push down prices to compelling double-digit discounts.

3. *Hunting for special situations.* The deep discounts on certain funds could narrow if some unique development occurs such as a change in management, liquidation of the entire portfolio, or conversion to open-end status. Special situations may not pan out, however, so be sure the fund can make a contribution to your portfolio before you buy.

As a general rule, a discount that's at least five to 10 percentage points deeper than its past average should cushion any NAV decline because a cheap stock doesn't have as far to fall as a pricey one. However, if the discount is wide but not abnormally so, it could easily widen further.

When Discounts Don't Narrow

Even if the discount doesn't narrow, you still can earn a decent return on a closed-end fund, especially if regular distributions are being made. The larger the payouts, the better. Suppose a fund trades at $8, a 20-percent discount from its $10 NAV, and that it distributes $1 for the year. By reinvesting these payouts at the market price, you buy more shares. In this example, if you reinvest at a price 20 percent below the NAV, you receive 25 percent more shares than if you had done the same at NAV.

Beware of Steep Premiums

In general, it's best not to buy shares at prices above the NAV. Single-country funds in particular sometimes trade at heady double-digit markups. They are like growth stocks that sell at outrageously high earnings multiples. Suppose ABC Country Fund is trading at a 30-percent premium due to investor euphoria. If sentiment sours as ABC's market plunges, that markup could evaporate and turn into, say, a 10-percent discount, resulting in a 45-percent loss on stock price, as seen in Table 9-4.

Table 9-4   The Risk of Buying at a Premium

	Original	Present	Change
Net asset value	$10.00	$8.00	-20%
Stock price	$13.00	$7.20	-45%
Prem. (+)/disc. (-)	+30%	-10%	

MARKET PRICE VERSUS NAV RETURNS

Total returns on closed-end funds can be calculated in terms of either market price or NAV. Morningstar, for example, offers both. NAV results show how the manager did and are comparable to mutual-fund performance. Conversely, market-value returns show how investors fared, and are impacted by changing discounts and premiums. However, your own results also depend on when you purchased shares, what you paid, and whether or not you reinvested any distributions, so they normally will differ from published figures.

"Leveraging Up" Your Return

The biggest advantage of investing in closed-end portfolios is the ability to purchase shares at a significant discount. As explained earlier, if you buy in at a 15-percent discount, you effectively are paying 85 cents for each dollar's worth of assets.

Consider the performance of a hypothetical no-load stock fund compared with an otherwise identical closed-end portfolio. Here are our assumptions:

1. The initial NAV of each is $20.

2. The mutual fund is bought at its NAV and the closed-end portfolio at a 15-percent discount, or $17.

3. Each fund is held five years and distributes $2 yearly.

4. At the end of five years each fund has a $22 NAV.

What are the results? The open-end fund produces an 11.6-percent annualized return. The performance on the closed-end portfolio depends on the amount of its discount or premium when you sell, as seen in Table 9-5. In most cases, it significantly outperforms the mutual fund. Only when its discount deepens to a huge 27.3-percent gap does it underperform.

Table 9-5   Total Returns on a Closed-End Fund with Different Selling Prices

Case	NAV	Selling Price	Premium (+) or Discount (-)	Annualized Return
1	$22	$23	+4.6%	16.8%
2	22	22	0	16.0
3	22	21	-4.6	15.2
4	22	20	-9.1	14.4
5	22	18	-18.2	12.7
6	22	16	-27.3	10.8

RIGHTS OFFERINGS

Closed-end funds sometimes raise more money from existing shareholders at what management feels is an appropriate time, commonly—but not always—during a bull market. The way they do this is by offering rights or options to buy more shares.

How Rights Offerings Work

Investors usually are issued one right for each share held, so a holder of 100 shares would receive 100 rights. The latter can be used to purchase additional shares at a predetermined subscription price, commonly 5 to 10 percent below a fund's market price or average price over a particular time. Several rights—typically three or more—are needed to acquire each new share.

Most offerings allow shareholders to exercise their option within several weeks. When the rights expire, they are worthless. Rights are issued in either *transferable* or *nontransferable* form. Transferable rights can be sold during the "ex-rights" period by shareholders who choose not to exercise them; nontransferable rights cannot.

Rights offerings should not be ignored. Even if you don't want to buy additional shares, you should take some action. Suppose you're strapped for cash or simply don't want to increase your dollar commitment to a fund. Or perhaps your shares are held in an IRA and you can't invest more. If the rights are transferable, you should sell them on the open market as soon as possible because the fund's price typically declines during the offering period. By doing this, you will lock in the value of the rights and avoid diluting your investment.

If the rights are nontransferable, you can do a little arbitraging on your own to capture at least some of their value. Simply sell the number of shares to which you are entitled, then buy them back at the lower subscription price by exercising your rights. The sooner you arbitrage, the more value you are likely to lock in. Remember that rights offerings can dilute the holdings of investors who don't act since additional shares are issued below the market price. If the fund sells at a discount of 10 percent or more, the dilution can be considerable.

MERGERS, OPEN-ENDINGS, AND LIQUIDATIONS

For various reasons, closed-end funds occasionally merge, sell off their assets, or convert to open-end status. For example, Nuveen & Co. in Chicago has merged many of its muni-bond portfolios with similar objectives, such as those investing in a specific state. The purpose was threefold: to benefit shareholders through economies of scale, to boost daily trading volume, and to create portfolios that are easier to manage.

Closed-end fund prospectuses often stipulate steps that can be taken by management to reduce or eliminate a large discount. These may include making a "tender offer" for some or all of the shares or converting to a garden-variety mutual fund. However, the wording of the prospectus may be somewhat vague, which can lead to shareholder disappointment if management doesn't take the remedial steps that investors were expecting. Taking action to reduce or eliminate a discount is usually just a possibility and left to the discretion of the fund's board of directors; but shareholders often get the impression that it will happen with certainty.

TEN CLASSIC BLUNDERS

Here are ten big mistakes investors often make with closed-end portfolios. By sidestepping them, you will greatly improve your investment odds.

1. *Rushing in.* Don't buy shares during initial public offerings. If you like the merchandise, wait for a discount to develop. With an existing fund selling at an attractive discount, don't jump in until you check its average daily trading volume. Placing a big buy order can drive its price up.

2. *Failing to check out the merchandise.* Closed-end portfolios are more complicated than their open-end siblings and have to be analyzed both as an investment company and as a stock.

3. *Blindly going for the deepest discount.* Investors are asking for trouble if they ignore other factors such as past performance, expenses, and trading liquidity.

4. *Buying last year's top performers.* These are often the more volatile sector or single-country funds, which easily can go into reverse.

5. *Placing market orders instead of limit orders.* The latter are instructions to your broker to buy or sell at a specific price or better. With a little patience, they allow you to shop for slightly better prices.

6. *Taking small positions in too many funds.* This can greatly increase brokerage commissions as a percentage of your investment.

7. *Trading too much.* Frequent brokerage transaction costs will hurt your performance.

8. *Being impatient.* You can hurt your results by selling too soon. Maintain some discipline and give the fund a chance to work for you.

9. *Falling in love.* A fund won't be heartbroken if you decide to sell. Assuming you purchased shares at a deep discount that subsequently narrows significantly or turns to a premium, consider taking profits if better values exist elsewhere.

10. *Betting the ranch.* Don't go overboard by loading up on speculative sector or single-country funds. Such investments commonly travel a bumpy road.

AT THE CLOSE

Closed-end funds demand understanding, discipline, and patience. The tendency of these investments to trade at premiums or discounts makes them more complex than regular mutual funds. In addition, timely information on closed-end funds can be harder to come by.

Our philosophy is that closed-end portfolios normally should be bought and held as intermediate or long-term investments rather than traded as short-term speculations. Investors who do best are those who choose their funds carefully and hold on to the best ones the longest, cutting loose any dogs along the way.

By picking a handful of quality stock funds at double-digit discounts, you likely will be well rewarded over time. You could build an entire portfolio out of closed-end products. Or you can use them as core holdings to profitably augment a mutual-fund portfolio, substituting them for other vehicles when compelling discounts exist.

CHAPTER 10

Global Investing

Diversification and growth. Those are two compelling reasons for placing some of your money in foreign equity markets. Spreading your assets across different companies and industries reduces risk. That's the major advantage of investing in mutual funds. But with an All-American portfolio, you still face the danger that the overall stock market will perform poorly.

Adding international exposure can decrease short-term risk while increasing long-run reward. That's because market leadership rotates from one nation to another. One bourse may be up 30 percent while another remains flat, as a third falls 25 percent. Different economies can be in different parts of the business cycle at any one time.

Don't get us wrong. We're not talking about chasing the latest overseas fad or hot market. No one can be certain which exchange will soar next year and which one will tank. But if investors gain exposure to many markets, they will ensure having at least some money in the next top performers. It also makes sense to have some of your assets in currencies other than the U.S. dollar, in case the greenback declines in value.

Spreading assets across the world's stock markets is particularly important for growth-oriented portfolios. Over long stretches, foreign stocks have performed handsomely. This was certainly true of Japan for many years, until a lengthy bear market began in early 1990 after a speculative bubble burst. And it will be true of many emerging economies of Asia, Africa, Eastern Europe, and Latin America.

With the tremendous growth of capitalism and free markets around the globe, today's investor has unparalleled opportunities. The long-term outlook for foreign equities is bright because most economies are growing more rapidly than ours—at least twice as fast in the cases of many developing nations. Robust economic expansion promotes escalating corporate profits and, ultimately, substantial capital gains for investors with patience. In addition, at any moment some markets offer better values than others, giving overseas buyers more places to search for bargains and pricing inefficiencies.

MUTUAL FUNDS: YOUR TICKET OVERSEAS

Mutual funds offer superb access to a wide spectrum of non-U.S. markets. For buyers of individual stocks, investing directly in foreign businesses is more complex and costly than staying within the United States. It is harder to obtain meaningful, timely information on foreign companies and to analyze financial reports and other data. Overseas markets, especially those in developing countries, are more volatile and less liquid than our own. Transaction costs can be very high. In addition, many markets are subject to far less regulation, including lower accounting standards.

Mutual funds provide the expertise of experienced portfolio managers, who often "kick the tires" by visiting companies and meeting with top executives, as well as suppliers, customers, bankers, politicians, and accountants. Field research becomes essential where published information is inadequate. It's easy to see why management fees can be higher for international funds.

PROMISING OPPORTUNITIES

With today's sophisticated communications, the world has become much smaller. Just about every hour of the day, stocks are being traded somewhere. The United States remains the world's biggest financial market, but its impact has gradually lessened. At the beginning of the 1970s, about 30 percent of the world's stock-market value existed outside the United States. By 1980, the proportion had risen to just over half, and in recent years it has climbed to about 60 percent. The proportion of global gross national product generated in foreign nations has registered a corresponding increase.

Excellent growth opportunities can be found in many stock markets around the globe, especially in those of emerging nations. And some of the world's biggest and best companies are based outside the United States. Examples include Mitsubishi, Nippon Telephone & Telegraph, Royal Dutch/Shell, Daimier-Benz, Nestle, and Unilever.

Reducing Risk with Low Correlations

As noted earlier, global investors can earn greater returns for a given level of risk. An internationally diversified portfolio tends to have less volatility than those with either a 100-percent U.S. exposure or an entirely foreign allocation. The reason for this is that different stock markets do not always move in tandem with our market or with one another. One might zig while another zags. The degree of price synchronization between markets—measured by the "correlation coefficient"—can be quite low, especially with emerging nations such as China, Colombia, Greece, India, Russia, Taiwan, and Turkey. However, a few bourses such as Hong Kong exhibit high correlation with the United States because their currencies are pegged to the U.S. greenback and their economies are closely intertwined with ours.

The correlation coefficient is a statistical measure computed from two "time series" of numbers, such as stock prices in the United States and those in Japan over a set interval. It gauges how closely the two series move together. A +1.0 correlation indicates a perfect positive association; a value of 0.0 reflects complete independence. That is, a zero correlation means that the price variations in the two countries are totally unrelated. The closer the correlation to zero, the weaker the stock-price relationship and the greater the diversification benefits.

Time series of stock prices in different countries are generally positively correlated, but the coefficients are typically well below 1.0. Researchers have found the relationship between the United States market and many foreign bourses to be less than 0.5. In fact, the correlations between our market and some emerging nations such as India and Turkey have even been slightly negative in recent years, which means that as stocks rise in one place, they have a modest tendency to decline in the other. Emerging markets tend to have the weakest links with America, offering a particularly thick layer of international diversification.

Table 10-1 shows some examples relating the S&P 500 to various foreign-stock indexes. The highest correlation, 0.50, is between the U.S. and the United Kingdom, as measured by the Financial Times 100. In contrast, the U.S. and Japanese markets have a low 0.16 coefficient. The link between the S&P 500 and the Morgan Stanley Capital International EAFE, an index that primarily reflects the world's developed markets, is a modest 0.36. Anything

Table 10-1   Correlations of Price Returns to S&P 500*

U.K., FT 100	0.50	IFCG Composite	0.20
Japan, Nikkei	0.16	IFCG Latin America	0.20
MSCI, EAFE	0.36	IFCG Asia	0.14

*In U.S. dollars for the 60-month period ending December 1996.
Source: International Finance Corp.

under 0.50 is considered low, but slightly higher numbers can still provide significant diversification benefits.

The weak ties between the U.S. and emerging markets are evident from the 0.20 correlation between the International Finance Corp. Global (IFCG) Composite and the S&P 500. The IFCG Composite tracks nearly 1,900 stocks from 31 developing markets.

Of course, with the growing trend toward globalization dominated by multinational businesses, the economies of the world are becoming more closely linked and interdependent. This means that different markets will tend to exhibit higher correlations. But it might be a long time before the major markets move in close sync with one another.

Low correlations do not necessarily remain low at all times, however. They may increase just when you want loose links the most—when U.S. stock prices are falling. The linkages among the world's bourses tend to strengthen in bad times. In fact, correlations can increase strikingly during severe global traumas such as the 1973-74 bear market and the October 1987 crash, when fear gripped investors worldwide. Markets also move more closely during shorter periods of global crisis such as during the build-up to the Persian Gulf war. All the world's bourses tend to tumble in sync during these infrequent routs. Fortunately, global meltdowns and crises are not an everyday occurrence. International diversification will serve you quite well most of the time.

Profiting from Inefficiencies

Although bargains are the exception rather than the rule, foreign markets often provide better shopping than in the U.S. In an efficient market, such as the New York Stock Exchange, new information is freely available and acted upon so rapidly that it's difficult to find a mispriced stock.

However, things are different in smaller, thinly traded foreign markets. Information is more costly and often difficult to obtain. It takes special skills, lots of experience, and dependable contacts to obtain and analyze facts and figures about obscure corporations in up-and-coming nations. But this provides plenty of opportunity for the smartest, most savvy global managers to outperform the crowd, especially if they have superior access to information and a better ability to analyze it.

Investor overreaction provides another way for global investors to prof-it. As sentiment shifts, it generates far wider price swings in small, thinly trad-ed markets, particularly if an environment of poor information breeds fear and uncertainty. As we'll see in Chapter 11, single-country closed-end funds sometimes bounce around a great deal, alternating between double-digit dis-counts and double-digit premiums. Astute investors can profit in this type of a setting.

OPPORTUNITIES IN EMERGING MARKETS

The world's economies and stock markets can be classified in three broad categories:

1. *Large, developed economies.* The top tier includes Canada, France, Germany, Italy, Japan, the United Kingdom, and the United States—the so-called "Group of 7" nations.

2. *Smaller (or second tier) developed markets.* This large group includes countries such as Austria, Belgium, the Netherlands, Singapore, South Korea, Spain, and Switzerland. Many are wealthy nations with technologically advanced economies. In general, the risks and poten-tial rewards of this group are not as great as in the emerging-markets category. Some countries in this group such as Singapore and Spain were considered emerging markets just a few years ago.

3. *Emerging or developing markets* such as Brazil, China, India, Russia, Turkey, and Vietnam. In contrast to 51 developed or industrialized nations, there are 158 emerging economies, according to the World Bank. Their dominant industries include those in agriculture, natural resources, and low-skill manufacturing. Stock markets in these places can perform very differently from one another and the U.S. market. In general, high volatility is found among members of this group, which we'll examine below.

Developing markets are nothing new. About a century ago the British viewed the U.S. as an emerging market, and their investment trusts bought shares of infrastructure companies here, especially railroads. At that time, the U.S. economy was a far cry from today's sophisticated nation.

In 1981, the International Finance Corp. established an Emerging Markets Database to track the performances of stock markets in developing countries. At that time, only a handful of nascent markets were open to for-eign investors. Since then, the number of accessible stock exchanges has grown dramatically, and they have become larger and more liquid. Emerging markets climbed from 4 percent of total global stock-market capitalization at the end of 1985 to 11 percent a decade later. Developing nations, in fact, are pushing up the total value of the world's stock markets, and that trend will continue.

Of course, deciding whether to classify a country as "emerging" can be subjective. There's far more heterogeneity among emerging markets than in the developed world. But, at a basic level, these economies exhibit one or more of the following three characteristics:

1. *Low per-capita income.* Most residents in these places either live at a subsistence level or earn up to only a few thousand dollars a year.

2. *An economy that has not yet been industrialized.* Farming and extractive industries such as mining or logging often predominate. These countries often lack adequate roads, telephones, and electricity.

3. *Underdeveloped financial infrastructure.* The total capitalization of an emerging nation's stock market is often a relatively small percentage of its gross domestic product. In addition, a handful of companies may dominate the exchanges. And there might be problems when trying to place or settle trades.

Favorable Investment Opportunities

Giant strides have been made over the past several decades in emerging nations. With improved health care, life expectancy has increased markedly. Adult literacy has risen phenomenally, and demands for education have skyrocketed. Industries considered mature in the U.S., such as banking, cement, or household appliances, offer exciting growth potential in developing

---

A Continent of Opportunity

Africa is the last inhabited continent to attract investor attention. Political tensions and illiquid stock markets have kept most individuals away until recently. But the climate is becoming much more investor friendly. Most of the capital flowing into the continent has been aimed at the South African stock market, the largest and most sophisticated in the region. However, opportunities also exist in such places as Morocco, Nigeria, Ghana, Zimbabwe, and Kenya, on which you can capitalize with a pan-African fund such as Morgan Stanley Africa Investment, a closed-end portfolio. In addition to substantial long-term growth potential, Africa's markets are likely to offer good diversification. For the most part, share prices in Africa move independently of those in the U.S.

economies. Technological change is progressing rapidly. Some areas, particularly Latin America, have extensive untapped natural resources.

Emerging markets represent a vast and exciting economic frontier offering a chance for generous returns to patient, risk-tolerant, long-term investors. Strong performance is possible because emerging economies and stock markets both are expanding rapidly. For example, with more than 900 million people, India has a growing interest in free enterprise and a large middle class with a healthy appetite for goods and services. The subcontinent has numerous stock exchanges that collectively list thousands of issues. The largest, in Bombay, counts more firms (which are mostly small) than any other exchange in the world.

Expenditures on infrastructure enhance the growth of developing countries as they did in the U.S. in the late 19th and early 20th centuries. Expanding economies usually depend heavily on revenues from key exports to fuel rapid growth. Low wages, abundant natural resources, and, in some cases, skilled workers provide a competitive edge.

Capitalism Takes Root

Much of the fuel for capital gains in developing nations has come from privatization, a shift in responsibility from the government to private enterprise for meeting basic needs in goods and services. Governments in recent years have been moving toward free-market economies partly by transferring shares of state-run enterprises into private hands. The entities undergoing transformation are often sizable organizations, which thus offer significant investment opportunities. New stock exchanges have been created to handle the growing number of publicly traded companies and to accommodate the inflow of capital from developed nations. Privatizations initially were more common in developed countries where socialism had taken hold, but in the 1980s many emerging nations became involved, with those in Latin America being first. Telecommunications, energy, insurance, banking, steel, and mining are examples of industries where privatizations have occurred.

Why do governments sell state-run enterprises? A variety of benefits exist. For instance, privatizations often result in improved organizational efficiency and profitability as well as more competition, which leads to greater consumer satisfaction. A well-run investor-owned company enjoys good access to talented individuals and can tap the financial markets as needs arise. In addition, government budget deficits are reduced because the sale of a state-owned business generates money and eliminates any drain that an inefficiently operated enterprise may have been. Free markets do a much better job of allocating resources than a bureaucracy.

SPECIAL RISK CONSIDERATIONS

International diversification can reduce your portfolio's volatility, as noted elsewhere. But investors still face certain dangers, particularly if they concentrate their assets in a few companies or stock markets. These risks can be grouped into four broad categories:

1. *Company-specific risk.* This is similar to the danger facing U.S. stock investors, enhanced by the fact that it can be more difficult to get information on foreign companies. Particularly in emerging markets, investors might come across management that is not experienced or trustworthy, a product market that is not well-established, or a company having an illiquid stock. The shares of certain outfits might not trade for weeks at a time and consequently may exhibit erratic fluctuations when trades occur. It's often more difficult to sell a position at an acceptable price than it was to acquire it.

2. *Country risk.* Economic dangers include relatively unstable governments, economies based on only a few commodities or industries, runaway inflation, and natural disasters such as earthquakes. In contrast to the large and diverse U.S. market, a large percentage of the total capitalizations of many countries might be concentrated in a handful of companies. Stock-market risks include high volatility and poor liquidity. Various events such as coups and drastic changes in government policies can send tiny illiquid companies spiraling

---

Japan's Speculative Bubble Bursts

Japan's stock market was one of the first to attract U.S. investors. During much of the post-World War II period, the Land of the Rising Sun experienced remarkable economic development and vigorous growth. The stock market reflected Japan's economic miracle, and the Nikkei index climbed to dizzying heights on explosive share volume. Japanese stock prices in the mid- to late-1980s represented a classic speculative bubble not unlike that of the U.S. toward the end of the 1920s.

The Nikkei hit an all-time high of 38,916 at the end of 1989. But then the bubble burst and the index headed straight south. In August 1992, the Nikkei had dipped to 14,309, a nadir 63 percent below its peak. Prices still remain well below their former levels. The rout of Japanese stocks underscores the need to diversify your foreign holdings across many nations.

downward, especially if their shares were overpriced in the first place.

3. *Currency risk.* If the dollar appreciates against the currency in which a foreign share price is denominated, your returns will be adversely affected. Conversely, a declining dollar will boost the value of foreign investments, including international mutual funds. Unexpected exchange-rate devaluations can cause major market meltdowns, as occurred in Mexico in 1994.

Mutual funds greatly reduce company risk through diversification. Country risk can be diversified by investing in a fund that holds stakes in many nations, in several different regional funds, or in an assortment of single-country portfolios. Currency risk also can be tempered to some extent by spreading assets among countries with different currencies.

UNDERSTANDING CURRENCIES

Yen, pound, franc, mark, peseta, peso, lira, and krona: International-fund managers deal daily with these currencies and more. In fact, the foreign-exchange market is the world's largest financial marketplace. Stocks trading overseas are usually purchased with the local currency. Thus, a foreign security combines both an investment in a company and a currency speculation.

Some individuals are fearful of investing in foreign stock funds because of the currency risk. It's exceedingly difficult to predict short-term fluctuations in exchange rates. But this danger is generally not a problem for long-term investors using international funds that diversify across many markets. That's because the favorable and unfavorable fluctuations more or less balance out over time. There's also a good argument for Americans who have the lion's share of their assets and career earnings in dollars to diversify internationally, as a hedge against a long-term decline in the greenback. A little understanding of the basics of the currency markets can help you sleep better with your foreign investments.

Currency Risk

Simply put, exchange-rate fluctuations can work for or against a U.S. investor in the following two ways:

1. If the dollar strengthens and the foreign currency weakens, the American incurs a loss.

2. If the dollar weakens and the foreign currency strengthens, the American realizes a gain.

Table 10-2   *Impact of Currency Fluctuations on Total Returns*

Case	Return on Japanese Security	Return on Japanese Yen	Total Return to U.S. Investor*
(1) Gain on security and yen	+20%	+10%	+32%
(2) Breakeven on security; gain on yen	0	+10	+10
(3) Gain on security; breakeven on yen	+10	0	+10
(4) Gain on security; loss on yen	+20	-10	+8
(5) Loss on security and yen	-20	-10	-28

*To calculate the U.S. investor's total return, you need to convert the percentage changes into decimals, add 1.0 to each, and multiply. For case 1: (1.20)(1.10) = 1.32. Then subtract 1.0 from the product to get 0.32 or 32%.

As with any other commodity or investment, currency prices or exchange rates reflect demand and supply. Suppose the rate of Japanese yen is 100 per dollar. If the demand for yen rises, the price for Japanese currency would be bid up and the exchange rate might move to, say, 90 yen per dollar. With the exchange rate at 100, each yen was priced at $0.01. With a new conversion rate of 90, one yen increases in value to $0.01111, representing an 11.1-percent gain.

Table 10-2 illustrates the impact of currency risk for an American investing in a Japanese stock. Fluctuations in the yen/dollar exchange rate can boost the return, as in cases 1 and 2; reduce it as in cases 4 and 5; or have no impact as in case 3, where the rate of exchange holds firm. Obviously, you can make a lot of money with foreign equities when the dollar depreciates. But if the greenback gains ground, your results would be harmed. A word to the wise: Never invest in a foreign-stock fund as a currency play. Predicting short-term fluctuations in exchange rates is simply too difficult.

The long-term trend in a currency's price reflects both political conditions and growth of the nation's economy. Strong, prosperous countries with a continuing trade surplus and low inflation tend to have strong currencies. The currency of a thriving nation is in demand for several reasons. For instance, an expanding economy generally attracts foreign investments in tangible assets such as real estate. In addition, economic strength often lifts interest rates, making the nation's bonds more enticing to foreigners. In both cases, outsiders need to buy the local currency to make their investments.

Purchasing-Power Parity

Although short-term currency fluctuations are hard to predict, there is a simple theory of long-run trends that provides useful insight for global investors. It's called "purchasing power parity," and essentially it says that inflation-rate differentials between countries can impact their currencies over long periods.

Here's a simple example. Country A normally has a 10-percent yearly inflation rate, while price levels in country B rise at a 6-percent clip. According to purchasing-power parity, A's currency should decline about 4 percent yearly relative to B's, representing the difference between the two inflation rates, assuming no trade restraints. If A's currency did not depreciate, what A exports to B would be overpriced while B's exports to A would be underpriced. The resulting demand for B's currency to purchase its cheaper goods leads to an increase in its currency relative to A's, until the latter's competitive disadvantage is removed. Basic common sense tells us that comparable goods should be competitively priced in the world economy.

Although the purchasing-power parity explanation is perfectly logical for long-run currency trends, the theory doesn't predict short-term fluctuations, owing to various complications. Rather, it simply illustrates that inflation-rate differentials between countries can impact their currencies over long periods and is best used as a rule of thumb.

Hedging Currency Risk

Mutual funds that target foreign stocks have the ability to reduce the threat posed by adverse currency fluctuations. They can hedge, or control unwanted risk, by initiating some type of offsetting position. In particular, they can use currency options, futures, or so-called "forward contracts."

Of course, a hedge also can lower a fund's return if the manager incorrectly anticipates a currency's move, which often happens. That's why managers usually hedge their portfolios only to a limited extent, if they hedge at all. You can find out about a fund's hedging activities by studying its prospectus, or by asking either your broker or the fund's customer representative.

As discussed previously, currency risk generally does not pose a significant problem for long-term investors using a well-diversified international mutual fund. That's because the favorable and unfavorable fluctuations balance out, more or less, over time. Thus, currency changes are not the major component of long-run returns. Our preference is for funds that remain unhedged because managers can add a lot more value by spending their time analyzing companies and stock markets, rather than trying to predict exchange rates.

Other Ways to Cope with Currency Risk

Fund managers can employ additional mechanisms besides hedging to deal with currency risk. Suppose a manager wants to invest in a country but expects inflation to increase and the country's currency to be devalued. He or she can reduce risk by investing in companies that export heavily to the U.S. or that sell goods priced in dollars. Such firms would benefit from a stronger greenback.

It's worth noting that a rising dollar is not necessarily bad news for stateside investors. Foreign-stock prices may rise on balance when the dollar strengthens because the products manufactured by non-U.S. firms will become more competitive vis-à-vis American goods. For example, the profits of many Japanese companies are tied to exports, so a strong yen can be devastating for them. The nation's exporters certainly would have a rough time if the yen consistently traded at 90 or less to the dollar.

AT THE CLOSE

Now you should have a good feel for the risks and rewards of global investing. Certainly there are important dangers to confront when it comes to individual companies, countries, and currencies. But profit opportunities also abound, and much of the risk can be cut through the diversification features of mutual funds. So where do you begin to build a global portfolio? Chapter 11 will help you sort through the options.

CHAPTER 11

Sizing Up World-Stock Portfolios

A generation ago, it was possible to travel around Europe on $10 a day. You bought a backpack, got a Eurail pass, found a buddy, and took off for the summer. If you were really adventurous, you headed to some other foreign location, shaving your expenses even further.

Those landmark travel days are over, but international destinations still offer many excellent values for mutual-fund investors. Most foreign economies are expanding faster than the U.S. economy, and their stock markets are not so thoroughly picked over. The result is an enticing combination of growth potential and bargains.

While international investing was still a rarity as recently as the early 1980s, today all but the smallest fund companies offer something in this arena. The huge foreign stock-fund menu includes ample numbers of open- and closed-end portfolios available in an impressive variety. Broadening your range of options even further are the relatively new single-country index portfolios that trade on stock exchanges. They constitute an interesting hybrid between open- and closed-end products.

World-equity portfolios fall into the following categories:

| Global | Regional | Small company | Sector |
| International | Single country | Emerging market | Index |

The groups are not necessarily mutually exclusive. For instance, a global or international fund could have a small-company focus, perhaps with an emerging-markets twist. A sector fund also could be global or international. If you want to invest in Japan, the world's second-largest market, you can choose among open-end, closed-end, small-stock, and index products. The problem facing most investors is deciding what kinds of foreign-stock funds they need. This chapter will help guide you through the selection process.

BROAD-BASED PACKAGES

For your initial financial foray outside of America's borders, you might want to venture somewhat cautiously into "global funds." These funds hold U.S. stocks in addition to an assortment of foreign equities. Because of their extensive diversification, they can be good choices for people with uncomplicated portfolios.

Global products differ in their exposure to stateside investments. Some limit the proportion of assets that they can invest either inside or outside of the United States; others simply go after the best opportunities wherever they exist. The domestic proportion may vary from less than 20 percent to more than half, so it's important for you to find out where the money is going. The details about how and where a fund invests can be determined by studying both its prospectus, which provides general guidelines, and a recent shareholder report, which gives a specific breakdown of the assets by country. Working within the general guidelines outlined in the prospectus, managers typically shift assets between the U.S. and foreign nations depending on their outlook for the different nations, companies within those markets, and currencies.

But the ability of global funds to amass large U.S. holdings is, in our view, a drawback. That's why we're partial to "international funds," which invest virtually all of their assets outside the U.S. Because of their more carefully defined stock-picking parameters, international funds are generally preferable to global products, which might be betting heavily on U.S. stocks at the wrong time. Also, when the latter make large shifts between U.S. and foreign companies, that can mess up your own asset allocation. At the same time, international funds offer better diversification than the more narrowly defined single-country or regional portfolios. T. Rowe Price International, Scudder International, Templeton Foreign, and Vanguard International

Growth are examples of some of the large non-U.S. funds with long track records.

Schwab and Vanguard are among the few firms with international index products. Vanguard Star Total International invests in three other Vanguard index products counting in excess of 1,500 stocks from more than 30 countries. About 14 percent of this broad portfolio's assets recently were allocated to emerging markets. The lion's share of the portfolio is structured to replicate the EAFE index. Another broad-based portfolio, T. Rowe Price Spectrum International is a "fund of funds" that holds a mix of that family's diverse international lineup.

With international funds, one important caveat is to check the portfolio weighting allocated to Japanese companies, since that nation accounts for such a large share of total world stock values. Some index funds, for example, have more than a third of their assets earmarked to Japan. During the 1980s, most funds with dominant Japanese stakes did phenomenally well, but through most of the 1990s, these portfolios lagged.

A fund's positioning in emerging markets or out-of-favor developed countries—such as Japan in 1997—often reflects the manager's ability to think independently. This is a desirable trait often seen in the most successful stock-pickers, especially in the international realm, which offers many more opportunities to be creative and add value. So if your international fund has over-weighted countries that its peers have underweighted or avoided, that's not necessarily cause for alarm.

MORE SPECIALIZED CHOICES

A tried-and-true international fund may be all you need to round out your holdings of domestic stocks and stock funds. But if you're a more dis-criminating shopper with a large nest egg and a lengthy time horizon, there are many more foreign products on the shelves. You may want to consider some of the following specialized offerings.

Small-Stock Funds

Because of illiquidity, the frequent lack of sound information, and other problems, most foreign-stock funds stick with the larger corporations. These are the ones that are easiest to find, research, and follow. Yet smaller compa-nies in general offer better profit potential. A modest but growing number of foreign-stock funds focus on these types of firms. The group includes Acorn International, Founders Passport, Montgomery International Small Cap, T. Rowe Price International Discover, and Scudder Global Discovery.

As in the domestic arena, small-company foreign funds typically are more volatile than their big-cap siblings. The trade-off is that they invest in stocks and in markets with good potential. And because they do not move in sync with U.S. stocks, they generate an added layer of diversification—probably better than that provided by mainstream foreign funds. Of course, a small-company global or international portfolio in itself does not offer a complete investment program. Lean toward these products only if you have a multiyear outlook, a fairly aggressive appetite for risk, and other international holdings.

Emerging-Markets Funds

The tremendous potential of the world's up-and-coming nations was discussed in Chapter 10. How can you make it work for you? The riskiest route to emerging markets is with single-country closed-end funds, which we will discuss later. A volatile country fund with a manic-depressive personality could be up 100 percent one year and down 50 percent the next, taking shareholders on a wild ride. Owning a fund with exposure to many emerging countries in different regions of the world greatly reduces your risk. Many of these worldwide portfolios have been introduced in recent years.

Such open-end funds are available from Fidelity, Lexington, T. Rowe Price, Montgomery, Robertson Stephens, Warburg Pincus, Templeton, Vanguard, and others. Closed-end emerging-markets portfolios include Morgan Stanley Emerging Markets, TCW/DW Emerging Markets Opportunity, and Templeton Emerging Markets.

Then again, you might not need a separate investment in developing nations. Traditional international funds primarily target developed countries but many have a slice of their assets in emerging nations. Managers typically will vary the emerging-developed balance as the fundamentals change. Take this allocation shift into consideration if you're thinking about buying an emerging-markets portfolio along with a core international fund.

NARROWING YOUR GEOGRAPHIC FOCUS

Many regional portfolios exist of both the open- and closed-end varieties. Most target either Europe, Asia, or Latin America. A few choices even are available for Africa. Vanguard offers regional index funds that focus on Europe and the Pacific. They track Morgan Stanley Capital International's Europe and Pacific indexes, respectively. Because of Japan's large market weighting, the Pacific portfolio recently had about 70 percent of its assets there, although that's down from 90 percent several years ago.

Investors buy regional portfolios when they have an especially positive outlook on a certain area of the globe. In particular, the perennially high economic growth in Southeast Asia has attracted considerable interest to that area. Because of their narrower geographic focus, regional portfolios generally are more volatile than broadly diversified global or international funds. But regional products offer an advantage over individual single-country funds in that you have a professional manager making the allocation decisions for you. Assets can be shifted from a falling market to a rising one. And by investing in three good regional funds, you can pretty much cover the entire international scene, although you retain the flexibility of weighting each region as you see fit.

Single-Country Funds

Dozens of funds confine themselves to the stocks available in one country. Most are closed-end but an increasing number of traditional mutual funds with a single-nation focus have sprouted up recently, including several Fidelity offerings. The relatively new WEBS portfolios are exchange-traded index products that track the more developed markets. More on these later. Countries targeted by single-country closed-end funds are listed in Table 11-1.

Despite recent increases, only a handful of garden-variety mutual funds invest in single developing nations. The closed-end format works better for stock selection in markets characterized by high volatility and illiquidity. As explained in Chapter 9, closed-end funds don't have to redeem shares, so they can retain assets even when their prices are gyrating wildly. By contrast, massive shareholder redemptions in an open-end portfolio could prove harmful to the fund and might even hurt the stock market if it's a tiny one. Conversely, closed-end portfolios in general have been out of favor for various reasons, which explains why more single-country open-end funds have debuted lately.

Buyer Beware

Individuals face considerable risk when investing in a particular nation. Prices of closed-end single-country funds can soar or plunge on the basis of three factors:

Table 11-1   Countries Targeted by Single-Country Closed-End Funds*

Argentina	Germany (3)	Malaysia	Spain (3)
Australia	India (4)	Mexico (3)	Switzerland
Austria	Indonesia (2)	Pakistan	Taiwan (2)
Brazil (2)	Ireland	Philippines	Thailand (2)
Chile	Israel	Portugal	Turkey
China (4)	Italy	Russia (2)	United Kingdom
Czech Republic	Japan (2)	Singapore	Vietnam
France	Korea (4)	South Africa	

*Denotes the number of funds available if more than one invests in the nation.

1. *The performance of the underlying stock market.* Many small bourses are illiquid and highly volatile. Political scandals, social upheaval, or other problems can send an unstable market into a tailspin. The prospectus of the closed-end Templeton Russia Fund, launched in 1995, contained nearly five pages of "risk factors and special considerations." Among the dangers mentioned was the pervasiveness of corruption and crime in that country.

2. *Currency fluctuations.* Changes in the dollar value of a foreign currency may lead to substantial short-term gains or losses. As discussed in Chapter 10, if another currency grows stronger against the dollar, the NAV of a foreign fund benefits. Conversely, if the currency weakens, the fund's per-share price is hurt.

3. *Discount-premium fluctuations.* Country funds have been known to alternate between double-digit discounts and premiums as investor sentiment swings from fear to greed, and vice versa. Table 11-2 illustrates this phenomenon.

For the speculator, country funds offer the opportunity for a "triple play" if the target market surges, the currency appreciates, and a wide discount evaporates or turns to a premium. The gains can be substantial even if only two of the three factors are at work. Naturally, these variables also can work in reverse.

To do well with single-country funds, you should hold at least a half dozen to ensure adequate diversification. This is doubly true if you lack a core position in a broad international portfolio. You also should make any such investments with firm buy and sell prices in mind. Because these funds are so volatile and can generate staggering losses, it's wise to follow a carefully constructed plan of attack.

Table 11-2
52-Week Discount (-)/Premium (+) Range for Selected Closed-End Funds*

Fund	High (%)	Low (%)
Brazilian Equity	+15.8	-28.4
China Fund	+16.6	-18.2
India Fund	+16.2	-10.2
Indonesia Fund	+27.0	-11.7
Japan OTC Equity	+21.2	- 9.1
Taiwan Fund	+24.5	-14.0
Templeton China World	+ 2.3	-20.9
Turkish Investment	+27.9	-10.1

*Ranges are for the 52-week period ended 12/27/96.
Source: Lipper Analytical Services Inc.

Trading Volatile Closed-End Funds

Funds with the most volatile NAV returns also tend to experience the wildest discount-premium swings. The more volatile the portfolio, the greater the odds that a steep markup will quickly evaporate or a gaping discount will close. Thus, the least stable single-country funds present the best opportunities for astute traders who keep a close eye on discount-premium fluctuations.

COUNTRY-SPECIFIC INDEX FUNDS

Perhaps you like the idea of making your own bets on individual nations but feel uncomfortable with the closed-end structure and its fluctuating discounts and premiums. If so, single-country index funds known as WEBS, or "World Equity Benchmark Shares," represent a nice alternative. Developed by Morgan Stanley, these portfolios offer access to 17 relatively large, developed stock markets. Table 11-3 lists these countries and the funds' trading symbols. We expect to see additional WEBS in the future. Each portfolio provides ample exposure to a nation's dominant corporations, just as an S&P 500 index fund provides a good grounding in U.S. stocks.

Like closed-end funds, WEBS trade on a stock exchange at varying intraday prices. Investors pay brokerage fees to purchase or sell shares, but there are no loads or deferred sales charges to confront. Yet the portfolios are open-end funds—the first to trade on exchanges. WEBS are similar in concept to the

Table 11-3   Directory of WEBS

Nation	Amex Symbol	Nation	Amex Symbol
Australia	EWA	Malaysia	EWM
Austria	EWO	Mexico	EWW
Belgium	EWK	Netherlands	EWN
Canada	EWC	Singapore	EWS
France	EWQ	Spain	EWP
Germany	EWG	Sweden	EWD
Hong Kong	EWH	Switzerland	EWL
Italy	EWI	United Kingdom	EWU
Japan	EWJ		

S&P 500 and S&P 400 MidCap "Spiders" covered in Chapter 8. All trade on the American Stock Exchange. They can be bought on margin and sold short by those so inclined.

As a Morgan Stanley product, WEBS replicate 15 individual countries within the EAFE index plus indexes for Canada and Mexico. The portfolios are based on a sampling or "portfolio optimization" technique, so an individual fund generally will own fewer stocks than the total contained in the benchmark.

In-Kind Investments and Redemptions

Individuals can't make cash investments and redemptions with WEBS as they routinely do with regular mutual funds. But large "in-kind" investments and redemptions can be made by major global banks and securities firms. This deserves some elaboration because in-kind transactions help ensure that prices don't move to premiums or discounts.

Here's how the process works: WEBS are issued by their distributor in "creation units." Each represents a basket of stocks corresponding exactly to those in the index, in composition and weighting.

Big institutional investors may be motivated to create new units or exchange their positions for underlying stocks in an effort to earn arbitrage profits. Suppose Australian WEBS are trading $1 a share below their net asset value. If so, an institutional investor that owns the Australia WEBS may choose to redeem, take its basket of stocks, and sell them in the market while simultaneously purchasing an equivalent WEBS position on the exchange. The result is that the institution would lock in a profit that's virtually risk free while helping to close the gap between price and NAV.

Comparing WEBS Against Closed-End Funds

In general, these indexed portfolios may be easier to evaluate and trade than conventional closed-end funds because they don't require investors to deal with fluctuating discounts and premiums. The following noteworthy differences also exist:

- *Each portfolio is passive.* WEBS normally remain fully invested and don't try to time the market or hedge currency risk. This results in lower management costs and greatly reduced transaction expenses.

- *They are relatively tax efficient.* Because they follow a buy-and-hold policy, index products distribute little if any realized capital gains. Most of any gains remain tax-deferred until you sell. By contrast, shareholders could face a significant tax bill when a closed-end fund makes a sizable distribution of profits in a good year.

- *They focus on developed markets.* The index-fund structure does not work for tiny, illiquid developing markets for which institutions would have difficulty pursuing an arbitrage strategy. You don't see index portfolios for countries such as Israel, Pakistan, Russia, or Turkey—at least not yet.

- *Large companies predominate.* Big stocks comprise the lion's share of each index portfolio. That's not necessarily true for single-country closed-end funds, which may choose to mix smaller companies into their portfolios. Many small firms offer excellent appreciation potential, but they also are relatively costly to research and trade.

More Index Specifics

The annual costs for individual WEBS vary based on factors such as the size of the portfolio. Generally speaking, their expense ratios average 1.4 percent or so, which is somewhat less than the typical expense ratios of actively managed single-country funds, but not at the rock-bottom levels as those on Vanguard's foreign index funds. One reason for this is that the expense ratios for WEBS include 0.25-percent 12b-1 fees. The fact that index funds incur expenses means that they will lag their respective benchmarks over time. The lower the costs, the smaller the expense-related tracking error.

Of course, a fund that just mimics an index may not necessarily be the way to go. A skilled manager who knows the country well can take advantage of inefficiencies, minimizing exposure to undesirable companies and over-weighting areas where good value exists. In fact, some promising companies might not even be included in the index. Active management often is worth its higher cost, particularly in the foreign-stock arena. Besides, if you can find a good closed-end country fund trading at a discount, why buy one of the index products at net asset value?

In short, the index portfolios can be dicey and must be used with care—just like their actively managed single-country cousins. They can be highly volatile and should be limited to a small part of your portfolio, if you utilize them at all. Above all, you should refrain from committing a large portion of your assets to a single foreign market. It's important to diversify among nations and geographic regions. Such products may have greatest appeal to investors with large portfolios who want to fine-tune their country allocations. Further information and a prospectus can be obtained by calling 1-800-810-WEBS. The Internet address http://www.websontheweb.com also can be used.

DO'S AND DON'TS FOR GLOBAL INVESTORS

The preceding sections on international funds of various types can be summarized in a half-dozen pointers. Let the following suggestions guide your thinking when adding a foreign component to your overall portfolio.

Do Determine Your Long-Run Allocations

Before committing any money, decide how you want to apportion your stock-fund holdings among U.S. and foreign markets, including both developed and emerging ones. Recognize that some exposure to up-and-coming countries is wise for appreciation potential but don't bet the ranch. Such investments demand patience and discipline. As a general guideline, target 20 to 40 percent of your total stock allocation in non-U.S. equities, depending on your time horizon and risk tolerance.

Do Put Broadly Based Funds at Your Portfolio Core

Diversified international funds with good long-term records can make an excellent portfolio anchor. They may even be all you need to round out your domestic holdings. Only if you want to do more fine-tuning should you consider more specialized products such as regional funds, single-country funds, and WEBS.

Don't Overpay for Your Global Exposure

Because foreign investing is more costly in general, it's easy to overpay for international funds. But doing so will undercut your long-term performance. You can avoid many problems by keeping these four advisories in mind:

1. *Don't buy closed-end funds at a premium.* Rather, buy them at a discount—the wider, the better. Volatile single-country funds can sell at haircuts of 15 percent or more. Find out about the discount-premium histories of any closed-end funds you're considering.

2. *Avoid funds of any type with high ongoing costs.* Index funds generally feature the lowest expenses. Note that a deep discount on a closed-end fund may be offset by a high expense ratio.

3. *Avoid trade-happy portfolio managers.* Favor low-turnover funds, especially in emerging markets. Trading costs money, and the impact is magnified in smaller stock markets. A stock's price can be unfavorably impacted through a manager's own actions when he or she needs to buy or sell quickly.

4. *Avoid hedgers where possible.* Currency fluctuations are extremely difficult to predict in the short run. Funds that do little or no currency
hedging enjoy a built-in cost advantage. It's better to accept some
additional short-term risk in return for greater long-term gains and
the certainty of lower expenses.

Do Keep Up

It's a good idea to stay reasonably up to date on major world stock markets, economies, and currencies—especially if you're planning to include single-country or regional funds in your asset mix. Both *Barron's* and *The Wall
Street Journal,* among other publications, provide useful articles and data in
their international-investing sections. For more of a multinational view, consider publications such as *The Financial Times* and *The Economist.* You should
evaluate the performance of specific foreign-stock funds against their peers
and against appropriate market benchmarks. A relevant measure for most
broadly diversified international funds is the EAFE index. Various stock-market indicators, including the EAFE, can be found daily in the "World Stock
Markets" section of *The Wall Street Journal.*

Don't Make Big Country Bets

Avoid the temptation to speculate big time on a hot market. Invest in at
least a half dozen different countries, to spread the risk. In addition, make
sure you don't end up with too much exposure to developing markets or in a
particular region of the globe. If you are using broad international funds, find
out if your manager is investing a substantial chunk of the portfolio in just one
or two markets. Know where your money is going.

Do Be Patient and Disciplined

These traits are essential prerequisites for successful global investing
because foreign markets can be exceedingly volatile and might generate disappointing performance for long stretches. It's important to view your non-
U.S. funds as a core part of your portfolio. You should be willing to hold them
for at least 10 years.

The more markets in which you have invested, the greater the chances
that one or two will experience a nasty plunge. If you hold single-country
funds, be sure you have the fortitude to ride out any prolonged setbacks. It
helps to assess any damage in terms of your overall portfolio. Perhaps a
volatile country fund is down 45 percent, but your total portfolio has suffered
just 10 percent. Focus on the latter figure as the more relevant. Of course, it's
a lot easier to absorb losses if you are properly diversified to begin with and
have not speculated big time on any specific markets.

AT THE CLOSE

Mutual funds are covering the world in a range of choices. Investors can pinpoint narrow areas of the map with single-country or regional portfolios, or they can survey vast distances with broad-based international and global products. They also can further slice up the terrain with small-stock and index investments, including WEBS.

The key to international investing is selecting an appropriate level of diversification, while keeping an eye on costs and understanding the impact of currency fluctuations.

CHAPTER 12

Hybrid and Specialized Products

If you spend time in a candy store, you quickly will realize you don't have to stick with the usual assortment of chocolates, lollipops, and gum. You also can dip your hands into more exotic jars filled with yogurt-covered almonds, guava-flavored suckers, and more. So long as there's a sugar-will, there's a way.

So too with mutual funds. Many portfolios start with a simple stock base, then add or subtract flavors to suit individual tastes. The result is a rich assortment of products ranging from stock-bond hybrids to funds that target single industries only.

HYBRID FUNDS

Mutual funds in this category are not strange mutants like something you might find on "The Island of Doctor Moreau." Rather, the "hybrid" designation merely signifies that a portfolio has a dual stock-bond heritage. In most cases these offerings bear a closer resemblance to stock portfolios. Included among the hybrids are balanced, convertible, and asset-allocation products. So-called "funds of funds" also are considered hybrids even though they may have a distinct equity or fixed-income flavor. When hybrid funds pass along dividends from the bonds they hold, they generally are most appropriate for tax-deferred retirement accounts, except for investors in a low tax bracket.

Balanced Funds

The most visible hybrid products, balanced funds are designed to provide one-stop shopping for people who want the ultimate in simplicity. They make an appropriate choice for individuals who can afford only one fund, since they offer diversification in both the bond and stock markets. They also make sense for investors who are just starting out and want something conservative.

These portfolios strive to achieve three goals: income, moderate capital appreciation, and preservation of capital. They do this by holding bonds, perhaps some convertible securities, and preferred stock, as well as common shares. They typically favor stocks over bonds by a 60-40 ratio, although the precise percentages vary. Generally, balanced funds hold at least 25 percent of their assets in bonds and 25 percent in stocks at all times. Although the group has earned a conservative reputation, individual funds sometimes dabble in such things as smaller stocks, foreign issues, and long-duration bonds to try to enhance returns.

Even though many families offer them, balanced funds are certainly not for everyone. You may be better off putting together your own "balanced" portfolio by investing 60 percent of your money in the best stock funds you can find and the other 40 percent in handpicked bond vehicles. You might even achieve lower expenses this way because bond funds normally cost less than stock funds—many have expense ratios well below 1 percent yearly— but balanced portfolios may carry costs as high as those charged by stock funds. A notable exception is Vanguard Balanced Index, which has a 0.20-percent expense ratio.

If you can afford to, you probably would be better off building your own tailor-made portfolio. That way you can select funds that specialize in small, medium, and large stocks, as well as foreign issues. By mixing up your equity holdings, you likely will experience better long-run performance. If you're in a high-tax bracket, you might want to channel your fixed-income assets into a municipal-bond fund. Even more appropriate might be a fund that buys bonds issued in your state if you live in a high-tax state such as California or New York. Such localized portfolios kick off income that's free from state as well as federal taxes while most balanced funds hold taxable issues only. Vanguard Tax-Managed Balanced is an exception. It invests about half of its assets in federally tax-free munis.

Convertible Funds

These portfolios are the ultimate in cross-pollination between stocks and bonds. That's because a convertible security is a bond or preferred stock that can be exchanged for a predetermined number of the company's common shares, at the holder's option. The "conversion price" represents the per-share cost of the stock if you decide to make the exchange. For instance, if a $1,000 convertible bond can be exchanged for 20 shares of stock, it would have a $50 conversion price (or $1,000 divided by the conversion ratio of 20).

Convertibles have a split personality. At times they act like stocks and at other times, like bonds. They offer the downside protection of fixed-income securities and the upside potential of equities. When a company's regular stock moves up in price above the conversion price, the convertible also will appreciate in value, albeit at a somewhat lesser rate because you pay a premium for the conversion privilege. Conversely, when the regular common shares plummet below the conversion price, the convertible provides a floor of protection. Because of these desirable attributes, convertibles have been called ideal investments. However, during a period of surging interest rates, they can be hit hard, declining in value like conventional bonds. This is called "interest-rate risk" and it is discussed fully in Chapter 13.

Fund managers pay attention to the relationship between the stock price and conversion price. When the former greatly exceeds the latter, a convertible security tends to trade more like the underlying stock. But when the common-share price is below that threshold, the convertible behaves more like a bond. Investors who buy these types of mutual funds should realize that some portfolio managers favor convertibles that behave like stocks, others concentrate on those that act more like bonds, and still others favor a mix. The higher a fund's yield, the more it emphasizes bond-like convertibles. It's also worth noting that convertible funds can differ in terms of the size of company they target. The market is made up mostly of smaller and medium-sized growth firms.

Convertible funds are somewhat similar to balanced portfolios because they both place a greater emphasis on income and capital preservation than the typical stock investment. If you don't mind going a bit off the beaten path, closed-end funds such as Bancroft Convertible and Lincoln National Convertible can offer good value, particularly at double-digit discounts. Fidelity, Putnam, and Vanguard are among the families that offer open-end convertible portfolios.

Asset-Allocation Funds

A portfolio manager's decision for apportioning investor dollars among stocks, bonds, and cash influences overall performance more than the individual securities selected. Asset-allocation funds diversify beyond equities into other categories. The idea is to reduce risk because different asset classes are less than perfectly correlated with one another—they don't all rise and fall together. Like a balanced fund, an asset-allocation product could serve as a complete investment program for people who can afford to own only one fund. Families offering these products include Crabbe Huson, Dreyfus, Fidelity, Fremont, Preferred, Strong, and Vanguard.

In general, these all-weather funds initially establish defined ranges for their holdings of stocks, bonds, and cash—the three primary asset classes. At the extreme, a fund would invest as little as 0 percent or as much as 100 percent in any category. They might also mix in some inflation-resistant securities, including gold, natural resource, energy, and real-estate stocks. For instance, USAA Cornerstone Strategy can invest from 22 to 28 percent of its assets in each of the following: U.S. stocks, foreign stocks, U.S. government securities, and real estate. In addition, it can stake up to 10 percent in gold stocks. This fund touches many bases, yet still has less leeway to shift assets into different categories than many competitors.

Most multiasset portfolio managers gradually adjust the category weights as prices and market outlooks change. Most funds have what's known as a "neutral mix," which indicates the portfolio's long-run normal allocation. For instance, Fidelity Asset Manager targets a 40-40-20 split among stocks, bonds, and cash even though it has the leeway to make considerable changes in its allocations. Conversely, the very conservative Permanent Portfolio maintains fixed commitments to its asset classes, which include gold and silver bullion, Swiss francs, domestic and foreign stocks, and U.S. Treasury bonds and bills. Permanent Portfolio, which began operations in 1982, is considered by some to be the grandfather of asset-allocation funds. Most rivals debuted following the crash of 1987.

Most all-weather funds have a global orientation. They diversify across stock markets and currencies as well as sectors, including common shares and bonds from emerging markets. Foreign stocks often perform very differently from U.S. equities, as discussed in Chapter 10.

Asset-allocation funds have certain shortcomings and have drawn their share of criticism. You need to exercise care if you want to invest. Here are the key problems:

1. *It's easy for a manager to mess up.* It's virtually impossible for anyone to make accurate near-term predictions in the financial markets on a consistent basis. The most flexible funds are simply aggressive market timers in disguise. But timing strategies don't work, as explained in Chapter 7.

2. *High turnover can pose problems.* Moving money around the asset-class spectrum leads to high transaction costs, adversely impacting performance and tax efficiency.

3. *Above-average costs dampen returns.* Asset-allocation funds tend to carry high costs. Hefty expense ratios are difficult to justify, especially at times when most of the assets may be in cash and bonds. We cited this concern earlier with balanced funds.

4. *Some funds may be overly cautious.* Certain managers maintain large positions in Treasury bills and precious metals. Such assets typically generate subpar returns and could be inappropriate if you're working with a long time horizon.

5. *You might not require allocation help.* Generally, you may be better off building your own portfolio of mutual funds and making any changes in this asset mix only when your circumstances change. Chapter 19 explores this subject. If you already hold a diversified assortment of funds, there's no need for an asset-allocation product.

Funds of Funds

The idea of having certain mutual funds invest in others has been around for decades. In fact, the approach received a bad name in the 1960s when an offshore company run by Bernie Cornfeld collapsed and brought down some stateside portfolios in which it held stakes. In 1970, Congress reacted to the fiasco by imposing restrictions on funds of funds.

Multifunds can be separated into two broad groups: those investing in nonaffiliated funds and those that hold an assortment of in-house products. Examples of the latter include T. Rowe Price Spectrum portfolios that buy stakes in several other T. Rowe Price products.

In theory, the overly diversified nature of funds of funds may produce mediocre results, and a possible double layer of fees puts a drag on performance. The added fees are those the "parent" fund charges for its allocation and bundling services. Exceptions include a few fund families that offer economical access to in-house portfolios, charging just one layer of fees. Vanguard Star, for example, imposes no management fee of its own. This balanced portfolio invests in an assortment of other Vanguard funds, and only the management expenses of these portfolios apply—on a pro-rata basis, not cumulatively. The T. Rowe Price Spectrum multifunds also impose just one layer of fees. Each invests in a mix of other T. Rowe Price products, offering a means of getting widespread diversification in a single purchase. Vanguard also has four Star LifeStrategy portfolios geared to people in specific age brackets. Each invests in other Vanguard portfolios.

Some multifunds move in and out of nonaffiliated funds as their market outlook changes. They share similarities with asset-allocation portfolios but invest in other mutual funds rather than directly in stocks and bonds. Two such portfolios with a market-timing orientation include Flex Muirfield and Rightime.

SPECIALIZED PRODUCTS

In sharp contrast to the hybrid portfolios, specialty funds take a narrow portfolio orientation. Some focus on a certain industry or on a geographic region of the United States. Still others follow well-defined social objectives and invest only in companies that satisfy their ethical criteria. Most people don't need specialty or sector funds. But it's still a good idea to be aware of what they can offer and, especially, of their pitfalls.

Sector funds are the most prominent type of specialized product. The concept behind industry-specific funds got a big boost in 1981 when Fidelity brought out the first of its Select portfolios. Invesco and Vanguard are among the other groups with sector products. But the concept is not a new one. For instance, Century Shares Trust has been investing the majority of its assets in the insurance industry since 1928.

Sector Choices

You can select from several hundred sector funds representing more than three dozen industry segments. But the total assets of all sector funds account for a relatively modest slice of the overall pie. Many such portfolios are small, with assets below $100 million.

The following are examples of available industry groups:

Air transportation	Gold and precious metals	Real estate
Automobiles	Health care	Regional banking
Computer software	Insurance	Technology
Environmental services	Leisure	Telecommunications
Financial services	Natural gas	Utilities

Fidelity counts about three dozen funds in its Select group. Normally, at least 80 percent of a portfolio's assets will be invested in its target sector. Each portfolio is classified as "nondiversified" and may invest up to 25 percent of its assets in a single stock. A unique feature of Fidelity's funds is their hourly pricing. This enables short-term traders to move in and out quickly, getting transactions executed at any of several prices during the day. About one-third of Fidelity's Select portfolios can be sold short by customers with margin accounts established at the firm's discount brokerage.

Be aware that there can be striking differences among funds investing in the same sector. They may hold different stocks and use nearly opposite strategies, as evidenced by their portfolio-turnover ratios or yields, or by the number of securities held. Some sector funds also may invest in foreign stocks. Thus, it's important to make close comparisons among peers before committing your money.

Sector-Fund Performance

When you peruse newspaper and magazine charts listing the best and worst performing funds, you invariably will see industry portfolios well represented. Table 12-1 contains the annual total returns of eight sector-fund groups, as reported by Lipper Analytical Services. You can learn a lot about the way these investments behave by comparing the ups and downs of the various groups. The gold-oriented portfolios, for instance, have exhibited the widest swings. And while utilities once had been thought of as a sleepy and safe industry, their returns got short-circuited in 1987 and 1994, when interest rates rose sharply.

Specific sectors can perform quite differently from the overall market and from one another, as evidenced in Table 12-1. For instance, in 1991 health/biotechnology funds surged 68.4 percent, natural-resource funds gained a paltry 1.5 percent, and gold portfolios slipped 3.6 percent.

Table 12-1   Yearly Total Returns of Sector Fund Groups (%)

Sector	1986	1987	1988	1989	1990	1991	1992	1993	1994	1995	1996
Gold oriented	37.3	37.7	-17.3	26.4	-23.5	-3.6	-15.8	88.0	-12.2	2.4	7.5
Environmental	22.5	-3.2	23.9	26.1	-5.1	16.6	-5.1	-2.4	-7.8	27.7	18.5
Financial Services	15.1	-11.5	19.0	24.5	-15.6	59.3	35.2	16.2	-2.7	41.5	28.0
Health/											
Biotechnology	16.6	-1.2	12.4	46.3	20.2	68.4	-6.7	3.7	4.3	47.2	13.4
Natural Resources	10.7	11.9	7.0	32.2	-8.2	1.5	1.9	27.0	-3.6	17.1	32.4
Real Estate	na	-7.7	15.6	10.6	-16.9	33.1	12.8	22.6	-2.9	13.9	30.9
Science &											
Technology	7.6	5.0	6.6	23.0	-0.5	48.8	14.4	24.0	16.4	39.5	19.1
Utilities	21.1	-8.5	14.8	28.6	-1.2	21.6	9.5	14.7	-9.1	27.4	9.9
S&P 500	**18.7**	**5.3**	**16.6**	**31.7**	**-3.1**	**30.5**	**7.6**	**10.1**	**1.3**	**37.6**	**23.0**

Source: Lipper Analytical Services Inc.

Conversely, in 1993 gold funds rocketed 88 percent while environmental funds declined 2.4 percent and the health funds inched up just 3.7 percent.

Sector funds attract people drawn to the latest "hot" industry or theme. If a family offers funds targeting many different sectors, it stands a good chance of having at least one star fund much of the time. But industries can undergo extreme ups and downs that won't show up in the broad market averages, and some sector portfolios can be as volatile as individual stocks. In fact, they can be hurt significantly by the performance of just one company because they hold far fewer stocks than their broadly diversified relatives. Unfortunately, high risk doesn't necessarily equate to high long-run returns, especially when you're not diversified. An industry could lag the overall market for many years, particularly if it's shrinking. Entire industries can become obsolete with technological change.

Why Invest in Sector Funds?

The arguments against industry-specific portfolios probably outweigh their benefits. Still, sector funds can make a nice alternative to investing in a few individual stocks within an area where you want special exposure. They also may be of some interest to larger investors who already own a diversified mix of funds. Here are several reasons why people might choose to buy shares in sector funds.

1. *To invest in the industry in which you work.* You know your business really well and either feel it has outstanding growth potential or think you can spot turning points. In such cases, a sector fund allows you to take a big stake with ease.

2. *To obtain concentrated exposure to a promising industry or theme.* Sector funds can be used to add a "kicker" to a broadly diversified portfolio. The funds have the potential to provide extraordinary returns, as evidenced by the health/biotechnology group from 1989 through 1991 and in 1995 (see Table 12-1).

3. *To do your own sector selection, weighting, and rotation.* A true hands-on investor might want to build a portfolio of different sector funds, reasoning that the manager of each is an expert in that industry. Most investors should avoid this approach, however, as the time required to monitor the holdings could defeat the purpose of buying mutual funds in the first place.

4. *To obtain above-average income with some growth potential.* Funds focusing on financial, real-estate, and utility stocks pay some of the heftiest dividends around.

5. *To hedge your portfolio.* A modest stake in a gold portfolio is sometimes recommended as a hedge against high inflation or other catastrophic occurrences. An energy fund could protect you against surging oil prices.

In fact, each industry group offers its own trade-offs among income, growth, stability, and other traits. What follows is a sketch of some of the dominant sectors.

Real Estate

These funds bet on real estate, specifically by purchasing shares in real estate investment trusts (REITs). REITs are exchange-traded companies that invest in various income-producing properties, including apartments, hotels, office buildings, and shopping centers. They have performed comparably to stocks in general over the past two decades, yet offer significantly higher income than, say, an S&P 500 portfolio.

Because of a fundamental shift in the way commercial properties are being financed, you could make a strong case for diversifying a portfolio with real-estate securities. While REITs have been around since the early 1960s, they only recently emerged as the industry's predominate vehicle for raising capital, replacing limited partnerships, bank loans, and other traditional means. REITs acquire and manage properties, thereby increasing their cash flows, which leads to a growing stream of dividends for shareholders.

Real-estate funds normally diversify their holdings across many states. Some even take a global slant. The typical real-estate fund takes positions in all of the major property types, primarily through REITs. A fund also might invest in related companies such as developers and building-supply firms. In addition, they may own stocks of companies in other industries with substantial real-estate holdings. By purchasing stocks rather than properties directly, real-estate portfolios offer investors the high liquidity characteristic of mutual funds. CGM, Cohen & Steers, Fidelity, and Vanguard are among the groups with products in the real-estate area.

Utilities

Mutual funds that target electricity providers offer far more stability than the typical sector product. Like bonds, utility stocks typically generate high income. But unlike bond interest payments, which remain fixed, utility dividends can grow over the years. Utilities represent defensive investments since their services are always needed, regardless of how the economy is doing.

Utilities have changed in character over the past few decades, however. Deregulation and competition have shaken up this once-staid industry.

Utilities have more freedom to increase their earnings but also face pressures to cut costs, including dividends paid to shareholders. Investors can no longer assume that all of these stocks remain suitable for "widows and orphans." You can't just buy them, put them away, and plan on collecting steady dividends for the next 30 years. Companies on occasion run into severe difficulties and may be forced to cut dividends—a scenario that could send their shares plunging. This makes a good case for using mutual funds to minimize the risks associated with individual companies.

Utility portfolios differ in composition and aggressiveness, although most emphasize income to varying degrees. Some make bets on the recovery of turnaround candidates, thus placing more emphasis on capital appreciation. Others stick with perennial industry leaders. The utility business consists mainly of electric, natural gas, and telephone companies. The funds mix the groups in various ways or specialize in one category or another. A few portfolios take a global orientation, investing in utilities domiciled in other countries.

Even though utility funds ordinarily are stable, they can be volatile at times. Like bonds, they are interest-rate sensitive. As you will see in Chapter 13, increasing rates depress the prices of high-yielding stocks as well as bonds. In addition, rising interest rates mean heavier borrowing costs for this capital-intensive industry, which puts a squeeze on profits. The flip side is that utility funds can generate robust returns during years when rates decline.

Gold and Precious Metals

Gold has a rich history and a special allure. But owning the metal as an investment has its drawbacks. You must contend with brokerage fees, dealer markups, and storage and insurance costs. Besides, gold bullion or coins do not produce income, as you would get from a stock or bond.

Gold funds offer a cost-effective way to participate in possible increases in the metal's price. They focus primarily on the stocks of gold-mining companies. Most gold-extracting companies are located in North America, South Africa, or Australia. Regional weightings vary among funds and some managers confine their investments to a single territory such as North America. Certain managers also hold modest amounts of gold bullion. Silver and platinum play a minor role in some portfolios.

Gold stocks and gold funds tend to exhibit more price volatility than does the metal itself. This is attributable to speculators moving in and out of funds and stocks as their sentiment shifts. Further exaggerating these movements is the so-called operating leverage of mining companies. Because mining costs are largely fixed, most of any rise in the price of the metal goes to each firm's bottom line. Suppose a gold-mining company has fixed costs of $100 million, which enable it to produce about 300,000 ounces of metal in a year. If gold sells for $380 an ounce, it earns a $14-million profit (the $114-mil-

---

Bear-Market Funds

A few mutual funds are designed to protect investors in down markets, either partially or completely. Some managers try to accomplish this by selling certain stocks short that appear overpriced, by stocking up on gold shares, or by making use of speculative options or futures strategies. The funds in this group are quite diverse and their performances difficult to predict. Our advice is to avoid bear-market funds, at least in sizable amounts. It doesn't make sense to hold them in up markets, while downturns are difficult to predict and relatively infrequent. Don't forget that the market has a bullish bias, rising in about seven of every 10 years. As noted elsewhere, you have to live with some short-term declines to realize long-term gains. Money you can't afford to risk doesn't belong in the stock market in the first place.

---

lion revenues minus the $100-million costs). If gold increases 10 percent to $418 an ounce, profits leap to $25.4 million, or about 81 percent. This large rise in profitability is possible because operating costs are unaffected. Of course, operating leverage is a double-edged sword, cutting heavily into earnings when the price of the metal takes a spill. Incidentally, mines with higher fixed costs exhibit greater operating leverage. This is true of the South African mines, and it contributes to the greater volatility of their shares.

Needless to say, gold funds by themselves do not offer a complete investment program. But you might want to allocate a small proportion of your assets, perhaps 5 percent, to a gold fund for diversification purposes. Gold sometimes moves inversely to the prices of stocks and bonds and occasionally performs very well during times of turmoil. You have to think of it as a kind of insurance policy and not get too upset about periodic losses. Outright speculation on gold is not recommended, as the metal's price is highly unpredictable.

The bottom line is that gold often fares poorly relative to mainstream stock-market investments. A random sampling of stocks likely will fare better over the long run than will a group of gold-mining companies. There are times when you should "just say no" to an investment, and gold fits squarely into that category most of the time.

Natural Resources

Like gold portfolios, natural-resource funds provide a hedge against inflationary surges. They concentrate on companies involved in oil and natural gas, precious and nonprecious metals, minerals, and paper and forest products. Examples include T. Rowe Price New Era, Fidelity Industrial Materials, Putnam Natural Resources A, Vanguard Specialized Energy Portfolio, and Petroleum & Resources, a closed-end portfolio.

Although there is no perfect inflation hedge, natural-resource funds tend to perform best when oil prices increase sharply. Some funds in this group are pure energy plays—they confine their holdings to companies in oil and gas as well as alternative energy sources such as nuclear and solar power. Be aware, however, that natural-resource portfolios sometimes lag in up markets during disinflationary times. Still, they represent a better choice than gold portfolios for long-term investors because their industries are more varied and economically viable.

Drawbacks of Sector Funds

So much for the attractions of sector funds. There are some reasons for steering clear of these vehicles.

1. *They are risky.* With a sector product, you give up diversification. Managers of such funds operate within an "investment straightjacket" because they must stick with their industry through thick and thin. Industry funds that catapult to the top of the performance charts one period might land near the bottom the next time around.

2. *It's easy to mess up trying to time purchases and sales.* Predicting near-term results for the stock market isn't easy, not even for industry groups. The problem is worse with precious-metals funds because of their heightened volatility. Many investors seem to try to time their sector picks more so than their diversified choices.

3. *Sector funds can contribute to superfluous diversification.* A fund's target sector may duplicate a large portion of another fund you already hold. For instance, utility, financial-services, or real-estate portfolios could largely replicate what's also in your equity-income or balanced fund.

4. *You may be overpaying.* Expense ratios often are higher for sector funds, in part because they typically are smaller. On average, you can expect to pay about 1.5 percent, according to Lipper. In addition, many sector funds impose sales charges, including the Fidelity Select portfolios. With a sector fund, there's no industry allocation and rotation, as in a typical diversified fund, so you may be paying more for less!

SOCIALLY RESPONSIBLE INVESTING

For decades, money has been used as a tool in promoting social change. People see investment dollars as a means to curtail tobacco or alcohol abuse, restrict the spread of weapons or gambling, and fight businesses that pollute the environment. The widespread withholding of investment capital probably helped to defeat apartheid in South Africa. Activists think it could work in other ways, too.

Such concerns gave rise to "socially responsible" or "ethical" funds, which screen out certain companies that their shareholders might find offensive. Examples include Domini Social Equity, Dreyfus Third Century, Neuberger & Berman Socially Responsible, Parnassus, and Pax World. As you might expect, there can be huge differences among these funds, both in defining problems and pursuing investment goals. For instance, one fund might invest only in companies that are particularly sensitive to the needs of women or homosexuals in the workplace, while another labors to promote low-polluting sources of energy. Ethical funds might be a good option for someone who otherwise would avoid the stock market entirely over philosophical objections.

But ethical funds also have several problems to overcome in the minds of mainstream investors, including the following:

1. *Excluding certain types of companies limits management.* This can hurt performance by reducing the number of profitable opportunities. But social activists counter that the most progressive companies typically are the most successful, too.

2. *It's impossible to totally screen out undesirable businesses.* Almost every company will mess up in some way—in its pollution problems, its hiring practices, or its manufacturing processes. For instance, a fund might shun tobacco companies but it may still invest in a communications company that derives some income from tobacco advertising; or a portfolio manager may avoid alcohol producers in favor of food processors that make salty, high-fat snacks.

3. *You may be overpaying.* Ethical investing remains something of a fringe movement, which means the mutual funds in this realm are on the small side. Many carry high expenses because they don't benefit from economies of scale.

4. *There may be diversification holes in the portfolio.* It's possible a fund may exclude companies in a range of important industries such as aerospace, chemicals, energy, plastics, and mining. In addition, ethical funds tend to avoid small companies and foreign corporations for which information on social concerns is harder to come by.

One suggestion we can offer to anyone concerned about these important issues is to invest in a broad-based mutual fund and donate a portion of your profits to your favorite cause or charity. Because it's difficult to define precisely what's socially responsible, most major fund groups don't offer ethical products. The response from investors has been lukewarm at best.

AT THE CLOSE

Investors enjoy an ever-widening selection of mutual funds that provide an entrée into the stock market, but not in the traditional sense. On the one hand, there are balanced, asset-allocation, and convertible portfolios—products that overlay bonds onto a heavy stock foundation. These investments tend to be fairly conservative and can make good all-inclusive choices. But you usually can do better mixing more narrowly defined investments.

At the other extreme, certain stock funds deliver very narrow diversification by limiting their holdings to companies in a specific industry. Sector funds can be highly volatile and should be utilized in moderation, if used at all. As a rule, sector investments tend to carry high costs and might duplicate what you already own in more widely diversified funds. Then there are "socially responsible" portfolios, which don't pursue an industry orientation but nonetheless limit their investment options. They remain most popular among people who feel passionately enough about ethical causes to stake their investment dollars on them.

CHAPTER 13

How Fixed-Income Securities Work

Bonds and bond mutual funds are like the shallow end of a swimming pool. They are a place in the investment world where you can cool off and splash around without much fear of drowning. Once you learn to swim well, you can paddle over to stock investments in the deep end, where there's more room to have fun. After you have tried the diving board, you might never want to leave the deep end. So too with the greater reward potential of stocks.

Nevertheless, bonds and bond funds still deserve your consideration, at least for a modest portion of your portfolio. These investments provide income, fairly good predictability, and more stability than equities. They also enhance diversification in an equity-dominated portfolio. But beyond these generalizations, fixed-income securities can vary markedly. What follows is a look at their many shapes and sizes.

MONEY AND CAPITAL MARKETS

Before reaching bond investments on the risk-return scale, you will find *money-market securities,* or short-term debt instruments. Such IOUs include Treasury bills, commercial paper, repurchase agreements, certificates of deposit, and Eurodollars. A common thread of each is that they all mature in one year or less. Repurchase agreements often come due the next business day.

By contrast, the fixed-income capital market, popularly known as the bond market, is the place for longer-term securities. It can be separated into six general segments:

1. Corporate debt

2. Treasury securities

3. Federal-agency debt

4. Mortgage-backed securities

5. Tax-exempt bonds

6. Foreign debt

Our major focus in this chapter is on bonds and the capital markets. Chapters 14 and 15 cover the many categories of taxable and tax-free bond funds. Chapter 16 deals with money-market securities and the money-fund arena.

WHY INVEST IN FIXED-INCOME SECURITIES?

Common stocks provide much better long-run returns than fixed-income investments. They're also a lot more exciting. So why bother with bonds? The reasons can be summed up in three terms: *liquidity, capital preservation,* and *income.* These attributes of bonds and bond funds give them certain advantages over stock investments.

1. *Liquidity.* Money-market funds provide a cash reserve to handle emergencies or take advantage of attractive investment opportunities. Bond funds with short maturities offer the same benefits at higher yields. Cash you might need within the reasonably near future could be invested in a short-term bond portfolio to minimize risk yet provide higher yields than on money markets.

2. *Capital preservation.* Bond funds generally fluctuate less than stock investments. The shorter their average term to maturity, the more stable the price. Capital preservation goes hand in hand with liquidity.

Of course, some fixed-income products can be pretty volatile. Investors who held bond funds during 1994 learned that lesson.

3. *Income.* Debt securities generally provide higher, more dependable payouts than stock portfolios. Municipal-bond funds offer yields that also are partly or wholly tax-exempt. They have grown rapidly in importance in recent years as a means to shelter income from Uncle Sam, especially as rival shelters dried up.

Bond-fund investors must choose between liquidity and capital preservation, on the one hand, and income on the other. The highest-yielding bonds are usually the riskiest and thus should not be relied on for safety or for ready money. Conversely, the more secure investments promise the lowest payouts.

BOND CHARACTERISTICS

Bonds have different features from stocks—at least a dozen unshared attributes. Their major characteristics can be summarized as follows:

1. A bond is a contractual commitment between issuer and investor. The "bond indenture," a disclosure document, spells out the terms of the contract.

2. Corporate and municipal bonds have credit risks of varying degrees. The creditworthiness of an issue is judged by independent rating agencies.

3. Bonds have a "par value," also known as the face or maturity amount. It is commonly $1,000 for corporates and $5,000 for municipals. Bonds that trade below par are said to be selling at a discount; those hovering above par trade at a premium.

4. Most bonds pay periodic interest, which is generally fixed and expressed as a "coupon" rate. The name derives from the old practice of clipping the coupon on a bond and mailing it in to receive the interest. Payments are typically made semiannually. An 8-percent coupon bond with a $1,000 face value would pay $40 every six months. In contrast, zero coupon bonds do not pay interest until redemption; instead, they're sold at a discount to their maturity value.

5. Bonds come due on a specific date. At redemption, investors receive a principal payment equal to the security's face value.

6. Mortgage-backed securities, such as Ginnie Maes, differ from other types of bonds. They pay both principal and interest monthly, as they

are self-liquidating. They do not have a specific maturity date. That's because prepayments by mortgage holders, which cannot be forecast precisely, will shorten an issue's life.

7. Bonds are generally "callable" prior to maturity. This means the issuer may choose to retire some outstanding securities if interest rates have fallen sufficiently. In essence, this allows the issuer to replace expensive debt with bonds paying lower interest. But investors would have to reinvest the proceeds at the lower, currently prevailing rates, making the call feature unattractive for them.

8. Bond yields move in the opposite direction from prices. This can best be illustrated in terms of current yield, which is defined as the annual interest payment divided by the bond's price. If an 8-percent coupon bond sells for $1,000, its current yield would be 8 percent. But assuming the price falls to $920, the yield rises to 8.7 percent ($80/$920). An increase to $1,080 would lower the yield to about 7.4 percent ($80/$1,080).

9. Bond prices vary inversely with market interest rates. Rising rates depress prices, while lower rates spark rallies. This is the flip side of the inverse relationship of yield to price. If interest rates increase, for example, yields on outstanding bonds must move up (and their prices fall) to stay competitive with rates paid by new issues of comparable bonds.

10. The "yield to maturity," or promised yield, indicates a bond's expected annual total return. It takes into account potential capital gains and losses. Suppose a 14-percent coupon bond that matures in 10 years is selling for $1,400. At maturity, the holder would receive $1,000, or $400 less than the present price. The current yield is 10 percent ($140/$1,400) but the yield to maturity is only about 8 percent. Simply put, the yield to maturity is less than the current yield in this example because it reflects the amortization or erosion of the $400 premium.

11. Bonds with longer maturities and/or lower ratings carry bigger risks. Riskier debt securities promise higher returns, but may not deliver them.

12. Short-term yields fluctuate more than yields on long-term debt. For example, rates paid by money funds historically have ranged from under 3 percent to over 18 percent, exceeding the yield variations on conventional bonds.

THE YIELD CURVE

This analytical tool shows graphically how payouts vary for different maturities of bonds. You can gauge the level and shape of the curve daily by looking at the "Treasury Bonds, Notes & Bills" column in *The Wall Street Journal* or by examining a similar chart in *Investor's Business Daily* newspaper.

Figure 13-1 contrasts a normal, upward-sloping yield curve with the rare downward sloping, or inverted, curve. The former indicates that longer-term bonds pay higher rates, as would be expected. For example, if 3-month Treasury bills yield 4 percent; 10-year notes, 7.5 percent; and 30-year bonds, 8 percent; the curve is positively sloped. If the curve climbs sharply upward, investors in general expect rates to rise. An inverted or negatively sloped curve means yields on bills exceed those on notes which, in turn, exceed those on bonds. The inverted pattern exists when rates are relatively high and investors expect them to come down.

As noted, an upward-sloping curve is the norm, showing that longer-term bonds yield more than shorter-term instruments. Longer bonds should pay more since they have a greater exposure to adverse price fluctuations. In addition, the risk of default is somewhat higher with long-term corporates and municipals since there is more time for the issuer to get into trouble.

The level and shape of the curve also may reveal where "yield-sensitive" investors are likely to be moving their money. As short-term rates fall and the

Figure 13-1   Two Yield Curves

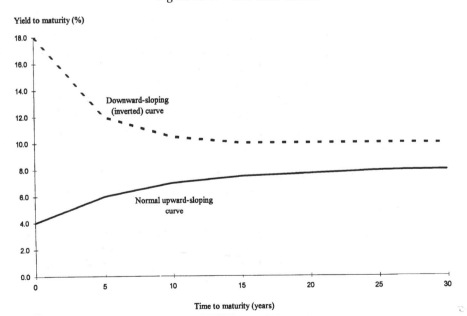

Yield to maturity (%)

Downward-sloping (inverted) curve

Normal upward-sloping curve

Time to maturity (years)

curve slopes upward, investors probably will go "further out" into longer-term bonds, attracted by the higher payouts. Usually, there will be a place where the curve is particularly steep, which might offer a good spot to pick up extra income without much additional risk. When short rates rise to where the yield curve becomes inverted, investors move out of bonds and into money-market funds.

PRIMARY RISK FACTORS

Bonds are generally less volatile than stocks, although they still can get hit hard during periods of higher inflation. They also carry a variety of other dangers, including some subtle ones that might catch the uninitiated off guard.

The following risk factors can affect bond-fund investors as well as people holding individual bonds. Portfolio managers can minimize some, but not all, of these dangers.

- *Interest-rate risk.* When rates rise, bond prices fall. The longer the maturity and the lower the coupon rate, the greater the vulnerability.

- *Inflation risk.* As explained in Chapter 6, inflation erodes the value of fixed returns. People who stash a large portion of their long-term wealth in debt securities face substantial inflation or purchasing-power risk, though they might not realize it.

- *Reinvestment risk.* When interest rates fall, so do the rates at which bond interest payments can be reinvested. This reduces bondholders' actual yields, since they will be earning less interest on their interest. Zero-coupon bonds don't make periodic interest payments and thus don't have any reinvestment risk.

- *Call risk.* This reflects the danger that a bond might be called or forcibly redeemed during a period of declining interest rates. People who see their high-yielding investments called likely will have to reinvest the proceeds in bonds that pay less. Fund managers can reduce this risk by holding issues with longer periods of "call protection."

- *Credit risk.* This reflects the possibility that the issuer will not make promised interest and principal payments on time or in full. Treasury securities are perceived to have no credit risk. The danger on corporate and municipal bonds varies, with lower-rated bonds being more treacherous. Diversification greatly reduces credit risk.

- *Liquidity risk.* Thinly traded securities, including many municipal bonds, carry this danger of not being easily salable. It means the fund manager may have to take a big hit in price if he or she must quickly unload an illiquid bond. This also can be a problem for junk-bond funds and even some higher-quality corporates.

Different fixed-income mutual funds are subject to the range of risks in varying degrees. Still other dangers that affect specific groups of bonds will be discussed later.

MORE ON INTEREST-RATE RISK

This peril confronts bond-fund investors directly, especially those in longer-term portfolios. Simply put, bond prices fall when interest rates rise. Table 13-1 illustrates that prices of longer-term bonds drop more dramatically as interest rates increase. This illustration displays the percentage change in price of a bond with an 8-percent coupon when interest rates change by one percentage point, up or down. For instance, when rates increase by one point, the 30-year bond falls 10.32 percent. This decline more than offsets the 8-percent interest income earned by the bondholder, resulting in a negative total return. If rates ease, on the other hand, the investor benefits from appreciation. The longer the maturity, the greater the potential for capital gains as well.

Using Bond Duration

Time to maturity is not the only determinant of a bond's interest-rate risk. This danger is also greater for bond issues with lower coupons. For example, a 30-year, zero-coupon bond that yields 8 percent to maturity would fall about 24 percent in value if interest rates rose one percentage point. Mutual funds that focus on long-term zero-coupon bonds exhibit the most volatility.

Table 13-1   Price Volatility Varies Directly with Maturity

Maturity (Years)	Bond Price Changes*	
	Rates *Increase* 1 Percentage Point	Rates *Decrease* 1 Percentage Point
1	-0.94%	+0.95%
3	-2.58	+2.66
5	-3.96	+4.16
10	-6.50	+7.11
20	-9.20	+10.68
30	-10.32	+12.47

*Assumes an 8-percent-coupon bond initially priced at par.

Duration is the best indicator of interest-rate risk because it considers the size of the coupon as well as the time to maturity. The idea behind duration is that bondholders recoup their investments little by little through the periodic receipt of interest payments and from the eventual repayment of principal. The longer this takes, the longer the duration, and the more price-sensitive the bond or portfolio is to rate changes.

More specifically, duration is a sophisticated measure of a bond's "average" life, considering its time to maturity, stream of interest payments, and current price. It provides a weighted average of the time to recovery of all payments to the bondholder. The duration for a coupon-bearing security is less than its time to maturity. For example, an 8-percent bond maturing in 30 years and selling at par would have a duration of a little more than 12 years. In contrast, the duration for a 30-year, zero-coupon bond is 30, its time to maturity.

The duration of a mutual fund is found by averaging the respective figures for the individual bonds it holds. Telephone reps at many fund companies can provide up-to-date numbers. Duration figures also can be found in Morningstar and Value Line reports. The higher the number, the more a fund's price fluctuates in response to interest-rate changes. For example, if rates increase by one percentage point, a long-term fund with a duration of 12 could be expected to fall about 12 percent in value. Conversely, an intermediate-term portfolio with a duration of 6 would decline only 6 percent in this

---

Interest-Rate Risk Also Affects Stocks

Like bonds, stocks rise and fall according to interest-rate swings. Both types of securities compete for investor dollars, so when rates rise, people move from equities into the fixed-income arena to capture the higher, more secure yields. Stock prices decline as investors sell out.

The impact readily can be seen on real-estate stocks, which pay relatively high dividends. During a period of rising rates, real estate investment trust share prices will tend to fall as investors sell. The lower prices would result in higher dividend yields, bringing the shares in line with prevailing financial conditions. Suppose a REIT pays a dividend of $4 a year and sells at $50, for a yield of 8 percent (or $4/$50). Now assume interest rates advance to the point where the stock has to yield 10 percent to attract investors. The price would have to fall to $40.

In addition, rising interest rates mean higher corporate borrowing costs, which erode profit margins, further depressing stock prices. Lower rates would have the opposite effect.

case. Be aware that duration gauges only the interest-rate risk of a bond fund, not other potential perils such as credit risk.

If the duration of a bond fund is high, its standard deviation usually is high. However, a high standard deviation does not necessarily translate into a lofty duration because the variability could come from some other factor such as adverse currency movements on an international fund, or deteriorating creditworthiness in the case of a high-yield portfolio. Duration, after all, measures interest-rate risk only. For this reason, standard deviation is a more comprehensive yardstick than duration because it reflects all sources of volatility.

INFLATION RISK AND REAL RETURNS

What you earn on a fixed-income security or portfolio after inflation has been stripped away is called the "real rate" of return. This simply reflects the growth in your wealth in terms of purchasing power.

Nominal fixed-income yields normally contain a built-in inflation premium, which varies with investors' consensus expectation for inflation at the time. The higher the consensus forecast, the loftier the level of interest rates in general. Changes in the inflation outlook lead to fluctuations in nominal yields.

Suppose a one-year T-bill yields 6 percent. If the consensus anticipates inflation of 4 percent for the next 12 months, you could expect to earn a real rate of about 2 percent. If inflation estimates increase, T-bill rates should rise correspondingly. The same holds for other fixed-income securities.

Suppose, however, that an investor purchased the one-year T-bill yielding 6 percent, but, to the surprise of many, inflation turned out to be 6 percent for the year. The real return would be zero. You can see from this illustration that a major risk faced by bondholders is that their yields may be too low because investors can underestimate future inflation. This could lead to extremely low or even negative real returns.

The discussion on nominal and real returns can be summarized as follows:

- The higher the real return, the better the actual performance, regardless of the level of nominal yields.

- Bondholders get hurt when they underestimate future inflation and yields turn out to have been insufficient.

- Bond funds become more enticing when their probable real rates appear generous. Real rates that exceed 4 percent are generally attractive. This may be a good time to increase your stake in these investments.

CREDIT RISK

Default danger affects corporate and municipal bonds. Since a bond is basically an IOU, investors must assess the possibility that the issuer might not live up to its promises. The credit risk of a bond can be gauged by examining its rating. Bond funds discuss credit risk in detail in their prospectuses. They also list the ratings of all bonds held in their annual and semiannual reports to shareholders.

Moody's Investors Service and Standard & Poor's Corp. are the two best known of the various independent rating agencies. Each grade represents an agency's assessment of an issuer's ability to pay principal and interest on time and in full. The agencies consider factors such as the issuer's general financial health and ability to generate enough profits to make bond payments. They also examine provisions in the bond's indenture that might affect the security offered.

In a broad sense, bonds fall into two general quality categories: investment grade and speculative. And within each main group there are a number of gradations.

"Investment-grade" securities carry any of the top four ratings of Moody's and S&P. For example, the S&P ratings are AAA, AA, A, and BBB. Nonrated bonds might also fall within this category provided a fund manager judges them to be of high caliber. Rating agencies may modify a letter grade to indicate finer distinctions. For instance, S&P alters its ratings with a plus or minus sign, so a bond rated A+ would outrank a simple A.

Within the investment-grade category, the triple-A and double-A designations represent *high-grade* issues. So-called "gilt edge" corporate or municipal bonds, rated triple-A, offer the most creditworthiness, although they would still carry a slight amount of default risk compared to Treasuries, which have none. Single-A and triple-B bonds are designated *medium-grade* issues. There is always the chance that a bond's rating could be lowered if the issuer's financial condition deteriorates; this would result in a lower price for the security. On the other hand, a bond also might see its rating upgraded.

"Speculative" issues are those below triple-B, again with various gradations. The lower the rating, the greater the risk. IOUs rated double-B or lower are known pejoratively as junk bonds. Convertible bonds generally carry ratings below investment grade, too. Moody's assigns some evaluations as low as single-C; S&P ratings can drop to single-D. Issues carrying such deficient grades probably are in default. As explained previously, the most important advantage of a mutual fund is the built-in diversification offered. Anyone who buys a single bond would need to be very concerned about credit risk. But this is not really a problem for a portfolio of bonds. By diversifying into 50, 100, or more issues a fund manager can reduce the overall default danger, even with junk bonds.

It's worth noting that fund managers won't always accept a bond's rating at face value. They often will dig into the company's financial statements and make their own assessment. The manager's expertise is especially important with a junk-bond portfolio, or when dealing with a significant number of smaller, nonrated issues. Some of these securities represent good values.

In analyzing the credit risk of a bond portfolio, you should consider its proportionate breakdown in the different letter-grade categories and the fund's average rating. For high-yield funds, this analysis is especially important. Be sure to check what percentage of the bonds carry ratings below triple-B. A percentage breakdown by credit quality can be found in the fund's prospectus or in the profiles compiled by Morningstar and Value Line.

A BONDHOLDER'S TOTAL RETURN

The total return earned on any investment during a year equals its income plus any price gains, and minus any losses. For multiyear periods, the interest earned on the reinvested interest exerts a big overall influence. Bondholders who don't understand this may be doing worse than they think. The following illustration demonstrates why the compounding effect is so important.

Suppose you buy a 10-percent coupon bond at par, or $1,000. The investment pays annual interest and matures in 25 years. You hold it to maturity. Would you realize a 10-percent yield to maturity, also known as the true compound rate of return? The answer depends on what you do with the interest payments, which total $2,500 over the 25 years ($100 per year times 25). Here's an analysis of the case:

- If you spent your interest checks when received, your yield to maturity would not even come close to 10 percent. It would be a paltry 5.14 percent.

- Instead, suppose you reinvested in a passbook account at 4 percent. You would accumulate $4,164.59 in interest, but your realized yield to maturity still would be only 6.79 percent.

- To earn the full 10-percent yield to maturity, you would have to reinvest each payment at 10 percent. The accumulated interest would amount to $9,834.71.

Thus, even when you buy an individual bond, you can't always tell what you will be earning. The important point to remember is that interest on interest—or compounding—is a powerful concept. The longer you hold onto a bond or bond fund, the more significant it becomes. By reinvesting all interest payments or distributions from a mutual fund, you will realize a better return.

In fact, it's easier for most people to reinvest income at favorable rates through bond funds. Why? Because the funds will credit you with fractional-share purchases, even on small dividends, usually without charging any loads or commissions. Try investing $20, $100, or even $700 in an individual bond. Also, bond-fund reinvestments are made instantaneously and automatically, with no action needed on your part. If you own some individual IOUs directly and don't need the income now, consider reinvesting your interest payments in a bond fund.

INTEREST-RATE FORECASTS

You could generate a fortune in the bond market by making accurate interest-rate predictions even most of the time. Unfortunately, that's easier said than done. What's the track record of professional rate forecasters? It's mediocre at best. Rate movements depend on changes in economic conditions, especially inflation. It's very difficult to make such predictions consistently, since there are too many unknowable factors.

The best strategy for most investors is simply to use bond funds to meet liquidity, preservation of capital, and income needs. Don't expect to build a fortune in the bond market by forecasting interest rates. For amassing wealth, stock portfolios provide much better opportunities.

Nevertheless, astute investors can generate slightly above-average results by reading the economic tea leaves and adjusting their portfolios accordingly. The manager of a bond fund may lengthen overall maturities a bit when he or she expects rates to fall and shorten when rates appear likely to rise. Some bond funds—the so-called "flexible" portfolios—enjoy considerably more leeway to alter maturities than others.

"FED WATCHING"

It's hard to look at the business news without reading something about the Federal Reserve, or "Fed," and its probable next move at an upcoming meeting. The Fed Chairman generally is considered the second most powerful person in Washington behind the President. The central bank strives to help the economy to grow at a steady real rate of about 2 to 2.5 percent yearly. The rate in question is the after-inflation increase of gross domestic product. Higher growth spells danger because it can ignite an inflationary spiral. To do its work, the Fed regulates expansion of the money supply, which has an important effect on the economy, inflation, and interest rates.

The Monetary Tools

As the nation's central bank, the Fed has three primary monetary tools at its disposal, namely:

1. *Open-market operations.* The Fed's most frequently used tool involves the purchase or sale of government securities (normally T-bills) in an effort to fine-tune growth in the money supply. When the Fed buys T-bills, it simply "writes a check," thereby boosting the money supply. Conversely, if the Fed wants to pursue a tight-money policy, it steps up its sales of T-bills. Proceeds from the sales of T-bills enter the central bank's account and thus reduce the money supply.

2. *Changes in key short-term interest rates.* The most visible aspect of monetary policy is a Fed decision to raise or lower rates. In this manner, the central bank signals its intentions in the interest-rate arena. The rates in question include the *discount rate,* which is what the Fed charges banks for overnight loans to build up their reserves, and the *federal-funds rate,* at which banks borrow from each other short-term.

3. *Setting reserve requirements for banks.* The Fed can change the amount of total deposits that banks must keep idle, in reserve. Lowering these requirements allows banks to loan a greater percentage of their total deposits to customers, thereby expanding the money supply. Small changes in this ratio can have a dramatic impact on the money supply. This tool is rarely used by the Fed.

Reining in Inflation

When growth accelerates to the point that the economy overheats, inflation becomes a problem. By influencing monetary policy and interest rates, the 12-member Federal Open Market Committee, of which the chairman plays a dominant role, can exert a dramatic impact on the economy, the stock and bond markets, and your mutual funds.

Suppose the nation is facing full employment and buoyant economic growth. In this scenario, the Fed can apply the monetary brakes as a preemptive strike against inflation. It will step up sales of government securities in its day-to-day, open-market operations, taking money out of circulation. If inflationary concerns are great enough, it can directly boost short-term interest rates by increasing the discount rate and, possibly, the federal-funds rate. Because these rates set the tone for the whole economy, the Fed's actions reverberate throughout the financial markets. In this case, they would lead to higher interest rates, falling bond and stock prices, and increasingly nervous investors.

In fact, investors often react to news that they feel will prompt the Fed to raise rates. Unusually strong employment numbers, for instance, may cause havoc in the bond market, driving the benchmark 30-year T-bond yield skyward. The stock market often reacts with a sizable drop as jittery traders quickly head for the exits. But long-term investors should not worry about this frenzied activity. If anything, corrections can present good buying opportunities.

Arousing a Sleeping Economy

Conversely, if the economy is slumbering in a recession and needs a shot in the arm, the Fed will pursue an easy-money policy and pump reserves into the banking system. It can purchase government securities in its open-market operations and reduce the federal-funds and discount rates, thereby stimulating credit, employment, and economic activity. Falling interest rates can do wonders for the stock and bond markets. Such a scenario unleashed the roaring bull market that began in 1982. The Fed in that year had finally succeeded in pushing inflation down from double digits to a respectable single-digit figure. In general, stable—not excessive—real growth remains the top priority.

Even though interest rates are hard to forecast, it pays to keep abreast of the Fed's activities. This will provide valuable insight into the reasons for the recent behavior of the stock and bond markets. Fed watchers hold that several consecutive increases (or decreases) in the discount rate can reverse a bull (or bear) market. This has led to indicators such as the bearish "three steps and a stumble" rule. The theory is that when the central bank boosts the discount rate three times in a row, stock prices tend to falter, although the relationship doesn't always hold.

YIELD SPREADS

We have already talked about inefficiencies in the stock market. Such opportunities also exist in the bond arena, and it's the goal of good fund managers to take advantage of them.

One way they do this is by monitoring "yield spreads," or differences in payout rates among individual bonds or groups of bonds. Don't confuse this with the difference between the bid and asked prices in a bond's quotation—also called the "spread." For example, suppose a portfolio of triple-A corporates yields 8 percent, while double-B corporates yield 10 percent. The spread is two percentage points or 200 "basis points." Each basis point equals 1/100 of a percentage point.

Yield spreads come in various categories:

- *Maturity spreads.* As noted earlier, the yield curve normally slopes upward, which means longer-term bonds typically pay more than shorter-term issues. Maturity spreads reflect the fact that longer-term IOUs are exposed to heightened interest-rate risk.

- *Quality spreads.* These refer to differences in yield among bonds with varying degrees of creditworthiness. For example, during a deepening recession, investors get nervous and you see a "flight to quality." The spread between, say, triple-A and double-B corporates widens as jittery investors shift their money from the latter to the former. When the economy is healthy, you would expect to see a much narrower differential.

- *Segment spreads.* Various types of bonds—Treasuries, agencies, corporates, and municipals—pay different yields. Segment spreads tend to expand and contract as sectors go in and out of favor. For example, you could expect to see the gap between Treasuries and corporates narrow during good times and widen during bad.

More illustrations could be provided. The point is that yield spreads change over time, and perceptive managers can profit from them. Abnormally wide or narrow differentials spell opportunity. For instance, during the worst of the 1989-1990 bear market for junk bonds, the gap between low-rated and high-grade corporates exceeded 10 percentage points. This was followed by a strong rally in the junk market beginning in 1991. A profit results when an abnormal spread returns to normal. Astute fund managers can exploit these opportunities.

BOND FUNDS VERSUS INDIVIDUAL BONDS

Many investors may not realize that bond funds don't behave exactly like individual bonds. A mutual fund is, after all, a managed portfolio. It has certain important differences from an individual debt security.

1. Unlike a bond, the typical fund has no maturity. The manager buys and sells on an ongoing basis, generating trading profits and losses and changes in the portfolio's yield.

2. The rate of return on a fund is more difficult to predict than that of an individual issue bought and held to maturity. However, an individual bond's return is often not that predictable either, as we have seen.

3. A fund's dividends are not fixed like the interest on a bond. The income could rise or fall with changing interest rates, or with different cash flows as investors enter or exit the portfolio.

This third point deserves elaboration. During a period of falling rates, your bond-fund dividend could be cut. This may be disturbing to some investors, but it's generally nothing to worry about because you also will be benefiting from appreciation. Income dividends are only part of the total-return equation.

Disadvantages of Bond Funds

From this brief discussion, it should be apparent that individual bonds enjoy an edge over managed portfolios in certain respects. Bond-fund drawbacks include the following:

1. *Expenses reduce returns.* The management fees and other costs to operate a fund can significantly lower your results. Chapter 14 takes a closer look at bond-fund expenses.

2. *Extensive diversification may be unnecessary.* You really don't need that many different bond issues to be well-diversified, assuming you stick with top-quality issues such as Treasury notes and bonds, agency securities, or high-grade munis or corporates.

3. *More predictable results.* As noted, you can anticipate more reliable returns with the right individual bonds compared to the typical, changing fixed-income portfolio.

Advantages of Bond Funds

Still, for many people, the fund route is the way to go. Smaller investors, in particular, will enjoy several benefits with a packaged portfolio compared to individual holdings. These selling points include the following:

1. *Easy access.* It is often difficult and expensive for smaller investors to deal directly in the bond market, which is oriented toward professionals. Transaction costs are higher and liquidity is lower for people buying and selling in relatively modest amounts. To succeed at bond investing, you need to shop around among different dealers for the best prices.

2. *Liquidity.* It is easier to take your money out of a fund without adverse price consequences than to sell thinly traded bonds prior to maturity. This especially applies to infrequently traded high-yield corporate debt and many municipal issues. Dealer spreads can be quite wide when it comes time to sell.

3. *Daily pricing information on funds.* By contrast, it can be difficult for you to get accurate quotes for many individual bonds. You won't find

prices or yields for most bonds in the newspaper—you have to go to a broker to obtain quotes. And even then, prices on a given bond can vary widely among dealers.

4. *Monthly income.* Bond funds generally declare dividends once a month. Conversely, individual bonds usually pay interest semiannually. Retirees looking to their investments for supplemental income might appreciate the monthly distributions.

5. *Ease of reinvestment.* Bond funds offer convenient reinvestment of dividends and capital-gains distributions, even for small dollar amounts.

Using Treasury Direct

The best argument for buying debt directly, rather than through a mutual fund, can be made in the case of Treasury securities—bills, notes, or bonds. There's no credit risk because all Treasuries are backed by Uncle Sam. That also means there's no research work or ongoing monitoring efforts required. Another nice feature is that you can buy without paying a commission if you use the U.S. government's Treasury Direct system.

The program is fairly easy to use. You deal through your nearest Federal Reserve Bank or branch. Investors place what's known as either a "competitive" or "noncompetitive" bid for an upcoming auction. Active professionals may submit *competitive bids* stating the amount of securities sought and their bid price. Conversely, individuals normally make *noncompetitive bids*. Under the latter arrangement, bidders pay a price equal to the weighted average price for the competitive bids that have been accepted. By placing a noncompetitive bid, you avoid the risk of bidding too high and losing interest or bidding so low that your order cannot be filled. When payments of interest and principal are due on your Treasury Direct holdings, they will be routed directly into your bank account by the Treasury, per your instructions.

You should keep the Treasury's offering schedule in mind. Auctions take place monthly for two-year T-notes and less frequently for longer-term issues. Your local Federal Reserve Bank or branch can provide further details and the appropriate forms. Plan on holding to maturity, however, to avoid the commission on a sale. You must sell through a broker if you need to liquidate prematurely.

For an information package on the Treasury Direct system you can phone the Bureau of the Public Debt at 202-874-4000 or your nearest Federal Reserve Bank or branch. Information also is available at http://www.publicdebt.treas.gov on the World Wide Web.

This allows for more efficient compounding, which can lead to higher returns over time.

6. *Professional management.* Fluctuating interest rates and other factors can make a buy-and-hold bond strategy perilous. Better returns often result from an actively managed approach. Good managers can react to opportunities in the fixed-income market and enhance performance. They also can unload lower-quality issues when their risks increase to unacceptable levels. For these reasons, bond funds often make more sense than individual holdings.

7. *Diversification.* Since a fund holds dozens if not hundreds of bonds, it exposes shareholders to far less credit risk than would be assumed by taking positions in one or a few issues. And, with their typical modest minimum initial investments, mutual funds make it easy to diversify among bond-market sectors.

Bond funds offer significant advantages over individual issues, but it is extremely important for their expenses to be low since fixed-income investments, on average, generate lower returns than stocks. Deciding between individual bonds or a bond fund is a personal choice and depends on the size of your portfolio, your objectives, the kinds of investments purchased, and your interest in doing the research. Of course, this doesn't have to be an "either-or" decision, since it often makes sense to use funds along with bonds.

AT THE CLOSE

Stock investments generate higher returns, but bond and money-market funds provide the stability, liquidity, and income that can help round out a portfolio. Plus, stocks and bonds don't always move in the same direction, providing good diversification opportunities.

The fixed-income market is characterized by many types of IOUs, which vary according to creditworthiness, yield levels, interest-rate risk, and more. A manager's ability to spot opportunities is a good reason to choose bond mutual funds over individual bonds. Yet expenses eat into returns, which means investors should lean to low-cost portfolios.

CHAPTER 14

Taxable Bond Funds

It's not enough to simply classify bond funds into the two basic groups of taxable and nontaxable. Within this huge universe, individual portfolios differ greatly in terms of the kinds of securities they hold, their risks, and their potential returns.

Various mutual-fund groupings generally reflect the ways in which bonds themselves are categorized. Fixed-income securities can be classified in four aspects.

1. *By term to maturity.* Short-term bonds come due in 1 to 5 years, intermediate-term IOUs in 5 to 10 years, and long-term issues in more than 10 years.

2. *By type.* Major classifications include coupon bonds, zero-coupons, mortgage-backed issues, and foreign bonds.

3. *By quality.* Default-free Treasuries top the list, followed by insured munis and gilt-edge corporates, then medium-grade munis and corporates, and finally speculative munis and corporates.

4. *By taxability.* Interest on municipals is tax-exempt at the federal level and may be at the state level. Yields paid on Treasuries generally avoid taxation by state and local governments.

Of the four groupings, one of the most critical traits is taxability. This chapter focuses on taxable-bond funds, and Chapter 15 examines the tax-exempt portfolios. There are, however, significant differences among funds within each of these two basic classifications. Figure 14-1 provides brief descriptions of the bond-fund categories used in this book.

Figure 14-1   Bond-Fund Categories and Their Objectives

TAXABLE PORTFOLIOS

U.S. government	Invest primarily in U.S. Treasury and agency securities.
Target maturity	Invest mainly in zero-coupon obligations maturing in a specific year.
Mortgage-backed securities	Invest primarily in the various mortgage-backed bonds such as Ginnie Maes.
Corporate	Hold investment-grade corporate debt, which is rated triple-B or higher. Some corporate funds restrict holdings to issues rated single-A or better.
High-yield corporate	Invest primarily in so-called "junk bonds," which are rated below triple-B.
Foreign bond	Invest mainly or exclusively in non-U.S. government and corporate issues.
Flexible bond	Can hold a variety of issues and can alter the mix.

TAX-EXEMPT PORTFOLIOS

National municipal	Invest in bonds from a number of different states.
Single-state municipal	Hold the bonds of one state so as to provide residents with income exempt from both state and federal taxes.
Insured municipal	Hold bonds guaranteed by an independent insurance consortium. Available in both national and single-state versions.
High-yield municipal	Invest in munis with lower ratings and higher yields.

GROUPING BY MATURITY

The two major dimensions of a bond portfolio are the types of IOUs that it targets and the average maturity or duration of its holdings. Funds may be categorized as short-, intermediate-, or long-term. The maturity classification gives you a general idea of the amount of interest-rate risk you would face, although such a designation is not always part of a fund's name.

But just knowing whether a portfolio is, say, intermediate-term is not enough because a given classification can cover a wide range of maturities or durations. So in addition to knowing a fund's general classification, it's important to understand its average maturity and, preferably, its duration. You then can compare the fund with its peers and have a better feel for its potential volatility. Also, recognize that managers can lengthen or shorten their portfolio durations as their interest-rate outlooks change. But they generally should not stray too far from the parameters for their category.

Table 14-1 provides approximate guidelines for four maturity classifications. These ranges are not cast in stone. For instance, a fund labeled as "intermediate term" may, at times, exhibit the characteristics of a long-term portfolio and vice versa.

U.S. GOVERNMENT BOND FUNDS

Federal government debt constitutes far and away the largest securities market in the world. U.S. Treasuries, issued by Washington to raise huge sums of money, are the staple of government portfolios. In fact, the Securities and Exchange Commission requires that these funds normally invest at least 65 percent of their assets in bonds issued or backed by Uncle Sam. The 65-percent threshold also applies to other bond and stock categories where a fund's name implies that it focuses on a particular type of security. Municipal-bond and money-market funds are subject to an even higher percentage.

Treasuries come in three forms: Bills mature in 1 year or less, notes in 2 to 10 years, and bonds in 30 years. Both notes and bonds are coupon-bearing.

Table 14-1   Fixed-Income Maturity Objective Guidelines

Maturity	Dollar-Weighted Average Maturity Range	Duration Range
Short	1 to 3 years	1 to 3 years
Short-intermediate	1 to 5 years	1 to 4 years
Intermediate	5 to 10 years	5 to 8 years
Long	11 to 25 years or more	9 to 12 years

Treasury bonds are either noncallable or callable, but only during the last five years of their lives. "Strips" are zero-coupon Treasuries, derived from notes and bonds, that have been separated into interest and principal components. Each individual payment effectively becomes a zero-coupon issue. For example, a 30-year Treasury would have 60 semiannual coupon payments and one principal payment.

Besides Treasuries, U.S. government funds buy agency and mortgage-backed securities. As the name implies, agency securities are issued by various federal organizations, such as the Government National Mortgage Association and the Tennessee Valley Authority, to finance their activities.

When evaluating a government-bond fund, you should examine the duration or average maturity and see how the portfolio is structured. Find out how the manager tends to invest any money that's not held in U.S. governments. As noted, SEC regulations allow managers to invest up to 35 percent of their assets in other securities.

Government-bond funds offer investors a break since state and local governments generally do not tax income earned on Treasuries. This exemption is not trivial if your state has a high tax rate. But the break applies only to Treasury bills, notes, and bonds, not to debt instruments from government agencies.

Inflation-Proof Bond Funds

A potentially revolutionary product debuted in early 1997 with the launch of an inflation-adjusted Treasury fund from American Century-Benham. This portfolio holds Treasuries immune from purchasing-power risk, which the government started to issue around the same time, modeled after inflation-indexed products in Britain, Canada, and a few other countries. Another portfolio, from Pimco Funds, debuted around the same time and holds bonds from the U.S. and other nations.

In short, the bonds' principal values are pegged to increases in the Consumer Price Index, rising over the years and ensuring that investor returns are not eroded by inflation. In the meantime, the bonds generate yields that remain fixed in percentage terms.

Because inflation-adjusted IOUs are more secure, they tend to pay slightly lower interest than comparable, conventional bonds. Thus, at the same time investors can sleep more easily, Uncle Sam can save money.

These bonds are not a panacea for inflation risk, however. During typical periods of moderate inflation, they will underperform straight Treasuries. Thus, the merit of inflation-adjusted Treasuries remains to be seen.

Incidentally, some longer-term government funds sell options against the bonds they hold to derive additional income. This yield-enhancement strategy works fine during periods of stable interest rates. But it cuts off appreciation when rates fall and prices rise, since holders of the options would exercise their right to buy the bonds from the fund at below-market prices. A later section on derivatives sheds more light on options and futures and how they're used by fund managers.

TARGET-MATURITY FUNDS

If you are looking for a fund that will make a fixed-principal payment on a specific date like an individual bond, target-maturity portfolios may be the answer. The funds in this small group pay no income until maturity because they hold zero-coupon Treasury strips all coming due in the same year, say 2020. As the zeros mature in the appropriate year, the proceeds go into short-term U.S. Treasuries that are held until the investors are paid off toward year-end.

To produce a competitive return, long-term zeros have to sell at prices substantially lower than their maturity values. That is, they trade at deep discounts. Suppose a Treasury strip comes due in 30 years for $10,000. If it yields 8 percent to maturity, reflecting comparable bond-market rates, it would now trade just under $1,000. The price gradually will appreciate over the years as the liquidation date gets closer. So too will the NAV of a target fund, although it might experience extreme ups and downs along the way. The target-maturity group consists mainly of the portfolios in the American Century-Benham Target Maturities Trust, which come due in 2000 and every fifth year thereafter until 2025.

Because they pay no periodic interest, zeros are highly volatile, as explained in Chapter 13 in the section on bond duration. The longer the time to maturity or duration, the greater the fluctuations. This makes zeros coming due many years out extremely sensitive to changes in interest rates. Suppose long-term rates rise by one percentage point. The 30-year zero referred to above would tumble about 24 percent in price. Conversely, if rates fall by one percentage point, that bond would appreciate 32 percent. Despite this volatility, if zeros are held to maturity, they can earn a predictable return. Zero holders face no reinvestment risk, since there are no periodic payments to reinvest.

Why Invest in a Target Fund?

Since strips are Treasury securities, they carry no default dangers. And the absence of reinvestment risk offers a major advantage, especially during times of falling interest rates.

Even though zero-coupon bonds pay no interest, the IRS still requires investors to pay taxes based on an "imputed" interest each year. The same applies to people investing in target-maturity funds, which make no cash distributions. You can avoid this problem if you hold a zero or target-maturity portfolio within a tax-deferred retirement plan. Otherwise, you would essentially face a modest cash-flow drain each year.

What kind of people use target-maturity funds? On the one hand, these funds make sense for conservative long-term investors who expect they will need money for a specific purpose at a certain time, such as to help finance retirement or a child's college education. On the other hand, zeros appeal to aggressive individuals who like to trade actively based on interest-rate forecasts.

Before you purchase shares of a target fund, determine its expected growth rate. This number should be available from the fund company. It is the compound annual return you can expect to earn if you hold the shares to maturity. In periods of low interest rates, these portfolios can make poor investments since their NAVs will be higher, their discounts smaller, and their expected growth rates lower. The reverse holds true when rates are abnormally high.

MORTGAGE-BACKED BONDS

This fund category traces its roots to 1970, when mortgage-backed obligations were introduced by the Government National Mortgage Association (GNMA) or "Ginnie Mae." The concept proved very popular, and these debt instruments have experienced explosive growth. Referred to as "pass-through" securities, mortgage-backed bonds generate relatively high cash flow since their principal is paid back gradually, along with interest, rather than at maturity, as with an ordinary bond.

Besides Ginnie Maes, mortgage-backed securities include Fannie Maes, which are obligations of the Federal National Mortgage Association (FNMA), Freddie Macs, issued by the Federal Home Loan Mortgage Corporation (FHLMC), and others. These various pass-through investments have little or no credit risk since the government either specifically guarantees payment of interest and principal, in the case of Ginnie Maes, or implies such backing with the others.

The "Pass-Through" Concept

Basically, a mortgage-backed security has characteristics of both a bond and a home loan. Here's how the concept works with Ginnie Maes. Pools of single-family mortgages with similar characteristics are assembled by a lender, such as a savings and loan. The lender delivers the pools to a securities dealer, who sells them to investors, including mutual funds.

The lender collects monthly interest and principal payments made by homeowners and forwards the money to the Government National Mortgage Association, which passes it along to investors. The agency makes payments regardless of whether homeowners have fulfilled their obligations—that's the federal guarantee.

Prepayment Risk

Because of unpredictable principal prepayments by homeowners, there's no way to tell exactly when a Ginnie Mae will mature. Most come due within 12 years, even though they're based on a pool of 30-year mortgages. Some loans get retired early when people sell their dwellings and move. Others are paid off prematurely as homeowners refinance their debts, especially during times of falling interest rates. Mortgage-backed securities yield more than Treasuries because of this prepayment risk. If rates drop significantly and prepayments surge, investors will be disappointed. They won't receive a capital gain, as they would from a conventional bond, and their principal will have to be reinvested at lower yields.

If rates rise, mortgage-backed securities will decline in price, like conventional bonds. Thus, a period of stable rates works best. These securities aren't as sensitive as long Treasuries to rising rates, however, because of their shorter durations.

CORPORATE BOND FUNDS

Funds in this broad category mainly hold investment-grade corporate IOUs rated triple-B or better. An individual fund might be substantially more speculative if it concentrates on the lower end of the investment-grade range or emphasizes the longest-term bonds available.

Conversely, high-quality corporate funds invest in debt issued by the nation's strongest, most secure companies. Most stick with bonds graded single-A or better, including some governments. But important differences exist between high-quality corporate-bond funds and pure Treasury portfolios. First, the former carry some credit risks. Second, as noted previously, the interest on Treasury securities is generally not taxable at the state and local levels. For both of these reasons, high-quality corporate funds tend to yield slightly more than government portfolios.

HIGH-YIELD BOND FUNDS

These portfolios invest in bonds with less than a triple-B rating, also known as junk securities. Some issues may even be near, or in, default. High-yield bonds have received plenty of attention by the media, based largely on their sizzling returns in the 1980s, their infamous 1989–1990 collapse and their subsequent rebound starting in 1991. High-yield issuers are found in a range of industries and include many large, well-known companies such as Bethlehem Steel, Kaufman & Broad, Kmart, Levitz Furniture, MGM Grand, and Revlon. Many others are small, obscure outfits you've probably never heard of.

High-yield bonds can be divided into two general categories: fallen angels and original-issue junk. The former include bonds that once carried an investment-grade rating but were downgraded as the company got in trouble. The latter were created by Michael Milken at Drexel Burnham Lambert starting in the 1970s. They include the bonds of small, emerging companies in relatively weak financial condition. In the 1980s, many of these issues were used to finance mergers and takeovers.

Why Invest in High-Yield Bonds?

Diversification into a unique asset class is the major benefit. High-yield bond returns tend to have relatively low correlation with returns of other bond groups during economic expansions as well as recessions. Here's why:

- When the economy is growing at a rapid clip, junk-bond issuers generally fare well. Conversely, if the Fed then raises rates to cool the expansion, interest-sensitive Treasuries and other long-term bonds can get hit hard, but the high coupons of junk bonds can offset their price declines. High-coupon issues are less sensitive to rate fluctuations because of their lower durations.

- In a recession, long-term Treasuries do well when interest rates decline and their prices rise. But the companies that issue junk bonds can be facing tumultuous times. Investors often respond by selling off their lower-rated holdings.

The potential for higher total returns is a second benefit of junk issues. The bonds tend to yield two to five percentage points more than gilt-edged debt securities. You can calculate the yield spread between junk bonds and high-grade corporates or Treasuries at any time using numbers from the "Yield Comparisons" box in *The Wall Street Journal's* "Credit Markets" column. When lower-rated bonds are out-of-favor, as during the 1989–1990 debacle, the spread widens considerably. It reached about 10 percentage points toward late 1990. We may never again see a gap that cavernous, however, as the high-yield market today is larger, of higher quality, and more liquid than it was prior to that collapse.

Junk Bonds versus Stock

High-yield bonds resemble common stock because they are sensitive to changes in the issuer's earnings, balance-sheet strength, and general fortunes.

A disastrous quarterly earnings report of a teetering corporation, for example, can send its debt spiraling downward. Conversely, unexpectedly good news can work wonders for a high-yield issue.

Because of their hefty income component, portfolios of junk bonds tend to be less volatile than those of stocks. Junk bonds also are less risky than the stock of a given company because creditor claims have priority over those of shareholders. In addition, the long-run returns of junk bonds are less than those of stocks, so it's reasonable to conclude the risks are lower, too.

Credit Risk

This is the major danger posed by lower-rated IOUs. Because of credit risk, the yield spread between junk and high-quality debt can be several percentage points. It is dangerous to hold just one or a few junk bonds. The same firm-specific risk that affects stocks also applies here. But credit risk can be reduced dramatically in portfolios that combine many different issues hailing from a good mix of industries.

Poor credit quality tends to become a problem for diversified portfolios only during periods of economic downturn. Prices could decline since a recession would lessen the ability of many highly leveraged companies to pay interest and principal. If several of these firms defaulted, the fund would be hurt. Even the threat of bankruptcies could push prices lower.

Here are two important questions to which investors in high-yield funds should seek answers:

1. How much credit risk does a fund intend to assume?

2. How much credit risk has the fund actually assumed?

The prospectus should provide answers to both queries in a useful summary breakdown of total assets by letter-rating category. You also can find this information in Morningstar and Value Line. In the illustration in Table 14-2, Fund A carries the least credit risk while Fund C is the most speculative. For nonrated debt, the prospectus will provide a breakdown of what the fund's adviser feels the agency-equivalent ratings would be.

A higher-quality junk fund will own predominately bonds rated double- and single-B, while holding only a limited number of issues graded less than single-B. Conversely, a lower-quality portfolio may allocate nearly all of its assets to double-B or lower issues, including a significant proportion below single-B. Some funds even earmark a modest portion of their assets to issues in default, which may offer an opportunity for substantial growth if the companies can emerge from bankruptcy.

Table 14-2   Asset Composition of Three Hypothetical High-Yield Funds

S&P Rating	Fund A	Percentage of Total Assets Fund B	Fund C
U.S. Govt.	4%	0%	0%
AAA	1	0	0
AA	2	0	1
A	3	0	1
BBB	33	0	8
BB	39	84	3
B	8	7	59
CCC	4	4	7
Nonrated*	0	0	13
Cash Reserves	6	5	8
Total	100%	100%	100%

*The adviser will provide its own assessment of the nonrated bonds. For hypothetical Fund C, the nonrated securities are judged to be comparable to: B, 9 percent; and CCC, 4 percent.

Liquidity Risk

Another danger faced by managers of high-yield funds is illiquidity. Many junk bonds are thinly traded, and their prices could plunge in the event a significant number of investors decided to sell. This poses problems for the fund. If the manager needs to dispose of a particular issue in a hurry, he or she may drive down the price in the process of selling. It's often difficult just to value illiquid high-yield bonds due to a scarcity of meaningful price quotes.

Liquidity risk was especially evident in 1990, when the high-yield market nearly collapsed on the heels of the excesses of the 1980s. Drexel Burnham, the principal market maker at the time, failed. The yield spread between junk and quality bonds widened. Despite paying double-digit rates, junk-bond funds suffered a negative 10.1-percent total return in 1990, according to Lipper Analytical Services. The price declines, in other words, more than offset the interest income. Many individual funds performed much worse.

But unusually high yields and low prices inevitably attract bargain hunters, and the junk market rebounded nicely in 1991. In fact, these funds were the best-performing bond category that year with a 37-percent total return, according to Lipper.

Investment Considerations

If you invest in a junk-bond fund, don't assume you will earn higher long-run returns than you might from a better-quality bond portfolio. The results of academic studies on the performance of lower-rated securities are mixed. There are no guarantees that a specific high-yield fund will outperform investment-grade portfolios, even over periods of 10 years or longer. In addition, high-yield investors don't get a "free lunch" because these IOUs are not consistently underpriced.

The returns earned on junk bonds are very much a function of the economic and market conditions prevailing during the period under study, and of the particular issues held in the portfolio. High-yield investing demands skilled management to cherry pick bargains, and some junk funds have much better track records than others. Management is a far more important factor with high-yield funds than with government and high-grade corporate portfolios, as returns on these latter investments tend to cluster closer together. A good junk-fund manager can add a lot of value, just as a superior stock buyer can.

Because of the heightened volatility of lower-rated bonds, dollar-cost averaging makes good sense with high-yield funds, as it does with stock investments. In fact, when a portfolio is down during a bear market in junk securities, you may even want to double up on your periodic investments, provided you have the time and patience to sit tight and wait for better times. Dividend reinvestment also works well with high-yield funds, providing an opportunity to pick up shares at lower prices, thereby reducing your average cost per share.

Before you invest in a high-yield fund, ask yourself the following questions:

- Is this a good time to buy into the high-yield sector, given the direction of the economy?

- Is the interest spread between junk and high-quality bonds sufficiently wide?

- Am I able to tolerate the greater volatility of a lower-rated portfolio?

- How would I react if the junk-bond market faltered?

High-yield investments certainly are not for everyone. But if they appeal to you, consider allocating 10 to 25 percent of your fixed-income holdings to the sector, with an eye on factors such as your time horizon and risk tolerance. For most people, a fund filled with lower-rated securities makes a lot more sense than investing directly in individual bonds.

FOREIGN-BOND FUNDS

More than half of the $20-trillion-plus market of world debt exists outside the United States, and the international share of the total continues to trend upward. As the label implies, foreign-bond funds invest primarily or exclusively in non-U.S. obligations. Government and high-grade corporates dominate the holdings of the group. Some funds invest only in governments.

Most foreign portfolios are subject to currency risk. They can lose money when the dollar appreciates, and gain when the greenback weakens. Chapter 10 includes calculations showing the impact of exchange-rate fluctuations on global investments. Current income is the major objective of most domestic-bond funds, but the foreign portfolios also try to obtain some capital appreciation, based on currency gains. Their managers look for the best interest-rate plays and a chance to profit from currency movements. The problem is that such movements are extremely difficult to predict.

In theory, foreign-bond funds can make good investments when it appears likely the dollar will weaken. But many managers hedge a portion of their assets against currency risk. Such hedging can easily mess up their potential to make a currency gain. A manager may place a bet thinking that the dollar will strengthen, but then it weakens instead.

Betting on Third-World Bonds

Most foreign-bond funds target debt securities issued in Western Europe, Japan, Canada, Australia, and other wealthy nations. But portfolios geared to developing countries in Latin America, Eastern Europe, Asia, and even Africa also are gaining a following. In fact, emerging-markets fixed-income funds achieved stellar results in 1996, outperforming all other fund categories with a 40.7-percent average gain, according to Lipper.

Third-World bonds offer certain advantages, including high-coupon yields, pricing inefficiencies, and little if any currency risk, since developing nations typically borrow in dollars. They also provide excellent diversification since the bonds' prices tend to fluctuate according to economic progress being made in the host country rather than in response to U.S. interest rates. However, the funds carry stock-like volatility and probably are too unnerving for the typical fixed-income investor.

Companies offering emerging-markets bond funds include Fidelity, T. Rowe Price, Scudder, G.T. Global, and Phoenix Duff & Phelps.

If you want international exposure, the best way to get it is with stocks, not bonds. Foreign-stock portfolios tend to do less currency hedging than their bond counterparts. Besides, stocks promise higher long-run returns than debt securities can deliver. The foreign-bond fund category is one you're probably better off avoiding, except in modest doses.

FLEXIBLE-BOND FUNDS

Chapter 12 discussed the hybrid asset-allocation funds that can invest in stocks as well as in bonds, varying the proportions depending on the manager's outlook. This section looks at flexible products that focus on different areas of the bond market. They also can be thought of as mixed-debt portfolios, since their managers are not restricted to securities of a particular quality, maturity, or type of issuer. They recognize that the bond market is not a homogeneous place.

These funds may appeal to investors who know they want a bond product but are not sure what kind. This way, a shareholder gets a variety of debt instruments in a single portfolio. A fund might include corporate bonds of various grades, and mortgage-backed securities, plus an assortment of Treasuries, and even some foreign issues. Thus, the portfolio is mixed in terms of credit risk, type of security, maturity, and possibly currency risk.

Well-managed flexible funds can take advantage of, or protect against, changing interest-rate and bond-market conditions. They offer the ultimate in fixed-income diversification. But with flexible portfolios, the experience and track record of the manager count heavily since the wrong moves can hurt performance badly. That's the obvious pitfall of giving the management of a mixed-bond fund too much room to maneuver.

TRACKING EXPENSE RATIOS

It's imperative to search for the lowest-cost funds because bonds, on average, return less than stocks. Performance results on bond portfolios typically cluster closely together, giving low-cost products a natural edge. Comparable funds can have expense ratios that vary by as much as a full percentage point, a difference in return of $10 for each $1,000 invested. The burden of high costs grows more acute during periods of low interest rates.

The overall average expense ratio for bond funds is about 1 percent. But wide variations exist. Numbers on individual portfolios range from near zero, where costs are temporarily being absorbed by the fund company, to a whopping 4 percent annually. Funds targeting foreign and high-yield bonds generally carry the highest costs while those focusing on U.S. governments and municipals have the lowest. Vanguard offers three Admiral bond portfolios that invest in Treasury securities. They feature very low 0.15-percent expense ratios. One reason for these rock-bottom fees is that each of the Admiral funds requires a $50,000 minimum investment. By raising the entrance threshold, Vanguard eliminates the costs of servicing small accounts and passes these savings along to investors. It also helps that Treasury securities are homogeneous and fairly simple to trade—a factor that allows for lower management fees.

Larger funds tend to feature lower ratios than smaller ones because the former benefit more from economies of scale. Bond index funds, particularly those offered by Vanguard, sport some of the leanest costs around.

WHAT THE MANAGEMENT FEE COVERS

Since you pay a fee for fund management, it's logical to wonder what you're getting in return. The investment professionals who run bond funds can do several things that most individuals can't or won't do:

- *Shop for the best deals.* It takes experience and clout to get the best prices and place trades at the tightest spreads.

- *Monitor credit risks.* An expert can spot issuers heading into trouble, long before a bond sees its rating downgraded. Conversely, a trained eye may see opportunities before others do.

- *Adjust maturities.* An active manager can move into shorter or longer bonds as situations warrant. However, some funds are not as flexible as others.

- *Reduce call risk.* Nobody wants to own bonds that are likely to be forcibly redeemed by the issuer. A manager can spot and replace vulnerable issues.

- *Research specialized issues.* Certain bond groups are difficult for individuals to analyze and understand, and may be characterized by a remarkable lack of information. Esoteric categories include mortgage-backed, foreign, high-yield, convertible, and even municipal securities.

- *Add value.* Temporary pricing anomalies sometimes exist within bond-market sectors, providing profitable opportunities. A good fund manager can find mispricings among riskier bonds and smaller, nonrated issues.

- *Employ ingenious strategies.* Professionals have more tools at their disposal than casual investors. A simple example is what's known as the "credit-quality barbell," a judicious mixing of quality extremes—U.S. Treasuries and junk bonds. This diversified combination can increase returns while holding risk to a reasonable level.

UNDERSTANDING YIELDS

What investors refer to as a bond fund's yield is technically known as the "ratio of net investment income to average net assets." Found in the financial-highlights table of a fund's prospectus, it provides a measure similar to the current yield on a stock or bond. The yardstick reflects income paid out over a year, excluding any capital gains or losses. Similar yields are reported by mutual-fund advisory services.

Because the yield figure tells what the fund's income has been, it's an important gauge for people looking for a monthly cash flow. These individuals should remember, however, that a fund's yield fluctuates whenever the NAV moves up or down, or the income distributions vary. Thus, a portfolio's yield isn't "locked in" as is the rate on an individual bond, a Treasury bill, or a CD. But in most cases, the payout percentage does not change drastically.

Nobody should ever buy a fund on the basis of yield alone. It tells only part of the story and can be very misleading. Total return provides a far more complete measure of performance. A high yield does little good if you lose a portion of your investment through principal erosion. In fact, high yields inevitably imply greater risk.

Determinants of Yield

Factors that affect a fund's payout rate include the following:

1. *Portfolio expenses.* Higher costs leave less for the bottom line. Funds pay their distributions after subtracting expenses, including any 12b-1 fees. Thus, the higher the expense ratio, the lower the yield, other things being equal. In fact, less-economical portfolios may be tempted to employ riskier strategies to pump up their returns so as to be more competitive. Conversely, be careful of funds that have very low expenses because of a temporary fee waiver by the adviser. A portfolio that can operate at low costs all the time makes a better bet.

2. *Average portfolio maturity.* The yield curve is normally upward sloping, reflecting the fact that bonds and funds with lengthier average maturities or durations generally pay higher yields, but they also carry greater interest-rate risk. A portfolio's maturity figure, or duration, reflects a weighted average of the various issues it owns.

3. *Quality of holdings.* As we've seen, bonds with lower credit grades normally produce higher yields, but they also expose investors to a heightened risk of default.

4. *Size of coupons.* Bonds with higher coupon payments typically kick off heftier yields, but there are pitfalls. Such issues also usually sell at premium prices, above their ultimate maturity value. Premium issues could be a bad choice if held to maturity, since those markups will evaporate. Plus, such bonds often are prime candidates for a call or premature redemption.

SEC 30-Day Yield

This is a superior measure for bonds selling at premium prices. Since 1988, the SEC has required funds to report uniform, annualized 30-day yields for use in advertisements and sales literature, and for telephone inquiries. The agency supplies an intricate formula that all fund companies must follow to calculate their payout rates. The computation assumes all bonds in the port-folio are held to maturity, or to the date at which they can be called, if a redemption is likely. So in contrast to the usual yield, the SEC's equation con-siders the amortization or erosion of both premiums and discounts. In other words, if a fund holds a lot of premium bonds, its SEC yield would be lower than the number obtained from a simple 12-month calculation.

In addition, the SEC formula considers any load charges an investor would pay to buy the fund, and it ignores any income the portfolio generates from writing options. The standardized 30-day yield, which is recalculated daily, can be obtained by calling the fund company. Money-market portfolios report a standardized 7-day annualized yield. Funds also must list their most recent 1-, 5-, and 10-year annualized return figures along with their yields, if they've been around long enough for all these numbers to be available. The reason total returns must accompany yields is that the former can be low or even negative when the latter might be high.

Don't Look for a Stable Payout

A mutual fund holds an assortment of securities and the mix is con-stantly changing with purchases, sales, bond calls, and redemptions. Market conditions are not fixed and investors are continually buying and redeeming shares. All of these factors make it hard for a company to pay out a constant monthly stream of dividends. If a fund tries to do so, it actually may do its shareholders a disservice.

For instance, some managers have gone so far as to pay a portion of the dividend out of principal. They "cannibalize" assets to avoid cutting their dis-tribution in times of low or falling interest rates. But this undesirable practice can hurt your investment. Fortunately, such an approach seems less common today, thanks to better reporting standards.

A WORD ON DERIVATIVES

Our discussion of bond funds would not be complete without a brief look at "derivatives," which became a hot topic in 1994 when a handful of supposedly staid bond and money-market funds sustained major losses. A *derivative* is a financial contract with a payoff based on the fluctuating price of some underlying instrument, such as a stock, currency, interest rate, or commodity. The word "derivatives" is a generic term like "investments," and as such covers many kinds of contracts.

Derivatives can be used in different ways, both to increase risk or reduce it. They often fulfill a useful purpose. Derivatives can be standardized, such as options and futures, or customized like collateralized mortgage obligations, structured notes, and inverse floaters. The price of a derivative could rise in the same direction as the underlying asset or move in an opposite direction. Derivatives often are inherently leveraged, making them more volatile than the primary security.

Here are some examples of how derivatives might be used by bond-fund managers:

- *To reduce or hedge an unwanted risk.* For example, a foreign-bond fund might utilize currency futures or options to minimize the danger of a strengthening dollar. This is an acceptable practice.

- *To make speculative bets on a market or security.* Since many derivatives are leveraged and highly volatile, they offer plenty of fast-moving action. Some fixed-income managers use them to place bets on rising or declining interest rates, at the risk of having red faces if rates move in the opposite direction.

- *To increase returns in an effort to offset lofty expenses, especially 12b-1 fees.* High-cost bond funds are at a competitive disadvantage. Derivatives can help juice up returns, but the manager must take on added risk in the process.

Most bond funds don't play games with your money. But a minority of fixed-income managers have accepted a higher risk/higher return tradeoff. Mortgage derivatives were a leading culprit in 1994. Any mutual fund that generates yields or total returns much higher than those of its peers must be considered suspect. Be especially wary of portfolios with both above-average performance and an above-average expense ratio.

The bottom line is that derivatives per se are not necessarily bad or evil. It's a question of how many derivatives a fund employs, and how they're used. Most prospectuses are written broadly enough to allow for the use of derivatives even though they may not be utilized often, if at all. To find out where a fund sits, you can call the company and ask about its derivatives practices. Better funds use them appropriately and in moderation.

AT THE CLOSE

Bond mutual funds are not a homogeneous lot. They vary by type of bonds held, by maturities, by creditworthiness, and other factors. Funds that generate taxable yields invest in government bonds, mortgage-backed securities, corporate IOUs, foreign debt, or a combination. Mutual-fund diversification is less necessary for secure Treasuries and most critical for lower-rated junk issues.

Expenses erode returns, so it's important to seek low-cost bond portfolios. It's also critical to understand how a fund's yield has been derived because high payouts often imply added risks or other problems.

CHAPTER 15

Shopping for Tax-Free Income

Few financial terms have as nice a ring as the words "tax free." And few investments can deliver shelter from Uncle Sam as well as mutual funds can. For most people, it's not a good idea to buy individual municipal bonds because that requires entrance into the heterogeneous, illiquid $1.2-trillion "muni" market. You should not even consider direct investment unless you have at least $100,000 to spend, the know-how to shop for the best deals, and the discipline to hold your bonds until maturity.

Tax-exempt munis are coupon-bearing securities sold by political subdivisions other than the federal government and its agencies. Issuers include states, counties, cities, airport authorities, and school, water, and sewer districts. Municipal notes come due in a year or less, while bonds have maturities extending beyond one year.

The appeal of these investments depends largely on your personal tax bracket. Individuals in higher brackets are the predominant buyers of municipal debt today. Munis generally are regarded as having fairly little credit risk, although they obviously rank below default-free U.S. government bonds in this regard. But because this is a huge and diverse group of about 80,000 issuers, there always will be some munis carrying high credit risk. In fact, a number of munis have faced serious problems in recent years. The late-1994 debacle in Orange County, California, is a case in point. Even though the county defaulted on more than $1 billion in debt, owners of large, well-managed tax-exempt funds had no need to lose any sleep.

TAX CONSIDERATIONS

The interest income paid by most municipal bonds avoids taxes at the federal level. Payments also would be tax-free at the state level on bonds issued within your state. A large number of single-state muni funds offer residents double tax-exempt yields and sometimes even a triple-tax exemption, extending to local taxes if applicable.

Municipal bonds can protect you to some degree against rising taxes. That's because tax hikes tend to boost the prices of munis and muni funds due to the greater value of the exemption. Conversely, if tax rates are cut, the investments become less valuable, depressing their prices and possibly inflicting losses on holders.

But the Tax Reform Act of 1986, which lowered rates, didn't hurt the municipal market. Why not? Because although tax rates dropped, the number of substitutes for sheltering income also narrowed. The net effect was an increased demand for the bonds, which pushed up prices and reduced yields. Investors who previously had bought munis or muni funds fared well on a total-return basis.

What effect will a flat tax have? In theory, the impact on the muni market could be enormous. If all types of investment income were made free of tax, as some proposals stipulate, the special appeal of municipal bonds would be wiped out. This could cause huge capital losses for municipal-bond fund owners, because the underlying bonds would depreciate until their yields roughly marked those on corporate bonds. But such a radical change in the tax structure is highly unlikely, at least anytime soon.

Finding Your Taxable-Equivalent Yield

Muni bonds, or funds, are not for everyone. For starters, they make sense only for money held outside of a tax-deferred retirement plan. Then, you need to be in a sufficiently high income bracket—the higher your bracket, the greater the appeal. Table 15-1 displays what are known as "taxable-equivalent yields," which illustrate the power of the sheltering effect. To use the chart, first determine your federal tax rate. Then read across that row to find the taxable equivalent of a particular tax-free yield.

Table 15-1   Taxable-Equivalent Yields

Federal Tax Bracket	If the tax-free yield is:				
	4%	5%	6%	7%	8%
	the equivalent pretax yield would be:				
15%	4.71%	5.88%	7.06%	8.24%	9.41%
28	5.56	6.94	8.33	9.72	11.11
31	5.80	7.25	8.70	10.14	11.59
36	6.25	7.81	9.38	10.94	12.50
39.6	6.62	8.28	9.93	11.59	13.25

This exercise will help you decide what advantage, if any, a tax-exempt bond fund would have compared with more mainstream choices of comparable risk. On an out-of-state muni or a national portfolio, the critical formula is as follows:

$$\text{Taxable-equivalent yield} = \frac{\text{Yield of municipal bond}}{1.00 - \text{Federal-tax rate}}$$

If a national fund pays 6 percent and you are in the 31-percent federal bracket, your taxable-equivalent yield would be 8.7 percent [0.06/(1.00 – 0.31)]. This means that you should invest in the national fund unless you can find an acceptable taxable-bond portfolio spinning off more than 8.7 percent.

A little income from a national fund often escapes state taxes. For example, if a New Yorker owns a national portfolio that has 8 percent of its assets invested in New York munis, that slice of the payout would avoid state tax. So would any of the fund's investments in U.S. territories such as Puerto Rico. At tax time, the fund will mail a sheet listing the percentages of its holdings in individual states and territories.

When comparing tax-exempt and taxable portfolios, it's important to look at funds of fairly equal credit risk and duration so you won't be comparing apples with oranges. Also, since capital gains on municipals are taxable, and losses deductible, it's only relevant to include yields, not total returns, on a taxable-equivalent basis.

In-State Taxable-Equivalent Yields

The above formula considers the impact of federal taxes only. As a result, it is valid only when:

1. You are analyzing an out-of-state bond or a national muni fund and will have to pay state taxes on the income.

2. You reside in a state that has no income tax such as Florida, Texas, or Washington or one that exempts interest on all munis from taxation such as the District of Columbia.

3. You are comparing a muni issued within your state to a Treasury note or bond. Income is not taxable at the state level for either the muni or the Treasury, so only the federal tax is relevant.

But suppose you want to compare a muni issued within your state to a corporate bond. You would need to know a second yield formula, computed as follows:

$$\text{Taxable-equivalent yield with federal and state taxes} = \frac{\text{Yield of municipal bond}}{(1.00 - \text{FTR})(1.00 - \text{STR})}$$

In this equation, FTR and STR represent your federal and state tax rates. The calculation assumes that state muni interest is tax exempt and that state taxes can be deducted on your federal return. With a 31-percent federal and an 8-percent state tax rate, a 6-percent payout on a state muni fund generates a 9.45-percent taxable-equivalent yield, calculated as follows:

$$0.06/[(1.00 - 0.31)(1.00 - 0.08)].$$

Capital Gains and Losses

Despite their alluring names, even the purest muni funds don't completely avoid taxes. That's because any capital gains on municipal bonds sold by the fund manager at a profit would be taxable to you. Losses, in turn, could be carried forward according to the usual IRS rules. The same is true of any gains or losses you might realize when selling a municipal-bond portfolio. This underscores one advantage of owning bonds directly over investing in a fund—with the former you face a tax possibility only when you sell.

Keep in mind that a large part of a muni fund's performance may be subject to taxation if bond prices have been rising in a particular year. Assuming you have owned shares during a year when interest rates declined sharply, you likely will have a gain to report.

The Alternative Minimum Tax

Not all municipals can claim to be tax-exempt. In particular, investors must watch out for "private-activity" bonds issued after August 7, 1986. The interest from these special IOUs could subject certain people to the federal alternative minimum tax. The AMT applies to high-income individuals who derive a significant benefit from certain deductions or exemptions called "tax preference" items. Private-activity bonds are explained later.

Tracking the Tax-Exempt Yield Ratio

An important yield relationship to watch is the one between tax-exempt and taxable bonds. If high-quality municipals yield 6 percent when comparable corporates are paying 8 percent, the ratio would be 0.75 (6 percent/8 percent). You can make a similar comparison between munis and Treasuries.

The higher the tax-exempt yield ratio, the lower the tax bracket necessary for municipals to start becoming attractive. Simply subtract the yield ratio from 1.0 to determine the marginal tax rate at which investors should be indifferent between the two types of bonds. This can be thought of as a break-even tax rate. For example, if the yield ratio is 0.75, investors in tax brackets above 25 percent (1.00 – 0.75) would prefer munis. But if the ratio were 0.60, the bonds would make sense only for people in a bracket above 40 percent.

The tax-exempt yield ratio changes inversely with tax rates. As rates fall, the appeal of munis diminishes and they must pay more to stay competitive. If there were no income taxes on investment income, the yield ratio would be 1.0 since a municipal bond would be paying roughly the same as any other debt security with a similar rating and maturity.

You or your accountant will know if you're wealthy enough to be affected by the AMT. If so, check to see to what extent, if any, a muni fund could produce dividends that might be taxable. Some portfolios invest in these bonds because of their somewhat higher yields. Others hold none. If you aren't subject to the AMT, there is nothing to worry about.

CHARACTERISTICS OF MUNIS

Munis come in two basic groups: *general obligation* or "GO" securities, and *revenue bonds*. The former are backed by the full faith, credit, revenue-generating ability, and taxing authority of the borrower. This makes them the more secure of the two categories, so they therefore yield less. However, many revenue bonds today are insured by a third party, which virtually eliminates their credit risk. Of course, insured issues yield less than their uninsured counterparts. Virtually all GO bonds mature serially. That is, they come due on staggered dates. Both types of munis customarily are issued in $5,000 denominations.

Revenue bonds account for most of the total value of munis issued in recent years. These bonds are used to finance specific revenue-generating projects such as bridges, toll roads, and publicly financed utilities and hospitals. The money earned by a project pays the interest and principal on the debt. Revenue bonds have a set term to maturity. Most come due well in the future, commonly 30 years. Thus, longer-term muni funds have a hefty proportion of their assets invested in these issues. The average maturities of these portfolios typically range from 15 to 25 years.

A special type of revenue debt is secured by payments made by a private user. These are the "private-activity" bonds mentioned earlier. Industrial-development bonds fall into this category. Buyers of private-activity securities generally do not have access to the resources of the municipality that issued the debt on the user's behalf. For this reason, the bonds tend to be of lower quality than other munis. Interest from private-activity bonds may be subject to the alternative minimum tax for wealthy investors. Not surprisingly, the issuance of private-activity debt has declined sharply since the Tax Reform Act of 1986.

RISK FACTORS

Munis face the same dangers that apply to taxable bonds. They're affected by interest-rate, credit, purchasing-power, call, and liquidity risk. In addition, munis can be harmed by a tax law change that would undermine the prices of outstanding issues. For instance, flat-tax fears depressed the municipal market in 1995.

Still, tax-exempt bonds generally can be considered highly secure investments. Like corporates, the various GO and revenue issues are graded for creditworthiness, by independent agencies such as Standard & Poor's and Moody's. Ratings on investment-grade munis range from triple-A down to triple-B. Some bonds are insured by very solid consortiums and thus sport a triple-A rating. But others—the high-yield or so-called "junk" issues—carry gradings of double-B and lower.

Many funds hold nonrated debt. These typically are smaller, less liquid IOUs that have not been graded by the rating agencies because it would not be worth the cost for the issuer to do so. Nonrated issues do not necessarily carry greater credit risk; they may be good investments and this is where a fund manager's talent comes into play. In fact, nonrated bonds can range in quality from triple-A to speculative.

In addition to rating individual issues, Moody's and Standard & Poor's also evaluate the general-obligation bonds of most states. State ratings can be found in *Moody's Bond Record* and *Standard & Poor's Bond Guide*, both commonly available in libraries. State ratings can and do change. Before you invest in a single-state municipal fund, get to know the overall credit quality of its debt. The grade on a state's GO bonds is a good place to begin, although it's not necessarily linked to the ratings of revenue bonds issued within that state.

Because individual munis subject investors to credit and liquidity risk, it's wise to use a mutual fund. Unless you are investing hundreds of thousands of dollars and thus are able to spread your assets over many issues, you probably will fare better with a fund and its diversified, professionally managed approach.

Fund investors should keep their eyes open for sector-concentration risk, however. Some portfolios invest a large slice of their assets in similar types of IOUs. A high-yield muni fund might stake 40 percent in hospital bonds, for example. Macroeconomic factors could harm a particular category of issuers. It's dangerous for a portfolio to have 50 percent or more of its assets in one or two sectors, no matter what they are.

CLASSIFYING MUNI-BOND FUNDS

Unmanaged unit investment trusts provided the earliest means for individuals to acquire a diversified portfolio of municipal bonds. The first tax-exempt UIT was introduced in 1961. Then the Tax Reform Act of 1976 allowed open-end funds to pass sheltered income through to shareholders.

To meet the SEC's definition of federally "tax-exempt," a fund normally must: (1) invest at least 80 percent of its assets in federally tax-exempt securities or (2) derive at least 80 percent of its income from such debt. Two basic ways to distinguish among municipal-bond funds involve maturity and credit quality.

1. *Maturity.* Most tax-exempt portfolios invest in longer-term munis. However, short- and intermediate-term funds exist, as do tax-free money-market portfolios. What you choose depends on how far out on the yield curve you want to go in terms of risk and return. Longer portfolios face the greatest interest-rate danger but could deliver the highest payoff.

2. *Credit quality.* Most funds hold bonds in the top four rating categories. But even here there are differences.

In addition, muni-bond funds are divided into national and single-state varieties.

National Funds

These portfolios hold IOUs issued in a number of states and thus offer geographic diversification. This is important since some states have riskier bonds than others. When examining a national fund, you might want to determine which states have the greatest representation in the portfolio and what their credit reputations are. But in general, you shouldn't worry much about default dangers.

Muni-bond interest from any state avoids federal taxes, but most of the income from a national portfolio would trigger tax at the state level. Suppose a Californian has money in a national fund that, in turn, has 7 percent of its portfolio in California bonds. Only that portion of the yield from the California bonds would be tax-exempt at the state level. National muni funds provide an annual breakdown of the percentage of assets invested in each state.

Single-State Funds

These products limit themselves to bonds issued in a specific state. Their portfolios thus enjoy a double exemption. Some funds might even generate a triple exemption, assuming they hold local bonds from cities or counties that impose personal income taxes.

Most single-state products were introduced in the late 1980s and early 1990s. By far the largest number cater to residents of California and New York—big states with high tax burdens. Other large states such as Massachusetts, Michigan, Ohio, and New Jersey also have substantial numbers of these products. All told, investors can choose from more than 600 single-state funds. Franklin, the largest manager of tax-free products, offers portfolios for more than 30 states, the biggest of which is the behemoth $14-billion Franklin California Tax-Free Income Fund.

Single-state funds in a number of places have had their problems, however. Certain states may not have a sufficient supply of munis at any moment for managers to build a suitable portfolio. In these cases, a portfolio may have to fill out its holdings with bonds from Puerto Rico and other U.S. territories, which also offer double tax-free income to mainland residents. There's even a fund that invests primarily in Puerto Rican municipal securities, offered by Franklin.

In addition to scarce supply, single-state funds in certain places may face lackluster demand for their shares, since the market of potential buyers is limited to just a small slice of the nation's population. Smaller portfolios normally have higher expense ratios, which squeeze returns, particularly in the case of bonds. Muni funds that lack sufficient assets sometimes are merged into larger, national portfolios. Another obvious drawback with single-state products is that you don't get the diversification you would with a national portfolio. This can lead to heightened risk.

It may seem puzzling that single-state funds exist for Florida, Texas, and Washington state, which currently have no income tax. In part, some residents may simply like the idea of buying into portfolios made up of bonds from their home states. Perhaps they figure a state income tax eventually will be imposed. In Florida's situation, even though there is no income tax, the state administers a small "intangibles" tax. Florida residents who hold munis from other states have to pay a levy on the income derived from those bonds.

Insured Funds

The highest-quality muni portfolios hold what are known as "insured" bonds, along with other top-grade issues. Simply put, these are obligations guaranteed by an outside underwriter as to the timely payment of interest and principal. The reputation of this additional party obviously is crucial. That's why fund managers generally use only those insurers rated triple-A by S&P or Moody's. If the issuer defaults on interest or principal payments, the insurance company would have to step in and meet the obligation, allowing investors to receive all scheduled payments in full. The insurance covers credit risk only, not interest-rate risk or any other dangers.

Since coverage has a cost, insured funds generally yield less. The difference in return varies over time but generally ranges from about 10 to 40 basis points (0.1 to 0.4 of a percentage point) each year. This can add up over time. Thus, you have to decide if the added protection is worth the cost. In general, a well-diversified portfolio holding high-grade munis offers sufficient safety for most people without extra coverage. Insurance is more important for people who invest in individual bonds than for those holding shares in a well-managed fund.

High-Yield Funds

At the other extreme, the so-called "junk" tax-exempt portfolios invest in lower-grade munis. Their managers hope to generate higher returns by finding bonds offered by issuers whose credit situation appears to be improving.

As with corporate high-yield funds, these products face heightened credit and liquidity risks. The least aggressive portfolios in this group might hold only a few junk munis, sprinkling them among stronger issues. Others may invest nearly all their assets in the most speculative areas.

Still, high-yield municipal-bond funds generally don't assume as much credit risk as their corporate counterparts. This reflects the fact that there simply aren't as many seriously troubled municipalities as there are companies.

Some junk funds may move a large part of their assets into better-grade bonds when the yield spread between the two narrows to the point where there isn't enough to compensate investors for the added risk. As a general rule, good managers venture into riskier securities only when they expect to receive a sufficient reward for doing so.

CLOSED-END PORTFOLIOS

Introduced in 1987, closed-end muni-bond funds have proven to be quite popular and now constitute the largest segment in the closed-end universe. All told, they number about 200, including national, single-state, insured, and high-yield varieties. With these quirky products you can sometimes buy a dollar's worth of selected munis for 90 or 95 cents. Their prices tend to range from discounts deeper than 10 percent to premiums of more than 10 percent, depending on investor sentiment, the outlook for interest rates, and specific characteristics of each fund.

Closed-end muni funds have several potentially attractive attributes compared to their open-end relatives:

1. They appeal to traders who like to buy at a discount and sell when the markdown narrows or turns to a premium.

2. Closed-end managers aren't forced to sell bonds to raise cash to meet redemptions during unfavorable times. In addition, because they don't need to maintain a cash cushion, they can remain fully invested in the hopes of generating a higher return.

3. Leveraged closed-end products can outperform unleveraged mutual funds during periods of stable or declining interest rates. Of course, to do this they assume more risk.

How Leverage Works

Most closed-end municipal-bond funds leverage their holdings by selling preferred stock. The preferred shares commonly amount to about one-third of the fund's total capitalization. The dividend paid on the preferred stock by the fund typically fluctuates with changes in short-term interest rates. Thus, the closed-end funds are essentially "borrowing" at short-term rates and "lending" long-term, since they will invest the proceeds in long-term muni bonds. Incidentally, affluent investors seeking tax-free income can buy the preferred shares in increments as low as $25,000.

Table 15-2 illustrates a case of favorable leverage. In this example, the manager borrows money at 4 percent, lends it out at 6.5 percent, and generates a 7.75-percent yield. As long as the short-term rate is lower than the return earned on the bonds, holders of the fund's common shares benefit from higher dividends. The municipal yield curve generally slopes steeply upward, so the strategy normally is profitable. The lower the short-term rate relative to long-term muni-bond yields, the better.

However, if interest rates rise sharply, leveraged muni investors are exposed to three risks:

Table 15-2   The Impact of Favorable Leverage on a Closed-End Fund's Yield

Closed-end fund capital structure		
Common	$200,000,000	(Held by fund shareholders)
Preferred	100,000,000	(4% interest cost)
Total portfolio	$300,000,000	(6.5% earned on munis)
Investment results		
Earnings on portfolio	$19,500,000	(6.5% of $300,000,000)
Preferred dividend	4,000,000	(4% of $100,000,000)
Available for common	$15,500,000	(Ignoring expenses)
Yield on common	**7.75%**	(15,500,000/200,000,000)

1. *Premiums on a closed-end fund can turn to discounts or, if discounts already exist, they could widen.* This results from selling by nervous investors.

2. *Rising short-term rates reduce the net income generated by the fund.* Suppose the 4-percent preferred yield paid by a fund rose to 6.5 percent, the same yield that the fund earned on its holdings of long-term munis. The profit from the leverage would vanish.

3. *Bond prices decline if long-term rates begin ratcheting upward.* This would lead to a drop in the fund's NAV, exaggerated by the leverage factor. Under extreme circumstances, the fund could try to minimize the damage by calling in its preferred stock at par, but its investments in long-term bonds would have to be sold at a loss to raise money to repurchase the preferred shares.

Investing in exchange-traded funds is tricky business and demands sophistication. Closed-end bond portfolios don't rank among our favorites. If you want to venture into the closed-end arena, you may find it more profitable to focus on stock funds, for two reasons: (1) closed-end stock products often can be bought at greater markdowns than their fixed-income counterparts and (2) stocks provide higher long-run returns than bonds. Nevertheless, if you think a closed-end muni fund might be your cup of tea, review the closed-end basics in Chapter 9.

UNIT INVESTMENT TRUSTS (UITs)

In contrast to both open- and closed-end funds, a unit investment trust is unmanaged, as explained in Chapter 2. It's a fixed portfolio with a finite life. Most UITs invest in munis. These products typically are owned by casual investors who deal with a full-service brokerage and desire a monthly stream of tax-free income. Buyers have several choices as to maturity and portfolio type. For example, you can find both insured and uninsured muni-bond UITs, as well as single-state and national portfolios.

The major selling point of UITs is that ongoing fees are normally low since the trusts are unmanaged and don't continually market their shares to the public. Some trusts, however, carry a deferred sales charge. Trading costs also are minimal, reflecting the lack of active management and thus transactions. However, these portfolios are supervised, so any problem issues can be sold.

For smaller investors, UITs might be preferable to investing directly in munis, but they don't compare favorably with open-end funds. Even closed-end portfolios offer a better deal, especially when they trade at attractive markdowns. Here are five arguments against unit investment trusts:

1. They impose front-end loads, which range as high as 5.5 percent. The sales charge can take a significant bite out of your return if you don't hold your investment long enough.

2. Trust sponsors often maintain markets in their products for people who want to sell prior to maturity, but this service isn't free. Spreads on bid and asked prices range from about 1.5 to 5.5 percent for the longest-term trusts. Some brokers may impose an added transaction fee.

3. You face a "dribble back" of your principal in future years as bonds are called, sold, or come due before the trust's stated maturity. Since new bonds are not bought in their place, this reduces the amount of cash working for you and thus your earnings. With long-term trusts, you may see a noticeable shrinkage in assets after 5 to 7 years. A portfolio may be liquidated prior to maturity if its assets fall significantly—say, to 40 percent or less of the original value.

4. There's no manager able to restructure the portfolio to take advantage of changing market conditions.

5. Investors will find a lot more information available on open- and closed-end funds. For instance, UIT shares aren't listed in newspapers.

If you nevertheless decide to take the plunge, shop around carefully and ask a lot of questions before investing in a UIT. For instance, you should find out how much call protection you're getting—preferably, at least 7 or 8 years with the longer-term portfolios. You also need to consider the quality of the bonds if the UIT is uninsured.

SELECTING A MUNI-BOND FUND

Shopping for muni-bond funds can be fairly difficult. In part, this reflects the fact that there are so many choices. The following points are worth heeding:

- Consider a single-state fund if you live in a high-tax state. But remember, these portfolios in general are riskier than the national funds because of their limited geographic diversification. In addition, they may have higher expense ratios and lower yields. For these reasons, it may pay to invest at least some of your tax-free money in a national fund.

- Insured funds may help you get a better night's sleep if you desire more security. But the extra protection carries a cost, which shows up as a lower yield than what's available on an otherwise-equivalent portfolio. Insurance usually makes more sense with a single-state portfolio than with a national one.

- The yield on a muni-bond fund is a telling indicator. A high-yielding portfolio usually will feature some combination of the following: a long duration, lower-rated holdings, derivatives, or leverage (if the fund is closed-end). Another factor that could give rise to higher yields is the presence of substantial amounts of alternative minimum tax issues. But these portfolios can be attractive if you're not subject to the AMT, which most people aren't. Finally, low expenses could explain a higher yield.

- Examine the fund's composition. Pay particular attention to portfolios with high concentrations in specific sectors, such as hospital or housing bonds. If a fund has more than half of its assets in one or two areas, be careful no matter what those sectors are.

- Read the newspapers and keep abreast of major national and state trends. This will help you spot threats to the bonds of particular states or sectors. Of course, with any managed fund, you should rely primarily on the portfolio manager to do the detailed analysis for you.

- If you plan to hold your municipal investment for many years and can accept fluctuations, consider a longer-term, uninsured portfolio for a higher potential return. Just remember that these funds could get hit hard if interest rates rise. Many unsuspecting investors got burned in 1987 and in 1994, when rates spiked upward. Widespread redemptions of muni-fund shares exacerbated the problem.

- Favor pure no-load funds with below-average expenses. Costs matter in the modest-yielding muni arena. For best results, find a fund with an expense ratio that is below 0.60 percent—the lower the better.

AT THE CLOSE

Investors enjoy ample choices when it comes to tax-free bond products. Several hundred mutual funds have sprouted in recent years to harness the tax-exempt yields paid by thousands of state and local political subdivisions on their debt. Most such bonds carry little default risk, helped by the taxing authority of municipal governments or the revenue-generating power of various public projects.

Muni-bond funds offer easy entrance into the tax-free bond market, where hefty trading costs, high minimum investments, and scarce information pose problems. Funds make most sense for high-income investors holding their shares outside of retirement accounts. Some simple formulas make it easy to compare tax-free and taxable bonds on an equal footing. Muni-bond portfolios don't skirt taxes entirely, since they will generate capital gains in good years.

After investors have bought into the tax-free concept, they still must decide how much credit and interest-rate risk to assume, and whether they want to trade the superior safety of a national muni fund for the heightened tax advantages of a single-state portfolio.

CHAPTER 16

All About Money-Market Funds

Safety, liquidity, yield, and simplicity: These are the hallmarks of "money-market funds," which deliver high stability by holding short-term IOUs issued by the federal government, corporations, municipalities, banks, and the like. The ingredients that fill out their portfolios include Treasury bills, commercial paper, repurchase agreements, jumbo certificates of deposit, and more. Because these various instruments require minimum investments ranging from $10,000 to $1 million and up, most people cannot afford to buy them directly.

Money-fund purchases can be made sporadically or through an automatic investment plan where the cash is transferred electronically from your bank account, paycheck, or Social Security check. Dividends are declared and credited to your account every day of the year and distributed monthly. You're entitled to all accrued interest when you redeem shares, which can be done without penalty at any time. Conversely, bank CDs traditionally require that you maintain the cash on deposit for a designated period and impose early withdrawal penalties if you don't.

You can benefit from holding money-market funds because they generate the highest short-term yields available. Since their debut in 1972, these investments have delivered better returns than those available at banks by offering small savers indirect access to prime short-term debt instruments. It also helps that fund-company overhead costs are lower than those of most banks, which have heavy investments in bricks and mortar.

The gap between yields on money funds and bank accounts was particularly large in the 1970s and early 1980s when Federal Reserve's Regulation Q was still in effect. This regulation, which was gradually phased out beginning in 1980, placed a ceiling on the rates banks could pay savers, so it penalized the latter and subsidized the former. It also created a benign environment for money funds to get started. Starting in 1982, banks were allowed to offer money-market deposit accounts, designed to compete with money funds. Even though banks now can pay whatever rates they wish, they generally can't match yields on money funds because of their higher operational costs.

The Derivatives Fiasco

The money-fund industry suffered its first real embarrassment in 1994 when more than a dozen companies had to ante up considerable sums of cash to make up for losses incurred by their funds through the indiscriminate use of risky derivatives. These actions prevented most such portfolios from saddling shareholders with any losses. But one small, institutional money fund "broke the buck" and liquidated because no one came to its rescue.

Derivatives are financial instruments that can be used either to control risk or to speculate. The price of a derivative fluctuates in response to changes in the value of some underlying security or index. Derivatives often are leveraged, leading to magnified volatility. The derivatives held by some money funds were used to juice up yields in the falling rate environment that existed prior to 1994. This worked well as long as rates continued to decline. But the tactic backfired in 1994, when rates suddenly spiked upward.

In the wake of that fiasco, the SEC stepped in and banned the use of the most dangerous derivatives by money funds. Derivatives are still used by the industry but no longer represent a major concern, particularly if you stay with the better and larger portfolios. For instance, some money funds own "floating-rate" securities with returns derived from short-term interest-rate benchmarks, but these instruments don't carry the kind of risk that can inflict principal losses.

The generally lofty levels of interest rates prevailing in the 1970s and 1980s made money funds a huge success, which, in turn, provided many people with their first introduction to mutual funds. They liked the concept and eventually ventured into stock and bond portfolios. At this writing, money funds counted combined assets of about $1 trillion, according to the Investment Company Institute. The group consists of nearly 700 retail and more than 300 institutional portfolios. The latter serve the needs of pension plans and other large investors. Some money funds are quite large. Dean Witter, Fidelity, Merrill Lynch, Schwab, Smith Barney, and Vanguard each have portfolios with assets of more than $10 billion. The Merrill Lynch CMA Money Fund is the behemoth of the group with assets of more than $40 billion.

Because of the stable nature of their investments, these funds are able to maintain a constant NAV pegged to $1 a share. Keeping track of your investment is simple. If you own 12,931 shares, your money-fund account is worth $12,931. Only your yield fluctuates. Thus, money funds are the safest of all mutual funds from a principal-risk standpoint. The $1 NAV is not guaranteed, though. Rather, fund companies simply try their best to maintain it, and they have done a nearly perfect job of not "breaking the buck."

MONEY-FUND APPLICATIONS

Money-market funds appeal to investors on several levels. Here are some common applications:

1. *As the "cash" component in your investment mix.* It makes sense to keep at least 5 to 10 percent of your investment portfolio in the form of ready money. And as you grow older, the cash allocation generally rises. Many retirees use money funds as a supplemental source of income.

2. *As a savings vehicle.* Cash being held for possible emergencies and to meet planned big-ticket expenditures over the next few years should be kept separate from your long-term investments.

3. *As a parking place.* Perhaps you have just received an inheritance or rolled over 401(k) money into an IRA. You're not yet sure how to invest the lump sum but need a safe harbor paying a decent return in the meantime.

4. *As a means of obtaining tax-free income.* Municipal money funds can be used in the ways listed above by people in higher tax brackets.

The checkwriting privilege is another attractive feature of money funds. Shareholders normally can write checks in minimum denominations of $100 or $500, and less in some cases. You continue to earn interest on the balance in your account until the check clears. Incidentally, writing checks on a money-fund account is not a tax hassle as it can be with a bond fund. That's because money funds maintain a constant NAV of $1, while bond portfolios don't. Therein lies the problem. With every check you write on a bond fund, you realize a taxable gain or loss, which you must report.

A systematic withdrawal plan is a convenient way to take cash out of your account regularly. Again, you don't have to worry about tax hassles created by a fluctuating NAV. Among other services, you can make redemptions by phone. Some money funds even provide access to your cash through an ATM. And in many cases you can wire large sums of cash between your bank and money-market fund for a fee.

Money funds also offer convenient access to a family's remaining stable of portfolios. You can deposit cash into a money fund, then switch to another product in the complex without filling out a new application. Be aware, however, of the minimum initial investments on any funds you plan to switch into. The requirements for money funds often are less.

PORTFOLIO BUILDING BLOCKS

Money funds invest in short-term debt, frequently coming due in 90 days or less. These securities often are sold at a discount to their face or maturity value. There is no actual interest payment in these cases. The size of the discount determines the purchaser's yield. For example, a U.S. Treasury bill maturing in 180 days for $100,000 and purchased at a $2,500 discount, or $97,500, provides a 5.2-percent annualized yield. The rate depends on the difference between the offering price and maturity value as well as the holding period.

Short-term rates exhibit wider swings over time than long-term yields. They are highly sensitive to anticipated changes in inflation and Federal Reserve policy. Key short-term figures can be tracked daily in the "Money Rates" box in *The Wall Street Journal* (part C). Because of their short maturities, and the fact that they typically are issued by large creditworthy borrowers, money-market securities bear an extremely low risk of default.

Here are the kinds of investments held by taxable money funds:

1. *Treasury bills.* The safest and most liquid of securities, T-bills are short-term IOUs of the U.S. government. They are auctioned weekly at a discount from face value in units of $10,000 to $1 million. They typically mature in 13 and 26 weeks.

2. *Federal agency notes.* Agencies are privately owned but publicly chartered entities such as the Federal Home Loan Bank System, the Federal Farm Credit Bank System, and the Student Loan Marketing

Association. They issue discount notes that feature the implied backing of the federal government.

3. *Commercial paper.* A money-fund staple, these short-term, unsecured IOUs are issued by large, creditworthy industrial and finance companies. Basically the corporate equivalent of T-bills, commercial paper is sold in multiples of $100,000, with maturities ranging from 30 to 270 days. Independent rating agencies grade these instruments for credit quality.

4. *Jumbo certificates of deposit.* Jumbo CDs are issued in exchange for a deposit of $100,000 or more by most U.S. banks. Maturities range from 14 days to one year, but certificates can be sold by the holder in the open market prior to their due date. Unlike "small" CDs that individuals purchase, they are not insured. The credit risk reflects the issuing bank's financial condition.

5. *Eurodollar CDs.* These dollar-denominated obligations resemble domestic bank CDs, except that they are issued by a foreign branch of a U.S. bank or by a foreign bank. Eurodollar CDs are less liquid and somewhat riskier than their domestic counterparts. They thus offer higher yields.

6. *Yankee CDs.* Large foreign banks that have branches in the U.S. issue Yankee CDs, which are dollar-denominated obligations sold on American soil.

7. *Bankers' acceptances.* These instruments arise from bank guarantees of international business transactions.

Repurchase agreements, or "repos," are another type of short-term arrangement used by money funds. Their unique features deserve an expanded explanation. What happens is that a borrower, typically a government-securities dealer, and a lender such as a money-market fund agree to sell and subsequently repurchase securities, commonly U.S. Treasuries. These securities serve as collateral, protecting the lender if the seller defaults. The borrower initiates the repo by agreeing to sell securities in its inventory to a lender and then buy them back on a certain date for a slightly higher price. Most repos are overnight loans. The lender's dollar interest return is the difference between the price paid and received.

Suppose a government-securities dealer has just bought $5 million of Treasury bills for a customer who will take delivery in two days. In the meantime, the dealer finances the position by selling the bills to a money-market fund and agreeing to buy them back two days later at a higher price, providing the fund with, say, a 5-percent annualized yield. Dealers enter into repo agreements because they have inventory on hand, reflecting the inability to precisely match the needs of their normal customers with suppliers.

Repos are the shortest-term money-market instruments and typically settle within one to seven days at a price tied to prevailing rates. Large amounts of cash are involved, typically at least $100,000. The repo investor's risk is the chance that the seller might not be able to buy back the instrument according to the terms of the agreement. Nevertheless, repos feature little credit danger because the loans are backed by government securities.

A handful of money funds specialize in instruments with average maturities of just a few days. By investing primarily in repos collateralized by U.S. government securities, these portfolios can quickly respond to changing interest rates. American Century-Benham's Capital Preservation Fund II is an example.

MONEY-FUND CHOICES

There are several kinds of money-market portfolios, classified by what they own. The group can be categorized as follows:

1. *U.S. Treasury.* These portfolios invest in Treasury bills. Consequently, these are the safest of all money funds. In addition, their income normally is exempt from state and local taxes. Because of their greater safety and state-tax exemption, Treasury portfolios pay slightly lower yields than other taxable money funds.

2. *U.S. government.* The funds in this group invest in notes issued by federal government agencies, in addition to Treasury bills and repurchase agreements. Agency securities carry a bit more risk than Treasuries because they don't have a direct backing by the federal government, only an implied one.

3. *General purpose.* These garden-variety money funds hold a range of instruments including commercial paper, government securities, CDs, and repurchase agreements. They normally pay the highest yields within the money-fund arena.

4. *Tax free.* Income from municipal portfolios is exempt from federal taxes. Part or all of the yield also may be exempt from state taxes, depending on the percentage of the portfolio that is invested in your state. The entire payout on state-specific funds skirts state as well as federal taxes for local residents. This explains their wide popularity.

A distinction also can be made between retail and institutional funds. The latter typically serve pension plans and other large investors and rarely deal with individuals. To keep expenses low, they require much higher invest-ment minimums, which result in larger account sizes. For example, Vanguard offers both retail and institutional versions of its Money Market Reserves Prime Portfolio. The institutional product has a $10-million minimum initial investment and a 0.15-percent expense ratio, compared with $3,000 and 0.32 percent for the retail product. Institutional money funds are available in both taxable and tax-free varieties.

Some retail portfolios impose higher investment minimums in an effort to weed out smaller shareholders and reduce costs. The T. Rowe Price Summit taxable and tax-free money portfolios require $25,000, and the Vanguard Admiral Treasury money fund has a $50,000 minimum. Fidelity offers three taxable money funds in its Spartan group that each have $20,000 minimums. Its nine Spartan muni money-market portfolios require $25,000 each. With the Spartan funds, charges for certain normally free services may be passed along if you maintain a balance of less than $50,000. These might include fees for writing checks, transferring accounts, and closing an account.

RISK AND RETURN

Money-market funds carry no government guarantees against loss. Conversely, the principal value of the typical bank savings account or CD is insured up to $100,000 by the Federal Deposit Insurance Corporation. Nevertheless, money funds are highly secure and thus represent an attrac-tive alternative to bank accounts, small CDs, and even money-market deposit accounts because they yield more. This yield advantage stems in part from the fact that money funds don't have to pay for FDIC insurance. Second, they have lower overhead because they generally don't maintain local branches or employ tellers who deal face-to-face with depositors. In addition, banks have many small accounts, which are relatively costly to maintain.

With the exception of Treasuries, the kinds of instruments that money funds hold have just a tiny amount of credit risk, and even this is minimized by diversification. The risk/reward trade-off is one of the best available because you earn a significantly higher yield—along with the other advan-tages discussed above—for taking on a very small amount of default uncer-tainty.

SEC money-fund regulations, which were made more stringent in 1991, restrict the kinds of securities in which a fund can invest, provide rules for diversification, and limit maturities. Except for U.S. government securities, a money fund cannot invest more than 5 percent of its assets in the paper of a single issuer.

The SEC also requires money funds to invest the bulk of their assets in the highest quality or "first-tier" commercial paper. Money funds can place no more than 5 percent of their assets in riskier "second-tier" paper. Most hold substantially less than that, if they have any. People who are still nervous about credit risk can invest in U.S. Treasury money funds.

Unlike bond portfolios, money funds have virtually no principal risk because their NAV is pegged at $1. And as noted above, the securities in which they invest characteristically face little, if any, interest-rate risk because of their very short durations. Thus, the returns on a money-market fund consist purely of income—there is virtually no capital-gains component.

Inflation and Income Risk

Money funds carry two primary forms of risk. They subject shareholders to inflation risk because their returns are vulnerable to purchasing-power erosion. Over many decades, for example, Treasury-bill yields have stayed only slightly ahead of the inflation rate. In addition, funds carry an added burden in the form of expenses. Thus, if a money-market portfolio is held in a taxable account, your after-tax return could easily be below the rate of inflation. For this reason, it's unwise to allocate a substantial percentage of your assets to money funds for the long haul.

A second danger, *income risk,* refers to the fact that the yields spun off by a money fund can fall sharply in a relatively short period, in tandem with declining money rates. Short-term yields are much more volatile than long-term rates over time. Table 16-1, which contains annual composite returns of the money funds tracked by Lipper Analytical Services, illustrates the ups and downs. Observe how returns climbed from 4.92 percent in 1977 to 17.16 percent in 1981, then declined to 8.69 percent in 1983. A decade later, they averaged a mere 2.62 percent.

Table 16-1   Yearly Returns of Money-Market Funds

Year	Annual Return	Year	Annual Return	Year	Annual Return
1996	4.80%	1987	6.17%	1979	10.92%
1995	5.37	1986	6.30	1978	7.25
1994	3.65	1985	7.77	1977	4.92
1993	2.62	1984	10.21	1976	5.11
1992	3.31	1983	8.69	1975	6.39
1991	5.70	1982	12.55	1974	10.79
1990	7.81	1981	17.16	1973	7.60
1989	8.85	1980	12.88	1972	0.38
1988	7.09				

Source: Lipper Analytical Services Inc.

It's easy to see how income risk works. Suppose you have $500,000 invested in a money fund that returns on average 8 percent for the year. Your income amounts to $40,000. Now suppose that a few years later your average annual return falls to 3 percent. The income from your $500,000 portfolio now would be just $15,000, a decline of nearly two-thirds. When rates are very low, some investors are tempted to boost their results by moving along the yield curve to higher-paying bond funds. But bond funds have unstable prices, and if rates should rise, their NAVs would decline. Our hapless investors would have been better off sticking with money funds.

Tracking Returns

Many publications list yields on money-market funds. *The Wall Street Journal* provides a table for both taxable and tax-free portfolios on Thursdays. *Investor's Business Daily* carries money-fund data each Friday. *Barron's* publishes a comprehensive weekly table of yields, average maturities, and total assets. Money funds report their annualized payout figures in two different ways: a seven-day average yield and a seven-day compound yield. The latter slightly exceeds the former due to the compounding effect of earning interest on reinvested interest. Both yield measures are net of fund expenses. You also can call the investment company to find out the basic information on its money funds, including their expense ratios. Current yield rankings of money funds are available online from IBC in Ashland, Mass., at no extra charge via the firm's address, http://www.ibcdata.com, on the World Wide Web.

Yields vary among money funds at any given time due to three primary factors:

1. The quality and composition of holdings in the portfolio.

2. The average maturity of portfolio holdings.

3. The fund's expense ratio.

Of the three, expenses are the most important because money funds face limitations on portfolio composition and average maturity. The SEC requires them to maintain average weighted maturities of no more than 90 days. Most keep their averages well below that limit, typically ranging from 30 to 60 days. The sooner that a fund's obligations come due, the easier it is to roll up to higher-paying issues during times of increasing rates.

At the extreme, a fund could have a one-day average maturity if it held only instruments that matured overnight such as repurchase agreements. But portfolios with short averages also would see their yields fall more quickly when rates decline. Predicting near-term interest-rate movements is extremely difficult, so it generally doesn't pay managers to make major shifts in their maturities.

TAX-FREE PRODUCTS

Municipal money funds are very similar to their taxable relatives. They offer stability of principal with an NAV of $1, daily accrual of dividends, and checkwriting privileges. These portfolios contain short-term tax-exempt debt known as municipal notes, of which there are several kinds. For instance, tax anticipation notes are used by cities, counties, and local-government agencies to meet their short-term cash needs while they are awaiting money from tax collections.

Tax-free money funds also invest in so-called "put bonds." These are bonds with longer maturities than the typical money-market instrument. However, the fund manager has the option to sell each bond at a specific "put" price well ahead of maturity, essentially making them short-term obligations. The rates paid on put bonds are adjusted as frequently as weekly to keep them in tune with changes in the level of short-term rates. These bonds have stable principal values because of the put feature.

Some tax-free funds hold private-activity securities subject to the federal alternative minimum tax or AMT. The proceeds from such an issue are directed at least in part to a private, for-profit company. The AMT applies primarily to high-income individuals and corporations that otherwise would be able to substantially reduce their regular tax liability with various deductions and other tax breaks. Private-activity munis pay a bit more than otherwise comparable munis to reflect their less-than-perfect exemption. Fewer than 1 or 2 percent of all taxpayers are subject to the AMT, but some feel that the proportion could escalate in future years.

Your federal tax bracket is what determines whether to invest in a taxable or tax-free money fund. If you also face a relatively high state tax rate, you may want to consider a single-state money fund. Such products are available for people who live in populous states with onerous tax rates, including California, Connecticut, Massachusetts, Michigan, Missouri, New Jersey, New York, Ohio, and Pennsylvania.

State funds offer double or even triple tax-free yields. For instance, a New York City resident could invest in a portfolio that kicks off income that's exempt from taxes at the federal, state, and local levels. But a possible drawback of single-state funds is that they provide less diversification than national money-market products.

It's a good idea to keep a watchful eye on the relationship between yields on the two types of money funds. The closer the taxable and tax-free yields, the greater the advantage of going with a tax-free portfolio. If your fund family offers both kinds of products, it's easy to make the comparison and switch when it becomes appropriate.

It's not hard to put the yields paid by taxable and tax-free money funds on an equal footing. All you need to know is your appropriate tax rate. The equations for calculating taxable-equivalent yields for both national and state products are found in Chapter 15.

CHECKING EXPENSES

Because money funds are fairly homogeneous, you may simply want to use one that's offered by your favorite family. After all, one of the advantages of a money fund is that it can serve as a link to stock and bond products within the same group.

However, if your family does not offer a suitable choice for your cash reserves, you may want to look elsewhere. Chapter 4 discusses the importance of expenses when selecting mutual funds. The cost factor is most important with money funds because these portfolios, particularly the tax-free products, have the lowest absolute returns of the various asset categories. Money-fund expense ratios normally range from about 0.2 percent to more than 1 percent. The average taxable portfolio recently charged 0.8 percent, according to Lipper Analytical Services. You want a fund that has a reputation for low expenses because each penny saved goes directly to the bottom line, adding to your yield.

Table 16-2 illustrates the considerable importance of low costs by comparing the results of two hypothetical money-market portfolios when yields are relatively high and when they are low. This is done by relating each fund's expense ratio to its gross income ratio—that is, gross investment income divided by average net assets. The higher the ratio of the former to the latter, the greater the amount of a fund's income that gets eaten up by costs. Note that expenses during both scenarios consume a far greater percentage of the

Table 16-2   Percentages of Income Consumed by Costs

	Gross Income Ratio	Expense Ratio	Net Income Ratio	Gross Income Consumed by Costs
Period of high yields				
High-cost fund	6%	0.8%	5.2%	13%
Low-cost fund	6	0.4	5.6	7
Period of low yields				
High-cost fund	3	0.8	2.2	27
Low-cost fund	3	0.4	2.6	13

gross yield for the high-cost fund. Also, the results are more pronounced when yields in general are low.

Typically, the most penny-pinching money funds are larger, established portfolios. Be aware of any fee waivers or "teasers," because they are temporary. If you invest in a fund that has had its fees reduced temporarily, check in regularly to see if the expense ratio has since been raised. A significant number of money-market portfolios do subsidize costs from time to time.

As an aside, money funds feature very high portfolio turnover rates, sometimes more than 1,000 percent. Such lofty figures reflect the short maturities of a portfolio's holdings. Money funds are not required to report their turnover rates, so you won't see them in the financial-highlights table. Even so, the portfolio turnover of a money fund is not a meaningful number for two reasons. First, it does not imply increased costs because brokerage fees are not normally incurred on the purchase or sale of money-market securities. Second, there are no capital-gains distributions about which to be concerned.

Are You Looking for a Little More?

Short-term bond funds can provide higher yields than money funds at the cost of a little interest-rate risk Short-term bonds mature within a 1-to-5 year span. Money funds generally avoid securities coming due beyond a year. Longer maturities normally translate into enhanced yields.

If you don't anticipate dipping into your cash reserves for at least 18 months, consider allocating a portion to a short-term bond fund. Of course, these portfolios aren't as safe as money funds because their NAVs fluctuate. How much riskier are they? Most short-term bond funds have durations of 2 to 3 years. The NAV of a portfolio with a duration of 3 years would fall about 3 percent if interest rates rose by one percentage point, as explained in Chapter 13. But higher returns normally more than offset the interest-rate risks, if you hold the fund for 18 months or more.

These products have more flexibility to maneuver than money-market funds so you need to analyze a portfolio carefully before investing. They may venture into riskier IOUs or lengthen maturities to boost yield. Also, you should favor only the lowest-cost products for best results. Finally, be aware that you face a taxable event when you redeem shares or write a check drawn against a bond fund because the NAV fluctuates.

AT THE CLOSE

Money funds make ideal vehicles for managing your cash reserves. They are nearly as safe as government-insured bank accounts, yet pay higher yields and offer convenient access to other funds in a family. You can still enjoy total protection against credit risk if you hold a money fund that invests in U.S. Treasury bills, while funds that own other types of short-term IOUs provide more generous payouts. If you're in a high tax bracket, you can derive a special advantage from a municipal portfolio.

Money funds are fairly homogeneous, and their managers don't have much opportunity to add value the way a good stock or bond selector can. The best money funds are sold by large, well-known families and feature expense ratios below 0.5 percent. You can say with a fairly high degree of certainty that low-cost products will continue to deliver the highest returns in the future.

CHAPTER 17

Mapping Out Your Retirement Strategy

People are living longer and sometimes retiring earlier. That combination makes proper planning more important than ever. Individuals generally require 60 to 80 percent of their working-years earnings to live comfortably in retirement. It's far better to have more than you might need than risk running short.

Mutual funds, with their built-in diversification, flexibility, and efficient services, offer outstanding advantages as savings vehicles. In fact, retirement-plan assets make up more than one-third of the fund industry's total. Most likely, the amount of retirement money invested in mutual funds will continue to grow.

Proper planning involves two primary phases: saving or investing during the working years, then carefully managing your assets during retirement. Contrary to what you might believe, the planning phase does not end when your employment does.

ACCOUNTING FOR INFLATION

It's essential to consider inflation when crunching your numbers. Otherwise, you may grossly underestimate your needs, especially if your planned retirement is many years away. Even inflation of 3 percent a year can be devastating for people with long time horizons and too much invested in low-yielding fixed-income securities. Today's dollar loses half of its purchasing power in 23 years at 3-percent inflation.

Table 17-1 shows the amounts needed in various periods to buy what $1 purchases today, assuming several rates of inflation. Suppose inflation averages 3 percent annually and you plan on retiring in 40 years. You would need $3.26 four decades hence to buy what $1 buys now. Thus, if you recently paid $20,000 for a new car, you could anticipate spending about $65,200 for a comparable vehicle in 40 years ($20,000 x 3.26).

RETIREMENT PLANNING 101

There isn't anything especially fancy about preparing financially for the future. Most people build their nest eggs from one or more of just three main sources:

1. Employer "defined-benefit" plans.

2. Social Security.

3. Personal savings and contributions to voluntary retirement programs, including workplace "defined-contribution" plans.

You don't have much control over the first two sources. In defined-benefit programs, your employer sets aside money on your behalf—based on your salary history and tenure with the organization—and should be able to tell how much monthly income you can expect. With Social Security, you compile a benefits credit based on your work and salary history. To obtain an estimate of what you can anticipate from Uncle Sam, phone the Social Security

Table 17-1   Sample Inflation Factors

Inflation Rate	Years in Future			
	5	10	20	40
3%	1.16	1.34	1.81	3.26
4	1.22	1.48	2.19	4.80
5	1.28	1.63	2.65	7.04
6	1.34	1.79	3.21	10.29

Administration at 1-800-772-1213. Ask for a "Request for Earnings and Benefit Estimate Statement," or Form 7004, which you need to complete and return.

Traditional defined-benefit plans, where the employer does all the funding and takes care of all the money-management details, are on the decline. It's anybody's guess what shape Social Security will be in 20, 30, or 40 years hence. That leaves personal savings as the most dependable leg of the three-pronged retirement stool. It's also the one over which you have most control.

Defined-Contribution Plans Are in Vogue

People seem to be getting the message. Employees are taking increasing responsibility for their retirement by participating in such programs as 401(k), 403(b), and SEP-IRA accounts. With these simple, flexible defined-contribution plans, workers, their employers, or both make deposits. The trend is toward growing use of employee-directed programs, where participants select from a menu of investments. This makes a knowledge of investing more crucial than ever. Unlike their defined-benefit predecessors, defined-contribution plans don't promise a specific stream of retirement income based on a formula. The final result depends on how much money was put into the plan and how well the investments performed.

How Much Will You Need?

You need to crunch some numbers to determine how much you should be socking away in retirement plans and separate investment accounts. Here are five simple steps to estimate what you might need:

Step 1: Forecast your total expenditures during the first year of retirement.

First-year needs differ widely among people, depending on factors such as area of residence and lifestyle. To be meaningful, your projection must reflect inflation and consider taxes. For example, if you spend $4,000 a month now including taxes and plan to retire in 20 years, you would need $8,760 per month in 20 years [$4,000 x 2.19 (from Table 17-1)]. This calculation assumes 4-percent yearly inflation.

You expect that in retirement you will need about 80 percent of what you spend now, so you scale back the estimate, rounding it to $7,000. Take those monthly expenditures and multiply by 12 to get your annual outlay, which amounts to $84,000 ($7,000 x 12).

Step 2: Estimate how much annual income you will receive from defined-benefit plans and Social Security.

Let's suppose this will amount to $40,000 in your case.

Step 3: Calculate your annual shortfall.

Your nest egg will supplement the expected inflows from defined-benefit plans and Social Security. Continuing the example, you forecast a need for

$44,000 in additional savings ($84,000 – $40,000) in the first year of retirement.
Step 4: Estimate how long you might live in retirement.

Life expectancies are rising, so be generous in your projection. Underestimating this amount can lead to serious financial repercussions. Table 17-2 shows the estimated years in retirement for people at various ages. A more complete life-expectancy table is available in IRS Publication 590. Consider adding 5 years to the forecasted amounts in this table because you have about a 50-percent chance of outliving the average. Continuing the illustration, let's say you and your spouse plan to retire at 65 and that at least one of you will live for another 30 years.

Step 5: Project how much you must save by the time you attain retirement age.

Multiplying the $44,000 annual shortfall by the 30 years you expect to live in retirement yields a grand total of $1,320,000. This estimate conservatively assumes that the return on your nest egg during retirement roughly equals the inflation rate.

Of course, it's difficult to be precise about the future, particularly if your planned retirement is several decades away. Nevertheless, you must rely on some ballpark figures to get the planning process started. Our simplified five-step projection does not go into the detail that a comprehensive analysis by a competent financial planner would, but neither one can provide a guarantee of what you will need.

This illustration is merely intended to be a first approximation in quantifying your future. Many people are shocked to see how much money they might actually need. Mutual-fund companies can help you make more precise estimates. For example, T. Rowe Price, Fidelity, and Vanguard will provide a comprehensive retirement-planning workbook on request. Vanguard also sells a detailed software package for running intricate calculations for a modest charge.

Table 17-2   Expected Number of Years in Retirement

Expected Retirement Age	For Individual	For Couple with Same Age
55	29	34
60	24	30
65	20	25
70	16	21

Source: Internal Revenue Service life-expectancy tables in Publication 590.

VOLUNTARY RETIREMENT PLANS

The best retirement programs allow you the flexibility of making large, deductible contributions that reduce your taxable income and tax bill. For example, if you're in the 40-percent combined federal and state tax bracket, each $1,000 you invest in an employer's 401(k) reduces your tax liability by $400, so your take-home pay falls by only $600. Your savings then grow tax-deferred until you make withdrawals. Here's a brief overview of popular plans.

Individual Retirement Accounts

IRAs are available to all wage earners under age 70½. They are ideally suited for young workers who will be making modest investments but have many years for their nest eggs to compound. You may contribute 100 percent of earned income up to $2,000 annually, or $4,000 for a couple. Nonworking spouses also can sock away $2,000 a year. Earnings grow tax-deferred for all IRA holders. Penalty-free withdrawals start at age 59½. A 10-percent tax penalty applies on withdrawals made before 59½ unless you become disabled or meet certain other criteria. Virtually all mutual-fund companies offer IRAs.

The Taxpayer Relief Act of 1997 promises to jump start enthusiasm for IRAs. The public's interest in these vehicles plunged following the tax act of 1986, when Congress ended the universal deductibility of IRA investments for all wage earners. The 1997 law raises some income thresholds below which workers can qualify for an IRA write-off, assuming they also participate in a pension plan at work. People lacking such coverage can receive a deduction, regardless of income. Plus, the new law makes it easier to qualify for a deduction even if your spouse participates in a workplace pension plan—a nice feature for homemakers. Previously, one spouse's participation disqualified the other from receiving a write-off. Another wrinkle of the legislation allows for penalty-free withdrawals from deductible IRAs if the money is used for college expenses or to buy your first home, though ordinary income taxes still would apply.

New Types of IRAs

The 1997 tax legislation added two new types of Individual Retirement Accounts—a revolutionary tax-free vehicle known as the "Roth" IRA, along with an education-oriented program that works much the same way, although designed for a different purpose.

The Roth account, named after Republican Senator William Roth, Jr., of Delaware, likely will prove highly popular. It allows individuals to sock away up to $2,000 a year, or $4,000 for couples, in an account for which no taxes would be due on earnings, assuming the money stays in place for at least five years and the recipient waits until age 59½ to begin pulling out cash. Although these accounts don't allow a deduction, the tax-free buildup could prove even more valuable, especially since money withdrawn from regular IRAs is taxed as ordinary income. Another nice feature is that investors can keep socking away money in a Roth IRA beyond age 70½, and they don't have to start withdrawals at that age—two departures from previous law. Roth IRAs are open to people with adjusted gross income below $95,000 (singles) or $150,000 (married couples). Above these limits, their availability phases out. Assuming you meet a lower income limit, you might be able to switch money from regular to Roth IRAs, although you would trigger ordinary income taxes but not a premature-withdrawal penalty in the process.

Education IRAs also break new ground in helping parents, grandparents, or others set aside money to meet a child's college costs, with tax-free compounding but no deductions allowed. Even an enterprising youngster can set up an education IRA as a custodial account. Within education IRAs, the maximum allowed annual investment is $500 per child, and contributions must end by the time that person reaches 18. Education IRAs are subject to the same income thresholds described above for Roth IRAs.

You can learn more about IRAs by calling the IRS at 1-800-TAX-FORM (1-800-829-3676) and requesting Publication 590.

SEP-IRAs

These easy-to-use investment accounts are designed for small business owners, especially those with no employees. They're formally known as Simplified Employee Pension-Individual Retirement Accounts. These self-directed plans allow you to put away a lot more retirement money each year than you could with just an IRA, although you face no minimums. Your investments can be cash generated from a side business. If you classify yourself as an employee of your business, you can contribute up to the lesser of 15 percent of your compensation or $30,000. SEP-IRAs are easy to use, and contributions can be deducted from your taxable income. SEP-IRAs are covered in IRS Publication 590, referred to above, and many fund companies will service your account.

Keogh Plans

These are advantageous for qualified self-employed individuals and any workers they may have. You can use a Keogh even if you are covered by a corporate pension plan, provided you have income from a separate business. They come in several designs including profit-sharing and money-purchase plans. Keoghs require more paperwork to establish and maintain than

SEP-IRAs, but you may be able to sock away more dollars each year than you could with the latter. As an employee of your business, you can generally invest up to the lesser of $30,000 or 25 percent of your compensation. Keoghs also are widely available from mutual-fund companies. For details, ask your fund-company representative or request IRS Publication 560, "Retirement Plans for the Self-Employed." Because of their greater complexity, it's generally advisable to consult an accountant or attorney if you are seriously considering a Keogh.

401(k) and 403(b) Plans

The popular 401(k) is a salary-reduction plan available through many for-profit employers. That is, you can elect to invest on a tax-deferred basis whatever cash you choose to have taken out of your paycheck. The maximum yearly contribution is linked to inflation and was $9,500 in 1997. A key advantage is that companies often invest money on behalf of their workers. A 401(k) plan should be your top priority for retirement savings if your employer matches a portion of your contributions.

Many nonprofit organizations, including charities and public-school systems, offer 403(b) programs. These plans, which are somewhat similar to 401(k)s, allow you to invest in either annuities or mutual funds.

With both 401(k) and 403(b) programs, you face a set number of investment choices, unlike the unlimited possibilities available through IRAs, SEP-IRAs, and Keoghs. Nevertheless, the trend for both types of workplace pro-

---

Don't Bet Heavily on Your Company

Some people fall into the risky trap of putting too much money into their employer's stock through 401(k) plans. Staking too much of your nest egg on any one company is tantamount to going out on a financial limb. This can be doubly dangerous if your employer is losing money or simply wants to restructure and your job security is threatened. Yet many companies encourage employee stock purchases because they provide support for the company's shares.

Generally speaking, stocks are the best long-term investment, provided you're well diversified and not overly exposed to any one company or industry. The mutual-fund industry's idea of well diversified is investing no more than 5 percent of assets in any one company. You could greatly exceed that by purchasing your employer's stock in a 401(k) plan. Why go out on a limb?

grams has been toward an increasing number of choices. For details about what's offered in your 401(k) or 403(b) plan, see the benefits representative at your workplace.

MANAGING YOUR NEST EGG

Obviously, the comfort of your retirement years will depend largely on how much money you have accumulated. This is why you need to follow a wise, profitable investment program. The following guidelines can help you compile a respectable nest egg:

1. *Choose a game plan.* Select the appropriate tax-sheltered retirement plan or plans, based on your circumstances. Summarize your goals in a short written statement.

2. *Get started.* Young people should start saving early in life, even if it's just a few hundred dollars a year. Older individuals who have neglected to invest for retirement should begin as soon as possible.

3. *Minimize the tax bite on lump-sum distributions.* If you receive a large chunk of cash from a company pension or profit-sharing plan, you should transfer it into an IRA to retain the tax-sheltering benefits. Mutual funds are attractive destinations for transfers because of their generally low annual fees, exchange privileges, and diversified investment options.

4. *Watch out for inflation.* Invest as much as you can in stock funds, to maintain purchasing power. Maximize your growth possibilities by putting some cash into small-stock and international portfolios, with their solid long-term potential.

5. *Avoid high-risk investments.* Speculation is the quickest way to lose wealth. Mutual funds, even those targeting volatile areas, generally offer more safety for retirement plans than a few individual stocks.

TAX-DEFERRED COMPOUNDING

This is the key to long-term wealth accumulation. By keeping Uncle Sam out of the way, your investments build up faster. All of the retirement options identified earlier offer tax-deferred compounding. It makes a lot of sense to have your money grow in this manner whenever possible.

Suppose you can earn 10 percent a year on a stock fund. If you contribute $2,000 to a deductible retirement plan, the full $2,000 goes to work for you. The future values of annual $2,000 investments for various periods appear in Table 17-3.

Table 17-3   Future Values of $2,000 Pre-Tax Annual Contributions*

Contribution Period (in years)	Deductible Retirement Account	Nondeductible Retirement Account	Taxable Account
5	$13,431	$8,596	$7,739
10	35,062	22,440	18,292
15	69,899	44,736	32,683
25	216,364	138,473	79,069
40	973,704	623,170	233,190

*Investments are made at the start of each year and earn 10 percent compounded annually before taxes. In the taxable account, both the investment contributions and earnings are taxed at a 36-percent combined rate. In the nondeductible account, only the contributions are taxed. The after-tax contributions equal $1,280 yearly. This example assumes an investor uses traditional IRAs rather than a Roth IRA.

Conversely, in a nonsheltered or taxable account, you would first pay taxes on your $2,000 of income, leaving a smaller sum to invest. Assuming a 36-percent combined federal and state bracket, your $2,000 would be reduced by $720 in taxes, leaving $1,280 to invest. In addition, your annual return would shrink. With a 36-percent bracket, the after-tax gain amounts to 6.4 percent.

With a nondeductible retirement plan, including the new Roth IRA, you pay taxes on the income you contribute, but that money then grows tax-deferred. Table 17-3 shows that even a nondeductible IRA is not that bad a deal.

One drawback with retirement plans, including traditional IRAs and 401(k)s, is that you pay taxes on withdrawals at ordinary-income rates, rather than as preferential capital gains. Still, years of tax-sheltered growth can help to minimize this disadvantage. Suppose that at retirement in 40 years, you withdraw $973,704 from the deductible account and pay taxes at a rate of 36 percent. You still would have $623,171 left over—the same amount as if you had used a nondeductible IRA—which greatly exceeds the $233,190 balance in the taxable account.

A better strategy from a tax viewpoint would be to take your payout in annual increments, waiting as long as you can after retirement before starting to draw money out. You *must* begin withdrawing from a traditional IRA by the time you reach 70½. But the longer you are able to wait, the longer the money keeps compounding tax-free. As noted earlier, you don't confront mandatory withdrawals from Roth IRAs at any age.

THE ADVANTAGE OF STARTING EARLY

The power of time is so great that a young person could invest modest amounts in a tax-deferred account for a few years, then stop and simply let the money build up. Given enough time, this approach still would result in a substantial sum. An investor who began later in life would have to contribute more for a longer period to compile an equivalent amount.

Table 17-4 illustrates the importance of time. At age 24, Monica began setting aside $2,000 at the beginning of each year in an IRA containing a growth-stock fund that returns 10 percent annually. She did this for 10 years, then stopped making further contributions and let her investment compound at 10 percent yearly for 30 more years. It amounted to $611,817 by the time she reached age 63. Notice that her contributions totaled only $20,000 ($2,000 x 10) so the earnings on her investment amounted to a whopping $591,817. That's the magic of compounding in action.

Conversely, Rita, Monica's twin sister, began saving $7,000 annually in a 403(b) plan when she turned 41. Her stock fund also returned 10 percent yearly. Rita made her deposits faithfully for 23 years. Her nest egg amounted to $612,481 when she turned 63, only $664 more than Monica's cache. However, Rita had to sock away a total of $161,000 ($7,000 x 23), or $141,000 more than Monica's modest $20,000. Rita didn't do badly but Monica fared much better.

Most people don't start investing for retirement until they reach their 30s or 40s, but anyone can get started much earlier. Teenagers even can open an IRA, if they have earned income from part-time or summer employment. Even if teens contribute just a few hundred dollars a year, it can make a substantial impact on their nest eggs by the time they reach retirement age. Suppose a 13-year-old invests $400 yearly in an IRA for six years. Assuming a 10-percent total annual return, those contributions, which totaled just $2,400, would compound to nearly a quarter of a million dollars by the time that forward-looking person turns 65.

Older investors can't turn back the clock, but they still may have a chance to earn a substantial amount through tax-sheltered growth. Life expectancies have increased significantly, and good stock funds can offer attractive appreciation potential prior to and during your retirement years. It's a fallacy to think you must withdraw all your money or switch everything into conservative investments at age 65 anyway. Chances are, you will be able to compound at least some of it for another 5, 10, or 20 years.

INCREASING YOUR PURCHASING POWER

Most IRA money in mutual funds has been committed to various categories of stock funds. Increasingly, people are recognizing that stock-market investments offer the best hope for avoiding the erosion of retirement dollars from inflation. Simply put, it's a well-documented fact that stock funds

	Monica's	End-of-Year	Rita's	End-of-Year
Age	Contribution	Value*	Contribution	Value*
24	$2,000	$2,200	$-0-	$-0-
25	2,000	4,620	-0-	-0-
26	2,000	7,282	-0-	-0-
27	2,000	10,210	-0-	-0-
28	2,000	13,431	-0-	-0-
29	2,000	16,974	-0-	-0-
30	2,000	20,872	-0-	-0-
31	2,000	25,159	-0-	-0-
32	2,000	29,875	-0-	-0-
33	2,000	35,062	-0-	-0-
34	-0-	38,569	-0-	-0-
35	-0-	42,425	-0-	-0-
36	-0-	46,668	-0-	-0-
37	-0-	51,335	-0-	-0-
38	-0-	56,468	-0-	-0-
39	-0-	62,115	-0-	-0-
40	-0-	68,327	-0-	-0-
41	-0-	75,159	7,000	7,700
42	-0-	82,675	7,000	16,170
43	-0-	90,943	7,000	25,487
44	-0-	100,037	7,000	35,736
45	-0-	110,041	7,000	47,009
46	-0-	121,045	7,000	59,410
47	-0-	133,149	7,000	73,051
48	-0-	146,464	7,000	88,056
49	-0-	161,110	7,000	104,562
50	-0-	177,222	7,000	122,718
51	-0-	194,944	7,000	142,690
52	-0-	214,438	7,000	164,659
53	-0-	235,882	7,000	188,825
54	-0-	259,470	7,000	215,407
55	-0-	285,417	7,000	244,648
56	-0-	313,959	7,000	276,813
57	-0-	345,355	7,000	312,194
58	-0-	379,890	7,000	351,114
59	-0-	417,879	7,000	393,925
60	-0-	459,667	7,000	441,017
61	-0-	505,634	7,000	492,819
62	-0-	556,197	7,000	549,801
63	-0-	611,817	7,000	612,481
TOTALS	$20,000		$161,000	

*Investments are made at the start of each year and earn 10 percent compounded annually.

Table 17-4   Twin Sisters Show How Starting Early Pays

provide far higher total returns over long stretches than fixed-income port-folios do.

Take the case of William, a 30-year-old, self-employed writer who wants to begin saving for retirement. He estimates that a growth-stock fund could return 10 percent a year and a conservative bond fund, 6 percent. William plans to retire at 65 and expects to invest $4,000 annually for the next 35 years in a Keogh plan. How much purchasing power can he accumulate with each investment?

William first needs to distinguish between nominal and real rates of return. The *nominal rate*, as discussed earlier, is the basic or "observed" rate of 10 percent on the stock fund. The *real rate* is an inflation-adjusted number that measures the *growth of purchasing power*. You can estimate it by subtracting expected inflation from the nominal number. With inflation projected at 4 percent a year, the real rate works out to 6 percent on the stock fund and 2 percent on the bond portfolio. Assuming William made his investments at the beginning of each year, the bond and stock funds would compound to the following nominal and real future values after 35 years:

	Future Values:	
	Nominal	*Real*
Bond portfolio	$472,483	$203,977
Stock portfolio	1,192,507	472,483

When you look at results in terms of inflation-adjusted real values, it becomes clear that you need to harness the higher potential of stock invest-ments to protect and enhance your dollars over the long-haul.

Even though stocks are more volatile than bonds, long-term investors benefit from time diversification, as we explained in Chapter 6. Younger peo-ple planning for a retirement decades away need not let the volatility concern them. They should focus instead on the multidecade upward trend in stock prices, perhaps using dollar-cost averaging to buy more shares in a fund when its NAV is down and fewer shares when it's high. In this sense, bear markets actually can benefit long-term savers, as we saw in Chapter 7.

Many types of equity funds can supply solid results for younger retire-ment investors, including small-cap, international, growth, and growth-and-income portfolios. Index funds also are attractive for retirement purposes because of their modest expenses, predictability, and very low portfolio turnovers. As explained in Chapter 8, a variety of index vehicles are available today, including those in the large-stock, small-stock, and international areas.

As people grow older, they tend to lighten up on equity funds and focus more on income. But it's generally unwise to move too far away from stocks, even at retirement, because bonds don't mix well with high inflation. A person retiring at 65 easily could live two or three more decades. People who call it quits at a younger age have even more time to worry about inflation. For these individuals, stock funds provide a hedge. One approach might be to redeem shares from a stock fund periodically to meet your income needs rather than to invest heavily in bond funds for their monthly income.

In short, it's difficult to manage with only fixed-income funds. True, you may need to have some bond holdings for income and stability, but you also require equities for growth.

MOVING RETIREMENT ASSETS AROUND

You have been reading about the merits of tax-deferred compounding. If you want to protect this tax advantage, you must be careful when taking a lump-sum distribution from an employer's pension plan.

A lump-sum distribution can occur for several reasons, including retirement, job changes, layoffs, or disability. In some cases, you might wind up with a significantly larger amount of money than you had anticipated receiving. Normally, you can contribute no more than $2,000 a year to a regular IRA. It takes time to build an account. Conversely, you might be able to move $50,000, $100,000, or even a lot more from a former employer's pension into an IRA at once.

Many people take a lump-sum distribution and simply pay taxes on it. It's often much better to keep this money under a tax-deferred umbrella, however. One option is simply to leave the account with your former employer, if it's permissible. This could make sense if the plan offered a good menu of funds. But moving the assets into an IRA may be better since you typically will enjoy even greater control of the money because it can be invested in whatever funds you want. If you haven't yet figured out which portfolio you want within a chosen family, simply park the assets in a money fund while you're deciding.

Consider moving the lump sum into a separate or "conduit IRA," so the money doesn't get mixed in with the contents of any other IRAs you may have. That way, if the opportunity should present itself, you can transfer the money back to a future employer's plan since it hasn't been commingled with other IRA assets.

Using a "Direct Rollover"

Moving money from workplace retirement plans can be hazardous from a tax standpoint. In addition to the usual 10-percent penalty if you cash out before age 59½, the IRS requires employers to withhold for federal taxes 20 percent of lump-sum withdrawals made from company pensions, including

401(k) and 403(b) plans, unless you initiate a "direct rollover." By direct, that means you personally can't touch the distribution check, which instead is payable to your chosen IRA custodian or new employer. To keep things simple and avoid the danger of paying taxes on the 20 percent withheld, you should use a direct rollover. Transferring assets directly from a qualified pension plan into an IRA is not a taxable event.

Changing IRA Custodians

Suppose you later decide you don't like Fund Family A and want to move your IRA to Fund Family B. In this case you could use either:

1. A "custodian-to-custodian transfer," where you don't handle the money at all; or

2. An "indirect rollover," where you receive a distribution check then reinvest it.

The IRS permits only one 60-day indirect rollover per IRA account in each 12-month period. If you use this method, be sure to reinvest the full proceeds before 60 days have elapsed to avoid a stiff IRS penalty. Conversely, with a custodian-to-custodian transfer, you face no 12-month limit on the number of moves you can make. This is the more efficient way to move an IRA and is recommended unless you need to use the money as a short-term loan within the 60-day window. To learn more about IRA rollovers and transfers, ask your tax adviser or fund company, or refer to Publication 590, mentioned earlier.

DIVVYING UP YOUR NEST EGG

Most investors have money both in and outside of tax-deferred accounts such as IRAs. How do you decide which investments to put in each? For starters, consider placing tax-efficient funds in ordinary taxable accounts. Your choices here might include index portfolios, which usually are tax efficient with their minuscule portfolio turnovers. Any profits you earn when you ultimately sell the fund would be taxed at a maximum 20 percent, down from 28 percent previously and well below the top ordinary-income levy. This assumes you hold your shares for more than 18 months. Conversely, on withdrawals made from a traditional IRA, you would pay taxes at the higher rate for ordinary income. The lower the capital-gains tax rate relative to the levy on ordinary income, the greater the potential benefit of keeping your investment in a taxable account. Some index funds managed by Vanguard and Schwab are specifically designed to be highly tax-efficient.

Certain managed stock funds that ordinarily are tax-efficient also might be held in a taxable account. These include small-stock funds that generate little or no income and feature low portfolio turnover. Conversely, investments that kick off high ·yields such as equity-income, utility stock, and high-yield bond funds are best suited for your traditional tax-deferred account. The same can be said of high-turnover growth funds that spin off lots of capital gains.

In addition, if you buy and sell funds fairly frequently, you are better off in a tax-deferred retirement plan—assuming, of course, that your transactions have been profitable. Should you encounter a painful losing streak, as many traders do, you won't be able to deduct any capital losses within an IRA. In any event, hopping in and out of funds is not recommended.

As a final thought, don't succumb to the temptation of socking away too much money in a retirement plan. Despite the tax-sheltering advantages, it's important to maintain sufficient liquidity for near-term cash needs. You can take money out of an IRA at any time, but you face a 10-percent penalty for premature withdrawals if you are under age 59½, unless you become disabled or meet certain other conditions. The impact of this penalty lessens, however, if you have been using tax-deferred compounding for many years, although the dollar size of the infraction would climb.

AT THE CLOSE

Taxes and inflation are the two biggest enemies of people saving for retirement. Tax-deferred accounts and common stocks offer the best ways to fight back. Tax laws change from time to time, but the principles of good retirement planning remain the same. The more assets you can keep away from Uncle Sam, the better.

In particular, take advantage of workplace retirement programs, deductible IRAs, and nondeductible Roth IRAs, in that order. But your total contributions to all IRAs cannot exceed $2,000 a year, or $4,000 for couples. Just be careful to steer clear of the tax penalties on these accounts, which can be substantial. Consider building your nest egg with mutual funds because of their broad diversification, professional management, wide investment choices, and other benefits. And get started as soon as possible.

CHAPTER 18

Sizing Up Variable Annuities

So far, we have examined tax-sheltered investing through voluntary retirement plans. There's another choice you should be familiar with: variable annuities, a moderately popular mutual-fund relative. What's "variable" is the investment return—these products fluctuate in price the same as any ordinary mutual fund does.

Variable annuities have increased in popularity ever since the Tax Reform Act of 1986 eliminated other types of shelters, including limited partnerships. However, the Taxpayer Relief Act of 1997 probably will harm annuity sales somewhat. Most variable annuities are sold by brokers or insurance agents who earn commissions. The products are more complex than mutual funds and require some explanation. There's also a small group of no-load annuities offered by several well-known families. Typical customers include long-term, retirement-oriented investors who already have contributed the yearly maximum to traditional retirement plans, such as IRAs, yet want an alternative to municipal bonds.

Although an annuity investment isn't tax-deductible, the money grows tax-deferred as it would in an IRA or qualified retirement plan. In that sense, it's similar to a nondeductible IRA such as the new Roth IRAs, but with no limit on how much you can sock away. As with any long-term saving vehicle, the sooner you get started with a variable annuity, the more compounding can work for you.

Like ordinary mutual funds, variable annuities offer built-in diversification and professional management. They really are just mutual funds with a thin layer of insurance that provides a minimum death benefit and an option to receive a stream of income for life. In addition, the insurance component allows investors to delay paying taxes on income and gains.

Don't confuse variable annuities with *variable life* or *variable universal life*. These are life-insurance products featuring mutual funds in which you invest your policy's cash value. Like variable annuities, these vehicles provide tax-deferred compounding until you withdraw money. But they are more complex products and carry a far greater insurance component than a variable annuity.

As you might expect, dozens of mainstream mutual-fund families manage variable-annuity portfolios. The list includes Fidelity, Franklin, Janus, Massachusetts Financial, Merrill Lynch, T. Rowe Price, Putnam, Scudder, USAA, and Vanguard. Typically, investors get a choice of fund types with an annuity, though the array doesn't compare in number to the lineup offered by a typical medium- or large-sized fund group. You can invest in one or several portfolios and move the money about as you choose, generally at little or no cost.

HOW ANNUITIES WORK

An annuity is a contract between an investor and a life-insurance company, which promises to provide future payments. Figure 18-1 identifies the major contract options.

An annuity can include up to three parties:

1. *Contract owner.* The person in control of all contract terms.

2. *Annuitant.* Often the owner, the individual who receives payments during the payout period.

3. *Beneficiary.* The person entitled to residual benefits from the contract when the annuitant dies.

Figure 18-1   Annuity Options at a Glance

PREMIUM PAYMENTS	BASIC PAYMENT OPTIONS
• Single	• Lump sum
• Periodic	• Irregular amounts as needed by owner
INVESTMENT RETURNS	• Annuity (as detailed below)
• Fixed	ANNUITY-PAYOUT CHOICES
• Variable	• Lifetime income
INVESTMENT CHOICES	• Lifetime with period certain
• U.S. stock	• Lifetime with installment
• Foreign stock	• Joint and last survivor
• Specialized equity	• Payments for a fixed period
• Hybrid	• Payments of a specified amount
• Bond	
• Money market	

Fixed Versus Variable

In terms of the investment component, annuities can be divided into two basic types.

Fixed annuities are guaranteed contracts, whereby the owner locks in an interest rate for a set period of a year or so. At the end of this time, the insurer designates a new rate. Usually, it's above the guaranteed base amount of interest that the company must pay under the terms of the annuity agreement. Like a bond or bond fund, a fixed annuity may fail to provide a satisfactory inflation hedge, thereby subjecting investors to purchasing-power risk.

Fixed-annuity assets are held within the insurance company's *general account*. This means the company's creditors can get their hands on the money in the event of trouble. For this reason, fixed-annuity purchasers need to check the rating of the insurer's financial health. You would want a company rated at least "A" by sources such as A.M. Best Co. and Standard & Poor's.

Conversely, with *variable annuities*, there's no such locked-in rate. How you fare depends on the performance of the portfolio you choose. In other words, the investment risk gets passed from the insurer to you, which offers you a chance of earning substantially higher returns than what's available on a fixed account. Variable annuities are sometimes called *self-directed* annuities because you have the ability to move money in and out of different portfolios, known as "subaccounts." The process works just like the popular telephone-switching feature offered by mutual-fund families.

Subaccounts

Technically, the person who invests in a variable annuity does not acquire a *direct* ownership interest in the underlying fund. Rather, that person owns a stake in a variable annuity "subaccount" through the sponsoring insurance company, which is the legal owner of the portfolio. Without going into more detail, suffice to say that this arrangement is legally necessary for the investor to get the tax-deferral advantage.

The subaccount is simply a division of a *separate account* that's not part of the insurer's assets. Each individual portfolio within the umbrella separate account is a subaccount. For example, if Fund Family A has six subaccounts, it would have six mutual funds within the wrapper. As measured by total assets, subaccounts are typically much smaller than comparable mutual funds, reflecting the greater popularity of the latter.

The insurance company maintains the subaccounts and keeps their assets "walled-off" from its general account. If the insurer gets into trouble, creditors can't lay their hands on the money. This represents an obvious plus for the variable annuity's investors, who don't have to worry about the firm's credit rating.

Each subaccount is a distinct portfolio, although it may mirror or "clone" an established mutual fund offered by the same company. In fact, subaccount managers are frequently the same individuals who oversee the family's regular mutual funds.

To make things even more confusing, some variable annuities offer so-called "fixed-rate accounts." They are not the same as a fixed annuity but give the variable investor a similar option.

These fixed options within a variable annuity pay a guaranteed rate of interest. They are part of the insurance company's general account and require you to make a commitment for a specific period, such as one or three years. For instance, you might go into a fixed option when rates are high to lock in a juicy level of interest. Or, they might appeal to someone who has just retired and wants stability. Since the fixed account lies within the insurance company's general account, the firm bears the investment risk, unlike with a variable account.

ACCUMULATION AND DISTRIBUTION

There are generally two phases in the life of an annuity:

1. *The accumulation, or asset-building, phase.* The longer this period of time before withdrawals start, the more tax-deferred compounding can work in your favor.

2. *The payout, distribution, or "annuitization" phase.* This is the period when the contract holder receives money. Normally, it occurs in retirement.

As with an IRA, annuity investors face a 10-percent penalty tax imposed on accumulated earnings on withdrawals made before age 59½. No penalty would apply for people who become permanently disabled or terminally ill. At or beyond 59½, you can either take your cash out in a lump sum or you can "annuitize," or establish a plan for taking periodic payments. You also can annuitize at a younger age without penalty if you choose to take income spread over your remaining life expectancy. A lot of people don't know about this painless early out feature, which also is available on IRAs.

When payments start, you as annuitant must pay taxes on the portion that represents earnings—at ordinary rather than preferential capital-gains rates. But you can elect to compound your money tax-deferred until age 85, if not longer, before making your first withdrawals. The specific age depends on the annuity. Conversely, traditional IRAs require that you begin making withdrawals by April 1 of the calendar year following the date you attained age 70½. As noted in Chapter 17, the Roth IRA is an exception.

Building a Nest Egg

You can purchase an annuity either by making a lump-sum investment or paying periodic "premiums." You buy "accumulation units" that are similar to mutual-fund shares. Hence, the "accumulation unit value" is analogous to a fund's NAV or per-share price. Unlike a mutual fund, however, a variable annuity pays no income or capital-gains distributions to investors, so its accumulation unit value builds up tax-deferred over the years, as is shown in the example of a nondeductible retirement account in Table 17-3.

In general, you can expect variable annuities to perform about the same as their mutual-fund cousins having similar objectives. Discrepancies could result, however, from factors such as differences in portfolio sizes, managers, and, especially, fees.

As noted, the annuity contains a minimum death benefit. This protects your beneficiary against any market losses during the accumulation period. In other words, if you as annuitant should die before payments begin, the beneficiary would receive the amount of your total contributions (less any withdrawals) or the current surrender value of the account—whichever is greater.

Some variable annuities offer a "stepped-up" death-benefit option, which would increase the base guaranteed amount payable to the beneficiary every few years. Once you annuitize, you lose this death benefit, however. By annuitizing, you set up a plan for receiving periodic distributions.

The death benefit really isn't an important reason for purchasing a variable annuity. It provides a modest security blanket for people who worry about low-probability, worst-case scenarios of losing money—and dying—within the first few years of buying a contract.

Drawing from Your Stash

Suppose you decide to annuitize rather than take a lump-sum payout or withdraw cash as needed; you can choose between a fixed or varying income stream. The fixed stream appeals to people who are more conservative. That's because the amount you receive on a variable stream depends on how well your investments performed. Specifically, the size of your monthly payments would hinge on four factors:

1. The total amount of your investment.

2. The length of your accumulation period.

3. Your investment performance, net of expenses.

4. The insurer's estimate of your life expectancy, if you opt for a lifetime annuity.

In addition to choosing between a fixed or variable income stream, you can select among several payout options, including the following:

1. *Lifetime income.* With this option, payments continue for as long as the annuitant lives. The risk is that the contract owner may die early since payments would cease at that point, regardless of the number or dollar amount received. This option may be good for a healthy single person with no dependent heirs.

2. *Lifetime with period certain.* Here, payments continue for a designated period, even if it exceeds the annuitant's life span. Suppose the period certain is 10 years and the annuitant dies after 5 years; the present value of the remaining payments would go to the beneficiary.

3. *Lifetime with installment or refund option.* Should the owner die before the principal in the account is depleted, the residual amount goes to the beneficiary, who has the option of taking it on a monthly basis. Suppose that the value of the annuity is $500,000 and the first payment is $2,500, with a total of 200 monthly payments. If the annuitant dies after 100 payments, the remaining 100 go to the beneficiary.

4. *Joint and last survivor.* Payments continue until the death of the last annuitant. This option is a popular one for spouses. The insurer doesn't guarantee that any minimum number of payments will be

made, which means that there is a financial risk that both parties might die shortly after annuitization begins.

5. *Payments for a fixed period.* Here, the insurer simply agrees to distribute cash for a set time span. This commonly ranges from 5 to 30 years with payments made monthly, quarterly, semiannually, or annually.

6. *Payments of a specified amount.* Finally, you can elect to have a specified amount paid out. In case you die before the contracted amount has been fully distributed, the remainder goes to your designated beneficiary.

Unlike regular life insurance, which protects you against the risk of a premature death, the lifetime payout options on variable annuities insure you (and your joint annuitant, if you name one) against the danger of outliving your retirement nest egg. It's worth noting that the insurance company may make a rather lengthy estimate of your life expectancy if you take the lifetime option. A longer estimate results in smaller monthly payments, since the company potentially is on the hook for a lengthy span.

Annuitization Perils

Choosing an annuitization option can be complicated and even somewhat risky. Once you decide, you can't change your mind because annuitization is irrevocable. At that point, you're basically relinquishing control over your money to the insurance company. The lifetime annuity is a good case in point, since the insurer will retain a substantial amount of money if the annuitant dies shortly after payments begin.

It's often much more sensible to withdraw money from your contract when you need it. Your requirements could change unpredictably in the future, and annuitization causes you to lose control of your nest egg. Making such a commitment makes sense only in special cases. For instance, it may be the best choice when the annuitant is incapable of handling his or her financial affairs.

Another potential drawback of annuitization is that it may subject you to a premium tax if your state collects one. At this writing, for example, premiums received by California residents were reduced by a 2.35-percent tax. Be sure to look into this situation in your state if you plan to annuitize.

SORTING OUT THE COSTS

Brokers and insurance agents, who account for most variable annuity sales, earn commissions of 6 percent or so for their efforts. These commissions are paid in advance by the annuity company at the time of sale. The firm then recoups its expenses by imposing *surrender charges*, which are similar to a back-end or "contingent-deferred sales charge" on a regular mutual fund. Front-end loads are rare. The amount might be 6 or 7 percent in the first year, dropping by a percentage point each year after that until it eventually phases out. However, surrender charges may kick in again under certain conditions—if you make additional investments, for example. With a "rolling surrender charge" the clock starts all over again whenever you put in more money—definitely an unpleasant feature.

Note that a surrender charge is only bad if you sell before it has been dropped. Variable annuities are supposed to be very long-term investments anyway, so it's wise to hang on for the long haul if you can. Of course, there's always the chance that you may need to yank out your money. That's why high-commission products are best avoided.

The ongoing charges of a variable annuity fall into two broad categories: insurance-related costs and fund costs:

1. *Insurance-related charges.* These costs consist of the so-called "mortality and expense-risk charge" or M&E, which generally ranges from 1.25 to 1.40 percent yearly. The mortality portion covers the death benefit and lifetime annuity perils that the insurer faces; the expense-risk portion covers a guarantee that your expenses will never exceed a specified amount. Distribution and other administrative fees also fall under this category. In addition, contract-maintenance charges of $25 to $35 a year are tacked on to the typical annuity. This charge normally applies only to smaller accounts.

2. *Fund expenses.* These costs include management fees and other outlays you would face with an ordinary mutual fund. As with funds, these charges differ by company and by investment category. In general, they're highest for international-stock funds and lowest for money-market products.

Combined, insurance-related charges and fund expenses average about 2 percent, according to Lipper. This seems rather high when you consider that plenty of good stock mutual funds can be found with expense ratios of 1 percent, or less. Of course, costs vary widely among annuity companies, so it pays to shop around. There are even some pure no-load products with no surrender charges and rock-bottom M&E charges. Vanguard, Scudder, Schwab, and T. Rowe Price are examples of companies in this group. As with commission-free mutual funds, you buy no-load variable annuities directly from the company. While you don't have a sales charge to worry about, you still have to examine the contract's total costs to make sure the annual expenses are reasonable.

An important question to ask about any variable annuity is how long it will take before the tax-deferred growth begins to outweigh your additional expenses, making you better off than with a regular mutual fund. The following factors lead to a shorter break-even time:

1. Lower costs.

2. A higher tax bracket.

3. Higher investment returns.

At the minimum, you should allow a variable annuity to compound tax-deferred for 15 to 20 years before making any withdrawals. Taking the time dimension to an extreme, a parent or grandparent could buy a variable annuity for a newborn child and let it grow for several decades. An investment of several thousand dollars could make that child a millionaire in his or her golden years, if it's invested in a solid stock subaccount.

The most appropriate variable-annuity investments include aggressive-growth, growth, growth-and-income, and international-stock portfolios since they will likely perform much better than fixed-income funds over time. A variable annuity is where the most aggressive part of your nest egg should be to offset the higher expenses, provided you can tolerate a risky component.

You also may have to stay put for a long time if you face stiff surrender charges. For this reason, you should be extra cautious before buying. Since you probably will switch among different funds within a family eventually, you want a group that offers an attractive menu, where all the investment choices are good performers. We advise going with a large, well-known complex that has a reputation for superior returns and reasonable expenses.

Although annuities are designed for retirement investing, you are not locked into a fund group forever. You can transfer from Family A to Family B using a so-called "1035 exchange." This is not a taxable transaction, as your money remains under a tax-deferred umbrella, but you do have to move your entire account balance. You can't transfer into an existing annuity with a 1035—a new contract must be established. Of course, normal surrender charges, if any, apply. A 1035 exchange generally takes from three to eight weeks.

WEIGHING THE CRITICISMS

The most important reason to buy a variable annuity is for the tax-deferred compounding. The higher your combined federal-plus-state bracket, the greater your benefit. But there are offsetting disadvantages that have made variable annuities vulnerable to harsh criticism on several grounds. Here are the major drawbacks.

Criticism #1: These products are too expensive.

Annuities and Index Funds

Index funds that feature low portfolio turnover and thus don't pay much in the way of capital-gains distributions are tax-efficient competitors of variable annuities.

Profits pulled out of an index fund are taxed at preferential capital-gain rates, assuming the shares have been held at least 18 months. Conversely, annuity earnings are taxed as ordinary income, usually at higher levies. This is a significant drawback for wealthier investors. In addition, index funds offer the advantages of simplicity, much lower ongoing costs, and access to your money without a surrender charge or premature-withdrawal penalty.

OUR POSITION: This can be a valid point, particularly if you don't stay with your investment long enough or don't invest in subaccounts that provide sufficiently high returns to overcome the added insurance-related costs. You may not need the modest insurance features anyway, even if you have dependents. In any event, you have to shop around carefully to find the best deals. No-load products are available from firms such as Vanguard, T. Rowe Price, Charles Schwab, Janus, Scudder, Jack White, and USAA.

Criticism #2: Annuities are oversold.

OUR POSITION: There's a lot of truth to this because the salesperson stands to earn a tidy commission, even if the product is not in your best interest. For instance, variable annuities often are pitched to senior citizens who don't have a long enough life expectancy to benefit from them. Or, if you already own an annuity, a broker, financial planner, or insurance agent might entice you to switch to the product he or she is pushing by claiming it's a better deal. Teachers and retirees are prime targets for this ploy.

Criticism #3: Variable annuities lock up your money.

OUR POSITION: The surrender charges and 10-percent penalty on distributions before age 59½ make it costly to pull money out of variable annuities prematurely. But you can move money among portfolios within the insurance wrapper, and you can transfer from one fund complex to another with a tax-free 1035 exchange. Teachers and some employees of nonprofit companies also can transfer money from a variable annuity to mutual funds if they open a 403(b) account. These transactions are not taxable events. Surrender charges and tax penalties discourage withdrawals, and underscore the long-term nature of annuities.

Criticism #4: Variable annuities offer fewer choices than ordinary mutual
        funds.

OUR POSITION: This is true, but you often can find enough investment options to suit your needs. Variable annuities should only be a portion
of your overall investment program anyway, so you should use them to supplement rather than supplant your other holdings. Contribute all you can to
the voluntary retirement plans first. Beyond this, consider buying tax-efficient
stock funds or muni-bond funds in ordinary taxable accounts rather than
variable annuities.

Criticism #5: They're too complex.

OUR POSITION: You certainly don't want to invest in something you
don't understand. Variable annuities are more difficult to analyze than ordinary mutual funds. You're definitely going to have to dig deeper into the
prospectus and research all the funds within the wrapper. The complexity
issue probably explains why most do-it-yourself investors steer clear of these
products.

Criticism #6: Earnings are taxed as ordinary income.

OUR POSITION: With variable annuities, you can't take advantage of
a capital-gains tax rate that might be significantly less than the levy you pay
on ordinary income. This is a valid criticism that also applies to distributions
from other tax-sheltered retirement accounts such as traditional IRAs, but not
Roth IRAs. In addition, when you die a variable annuity would pass to your
beneficiaries but they couldn't take advantage of the so-called tax-free "step
up in basis," as they could with positions in appreciated stocks and stock
funds in ordinary accounts. The "basis" in an investment is the amount on
which you don't owe taxes. The higher this figure, the better. Suppose you
owned an index fund that you held for many years, with a basis of $100,000,
reflecting the amount of your investments over the years. If at death, the portfolio had a fair market value of $200,000 and was held in a nonretirement
account, your heirs could step up the basis to $200,000, escaping any tax lia-
bility on the $100,000 in unrealized appreciation. They would not get the same
tax break with variable annuities. This makes annuities inferior tools for
building up assets that you can pass along to your heirs.

Criticism #7: Tax laws could change unfavorably.

OUR POSITION: On several occasions in recent years, legislation has
been proposed that would have changed the federal tax status of annuities for
the worse. It's difficult to predict what kinds of regulatory alterations will
occur in the future and how they might affect annuity owners. It is also possible, albeit highly unlikely, that any legislative change could be retroactive.

Variable Annuities: A Tougher Sell

Variable annuities wound up as big losers following enactment of the Taxpayer Relief Act of 1997. For starters, the appeal of annuities dimmed as a result of enhancements that made regular, deductible IRAs more attractive by comparison. Even more significant was the creation of Roth IRAs, a type of nondeductible account in which investment dollars grow tax free, with no taxation upon withdrawal. By contrast, cash pulled from an annuity is taxed as ordinary income. One drawback of both types of IRAs is that you still can sock away just $2,000 (individuals) or $4,000 (couples) a year, as before. With annuities, you can invest as much as you want. But that's also the case with index mutual funds and other highly tax efficient funds held outside of a retirement account. These investments got a big boost from the 1997 legislation in the form of lower capital-gains rates. On balance, the 1997 tax-law changes put pressure on annuity sellers to reduce their fees.

Before sinking a large investment into a variable annuity, seek competent advice from a tax professional or financial planner.

GETTING INFORMATION

For daily unit price, yield, and performance information on individual variable portfolios, you can call the sponsoring fund company on its toll-free 800 number. You won't find daily prices in the newspaper since the subaccounts are not publicly traded, although *Barron's* and *The Wall Street Journal* list unit values and recent total returns on a weekly basis. More complete information, including a breakdown of expenses and total returns over various periods, appears in *The Wall Street Journal's* quarterly mutual-funds survey. Subaccounts are grouped under the name of the applicable insurance company.

Both Lipper and Morningstar track the performances of variable annuities. Morningstar's software product, *Principia for Variable Annuities/Life*, covers more than 5,400 subaccounts. It's updated monthly.

CAVEAT EMPTOR

Tax deferral is valuable, but you shouldn't overpay for it. Because of the higher costs associated with annuities, you should first invest as much as you can in regular retirement plans, such as 401(k), IRA, and Keogh accounts. If you still have money to put away, then you can start thinking about a variable annuity. Normally, you wouldn't want to hold a variable annuity inside an IRA or similar account, because those plans already provide tax deferral.

But in the right situation, a variable annuity can be beneficial. The more years you're working with, the better your likely results. Ideally, you should plan to leave your money alone for several decades before making any withdrawals. With most annuities, you aren't required to take any money out until you reach age 85, or even later in some cases.

Another possible use of a variable annuity is for someone who has started saving for retirement at a late date and wants to catch up. If this person can let the money compound for at least 10 years before dipping in, an annuity could work nicely because there is no limit on contributions.

One attractive feature of variable annuities is the brief grace or "free-look" period that they offer, during which you can cancel your purchase if the contract doesn't suit you. If disappointed, you can exit after a few days without any penalty. Keep this provision in mind, as it could come in handy.

AT THE CLOSE

Variable annuities are a moderately popular, if oversold, retirement vehicle. These products wrap traditional mutual funds within an insurance package that allows earnings to escape taxes until money is withdrawn. Annuities offer various ways to make investments and take payouts. These features, along with an additional layer of insurance-related costs, make them more complicated than straight mutual funds, which partly explains their lukewarm reception among do-it-yourself investors.

As a rule, variable annuities should rank as your fourth or fifth tax-deferred option, behind 401(k) plans and IRAs, and possibly even municipal-bond funds or stock-index funds.

Analyzing a variable annuity is similar to researching a regular mutual fund, but you should do a more thorough job since you're dealing with a more complex product and possibly making a longer-term commitment. Read the prospectus and shareholder reports carefully, along with the "Statement of Additional Information" if you want further details. As with ordinary funds, fees and past performance are highly important.

CHAPTER 19

Allocating Your Assets

After watching bank yields decline for years, an investor in the early 1990s switched some money into a municipal-bond fund. He quickly developed a taste for tax-free income and principal gains, so he moved even more money into the same fund. Then he started switching cash into muni portfolios that paid the loftiest yields—funds that were carrying greater risks. But by the time he had transferred most of his assets into muni funds, Murphy's Law caught up with him and bond prices in 1994 took a nasty spill. Sadder but wiser, the investor came away with the realization that too much of a good thing can be bad, or at least imprudent.

This person would have been smarter to follow an asset-allocation approach. Simply put, it is a strategy for dividing up your portfolio into various investment classes, with stocks, bonds, and money-market securities being primary. Foreign stocks and bonds also play a big role in most asset-allocation schemes because of the desirable benefits of international diversification, which we explored in Chapter 10. Real estate and precious metals are among the other categories that can be used.

The goal of asset allocation is to earn the best possible returns at a prudent level of risk. Preservation of capital is an important objective. Essentially, you forgo the possibility of occasional spectacular gains in favor of greater consistency and less downside exposure. The ups and downs are less extreme because not all of your holdings will be rising or falling together. One asset class may zig while another zags. As we'll see, the asset-allocation decision is clearly the most important one you make as an investor.

AN "ALL-SEASONS" MIX

Asset allocation brings to mind the similar yet distinct concept of *diversification*. It's built around the notion that you should hold ample securities within a particular asset class—say, domestic stocks—to avoid losing big time if your future Microsoft goes belly up. In this sense, a single mutual fund, which may hold 100 companies, offers pretty good diversification. If a few stocks turn out to be real lemons, the overall portfolio won't necessarily suffer because many other companies may prove extraordinarily profitable, offsetting the losses. Diversification protects against company-specific or *unsystematic* risk; that is, the chance that an individual firm will turn out to be a dud. But diversification among domestic companies alone can't shield you against market risk, no matter how many you own.

Suppose you staked everything on a blue-chip fund that tumbled 30 percent in a bear rout. You obviously would be worse off than if, instead, you had allocated 50 percent of your portfolio to a money-market fund, in which case your overall mix would have fallen by just half as much, or 15 percent. The tradeoff is that the money-fund position would hold back your returns in good times.

That's a simple illustration, but it shows how asset allocation works, by leveling the peaks and valleys of your portfolio's value. The aim is to provide some protection against adverse developments that can hit a particular category of securities harder than others.

A mutual-fund portfolio containing the right mix of stock and bond categories will experience reduced volatility yet still produce the favorable long-run growth you get with equities. It offers an "all-seasons" mix that should at least help you get a better night's sleep even during the severest of bear markets.

Asset allocation has a lot going for it. Here's why:

1. Research has indicated that at least 90 percent of a portfolio's performance depends on the various asset classes it contains and their weighting. Less than 10 percent of the return is determined by the individual investments held within each asset class.

2. Putting together the right mix of asset classes also can greatly reduce a portfolio's total risk. That's because various asset categories carry different degrees of risk, and the correlations between any two classes can be fairly low. For example, correlations between the U.S. stock market and other world markets are often less than 0.5, indicating only a modest performance connection. A correlation of 1.0 indicates a perfect positive association of returns whereby two markets would fluctuate in complete harmony like a couple of synchronized swimmers. Conversely, a reading of 0.0 suggests no correlation of returns, or completely independent performance.

3. Asset allocation helps you maintain discipline. You don't have to guess what the financial markets are going to do next, so your emotions won't get the best of you. Maintaining relatively stable commitments to stocks, bonds, and cash will surely lead to better risk-adjusted returns over the long-haul than frequently giving in to your impulses.

QUESTIONS TO PONDER

Contemplate the following questions before deciding on what asset classes you need, and how to weight them:

1. *What is your age?* Chapter 1 provided three age-specific guidelines for determining your target stock allocation. Specifically, they are: 120

Few Asset Classes Are Spared During Global Crashes

Asset allocation doesn't always work as well as you might expect, at least over the short term. A severe global bear market is a good case in point. Small and large stocks in both emerging as well as developed markets can get clobbered, although some areas will be hit less severely than others. If the rout was triggered by rising interest rates, bonds will take a beating, too. Cash likely would be the only safe haven.

Fortunately, these chaotic periods tend to be rather brief, like the October 1987 crash. During longer stretches asset allocation works quite well. You can spot multiyear periods when either U.S. or foreign stocks have the upper hand, or when large or small companies are in vogue. It's rare for different asset categories to move in lockstep for long.

minus your age in stocks assuming you have a high risk tolerance, 110 minus your age (for moderate risk tolerance), and 100 minus your age (low risk). So, a moderate 40-year-old would invest 70 percent in equities (110 – 40) and split the remaining 30 percent between bonds and cash.

2. *What are your objectives?* Here you ponder what you're trying to accomplish by investing, and how much time you have to do so. Your age and the size of your nest egg are major factors. Some people may have several objectives, ranging from buying a home, to college for the kids, to retirement. Perhaps you already are retired and need monthly income in addition to modest growth.

3. *What is your risk tolerance?* For any investment plan to work, you have to stick with it. This involves knowing yourself and pondering how upset you might be if your portfolio lost perhaps a third of its value in a year. If you couldn't tolerate this, you certainly wouldn't want to allocate everything to the stock market. A good understanding of how financial markets and mutual funds work can go a long way toward calming frazzled investor nerves. The questionnaire in Chapter 1 can help determine your risk tolerance.

4. *How big is your nest egg?* Take an inventory of your assets and earnings potential. This can have a major impact on the kind of portfolio you can afford to build. With more money available, you may want to mix in more funds and categories.

5. *How involved do you want to be with your investments?* Assess your enthusiasm level for spending time establishing and rebalancing your portfolio. Are you willing to hone your knowledge of investments, or do you want to keep things as hassle-free as possible?

6. *What is your tax situation?* Your tax bracket can have a major influence on the investments you hold. You need to determine which mutual funds to put in tax-deferred retirement plans and which to leave in ordinary accounts.

This discussion of portfolio building is geared to people who do not make huge changes in their holdings as the market outlook changes. The idea is to draw up an allocation that you can stick with through the years. That's why we suggest looking at it as an all-seasons mix designed to serve you until there is a major change in one or more of the six factors listed above.

A LIFE-CYCLE APPROACH

For most people it makes sense to have a portfolio that gives some representation to each of the three main asset classes. As we've explained, the idea of asset allocation is to avoid making big bets on a particular category such as emerging-market stocks or high-yield bonds. By holding a mix, you can smooth out the ups and downs. The way you allocate depends largely on your age, time horizon, and objectives.

Table 19-1 displays possible asset-class ranges for investors in different stages of life. Of course, these ranges might not be appropriate for everyone in a specific age group, particularly for a person facing unique circumstances. That said, most people in their 20s, 30s, 40s, and even 50s are striving to accumulate capital for retirement. For investors in later age groups, conserving and spending capital become increasingly important.

Incidentally, it's not wise to include the cash in your long-term investment portfolio as a reserve for emergencies or big-ticket expenditures you plan during the next five years. That cash should be kept separate in a savings account that is invested in conservative instruments like money-market and short-term bond funds. The reason for this separation is that cash should play a normal role in your long-term investment portfolio, albeit often a small one. After all, income-oriented investments can provide a modest security blanket by adding stability and toning down the volatility of your stock and bond mix.

In addition, bond holdings are a useful ingredient because they return more than cash but have less volatility than stocks. Equity funds could lose more than 40 percent of their value in a severe bear market, but bond products are unlikely to drop even 10 percent, including interest income.

Stocks play a major role in most portfolios because of their desirable long-term growth potential. Even senior retirees, those in their 80s and 90s, should consider holding at least 10 percent of their wealth in stocks to provide

Table 19-1   Broad Asset-Class Ranges Based on Objectives

Objective	Stage in Life Cycle	Target Ranges		
		Stocks	Bonds	Cash
Maximum gain	Early career	80 - 100%	0 - 10%	0 - 10%
Growth	Mid career	70 - 80	10 - 20	5 - 10
Conservative growth	Late career	60 - 70	15 - 25	5 - 20
Growth and income	Early retirement	50 - 60	15 - 30	10 - 20
Income	Regular retirement	15 - 50	40 - 75	10 - 35

modest appreciation potential, thereby reducing the likelihood that they will outlive their nest eggs. Of course, these individuals should emphasize the more stable stock products, from the equity-income and growth-and-income categories.

Divvying Up Your Stocks

Since stocks should be the cornerstone of your portfolio during asset-building years, it pays to explore how an equity mix can be established. Table 19-2 shows broad-brush guidelines for growth-oriented investors.

Note that the percentages in Table 19-2 relate to your total stock allocation, whereas the numbers in Table 19-1 were percentages of your total nest egg. The rationale for dividing your equity holdings is to achieve a better risk-adjusted return. Different equity groups are less than perfectly correlated with one another, just as stocks don't move in sync with bonds and cash. Thus, one part of your stock collection could be shining while another is barely holding its own. That's the whole idea behind asset allocation.

The stock-category ranges in Table 19-2 are only a starting point, however. You confront a number of other considerations in establishing your equity mix, especially if you're working with a lot of money.

1. *Should you include index funds?* Many managed funds underperform their benchmarks. Besides, active management is more expensive. For these reasons, you may decide to hold a passive equity core, perhaps 25 to 50 percent of your stock allocation.

2. *Growth, value, or both?* It's important to blend your styles, as explained in Chapter 3. Growth and value investing tend to do well at different times. Rather than try to predict which one will be in vogue over the next few years, you might want to include funds that follow both approaches. With a larger portfolio, this is easier to do.

Table 19-2 Divvying Up Your Equity Allocation

Objective	Domestic Market		Non-U.S. Markets	
	Large Cap	Small Cap	Developed	Emerging
Maximum gain	25 - 35%	25 - 35%	25 - 35%	5 - 20%
Growth	35 - 50	20 - 30	20 - 35	0 - 10
Conservative growth	60 - 70	15 - 20	15 - 30	0 - 5
Growth and income	75 - 100	0 - 5	5 - 15	0 - 5
Income	90 - 100	—	0 - 10	—

3. *Do you want some of the more specialized types of stock investments?* You could add a mid-cap fund or perhaps use it in place of a small-stock fund. Conversely, you could step further out on the risk/return limb with a micro-cap fund.

4. *How about international choices?* You may want to mix in a foreign fund that specializes in smaller firms, specific regions, or even single countries. More sophisticated investors may even desire a few single-country closed-end funds or exchange-traded WEBS. Many possibilities exist.

5. *What about gold and real estate?* You may want to include a little gold or real estate in your target mix. This can be done with a specialized mutual fund, as discussed in Chapter 12. Just keep any gold investments to no more than 5 percent of your portfolio, as gold has a poor long-term track record. A real-estate fund would make a more promising choice.

You might want to pass on some categories altogether, such as global or hybrid portfolios. With a mix of domestic and international funds, you probably don't need a global investment anyway. Besides, global funds often alter their ratio of U.S. and foreign holdings in a way that you can't control. With pure foreign-stock funds, you will always have a better idea of your split between U.S. and overseas markets.

The same logic applies to hybrid portfolios, such as balanced, asset-allocation, and funds of funds. These products are more appropriate for people looking for one-stop shopping because they incorporate a mix of asset classes.

Adding Ingredients

If you've got a good-sized portfolio and you have become a fund junkie, there's nothing wrong with spicing up your mix—within reason. Some possible portfolio kickers include:

1. *More volatile sector funds, such as health-care portfolios.* If you target industries that have gone out of favor, you can generate profits by waiting for them to rebound.

2. *Single-country closed-end funds.* You can pick up bargains at deep discounts when investor sentiment has turned negative.

3. *Individual stocks.* There's nothing wrong with complementing your mutual-fund holdings with shares in promising companies. As long as you hang on to stock positions, you can delay paying taxes on any capital gains.

To reap the advantages of asset allocation, you would be wise to limit any money you allocate to the above vehicles to 10 percent or less of your portfolio. The main problem with these spicier investments is that they can cause otherwise calm investors to lose control of their emotions and trade too frequently. In addition, they represent more concentrated bets that may border on speculation.

Divvying Up Your Bonds

Bond funds also come in various flavors. The main distinction is between taxable and tax-free portfolios. Either way, bonds add a dimension of stability, even for people seeking capital appreciation who don't need the monthly income.

Among other combinations, you might consider holding junk-bond funds as well as portfolios of government bonds because the two types of debt fare well under different economic conditions and face different risks. High-yield bonds perform best when the economy is healthy and expanding because the earnings and balance sheets of their issuers improve. Conversely, government bonds can be hit hard by rising interest rates during periods of economic growth.

Then there are foreign-bond funds, which offer the same types of diversification benefits that you find with stocks. However, these investments can be treacherous for a couple of key reasons, including hedging and high expenses. Managers of foreign-bond funds often hedge against exchange-rate risk. Hedging is costly and sometimes impairs currency diversification. It's safe to say that bond-fund managers hedge more than their equity counterparts. Also, foreign-bond funds charge higher expenses than you would find on most domestic-bond portfolios. Since expenses weigh especially heavily on bond returns, this can be a major drawback.

REBALANCING TO YOUR TARGETS

Once you have chosen asset classes, you need to determine their respective weights. For your strategy to be effective, you should adhere to these targets for at least 5 to 10 years, or until your situation changes. Resist the temptation to wander too far from your long-run weightings. Asset allocation needs discipline to work.

Of course, your actual portfolio composition will change modestly with movements in stock and bond prices, and the additional investments that you make, perhaps through a dollar-cost averaging program. Or, if you're retired, you might need to withdraw income and principal periodically. To correct for these influences, you simply rebalance the mix back to the original targets as necessary, perhaps once a year or so, or after the market has moved sharply.

Avoiding "Risk Creep"

The purpose of rebalancing your mix is to keep your risk exposure in line with your original allocation. Failing to do so may lead to so-called "risk creep." This phenomenon can occur when appreciation in one category causes it to become significantly overweighted relative to another. Stock funds frequently start to crowd out bond and money-market holdings, which don't grow as much over time. When the stock market eventually heads south, as it will sooner or later, your portfolio will take a bigger hit if equities were substantially overweighted. Remember that rebalancing features an automatic buy-low, sell-high mechanism.

Since many small adjustments complicate recordkeeping and can trigger taxable gains, it's best to defer reallocations until the percentages deviate sufficiently from their targets.

There are three ways to rebalance a portfolio:

1. You can sell an appropriate amount of an overweighted asset and transfer the proceeds into a neglected category.

2. You can add cash to an underweighted class.

3. You can reinvest distributions from one fund into another.

Table 19-3 illustrates shifting values and weights in a growth-oriented portfolio. In this case, the investor's domestic stock holdings start to overwhelm the foreign equities, bonds, and cash. Since the new weights differ significantly from the original target allocations, it's time to rebalance.

Table 19-4 illustrates the rebalancing process. The "dollar changes" column shows the amounts of each fund that must be bought or sold to restore

Table 19-3   Shifting Values and Weights

Fund Category	Initial Allocation		Unbalanced Portfolio	
	Value	Weight	Value	Weight
Large domestic equity	$30,000	30%	$55,000	35%
Small domestic equity	20,000	20	42,000	27
Foreign equity	30,000	30	35,000	23
Bond	10,000	10	12,000	8
Money market	10,000	10	11,000	7
Totals	$100,000	100%	$155,000	100%

Table 19-4   Rebalancing to Original Target Weights

Fund Category	Dollar Changes	Rebalanced Portfolio Value	Weight
Large domestic equity	-$8,500	$46,500	30%
Small domestic equity	-11,000	31,000	20
Foreign equity	+11,500	46,500	30
Bond	+3,500	15,500	10
Money market	+4,500	15,500	10
Totals	-0-	$155,000	100%

this investor's target weights. Rebalancing essentially prompts you to lighten up on funds that have appreciated and to invest more in those that have dropped. It's a contrarian approach that forces you to sell what is in favor and buy what is not.

Rebalancing plans have two potential drawbacks, however:

1. *You might incur a tax liability when you sell appreciated funds.* To avoid this, you might choose to rebalance gradually by reinvesting distributions from your hot funds into your laggards. Or you can channel all new investment dollars into the lagging funds. Of course, if your investments are held within a tax-deferred retirement plan or variable annuity, selling presents no such problems.

2. *By scaling back on winners, you curtail your potential for further gains.* This can be a problem during an extended bull market. Nevertheless, the adjustments called for by an asset-allocation plan are generally modest and make much more sense than an aggressive market-timing program, which might prompt you to abandon stocks completely.

HOW MUCH FLEXIBILITY?

The illustration in Table 19-3 assumed fixed weights. As the word "fixed" implies, the targets generally will not change over time. Conversely, with flexible weights you can vary your allocations based on current market conditions and a forecast of future trends. If you use flexible weights, it is prudent to set upper and lower limits to form a range. Table 19-5 illustrates asset-allocation boundaries for the scenario in Table 19-3. Note that small domestic stocks and foreign equities are slightly overweighted and underweighted,

Table 19-5   Asset-Allocation Boundaries

Fund Category	Target Range	Present Allocation
Large domestic equity	25 - 35%	35%
Small domestic equity	15 - 25	27
Foreign equity	25 - 35	23
Bond	5 - 15	8
Money market	5 - 15	7

respectively. This means rebalancing is called for, but perhaps on a gradual basis because the deviations are not excessive.

Don't build in too much flexibility, however, because that would defeat the purpose of asset allocation, which is to stick with a reasonable all-seasons mixture. You don't want to become a de facto market-timer, making big bets on the direction of stocks or interest rates. All anyone knows for certain about the future returns of stocks, bonds, or cash is that they will fluctuate.

There's no magic formula for adjusting your asset-class weights to conform with the near-term market outlook. So it's not surprising to see plenty of disagreement when you study brokerage recommendations. *The Wall Street Journal* tracks asset-allocation recommendations of a group of major brokerages on a quarterly basis. You will observe that the pros can differ significantly on their recommended stock/bond/cash mixes, and the advice from a given firm can change dramatically from one quarter to the next with varying economic and market conditions. Don't get caught up in the confusion. Since the future is unknowable, you're better off sticking with an all-seasons mix based on ascertainable factors such as your age, personal financial situation, and risk tolerance.

That said, there's nothing wrong with a moderate amount of fine-tuning. Ranges give you some "wiggle" room. For instance, you can move to the upper end of your foreign-stock weighting if you feel particularly bullish on that asset class. But be careful not to drop below the lower bound, even if the outlook calls for caution, since stocks are a long-term commitment. Another benefit of using ranges instead of fixed weightings is that you may find yourself making fewer trades, which can simplify your tax situation and record-keeping.

AVOIDING BONDS

Do bonds always have to be in the equation to allocate your assets effectively? Not necessarily. You can made a good case for sticking exclusively with the right mix of stocks and cash. It might even simplify your financial life a bit.

Even without any bonds, you still can get a good long-run return provided you have a generous stock allocation. Unlike bond investments, the amount you have invested in cash can't decline in value when interest rates rise because a money-market fund bears no interest-rate risk. A climate of increasing rates is bearish for both stocks and bonds but will actually boost returns on money-market instruments. Yet another reason to favor cash over bonds is that redeeming shares from a money fund won't trigger a taxable event because these investments maintain a stable NAV of $1. This could be attractive if you want to use a flexible weighting plan.

If you choose to avoid bond funds altogether, make sure you find a money-market portfolio with a very low expense ratio, preferably below 0.50 percent. That way, you will squeeze out a bit more income from your low-yielding cash reserves.

A COLLEGE PORTFOLIO

As every parent knows, the cost of a college education can easily top $20,000 a year, especially when a child is going to an out-of-town private institution. For years, college costs have been growing at a rate higher than inflation, with little moderation in sight. Thus, proper planning is essential. Designing an appropriate asset allocation for a child's higher education largely depends on how old the child is when you begin. Obviously, the earlier you start, the more effectively time can work for you. Figure 19-1 contains some age-specific guidelines.

A simple way to make gifts to your child is through either the Uniform Gifts to Minors Act (UGMA) or Uniform Transfers to Minors Act (UTMA), depending on your state's law. The best time to begin an automatic monthly investment program is when your child is an infant. As indicated in Figure 19-1, you can stress maximum capital appreciation in these early years. Broadly diversified index funds make excellent choices because they offer low costs, the assurance of doing as well as the market, and tax efficiency. As discussed in Chapter 17, the Taxpayer Relief Act of 1997 created a new type of IRA designed to help pay for a child's higher education.

The important thing to remember about a college savings program is to change your investment mix as the child grows older. You need to shift to more conservative assets when the child reaches his or her early teens. When your child reaches high school, you probably should shift to an income-oriented portfolio because there is less time to recoup any losses. Ultimately, by the time college expenses begin, you will want to own nothing but money-market and short-term bond funds.

Figure 19-1   Guidelines for College Portfolios*

Objective	Age Range	Comments
Maximum growth	Up to 5 years	Equity funds should be given top priority because there's plenty of time.
Growth	6 - 12 years	Growth is still important but you want to become more conservative now.
Income	13 - 17 years	Shift from conservative equity funds into fixed-income funds with short maturities 4 or 5 years before college.
Capital preservation	18 and beyond	Keep cash needed for the first year's costs in a money fund. Hold cash needed for remaining years in a short-term bond fund.

*Assuming an entrance age of 18.

MANAGING YOUR NEST EGG IN RETIREMENT

People are living longer and often retiring earlier. This means that the typical retiree needs to balance income requirements with some capital appreciation to safeguard his or her wealth from the corrosive effect of inflation. Retirement can be a lengthy phase, perhaps lasting three decades, so a person's asset allocation can be expected to change during this period. Here is the basic pattern:

1. *Early retirement.* People who stop working at relatively young ages will need income from their investments because they won't be able to receive Social Security retirement benefits until age 62. They also require plenty of appreciation potential because they may live for three or more decades.

2. *Regular retirement.* People who retire with Social Security payments still may require both investment income and appreciation if they hope to maintain the same lifestyle they enjoyed in their working

years. That said, a person's income and capital-preservation needs rise with age, while growth requirements lessen.

The kinds of stock and bond funds suitable for retirement likely would be different from those appropriate at younger ages. Funds holding U.S. blue-chip stocks should receive the greatest weight, primarily those in the equity-income and growth-and-income categories, but you might own little or nothing in the way of small-stock investments. Stakes in international or domestic mid-cap portfolios might be suitable in modest amounts. The same can be said of real estate or utility sector funds because of their income potential.

As for your fixed-income allocation, consider intermediate- rather than long-term bond funds. The former can be expected to return about 80 percent of what you could realize from the latter, but with a lot less interest-rate risk. Municipal-bond funds are popular with many retirees, as are mortgage-backed securities, such as Ginnie Maes, because they provide high monthly income with relatively low volatility. Small stakes in junk-bond funds can round out your portfolio.

AT THE CLOSE

Your asset allocation is the most important decision you make as a mutual-fund investor. Choosing the right categories weighs even more heavily than the actual funds you pick. The idea is to select an asset-class mix that suits your needs and temperament, then stick with it for at least 5 to 10 years or until your situation changes.

It's wise to rebalance your portfolio periodically to stay on target and avoid possible risk creep. As a rule, check your allocation at least once a year or after the market has made a substantial move. Then make changes as necessary.

An asset mix that's designed to weather all types of market conditions will help you maintain discipline and enable you to feel more secure during tumultuous periods. In the long run, it's the performance of your overall portfolio that counts, not the inevitable short-term losses of individual funds. With adequate diversification, gains in one area help offset losses in another.

CHAPTER 20

Dealing with Your Fund Family

You can still find good solo funds, but families are what the mutual-fund business is all about these days. Small operations often have trouble gathering sufficient assets to realize economies of scale, which translate into lower costs for shareholders and higher profits for the management company. The number of fund complexes has grown from a little more than 100 in 1979 to more than 400 today, according to the Investment Company Institute. However, the biggest families have become more dominant, and the trend is toward larger groups, based on the economic rationale of building assets and thus boosting profits.

The ideal fund family would have four attributes: a wide selection of portfolios, consistent top performers in most categories, rock-bottom expenses, and a broad range of high-quality services—including the friendliest, most knowledgeable telephone reps imaginable. If you could find this ideal family, there would be no need to keep any money anywhere else. Needless to say, you probably won't find one superior group that makes the grade in all respects, although there are certainly several first-class outfits.

At the bare minimum, most families offer at least one money-market fund, one bond portfolio, and one stock fund. In fact, some groups have two dozen or more choices. The largest family, Fidelity Investments, boasts more than 250 funds and over $450 billion in assets. The Vanguard Group, the second-largest family, offers about 100 funds and has more than $250 billion in assets.

In picking your first or primary family, select a group that features at least one reasonably good choice in each of the following six areas: investment-grade bond, tax-exempt bond, growth stock, growth-and-income stock, small stock, and international equity. A good way to begin is to put your dollars in the family's money fund. Then, gradually move cash into riskier portfolios as you become more familiar with them.

Should you stay exclusively with one family? Yes, if you wish to make life simpler. Eventually, though, you may want to branch out to a few other families, especially as your holdings become larger and more diversified. You might look at smaller, more specialized groups or even solo funds that have something special to offer. The advantage of going with several management firms is that you can pick and choose the best of what each has to offer.

GETTING STARTED

When buying no-load mutual funds, you can either invest directly with the fund company or open an account with a discount brokerage. This chapter focuses on dealing directly with the company, and Chapter 21 explains the brokerage route, which offers convenient access to many different families.

Titling Accounts

When filling out a fund company's account registration form, the first thing you will be asked is how you want the account registered. For non-retirement holdings, there are two basic forms of ownership: separate and joint. These allow for several forms of registration, as identified below. Selecting the correct form of registration is important because it can help smooth the handling of your estate. If in doubt about the following designations, consult an attorney or your fund group's estate-planning specialist.

- *Individual*: This establishes a separate account for yourself. When you die, this account becomes a part of your estate, and the assets are distributed according to the terms of your will or trust.

- *Joint Tenants with Right of Survivorship*: This is the most common form of joint account but not necessarily a good one. Each owner has an equal and undivided interest in the account. As such, each tenant can transact account business without the other's consent—for better or worse. The arrangement is commonly used by husband and wife but also can be extended to children, parents, and so on. When one owner dies, the entire account transfers to the survivor without probate. That's what "with right of survivorship" means.

- *Tenants in Common:* Unlike joint tenants with right of survivorship, the co-owners in this arrangement aren't required to hold equal interests. Another difference is that when one owner dies, that person's assets are disposed of according to instructions contained in his or her will. Tenancy in common is not widely used and requires an underlying legal document specifying each party's ownership interest. You should keep a copy of this document with your will.

- *Gift or Transfer to Minor:* This allows an adult to buy shares for a minor child, naming the parent or someone else as "custodian." These accounts can be established under either the Uniform Gifts to Minors Act (UGMA) or Uniform Transfers to Minors Act (UTMA), depending on your state of residence. Keep in mind that gifts are irrevocable, and that the child gains control over the account when he or she reaches the age of majority.

- *Trust:* This is a legal arrangement whereby property is held by one party, the "trustee," for the benefit of another, the "beneficiary." Many types of trust are possible. A revocable "living trust" is an increasingly common vehicle that allows you to change key features like your choice of beneficiary—or even cancel the document altogether while you're still alive. One advantage of trusts over gifts, especially when dealing with immature or spendthrift heirs, is that you can stipulate conditions for how and when the account's assets will be distributed to them.

- *Corporation, Partnership, or Other Entity:* Many possibilities exist for companies or other organizations, including nonprofit institutions. For these forms of ownership, a taxpayer ID is required by the IRS.

The Perils of Joint Tenancy

As noted above, joint tenancy with right of survivorship is a common way to register mutual-fund accounts. Many couples feel secure using it without a will. They shouldn't. You still need a will to cover special circumstances, such as the risk, albeit small, of both you and your spouse dying together. And in the more typical case, when one spouse dies first, a will is needed to designate how the property will be disposed when the survivor passes away. You also might require a will for other reasons, such as to provide for the care and financial oversight of minor children.

Joint tenancy can complicate things for blended families where there are offspring from previous marriages. Furthermore, your spouse can sell assets without your knowledge or approval. A parent, child, or other party can do the same if listed as co-owner. Similarly, if your joint tenant goes bankrupt or loses a lawsuit, creditors can go after the account's assets. Be aware that a joint-tenancy relationship supersedes any instructions to the contrary in a will. That means your property would pass to your joint tenant at your death, even if you have indicated otherwise in a will. Other pitfalls also exist, so you need to think carefully about using this form of ownership. It's smart to consult an estate-planning attorney about registering your accounts, particularly if you have substantial assets.

Advantages of Community Property

Married couples should consider holding title to their mutual funds in community property form, if they live in a state that allows this form of ownership. Arizona, California, Idaho, Louisiana, Nevada, New Mexico, Texas, Washington, and Wisconsin all do. Community property refers to property acquired by the effort of either spouse during their marriage while living in a community-property state. Each partner has an equal interest in the assets. Property obtained by only one spouse (through gift or inheritance, for example) is not considered community property.

When one party dies, the survivor is entitled to one-half of the account balance. The other half passes in accordance with the will of the deceased spouse. Community property receives favorable capital-gains tax treatment on appreciated assets. The cost basis is "stepped up" to the fair market value at the date of death. The basis in an asset is the amount on which capital-gains taxes are not due, so a higher figure is preferable. This stepped-up basis applies to all community property, not just to the half included in the deceased spouse's estate.

If you live in a community-property state and choose to establish a community-property account with your spouse, simply indicate on your mutual-fund registration form that your joint account should be listed as "community property" rather than "joint tenants with right of survivorship." Some enlightened states such as Arizona also allow a relatively new form of ownership called "community property with right of survivorship." It offers the favorable tax treatment along with a probate-free transfer of assets. But be forewarned: Some fund groups still are not familiar with this option and might resist your using it.

SHAREHOLDER SERVICES

When choosing among fund groups, performance may be the single factor that most sways your decision. But the group you select should also have reasonable expenses and the kinds of services you will use. Performance and expenses have been dealt with earlier. The following pages provide greater details on the full range of services available.

All the big fund companies are paying more attention to this end of the business. They know people simply won't tolerate incapable telephone reps, poorly written reports, or other signs of inferior service. Figure 20-1 lists the services you need to be familiar with. Obviously, some features are more important than others.

To find out what's offered, consult the shareholder-services sections of the prospectus. These sections generally are found near the back of the brochure. Different groups present the information in various ways, but all the facts you will need to get started are there. You can learn the procedures for opening a new account, purchasing additional shares, and exchanging and redeeming shares. And depending on the company, you might find out about additional features such as asset-allocation plans that tell you where to put your money, periodic newsletters, telephone devices for the hearing impaired, local investor centers, personalized attention for large accounts, managed accounts for large investors, and discount-brokerage services.

The prospectus also spells out other, related information that you may need to deal effectively with your group. For example, it explains details on dividend and capital-gains distributions, limitations on fund switching, minimum account balances that you must maintain, and any special conditions placed on especially large redemptions. If you need further clarification after going through the prospectus, you can always contact a shareholder rep.

Figure 20-1 Mutual-Fund Shareholder Services

---

1. Retirement plans
2. Automatic investment
3. Automatic reinvestment
4. Transactions by phone or computer
5. Check writing
6. Systematic withdrawals
7. Periodic account and tax information
8. Shareholder reports
9. Information by phone or computer
10. Educational literature and newsletters

Retirement Plans

The prospectus tells whether the fund group allows investments in IRAs, SEP-IRAs, and profit-sharing and money-purchase pension plans. Make sure the plans you want are available. Bigger families typically offer the full gamut of retirement vehicles. Smaller ones often do not.

Be aware of annual custodial fees. Charges for mutual-fund IRAs are typically modest, but they can add up quickly if you own several portfolios. For instance, one family might charge $10 for each portfolio held. Conversely, the IRA fee might phase out once your account reaches some minimum threshold such as $5,000.

It's worth noting that fund companies usually lower their required initial investment for an IRA. For example, the normal minimum might be $3,000 but only $1,000 for an IRA. In this sense, many funds are more accessible through retirement accounts.

Automatic-Investment Plans

Often the simplest strategies are the best and most profitable. A surefire way to make more money with a good fund is simply to get more dollars into the pool working for you. Automatic-investment plans allow you to invest a fixed sum periodically, say $100 a month, in a designated fund. The amount typically would be debited to your bank account. To establish this program, you complete an authorization form and send it to the fund company along with a blank check marked "void." Virtually all groups offer automatic investing. Some families also let you divert the money directly from your paycheck, with your employer's consent.

Automatic-investment plans offer an ideal way to dollar-cost average by making saving a simple, ongoing process and by encouraging discipline. If you don't see the money before it's invested, you're less apt to miss it. Since they're automatic and ongoing, the plans also can encourage investment in depressed markets when many people don't want to have anything to do with stocks. This, of course, is the best time to buy. However, you can change or terminate the service at any time.

As an incentive for new shareholders, many fund companies will waive their customary dollar minimum if you sign up for their automatic-investment plan. That way, you can start gradually with just $50 or $100 monthly.

Automatic Reinvestment

Virtually all funds allow you to reinvest dividend and capital-gains distributions in additional shares. Typically, you can select one of the following three options:

- Reinvest both dividends and capital gains.

- Receive dividends in cash but reinvest the gains.

- Receive both dividends and gains in cash.

The reinvestment service is an excellent way to build wealth through the magic of compounding. Over time, a large proportion of your profits may derive from this effort. Most funds allow you to reinvest both forms of distribution into additional shares at NAV, without paying any sales charge. Thus, this is an economical, efficient service—and one that's not always available with individual stocks.

Some funds go a step further and allow you to reinvest the distributions of one fund into another portfolio within the group. Suppose you are in the ABC Family, and have a large investment in the income fund. You might reinvest all payouts from it into ABC's growth-stock product. This type of service offers great flexibility, and it's a relatively painless way to diversify into more speculative products.

Transactions by Phone or Computer

You can buy or sell shares in a fund by calling a telephone representative, who will instruct your bank account to be debited or credited, assuming you have already established this service with both the bank and fund company. Phone transactions generally are subject to minimum dollar amounts. Purchases may be subject to a maximum.

Keep in mind that whenever you buy shares in a fund for the first time, you are supposed to have the prospectus in hand. If not, the company will process the order and mail it with the first transaction confirmation. Even so, it's a good idea to obtain prospectuses for all the portfolios in the family that you could conceivably want to own. More groups are combining information on several portfolios into a single document. For example, they might list all the international funds in one prospectus.

Transactions by phone are available through banks that are members of the Automated Clearing House (ACH) network. Generally, you will be buying at the next day's price if you place your order before 4 P.M. Eastern Time, unless you prearranged to have money wired from the bank and it reaches the fund company before the market closes—in which case you would receive today's price. You will be billed by the bank for the cost of the wire.

Usually, you don't need to move all that fast when investing in a mutual fund, but suppose you're in a hurry for some reason. Many companies will let you open a new account without having an application on file, provided you submit one promptly. To do so, you need to call the group, provide certain information about yourself, obtain an account number, and give your purchase instruction. Then, tell your bank to wire the money to your new fund account. The shares would be priced on the day your bank wire is received. It's wise to have a prospectus in hand when you do this, and the telephone rep will generally ask if you do. It doesn't make sense to jump into a fund without some familiarity with it.

Many larger fund complexes operate 24-hour "transaction lines." These enable you to determine account balances, exchange money between portfolios, and, in some cases, make purchases and redemptions through a bank account without speaking to a representative. You use a PIN number to access your account with a touch-tone phone.

Increasingly, fund groups are offering online transaction capabilities, account information, prospectuses, and other literature for clients equipped with a personal computer and a modem. One benefit of using a computer is that you can pull up the entire history of your account. Chapter 24 explores the various ways in which computers can be used by mutual-fund investors.

The "exchange privilege" allows you to transfer money between funds within a particular family by phone or computer. It's the quickest, most efficient way to sell shares. Suppose you want to redeem $5,000 from a stock portfolio. You can simply switch that balance to a money fund, then draw a $5,000 check on the latter. Usually, you can switch for free, although some families charge $5, and a few charge $10. In addition, there may be a limit on the number of exchanges you can make in a year. Families frown on hyperactive switchers, because when investors shuttle big sums between different portfolios, this poses obvious management problems and can hurt other shareholders. Check with your group about the number of allowable switches.

It's important to recognize that an exchange between funds is a taxable event unless the money is held in a retirement account. The reason it's taxable is that you're selling one fund and buying another, generating a gain or loss on the investment sold.

Redemptions through the mail are time consuming and require more effort on your part. That's why proportionately fewer shareholders are doing them these days. Your redemption letter must include the pertinent details, and you may need to have your signature guaranteed. And since a number of days will elapse before your shares are sold, you risk a falling NAV during this period.

Check Writing

Typically, you can write checks against money-market and bond funds, but not against stock portfolios. Many groups impose a minimum of $100 to $500 on each check. This service can be an efficient way to redeem part or all of your shares, or to pay large bills. Many families will return canceled checks, an added benefit that may help you with recordkeeping.

One caveat involves taxes: If you write a check on any bond fund, including municipal portfolios, you likely will trigger a taxable event. That's because bond funds have fluctuating net asset values. With each check, you're basically redeeming a portion of your shares. This would not be a concern with money-market funds, which maintain a constant price of $1.

Withdrawal Plans

Many groups offer voluntary, systematic programs to take out money. To use them, you need to have a certain minimum amount invested, usually $10,000, and must withdraw a specific minimum, say, $50. Withdrawals can be made monthly, bimonthly, quarterly, semiannually, or annually. You can have the check sent to your home, your bank account, or to another person. You can change the amount of the withdrawal or terminate the plan whenever you wish.

The advantage of setting up a withdrawal plan with a stock fund is that your remaining balance can continue to compound at a higher rate, allowing you to draw out cash over a longer time horizon. But if you expect to take all your money out within just a few years, you are probably better off using a bond fund, to minimize the risk of losing principal. Chapter 22 takes a closer look at withdrawal plans.

Periodic Statements and Tax Information

One advantage of a mutual fund is that it can greatly reduce the amount of paperwork you need to compile. It's certainly a lot easier to keep records for a single fund than it would be for many individual stocks. Still, the paperwork still can be a headache if you're not well organized and misplace or lose statements.

Your fund company will supply you with various documents. Five common documents are described in the following list.

1. *Confirmation statements.* These list details of each transaction, including purchases, sales, and exchanges. You should retain all confirmation statements—at least until you receive the year-end account-activity summary—as they contain information needed to figure your taxable gains or losses.

2. *Account-activity statements.* These updates are sent out on a monthly, quarterly, or annual cycle, depending on the fund type. You also will receive one after each distribution. For a bond fund that pays monthly dividends, you would get one every month, reflecting year-to-date activity. The year-end summaries list purchases, redemptions, distributions, and all other transactions. Fund companies usually are very efficient and accurate, but it can't hurt to check for discrepancies between your confirmations and activity statements.

If you own more than one fund in the same family, the group might list your proportionate investments in different funds, which can be used to figure your asset allocation. Some statements, such as those provided by T. Rowe Price, even show the percentages invested in stocks, bonds, and cash as well as the percentages in each portfolio. You can compare your current allocation with the breakdowns on previous statements to see how your mix has changed.

3. *Form 1099-DIV.* This lists the amounts and tax status of income and capital-gains distributions paid to you throughout the prior year. Typically, they're mailed in late January. The Form 1099-DIV provides information you need to report on your tax return, even if you reinvested distributions in additional shares. Funds holding foreign stocks or bonds also may report any foreign taxes paid on your 1099-DIV, allowing you to deduct those taxes or claim a credit for them.

4. *Form 1099-B.* You receive this form, typically by early February, if you sold shares or wrote checks. It contains a copy of the information reported to the IRS on your sales or exchanges during the prior year. You use this statement to determine your taxable gains or losses.

5. *Form 1099-R.* This contains information on distributions from retirement accounts such as IRAs and annuities. Any federal taxes withheld are listed. Fund companies also mail this form in January but you would get one only if you received a retirement-plan distribution.

People who have been with a fund for many years may find they have lost some of their records. If this happens to you, don't hesitate to contact the company. You might have to pay something to have the firm dig up this information, but usually the cost is modest.

Shareholder Reports

Fund companies must send you at least an annual and semiannual report, although many also report quarterly. The yearly and six-month documents contain a statement by management as well as a list of the current portfolio holdings and changes. Quarterly reports typically offer less information. Morningstar assigns a letter grade—ranging from A to F—to each company's reports. The ratings reflect factors like candor, substance, timeliness, and organization. A high rating may indicate greater emphasis on shareholder services, according to Morningstar.

Information by Phone or Computer

You can obtain current price and yield data by telephoning fund companies, most of which provide toll-free numbers. Usually, you must call during East Coast business hours, although many complexes offer 24-hour phone lines, or at least extended hours. Fidelity offers different prices each hour on its 36 sector portfolios. Otherwise, mutual funds are priced once a day, at the market's close. Thus, it makes sense to make your purchases, sales, or switches shortly before the market's close. That way, you'll have a better idea whether the fund's price is up or down that day. Even if you place your transaction in the morning, you still get the market-closing NAV.

Telephone reps at no-load and many load companies will answer questions about your account, and they can provide information about the funds offered by the complex. They also may be able to offer help with various questions on such topics as retirement plans, risk, and managing investments. However, they steer away from giving specific investment advice or recommendations.

Incidentally, you may encounter some delays when you call a fund company. This could be a particular problem for a smaller yet successful family that is experiencing rapid growth. Good times to call are generally early in the morning and later in the afternoon. Lunch time on the East Coast is usually the worst time, and you might have trouble during the hour prior to the market's close.

Many fund complexes have established Web sites, providing easy access to current information by computer users. You can get up-to-date account values and summaries of recent activity without having to place a call or wait for your next statement. You can track the performances of funds you own and view your recent asset allocation. Some Web sites also include online "calculators" that let you compute future investment balances, retirement needs, college costs, and so on.

Educational Literature and Newsletters

Most fund groups also provide educational literature to shareholders. This includes pamphlets or guides covering topics such as retirement planning, fixed-income investing, international investing, variable annuities, and even bear markets. Some families also distribute a periodic newsletter with news and performance data on the funds, and perhaps a manager profile or two.

AT THE CLOSE

In dealing with your fund company, make sure it offers the services you want. Popular programs include automatic-investment plans, dividend reinvesting, retirement accounts, and check writing.

Once you sign up for these services, check to make sure they're working as you would expect. If there's a problem, resolve it promptly. With telephone switching in particular, you don't want to hit a snag the first time you really need to use it.

Also, make sure your holdings are titled properly. The way you register an account will determine to whom your assets will pass at death. In particular, you might want to rethink using "joint tenants with right of survivorship" if you currently are doing so.

CHAPTER 21

Fund "Supermarkets" and Investment Advisers

One-stop shopping has become popular with busy investors on tight schedules. Many people buy mutual funds from an assortment of families at their favorite brokerage. Fund-family ties and loyalties are not as strong as they once were. The financial "supermarket" arrangement allows people to cherry pick the best funds from different groups, with a minimum of hassle. The same people who buy their mutual funds from brokerages might also own some stocks or closed-end funds in the same account.

The great bull market of the 1980s and 1990s has made many Americans wealthier; at the same time, the financial world has grown more complex. This has created an ever-increasing thirst for investment knowledge and, in many cases, professional advice. Financial supermarkets cater to people who feel comfortable making their own investment decisions. Still, a large number of people continue to seek help in a more traditional manner, through full-service brokerages. This chapter also provides guidance for obtaining advice if you want it.

THE SUPERMARKET CONCEPT

All told, several thousand no-load and low-commission funds from several hundred families are available at no transaction costs through more than a dozen discount brokerages such as Charles Schwab, Fidelity, and Jack White. The idea of offering a no-transaction-fee smorgasbord was introduced by Schwab in 1991. Since then, many other discounters have instituted similar programs and the competition has intensified, benefiting the consumer. As investors have become more computer-literate, many discounters have made themselves accessible through PCs and are offering online trading.

Discounters offer two basic programs: no-transaction fee (NTF) funds, and portfolios that can be bought at a fee. With the latter, a fee applies to both purchases and sales. Most people obviously are more interested in the no-cost alternative. Figure 21-1 lists discount brokerages that offer mutual-fund programs.

The fees and other details of trading mutual funds differ. For instance, most discounters limit the amount of buying and selling you can do. To get free switching privileges, you might be required to hold a fund for more than 90 days—otherwise you are charged for the sale. By contrast, there are no such limits on transaction-fee funds because you pay for each switch. In addition, the lists of NTF funds differ among firms, and it's common to see changes in the assortment of portfolios offered at individual discounters. Fortunately, most have been increasing their lineups. You obviously want to deal with a brokerage that has the widest selection of NTF funds and families.

For transaction-fee funds, minimum costs range from about $25 to $45 per trade. As the size of your trade increases, the fee percentage goes down. Fee schedules differ among firms, so you have to shop around. For the most part, transaction fees, if any, are fairly reasonable, particularly if you deal in

Figure 21-1
Selected Discount Brokerages Offering Mutual-Fund Supermarkets

Broker	Phone Number	Broker	Phone Number
AccuTrade	800-882-4887	National Discount Brokers	800-888-3999
Barry Murphy	800-221-2111	PC Financial Network	800-825-5723
Charles Schwab	800-435-4000	T. Rowe Price Discount	800-638-5660
Fidelity Brokerage Services	800-544-8666	Scudder Brokerage Services	800-700-0820
Jack White	800-233-3411	USAA Brokerage Services	800-531-8628
Kennedy, Cabot	800-252-0090	Vanguard Discount	800-992-8327
Lombard Brokerage	800-688-3462	Waterhouse Securities	800-934-4443
Muriel Siebert	800-872-0711	York Securities	800-221-3154

large dollar amounts of $10,000 or more. Another key determinant of cost is whether or not the fund has a load.

Do you want to buy or sell your fund at today's price? If so, keep in mind that many no-load funds require that you place a trade by 2:30 P.M. Eastern Time to get that day's NAV. But exceptions do exist. In particular, if you're trading with Schwab or Fidelity, the cut-off time for their proprietary funds is 4 P.M. Eastern Time. Because cut-off times vary, it's important to check with your firm.

How can discounters afford to offer NTF programs? The answer lies in dealings between brokerages and fund companies. Discounters charge fund groups a distribution fee of 25 to 35 basis points a year, equal to $25 to $35 for each $10,000 in total assets held. In addition, the programs attract new customers, so a discounter could reap other business from one-stop shoppers. That is, a person might want to hold some stocks, bonds, or closed-end funds in their accounts as well as mutual funds. And during troubled markets, when people switch from stock funds to cash, they typically will have to use the money fund offered by the discounter, allowing the firm to generate management fees.

How do mutual funds benefit? A brokerage's program can offer a way for small, obscure families to gain visibility. If the fund has a good track record, this will become apparent to a wide group of investors, perhaps allowing it to attract a phenomenal inflow of new cash. In addition, the discounter will take care of such details as sending customers literature, answering their questions, and servicing their accounts. This results in savings for the fund company.

Pros and Cons for Investors

By keeping your funds with a discounter, you enjoy a number of potential advantages, in addition to being able to buy and sell at no cost. These benefits include the following:

1. *Consolidating records.* With a single brokerage, recordkeeping for your various funds and other investments gets condensed onto one monthly statement, which greatly simplifies the paperwork.

2. *Avoiding multiple custodial fees.* A single account is especially advantageous for IRA investors, who can avoid the overlapping fees that would otherwise result from maintaining investments at different complexes.

3. *Moving from family to family.* Transferring cash among fund groups requires time and effort. With a discounter, you can readily sell one fund and buy another in a different family on the same day.

Rebalancing your portfolio to your target asset-class weights need not be a chore.

4. *Making tax swaps easily.* Because switches are simple, it's no problem to lock in deductible capital losses where appropriate. You can claim a tax loss on an aggressive-growth fund in Family A by selling it and then immediately purchasing a comparable portfolio in Family B. Since you are buying a different fund—regardless of how similar it might be—the transaction would not be considered a wash sale by the IRS.

5. *Borrowing to boost returns.* You can tap your margin account if you need money for a brief period. Your cost would be far lower than it would for a credit-card loan. You also can borrow cash in this manner to leverage your holdings when you expect prices will rally. You can't use margin if dealing directly with a family. However, margin accounts have their dangers, as we will explain.

What are the disadvantages of fund supermarkets? Frankly, it's hard to find many. On balance discounters provide a useful service, although a few pitfalls, such as the following, may exist.

- *The number of NTF funds offered by any discounter is limited.* While the bigger supermarkets make available a wide selection, you may not find a particular portfolio that you're seeking. Some people maintain accounts at two discounters so they can have a broader range of choices.

- *Supermarkets raise fund costs.* This is probably true, but you get a valuable service in return. Besides, people who buy NTF funds direct from a family generally also would incur any higher costs and thus subsidize their counterparts in the supermarket. Of course, if an NTF program helps a small family amass more assets, the per-share costs may drop as a result of economies of scale. But this happens only if the fees are based on a sliding scale. It's worth noting that some new funds might add a 12b-1 fee to cover their eventual participation in discounter programs.

- *You may be tempted to trade excessively.* The ease with which you can buy and sell funds can prompt some people to hop in and out of investments more than they should. A long-term buy-and-hold strategy works best, unless there is a definite reason to bail out.

- *You may be tempted to speculate on margin.* Admittedly, this isn't a problem for most individuals, but those with speculative tendencies could succumb to the lure of fast profits.

THE PERILS OF MARGIN

You can buy most mutual funds held in your taxable account on margin when you deal with a discounter. Borrowing against a brokerage portfolio is definitely risky and not recommended under normal circumstances. Margin accounts work the same way with mutual funds as they do with stocks and closed-end funds.

Specifically, you can leverage your investment by borrowing up to 50 percent of the cost of your purchase. The brokerage loans you money at a rate that fluctuates with the going level of interest rates. This charge is based on the broker "call money" rate, which is quoted daily in the "Money Rates" box in *The Wall Street Journal*. Your broker typically charges you a somewhat higher amount. Margin interest can be deducted from investment income for tax purposes.

A double-edged sword, margin magnifies gains and losses. Suppose Joe Speculator wants to purchase 10,000 shares of Fund A, a volatile sector portfolio, at an NAV of $8 using 50-percent margin. The total cost of his position is $80,000, half of which is borrowed. Joe's equity in the account is $40,000, the minimum amount of cash he must come up with initially. Table 21-1 illustrates Joe's initial position. We're assuming he holds no other investments with his discounter (to keep the arithmetic simple).

As noted, Joe's *equity* equals the value of Fund A minus the amount owed the broker or $40,000 ($80,000 – $40,000). Initially, his stake is 50 percent of the $80,000 value. Now assume that the fund falls 25 percent from $8 to an NAV of $6. Ignoring any accrued interest liability, Joe's equity would plunge 50 percent, from $40,000 to $20,000. Table 21-2 shows his new balance sheet.

Table 21-1   Initial Position in Joe Speculator's Margin Account

Assets		Liabilities and Equity	
10,000 shares of Fund A @ $8	$80,000	Broker loan	$40,000
		Joe's equity	40,000
Total	$80,000	Total	$80,000

Table 21-2   Subsequent Position in Joe Speculator's Margin Account

Assets		Liabilities and Equity	
10,000 shares of Fund A @ $6	$60,000	Broker loan	$40,000
		Joe's equity	20,000
Total	$60,000	Total	$60,000

The margin is now only 33.3 percent ($20,000 equity/$60,000 value of Fund A). Danger looms because Joe will face a "margin call" if his equity drops too low. This is a demand to quickly deposit additional cash to meet your brokerage's requirement. For instance, if your margin falls below 30 percent, your firm may insist that you bring your equity up to 35 percent. If you can't come up with the money, you may be forced to sell a part of the investment at a loss.

Conversely, if the fund does well, margin magnifies your profits. Nevertheless, leveraging is highly speculative and, like other risky activities, can be addictive. It can lead to the potential destruction of a tidy nest egg. Certain funds such as sector, single-country, and capital-appreciation portfolios are risky to begin with. If you double up on the risks by using, say, 50-percent margin, the results can be devastating.

You don't need to borrow the full 50 percent as illustrated above. By borrowing less, you reduce the risk. Regardless of the percentage, keeping a fund margined for a long time means that you are paying more interest for the loan. This is a problem if the investment doesn't perform well.

Selling Short

This technique can be used by people who expect a security's price to decline. Simply put, the idea is to sell high now and buy back low later. Thus, it's the reverse of the normal process of buying today and selling tomorrow. But you need to borrow shares from your brokerage to get the process rolling. Suppose you short a stock at $10 a share, and it plunges to $6. You would make $4 a share when you close your position by repurchasing and returning the shares. You need a margin account to sell short. You must leave the proceeds of the short sale in your account and make a 50-percent deposit. And there are other technicalities, such as maintenance margin requirements, to deal with.

Exchange-traded WEBS and Spiders can be sold short, as can many closed-end funds, if sufficient shares are available from your broker. A few mutual funds can be shorted, including about 12 of the Fidelity Select sector portfolios. Discounter Jack White also offers a program for shorting funds.

Just keep in mind that short selling represents a highly risky strategy. You can incur substantial losses if your investments rise instead of fall, as many disgruntled short sellers have learned while trying to predict the end of the long bull market.

DEALING IN EXCHANGE-TRADED FUNDS

Certain types of diversified portfolios trade like stocks. These exchange-traded funds include closed-end portfolios, WEBS, and Spiders. By dealing with a discount brokerage, you typically can get a break on commissions compared with what you might pay at a full-service firm, but there's more to transaction costs than brokerage fees. Publicly traded funds are trickier to buy and sell than mutual funds because their prices bob up and down during the day. In addition, if you place a large order, you can move the price higher or lower, making your execution less favorable. This section contains some tips to help you get the best possible deal.

Be liquidity conscious. Unlike mutual-fund investors, people who buy or sell any exchange-traded product need to be concerned about liquidity. This refers to the ability to buy or sell a security in a reasonably large quantity without pushing its price up or down in the process. Liquidity depends on the size of your order relative to the investment's usual daily share volume, so it might pay to track the trading activity. But usually there's little to worry about unless you are placing orders of at least several hundred shares.

Check the bid-asked spread. Closed-end funds and other exchange-traded products always have two different prices—the "bid" and the "asked" price. The difference represents the so-called dealer markup, which commonly runs $1/16$ of a point or 6.25 cents a share, but which sometimes can go higher. In general, you want to buy securities with narrow spreads.

Use limit orders. By placing this type of order to buy or sell, you know in advance what price you will pay or receive. The order gets executed only if the price hits your specified target or moves to a more advantageous level. Limit orders can be entered either as *day orders* or on a *good-till-canceled* basis. The former expire at the conclusion of that day's trading, whereas the latter remain in effect for perhaps two months, depending on your brokerage's policy. For instance, if you want to buy a fund at a price of $9 a share when it has been trading at around $9$3/4$, you might want to place a limit order, probably on a good-till-canceled basis.

Going all or none. You can also place an *all-or-none* restriction on a limit order, which means you won't accept a partial execution. On orders executed piecemeal over, say, a three-day period, your commissions would be higher than if the entire transaction was completed at once. People use all-or-none restrictions to hold down commissions. Just be aware that with larger orders, it can be difficult to get the entire block executed at your desired price.

DO YOU NEED ADVICE?

Many people require some financial guidance, whether they realize it or not. Of course, the more you can do by yourself the better, because you will save on fees and commissions, and take responsibility for your own actions. Investing in mutual funds doesn't have to be that difficult or time consuming. It requires common sense and a general understanding of how the investment markets work. Mutual funds are professionally managed in themselves, so every time you invest in one you're essentially hiring an adviser. When you build a portfolio, you have a team of professionals working for you.

But in many cases advice makes sense, especially if you have a busy schedule and a large nest egg. Or perhaps you just want a second opinion on your decisions. In addition to asset allocation and investment management, you might want guidance in areas such as taxes, estate planning, insurance, and even real estate.

Beware of Smoke and Mirrors

If you do hire an adviser, it's still important to learn as much as you can about mutual funds and investing. You should have a good understanding of the risks and rewards of the three basic asset classes so you can judge the recommendations offered. The best brokerage or money-management customers are those who can intelligently choose reputable advisers and then evaluate what that person is doing on an ongoing basis. Most advisers are honest and competent, but the small number of phonies can wreak havoc on your portfolio. The following dialogue between a prospective client and a smooth-talking charlatan with a soothing personality illustrates the pitfalls.

CLIENT: I recently inherited $1 million. I'm 50 years old, have limited investment knowledge, and have saved relatively little for my retirement. Now I want to play catch up. I'd like to build the $1 million into a much bigger sum and retire in style in five years when I turn 55.

ADVISER: I'm glad you contacted me. You're certainly not alone in wanting money-management advice. I have a proprietary trend-following system that can provide total returns of 20 percent a year with virtually no risk. I'll put most of your assets into the best aggressive-growth funds, leverage the position with margin, and let your money multiply. As a hedge, I'll also keep about one-fourth of your portfolio in gold and silver bars, which can only go up in case inflation heats up and the dollar loses its value, as will happen sooner or later. I'm an excellent market timer, and I'll bail out of any stock fund that's ready to take a plunge. My clients were totally out of stocks during the October 1987 crash. So you'll experience virtually no risk. I'm sure you'll sleep well at night having me in control of your nest egg.

CLIENT: Wealth without risk! How much do you charge?

ADVISER: My yearly fee is 3 percent of the value of your portfolio. Because my proprietary system provides much higher returns than my competitors can earn, I charge a bit more.

CLIENT: Your system sounds almost too good to be true. Can you provide me with the names and phone numbers of a few clients so I could talk with them about your services?

ADVISER: I respect my clients' privacy. You wouldn't like to be bothered with lots of phone calls in the future about my services, would you? Besides, I've just finished some extensive computer simulations that backtested my system, and it has worked with 98-percent accuracy over the past 50 years. I'll show you the computer printouts but I can't let you have them because my proprietary trend-following system is top secret. What more evidence do you need?

CLIENT: None.

While the above dialogue may seem off the wall, it does bring attention to red flags to watch for when checking out prospective advisers. They include the following:

- Unscrupulous salespeople often promise unrealistically high returns. Remember that stocks have provided about 10 percent annually over the long haul before netting out inflation and taxes.

- Promises of wealth without risk should be greeted with skepticism. Only the lowest-returning investments carry high principal stability.

- Buying on margin is highly risky, as we have illustrated earlier in this chapter. Other leveraging tactics, such as the use of options or futures contracts, can be even more damaging.

- Market timing doesn't work consistently, as we have seen in Chapter 7. Backtesting and computer printouts don't offer proof.

- You should never allocate more than 10 percent of your assets to gold or other metals, if you invest in them at all. Pitches based around hyperinflation are designed to exploit your fears.

- You should steer clear of advisers who won't provide references. An even more alarming signal would be a lack of printed documentation.

Checking Credentials

One advantage of dealing with investment brokers for advice is that they must be licensed and their activities monitored by regulators. Complaints and disciplinary actions will show up on a broker's Central Registration Depository or CRD report, which you can access for free through the NASD (800-289-9999) or your state securities office. If a rep does not have a CRD report, it may mean the person isn't licensed and you should beware.

Before hiring a self-described money manager, make sure that person is a registered investment adviser (RIA) with the Securities and Exchange Commission, as required under the Investment Advisers Act of 1940, or with the appropriate state agency. RIAs must file periodic reports with their federal or state oversight agency, and their records are subject to routine surprise audits for no cause at least once every few years. If the adviser oversees less than $25 million, he or she generally will fall under the audit oversight of state officials. If the person manages more than $25 million, the SEC will perform the oversight function.

The Investment Advisers Act of 1940 does not ensure competence, however. The SEC does not require an examination, but rather the act is designed to protect investors against fraudulent and unethical practices by requiring disclosure to potential clients and periodic review of adviser activity. Federally registered advisers generally must file Form ADV, formally known as the Uniform Application for Investment Adviser Registration. Before you engage a money manager, make sure that you are given a copy of his or her Form ADV Part II. State disclosure rules vary.

The educational background and credentials of an adviser also are of considerable importance. Some money managers list a lot of letters behind their names, but they might not all be meaningful. A lawyer or Certified Public Accountant might be highly knowledgeable in his or her profession but could lack expertise in investments. So you need to be careful in your selection.

For advisers who describe themselves as financial planners, here are some credentials to watch for:

Certified Financial Planner. Individuals holding a CFP designation must meet the education, experience, and ethical requirements set by the Certified Financial Planners Board of Standards in Denver. They must pass examinations on relevant subject matter. Call the Institute of Certified Financial Planners' consumer assistance line (800-282-PLAN) for CFPs in your area. The CFP mark is the single most relevant designation in this field. In addition, the Atlanta-based International Association for Financial Planning (IAFP) will provide a list of planners in your area who are legally registered to perform various services related to the field of financial planning. Call 800-945-IAFP to get the names of five planners nearby.

Chartered Life Underwriter and *Chartered Financial Consultant,* commonly known as CLU and ChFC, respectively. These are insurance designations held by people trained by the American College in Bryn Mawr, Pennsylvania. A person holding one or both of these marks may steer you into insurance-related products such as variable annuities and universal variable life, so be careful. Nevertheless, they are respected designations.

Personal Financial Specialist. The PFS designation is provided by the American Institute of Certified Public Accountants to CPAs who have had additional training in financial planning. Call 800-TO-AICPA and ask for the names of CPAs in your area who have earned the PFS mark. These individuals often have expertise in tax planning.

A Checklist for Interviewing Candidates

Ask your accountant, attorney, or a respected business colleague for the names of reputable financial advisers in your area. Referrals often are the best way to find a competent professional. At a minimum, you should look for someone with a CFP, ChFC, or PFS designation. Education and prior experience also are important.

Pay close attention to how the adviser will charge you. The manner in which fees are imposed and the overall cost depend on the kind of service you want. For example, a fee-only financial planner might charge $100 an hour to prepare a comprehensive financial plan or 1.25 percent of the value of your portfolio yearly to manage your assets. If you deal with stockbrokers, insurance agents, or other individuals who are compensated solely on the basis of commissions, you need to beware of possible conflicts of interest. They may try to steer you into products that are most lucrative for themselves. For example, they might try to get you to buy a variable annuity instead of recommending that you invest more in your company's 401(k) plan.

Contact the adviser and arrange for an interview. Typically, this session will be free, but you might want to confirm this before making an appointment. Here are 12 key questions to ask candidates during the initial interview.

1. *Are you a registered investment adviser with the Securities and Exchange Commission or with the state agency that regulates advisers?* Be suspicious if the answer is no, especially if the person is operating a one-man shop. To save time, you might want to ask this question by phone before arranging a face-to-face interview.

2. *Explain your fee schedule.* Ask if the person charges a flat fee, or whether he or she is compensated by commissions from products sold. The adviser might receive both fees and commissions.

3. *Explain your investment philosophy.* Find out if the adviser will have you adopt an asset allocation plan and stick with it, or whether market timing will be recommended. Does the adviser have a penchant for certain investment styles or asset categories? If he or she favors precious metals, watch out.

4. *Which discount brokerage or fund complex do you use and why?* You normally will be asked to open an account at a discount brokerage or at a mutual-fund complex, with the adviser being granted a limited financial power of attorney to execute trades in your account. These

questions typically would not apply when dealing with full-service brokers.

5. *Do you place limit orders when you buy exchange-traded funds or stocks?* While the adviser may just stick with garden-variety mutual funds, this is still a good question to ask because it can indicate if that person is making an extra effort to get a good price.

6. *How do you feel about index funds?* As Chapter 8 explained, it's very difficult to select actively managed funds that will beat the market. If the adviser agrees and shows respect for indexing, consider this a plus.

7. *How have you done for your clients in the past?* Ask for the names and phone numbers of at least three references that you might contact.

8. *What are your credentials?* Ask about professional designations such as the CFP designation, relevant college degrees, prior employment, and number of years of investing experience. Be skeptical of someone who has scant work history.

9. *What professionals do you work with?* Ask for the names and phone numbers of lawyers, tax specialists, and accountants with whom the person has had business dealings.

10. *How would you help me?* Ask about the adviser's most beneficial services and make sure an overall individualized financial plan is included. Also, ask the person whether he or she will teach you more about investments.

11. *Would you have total control of my investment account?* Find out if the person will consult with you before making revisions in the portfolio. Be suspicious if the adviser simply wants to make trades as he or she deems appropriate.

12. *What kinds of communications can I expect to receive?* Ask about trade confirmations, periodic account statements, and even prospectuses and other marketing literature.

If an adviser gives seminars, attend one to get a better feel for his or her knowledge level and communication skills. Since your relationship with a financial adviser could be long-term, you need to make sure the chemistry is right. Choose an adviser with whom you feel comfortable. The person should take the time to listen to you and provide complete answers to your questions.

How Will You Benefit from an Adviser?

If you need help with investments, your adviser will need to find out information about your financial situation, then help you set up a mutual-fund portfolio, as covered in Chapter 19. Reread Chapter 19 and see if you would feel comfortable doing these things for yourself. The main idea is to establish appropriate asset-class weights, then build a portfolio with suitable funds. If you feel uncomfortable selecting actively managed funds, you can always put together a suitable mix of index products.

It's not a good idea to use an adviser who advocates market-timing or even one who believes in actively buying and selling funds. Generally when you establish your asset-class weights and pick some core funds, you want to stick with them for a long time. So the main jobs a good adviser would perform would be in helping to establish the initial portfolio, then monitoring it. Chapter 19 also explains how the portfolio should be rebalanced periodically to avoid risk creep.

Perhaps you mainly need advice with taxes and estate planning. In that case the services of a good CPA and an attorney could suffice. Remember that advice costs money. In addition, it's unlikely that your adviser would be able to consistently beat the long-run average return on stocks, which has been about 10 percent a year. Most fund managers have trouble beating the market, so you would expect this also to be true of personal financial advisers, especially since there's an added expense involved. If the market's 10-percent long-run historic return is reduced by fund expenses and transaction costs, amounting to perhaps 2 percent, plus an adviser's fee of 1 percent or more, you may be netting only about 6 or 7 percent—and that's before taxes and inflation. On the other hand, many people may do much worse on their own, so money-management services can make sense for them.

Wrap Accounts

As another advice channel, consider the so-called "wrap account" or portfolio-management programs offered by some fund companies and brokerage firms. These programs wrap or bundle various costs into a single account fee. Fidelity, SteinRoe, Dreyfus, and Strong are among the fund complexes offering this service. Brokerages with mutual-fund wrap programs include Smith Barney, Merrill Lynch, Linsco/Private Ledger, and Prudential. The minimum initial investments vary from about $25,000 to $250,000 or more. The annual charges also vary but can be fairly stiff, say, 1.5 percent or more. The wrap format does not include the operating expenses and brokerage commissions that the funds themselves incur. So if these outlays total 2 percent or so and you add a 1.5-percent wrap-account fee, you face a hefty 3.5-

percent yearly burden. Another issue to consider with a wrap program is the stable of funds that will be available. It should include plenty of good choices that have reasonable expense ratios.

Recently, full-service brokerages such as Smith Barney, PaineWebber, Prudential, and Merrill Lynch have instituted no-load fund supermarkets in an effort to compete with the extraordinarily successful discounter programs discussed earlier in this chapter. This represents a major change in the way mutual funds are distributed. These full-service firms don't lose revenue by offering no-load products, as one might think. Rather, they offer the no-commission portfolios within a wrap account, charging the client 1 to 2 percent yearly for asset-allocation assistance and investment advice.

AT THE CLOSE

Mutual-fund supermarkets are an important part of the investing landscape. They offer convenience, flexibility, and a wide array of choices. They allow you to consolidate all of your holdings under one roof—an attractive feature if you also own some stocks, closed-end funds, and other securities. As negatives, the convenience of fund supermarkets might encourage you to trade excessively or make use of potentially risky strategies involving margin and short selling.

Assuming you open a brokerage account, you should become familiar with tactics that might allow you to execute trades at preferable prices on closed-end funds, WEBS, Spiders, and the like. These tactics include various types of limit orders. Speaking of brokerages, you might decide that you need some help with your financial affairs. You may want to consider using a broker, money manager, financial planner, accountant, or lawyer, especially when your need for help overlaps into areas such as estate planning and taxes. A good adviser can help pick funds suitable for your goals, then monitor your holdings. But you should select a professional carefully, with an eye on costs, character, and credentials.

CHAPTER 22

When and How to Sell

A young man from a Midwestern state was having a love affair—with a mutual fund. He inherited the investment from his grandmother and forged an emotional bond with it in no time. While there's nothing wrong with long-term investing, the grandson learned his lesson too well, retaining the fund even after it had changed its name, added a 12b-1 fee, switched managers, flirted with an options-writing strategy and, in short, sunk to mediocrity. When the man eventually sold out after about a decade, he collected a tidy profit. But he could have fared better by shopping for a superior replacement after the first of the red flags went up.

SHOULD YOU BAIL OUT?

Certainly, there are times to think about selling some or all of your shares in a mutual fund. It pays to reevaluate your holdings at least once a year to make sure they still mesh with your objectives and offer good potential. In making this decision, you need to look at the same factors you considered when buying, only in reverse. The reasons for contemplating a sale can be divided into two groups: fund-specific and personal.

Fund-Specific Motivations

You will want to get rid of investments that aren't living up to your expectations. The reasons for being dissatisfied with a mutual fund likely will fall into one of these five categories:

1. *Hot hands turn icy.* If the fund has lagged its peers for perhaps 18 months, it might be time for a change. You also should check to see how the fund has fared relative to an appropriate index. For example, you might compare a utility fund against the Dow Jones Utility Average, a growth-and-income fund against the S&P 500, or a small-stock portfolio versus the Russell 2000.

2. *Expenses mount.* An expense ratio that is climbing noticeably not only costs you money but could be symptomatic of other serious problems. High expenses might result from the imposition of new charges, such as a 12b-1 fee that didn't exist previously.

3. *A revolving door.* A change in management might be another cause to sell. You need to find out the explanation for the move, and the background and qualifications of the person taking the helm. Changes usually are of less consequence when a fund is jointly managed by several individuals, and only one of them leaves.

4. *Assets surge.* A fund that has grown so big that its style has changed also might be a candidate for selling, especially if the manager has shifted from, say, small stocks to medium and large issues. Of course, larger size also results in important economies of scale. What you need to decide is whether management can continue to keep up the good work.

5. *A "no vacancy" sign goes up.* Pay particularly close attention to performance if a small-company fund has grown to the point where it closes to new investors. If performance continues to falter, consider selling. With a closed fund, management no longer benefits from large inflows of investor cash, which probably contributed significantly to the good returns of earlier years. Conversely, shutting out new investors also can help to boost performance.

Personal Reasons

Sometimes, you will want to sell funds that are still looking good. Here are some justifications for making such a move:

- *To enhance liquidity.* For many reasons, you might require more cash, or at least an increasingly conservative portfolio. Perhaps you're just a few years from retirement and desire reduced volatility. If so, it could be time to trim back your stock holdings.

- *To lessen risk creep.* In Chapter 19, we discussed the need to reduce your equity exposure if stocks have been climbing. Suppose your normal allocation ranges from 70 to 80 percent, but now it's up to 90 percent. It may be time to rebalance, especially if valuation yardsticks such as the market's dividend yield and P/E ratio are flashing warning signals.

- *To lock in a tax loss.* Suppose you hold a fund that has declined and you can use this to offset some capital gains on other investments. If so, you might want to sell. You could always buy back the shares at a later date, provided you wait at least 31 days before reestablishing your position to avoid the so-called wash-sale rule. On the other hand, you could invest in a similar fund without waiting and not violate the rule.

- *To reflect a change in tax bracket.* Perhaps you received a promotion or an inheritance, or you moved to a state with a high income-tax rate. Factors such as these can cause a jump in your tax liabilities. If so, you might want to switch some cash to muni-bond funds, tax-efficient index portfolios, or a variable annuity.

Eliminating Clutter

Owning too many investments can be a problem for some people. Individuals who don't have a plan and like to collect things may wind up with modest positions in a couple dozen mutual funds along with a smattering of stocks and bonds. Many of these funds likely will have similar objectives, leading to unnecessary duplication. The required housekeeping and tax-related work can be cumbersome. Annual custodial fees on different IRAs can add up. It's time-consuming to monitor each individual position, and there might be deadwood that should have been cleared out long ago.

If this describes your situation, consider paring the set of funds down to a manageable number, perhaps as few as five. Money-losing investments should be pruned, along with those that are unsuitable. Your performance likely will improve, and your financial life will be a lot simpler. Plus, it will be much easier to keep a watchful eye on your asset allocation.

Arguments for Staying Put

So much for the justifications for jumping ship. You may be better off not selling in many situations. Here are a half dozen "don'ts" to consider in this regard.

1. *Don't sell simply to lock in gains.* Profits really start to compound after many years. Just because a fund may have flourished for a while does not mean that it's going to stumble in the future, although volatile specialized funds might be an exception.

2. *Don't sell on the basis of a bad quarter.* To succeed, you have to think long term. View temporary setbacks as buying opportunities.

3. *Don't sell because you fear a plunge.* The stock market will fluctuate, but you can't pinpoint when it will take a nose dive. It's better to compile a portfolio that you're comfortable holding through thick and thin. If you have allocated your assets properly and have sufficient emergency money, you shouldn't worry.

4. *Don't sell just after a big plunge.* This is often the worst thing to do because you will lock in a loss—and miss the chance for a rebound. Panic selling rarely pays. Instead, view setbacks as buying opportunities.

5. *Don't realize large gains unless you must.* Think twice about selling a good fund held in a taxable account on which you have a hefty unrealized capital gain.

6. *Don't sell solely on the basis of one recommendation.* The advice may be wrong, and you will have to decide what to do with the proceeds. You could wind up making two mistakes: selling a fund you should have kept and buying one that was best left alone.

The increased popularity of discount brokerage programs discussed in Chapter 21 has made it easier and cheaper than ever to switch funds. Resist the temptation to sell on impulse. If you are disturbed about the performance of a fund, at least do some research first.

WITHDRAWING GRADUALLY

You don't need to sell your entire position in a fund in one fell swoop. A position can be liquidated bit by bit over many years, as when meeting a need for living expenses in retirement. In fact, it's useful to think in terms of systematic withdrawals when making long-range financial plans. Withdrawal plans are not covered in detail in many personal-finance books or in fund-company literature, yet the topic merits a close look.

First, you need to make some projections, perhaps with the help of a computerized spreadsheet or Table 22-2. You can get a good estimate of how long your capital will last under different assumptions using annual redemptions, even though you may want to take out money more frequently. The estimates in our illustrations are conservative numbers because they assume withdrawals are made at the beginning of each year, rather than monthly or at year's end.

The success or failure of a withdrawal plan will depend on several key factors:

1. *The size of your nest egg.* The more you have to work with, the better. Chapter 17 presented a method for making a ballpark estimate of the cash you will need at retirement.

2. *Your annual withdrawal percentage.* The less you spend each year, the better. Keep this amount as low as possible to avoid running out of capital too soon.

3. *The expected "real" return on your fund.* This equals the projected nominal return on your fund minus the expected inflation rate. It's essential to factor inflation into your analysis.

4. *The frequency of withdrawal.* You can take money out monthly, bimonthly, quarterly, semiannually, or annually. Each time you make a withdrawal, however, you're selling shares, which results in a taxable event. Withdrawing just once a year and parking the proceeds in a money fund that can be tapped as needed will simplify things when it comes time to figure your taxes.

How Long Will Your Capital Last?

If you plan to withdraw money from a fund at a faster rate than it's growing, you need to ask the same crucial question that confronts Marilyn, who just retired at age 62. She wants to take out 10 percent of her $500,000 original capital from a balanced portfolio that she conservatively expects will provide an 8-percent yearly return. The withdrawal will be made annually at the beginning of each year. In addition, Marilyn will adjust her withdrawals for inflation by increasing them by 4 percent yearly. So she will pull out $50,000 initially, $52,000 ($50,000 x 1.04) the next year, and so forth, as seen in Table 22-1.

Table 22-1   Marilyn's Inflation-Adjusted Withdrawal Plan

Year	Withdrawal*	Year-End Balance	Year	Withdrawal*	Year-End Balance
1	$50,000	$486,000	7	$63,266	$319,757
2	52,000	468,720	8	65,797	274,278
3	54,080	447,811	9	68,428	222,317
4	56,243	422,893	10	71,166	163,244
5	58,493	393,553	11	74,012	96,370
6	60,833	359,338	12	76,973	20,949

*Made at the beginning of each year.

The year-by-year analysis in Table 22-1 tells us that Marilyn's capital would last a little more than 12 years. Table 22-2 shows the same thing for this case and many other scenarios. Here's how to use the second chart:

1. Look in the 4-percent yearly return row, which in Marilyn's case is a "real" return determined by taking the fund's 8-percent nominal gain minus the 4-percent projected inflation.

2. Move over to the 10-percent column, which reflects the initial withdrawal rate. The intersecting number in the body of the chart provides the number of years your capital will last. In Marilyn's case, it is the same "12" found the long way in Table 22-1.

Table 22-2   Number of Years Your Nest Egg Will Last

Real Yearly Return	|	Initial Withdrawal Rate*										
	5%	6%	7%	8%	9%	10%	11%	12%	13%	14%	15%	16%
1%	22	18	15	13	11	10	9	8	7	7	6	6
2	25	19	16	14	12	11	9	9	8	7	7	6
3	29	22	18	15	13	11	10	9	8	7	7	6
4	37	26	20	16	14	12	10	9	8	8	7	7
5	62	32	23	18	15	13	11	10	9	8	7	7
6	**	49	28	21	17	14	12	10	9	8	8	7
7	**	**	40	25	19	15	13	11	10	9	8	7
8	**	**	**	33	22	17	14	12	10	9	8	8
9	**	**	**	**	28	20	16	13	11	10	9	8
10	**	**	**	**	**	25	18	14	12	10	9	8
11	**	**	**	**	**	**	22	16	13	11	10	9
12	**	**	**	**	**	**	32	19	15	12	11	9

*Withdrawals are made at the beginning of each year.
**Capital will last indefinitely.

If Marilyn wants to stretch her money, she either must withdraw less or seek a more generous return by switching to a higher octane all-equity portfolio. For example, suppose that she cuts her initial withdrawal rate from 10 percent to 7 percent. With this 3-percentage-point reduction, her money would last 20 years (Table 22-2). And if she could live with a 6-percent withdrawal rate while earning a 6-percent real return (10 percent nominal less 4 percent inflation), her capital would last 49 years (Table 22-2). You need to worry about exhausting a nest egg faster only if your withdrawal rate exceeds the portfolio's real rate of growth. The latter should approximate 6 percent if you hold a good equity fund in normal times.

Note that Table 22-2 also can be used in cases where your withdrawals will be constant, not just inflation adjusted. For instance, if Marilyn wanted to take out 10 percent of her initial capital on an annual basis ($50,000 each year), her nest egg would last 17 years with an 8-percent nominal return, instead of the 12 years we found when a 4-percent annual inflation factor was built in. As a practical matter, however, it is best to reduce the fund's expected return by a projected inflation rate. Otherwise, you risk withdrawing too much and crimping your living standards in future years.

Table 22-2 also can help determine an appropriate withdrawal rate, based on how long your capital must last. Suppose your nest egg must endure for at least 20 years, during which you expect 4-percent inflation. How much can you safely withdraw? If you estimate that your stock fund will generate at least 5 percent in real terms, you could take out up to 7 percent annually, under which scenario your principal should hold out for 23 years. It would be safer to tap the account for a bit less than 7 percent to provide some margin for error in case the returns don't live up to your expectations.

Choosing Appropriate Funds

Withdrawal programs work best with stock funds, unless you will be pulling out cash over a relatively short span such as 5 or 6 years. Equity-income and growth-and-income funds are good choices because they offer more stability than, say, small-cap investments, yet still offer solid growth potential. An S&P 500 index fund makes an ideal withdrawal-plan candidate because of its growth-and-income orientation, rock-bottom expenses, and tax efficiency. You can hold an index fund for years without having to worry about an active manager turning the portfolio into a laggard. Balanced funds also make suitable choices provided more than half the portfolio is in stocks.

But volatile capital-appreciation, sector, and single-country portfolios are generally poor choices. These funds can plunge as fast as they can surge. Withdrawing money after your account has sustained a massive setback obviously might lead to problems. This situation can be hard on your wallet and on your nerves.

Other Options

Consider the following, relatively simple methods for setting up a withdrawal plan.

Fixed period. With this approach, you liquidate your entire account within a predetermined number of years. It works well with traditional IRAs, since you must start taking distributions by April 1st of the year following the year you turn 70½. Such withdrawals are based on an individual's or couple's estimated life expectancy. Suppose you must withdraw money from an IRA over a 15-year period. In the first year, you would take out 1/15th of the account balance, followed by 1/14th in the second year, and so on. You would determine each annual withdrawal by dividing the account's value at the end of the prior year by a life-expectancy estimate that declines by 1.0 each year. IRS Publication 590 details the rules governing IRAs and contains the life-expectancy charts you will need to calculate withdrawals. To obtain your free copy, call the IRS at 1-800-TAX-FORM (1-800-829-3676).

Fixed percentage. Yet another option is to withdraw a set percentage of your account, say 8 percent, each year. Your monthly payments would vary somewhat, depending on fluctuations in the fund's NAV and changes in your balance. You would receive larger payments when the NAV is high, smaller ones when it's low.

Fixed share. Rather than take out a target dollar amount or percentage, you could redeem a fixed number of shares, say 100 monthly. The drawback here is that the cash amount would fluctuate each month, yet this is really a superior approach since it is a variant of the dollar-cost averaging principal explained in Chapter 7. That is, you receive more money when the NAV is high and less when it's low. Conversely, by withdrawing a fixed-dollar amount, you sell more shares when prices are low and fewer when they're high.

Since most people want to receive a constant monthly cash stream, fixed-share plans are rarely used despite their conceptual advantage. Further, this option might not be offered by your mutual-fund company. But you could implement it yourself, with a little work. All you would need to do is call the fund group, instruct the representative to sell the appropriate amount of shares, and have the proceeds transferred to your money-market portfolio.

Keep in mind that the estimates you make for any withdrawal plan should not be carved in stone. Retirement planning requires a periodic reevaluation of your situation, at least on an annual basis. You need to make a revised estimate of how long your capital might last, on the basis of the numbers in Table 22-2 or your own computer analysis. If possible, keep your withdrawals on the conservative side, to allow your remaining balance to grow as much as possible.

Withdrawal programs probably are most commonly used by retirees and widows. But they also can make sense in various other cases. For example, a plan could provide regular payments for a son or daughter in college. In general, it's best to stick with more conservative, income-oriented equity funds in a withdrawal plan, even when the recipient is a younger person. More volatile portfolios could lead to bouts of insomnia.

One final note on withdrawal plans: You've got to keep good records for tax purposes, so you can determine the gain or loss on each redemption. You need to decide on a logical method for matching up sales with purchases. The average-cost approach is typically used. As noted above, more frequent withdrawals will entail more paperwork.

Alternatives to Withdrawal Plans

If you have a large amount invested in a mutual fund, you may be able to generate a sufficient cash flow simply by taking your income dividends in cash. Receiving cash distributions is easier than using a withdrawal plan, as it greatly simplifies your accounting for tax purposes. Your annual Form 1099-DIV will list the taxable distributions. You don't need to be concerned about matching purchases of shares with sales as you would under a withdrawal plan.

As another alternative, you could always redeem shares at opportune times. You can try to time your redemptions, selling shares when the NAV is relatively high and transferring the proceeds into a money fund to spend as needed. This approach may work better if you're meeting at least some of your cash needs through monthly dividends.

AT THE CLOSE

The sell decision is often more difficult than the initial decision to buy. It's complicated because several factors are involved, including emotions. Frequently hopping in and out of funds is definitely a bad strategy. People who do so usually fare worse than individuals with discipline and patience. You should have a well-conceived investment plan that you follow consistently over the years. By sticking with it, you are less likely to be swayed by short-term market developments.

Withdrawal plans, if set up with care and then monitored closely, can be an effective way for retirees to systematically sell a modest amount of their nest egg each year. The major risk you have to guard against is outliving your assets, so be conservative in setting your withdrawal rate. It's a good idea to reevaluate your situation every year or so. Do some revised number crunching and make adjustments as needed.

CHAPTER 23

Tax Considerations

Mutual funds were designed to make investing simpler, and they do a good job for the most part. But some shareholders may have their doubts at tax time, particularly people who own a bevy of funds and have done lots of buying and selling. Figuring taxes on nonretirement accounts can become rather complex, even for those who maintain meticulous records.

There's nothing like a roaring bull market to warm an investor's heart. But the taxable distributions can throw a damper on the party because mutual funds must spin off their income and net realized gains yearly. That's why it's wise to invest all you can in tax-deferred retirement plans such as IRAs and 401(k)s. That way, you will reduce the number of tax-related calculations you need to make annually, and you'll postpone paying Uncle Sam for perhaps many years.

In deciding how to allocate dollars between taxable and sheltered accounts, you need to pay close attention to each fund's tax efficiency, which refers to the percentage of pretax profits that you pocket after settling with the IRS. We will provide some suggestions in this regard later in the chapter, but first it's important to understand the basics of mutual-fund taxation.

SORTING OUT DISTRIBUTIONS

There are three basic types of distributions that a fund can make, each with its own tax implications. The different categories are itemized in separate boxes on Form 1099-DIV, which fund companies mail to shareholders by late January for use in preparing tax returns. Fund companies also provide the IRS with a copy of your 1099-DIV. Here's a rundown on distributions.

1. *Ordinary dividends.* You pay taxes on ordinary dividends, based on your income-tax rate. The amount distributed consists of taxable interest and dividend payments, net of management fees, administrative costs, and any 12b-1 fees. In addition, the fund's net short-term capital gains are included here because they, too, are taxed at the same ordinary rate. Short-term gains reflect profits on securities held by the fund for 18 months or less.

2. *Capital-gains distributions.* This box on your 1099-DIV includes the net long-term capital gains, if any, on the fund's stock or bond holdings. Long-term gains refer to positions held for more than 18 months. Such profits are taxed at 20 percent for those in a 28 percent or greater tax bracket. The rate drops to 10 percent for people in the 15 percent bracket. Thus, they are desirable for people in higher federal tax brackets. If your bracket is 28 percent or lower, however, your capital-gains tax rate is the same as your ordinary-income levy.

3. *Nontaxable distributions.* These are simply dividends paid out of principal and therefore usually not taxable. They reduce your cost basis, which should be taken into account when you sell shares. Note that nontaxable distributions are not the same as tax-exempt dividends.

Incidentally, if a fund's realized losses exceed its gains in any year, the net loss would not be distributed as a credit or deduction. Rather, it would be carried forward by the company to offset net gains in future years. When a fund does realize gains, losses carried forward from prior periods can be a boon for shareholders. Volatile products, such as gold and single-country portfolios, frequently have loss carryforwards. But make sure you don't buy a perennial loser just to get this benefit.

Beware of Upcoming Distributions

Keep the capital-gains distribution date in mind when you invest in a fund during the final quarter of the year, unless your shares are held in an IRA or other tax-deferred account. Most stock funds declare capital gains in late fall, then pay them in December or January. These distributions can be huge if the stock market has raced to new heights during the year.

According to the Internal Revenue Code, distributions declared in October, November, or December are considered paid on December 31, even if payment isn't made until January. Thus, taxes will be payable for the current year. You can determine the distribution date by calling the fund's toll-free number and asking a shareholder rep. Also find out the "ex-distribution date," the "payable date," and the dollar amount involved. The day before the ex-dividend date is called the "record date." You get the dividend if you buy on the record date, but not if you buy on the ex-dividend date.

If you're making a sizable investment and your shares are held in a taxable account, it's often best to wait until the fund goes ex-dividend. By delaying your purchase, you avoid having to pay taxes. Otherwise, you would be buying somebody else's tax bill. The NAV will fall by the amount of the payment on the day the fund goes ex-distribution, so the only thing you gain by getting it is a tax liability.

Here's an example. Suppose you invest $10,000 in 1,000 shares of XYZ Equity in early December at its NAV of $10, shortly before it goes ex-distribution. The fund has done well this year and in a few days it will pay a $2.50-per-share distribution. You have just acquired a $2,500 gain on which you will owe taxes come April 15. If you had waited a few days until the fund went ex-distribution, your $10,000 could have acquired 1,333 shares at the $7.50 ex-dividend price and you would have sidestepped the immediate $2,500 tax liability.

People often forget to check on upcoming distributions. Suppose you suddenly find yourself saddled with a large, unexpected capital-gains bill from a fund in which you just made a sizable investment near the end of the year. To relieve yourself of the immediate tax liability, you can offset this by selling your shares at a loss—which equals the decline in NAV resulting from the distribution—before year end, and reinvesting the proceeds in a similar portfolio. By purchasing a different fund, you avoid the so-called "wash-sale" rule, which we discuss later in this chapter.

There may be some cases in which it is insignificant or even advantageous to purchase shares shortly before an ex-distribution date, however. Examples include situations when you are making a periodic monthly investment of just $50 or $100, when the distribution itself is rather small, or when you have realized losses during the year that would offset the payment.

Dividends on Non-U.S. Securities

Funds that invest in foreign stocks and bonds may distribute income to you that has been subject to foreign-tax withholding, thereby reducing your dividend. If your fund is held in a taxable account, you may be entitled to a tax deduction or credit. The amount of foreign tax paid will be listed in a box on Form 1099-DIV. A *tax credit* provides a direct offset against your tax bill, while a *deduction* merely reduces your taxable income. Credits thus are more advantageous. Taking a deduction is fairly simple. But if you want a credit, you must complete IRS Form 1116, which can be a headache. You aren't entitled to either a credit or a deduction on shares held in a tax-protected account such as an IRA, so you can make a case for holding your international funds in a taxable account.

SELLING SHARES

Good records are essential when you sell shares. The first point to remember is that any time you reinvest a distribution, you are making an additional purchase in the fund that adds to your cost basis. So when you sell, you should increase your basis to include initial and subsequent cash investments, plus all reinvested distributions. The higher the basis, the lower your tax bill.

If you have held a fund for many years, you might have to add dozens of purchases and distributions. But you need to include it all. If you don't, your cost will be understated, resulting in too large a taxable gain or too small a deductible loss. In addition, keep in mind that gains and losses on sales or exchanges of municipal-bond portfolios are taxable events that are treated the same as for other mutual funds. The tax exemption applies only to the dividends you collect from net investment income.

Selling in Stages

If you sell your shares in dribs and drabs, the calculations can become more complex than when you liquidate all your shares at once. Under the tax laws in effect at this writing, the IRS allows any of the following four methods to determine cost basis:

Don't Be Subject to Backup Withholding

One box on your 1099-DIV is titled "Federal Income Tax Withheld." You don't want anything to appear in this box but it might. In some cases the fund company may withhold 31 percent of your taxable distributions and any redemption proceeds on behalf of the IRS. Why? Perhaps you didn't provide the fund company with your Social Security number, supplied an incorrect Social Security number, or neglected to report dividends you received in the past. And there's always the possibility that the firm made a mistake. If so, contact the IRS at (800) 829-1040 as soon as possible to rectify the situation.

---

1. First-in, first-out (or FIFO)

2. Specific identification

3. Average cost—single category

4. Average cost—double category

Once you elect a method for a specific fund, you need to continue using it unless you obtain permission from the IRS to change. You need not, however, employ the same method for all of your funds.

First-in, first-out. The FIFO approach is based on the simple assumption that the earliest shares purchased were the first to be sold. This will be your best option only if the older shares were acquired at the highest price, which usually is not the case. The IRS will assume you are using FIFO unless you specify that you have chosen one of the other three methods. The information in Table 23-1 can be used to illustrate FIFO. On January 14, you sell 1,000 of your 2,675 shares of Fund A at $16. Which shares are you selling? Unless you indicate otherwise, the IRS assumes they're the initial 1,000 you acquired at $10 two years ago on March 15.

Specific identification. In general, this method makes the most sense and often results in the lowest tax liability. To sell specific shares, you need to inform the fund company of your intentions in writing prior to the time of sale. You also must keep some form of written documentation from the fund company of the shares sold. You identify the shares to be sold by the acquisition date. Using the data in Table 23-1, it would be best to sell 1,000 of the 1,500 bought on June 12 last year at $15, since the higher cost basis would lessen your taxable gain. In addition to being greater than the $10 purchase price under FIFO, this basis also exceeds the $13.01 value for the average cost–single category approach. Note that your short- and long-term capital-gains rates also come into play when deciding which shares to specify.

Table 23-1   Fund "A" Transaction Record

Date	Transaction	Shares	NAV	Value
Two years ago				
March 15	Initial purchase	1,000	$10	$10,000
December 31	Reinvested distribution	50	11	550
Last year				
June 12	Subsequent purchase	1,500	15	22,500
December 31	Reinvested distribution	125	14	1,750
This year				
January 14	Partial redemption	(1,000)	16	(16,000)

Average cost–single category. This is the most popular method. You simply group all shares together, sum your costs, and divide by the total number. In the example in Table 23-1, where 2,675 shares were purchased at a total cost of $34,800, the average cost per share works out to $13.01. To determine your basis, simply multiply the number of shares sold by their average cost. With this method, the shares you have held longest are deemed to be sold first. If these shares were held for more than 18 months, the long-term capital gains rate would apply. Many fund groups now calculate an average cost for each shareholder. This can make recordkeeping simpler for some individuals. Your average cost obviously changes as you make additional purchases and reinvestments. The average-cost method often isn't the best choice for minimizing your tax bill. But you may have to go with it if you didn't maintain good records of when, and at what prices, you bought and reinvested. It's also the most practical approach if you have sold relatively small lots frequently, as with a systematic withdrawal plan.

Average cost–double category. This version of the average-cost method allows you to separate short-term and long-term shares. The former are those you've held for 18 months or less; the latter for more than 18 months. The cost for each category is averaged separately. When you sell, you can specify whether you are liquidating long-term or short-term shares. In our example in Table 23-1, the average cost is $14.81 for the short-term shares (those acquired during the past 18 months) and $10 for the long-term ones. To minimize your tax bill, you must consider your short- and long-term capital gains tax rates when determining which shares to specify.

This method could benefit investors in high tax brackets who do a lot of short-term trading, which we don't recommend. If you use the double-category method, you need to tell your fund company whether you're going to be selling long- or short-term shares and then obtain written confirmation to file away with your tax records. If you don't specify, the IRS presumes you would be selling from your long-term group. Needless to say, using the double-category method can be a big headache.

Locking-In Losses

No one likes losing investments, but like dark clouds they can have a silver lining. You have good reason to dump a fund that has lost money if you can use the loss to offset realized gains from other positions. In addition, up to $3,000 per year of net capital losses can offset ordinary taxable income under laws in effect at this writing. If your deficit is larger, the unused portion can be carried forward to future years. Naturally, you always have the option of doing nothing. If your loss is not sizable and you plan to hold your fund for years, you may be better off staying put.

If you are sitting on a large loss yet still feel your fund is a good long-term holding, you could always sell the shares and buy them back at a later date. One drawback is that you must wait more than 30 calendar days to avoid the IRS' so-called wash-sale rule. Another problem is that your fund's NAV could rise while you're waiting. Technically, a wash sale occurs if a security is repurchased within 31 days after it is sold, thereby "washing out" any right you might have had to deduct the loss. This rule also prohibits you from buying shares within the 30 calendar days prior to your tax-loss sale. So, in total, it covers a 61-day period, with the date of sale occurring at the midpoint.

To avoid a wash sale, you could invest immediately in another fund with a similar objective. There's a good chance that both would recover at about the same time and rate if they have comparable portfolios. Tax swapping is especially convenient if you're dealing with a discount brokerage.

Tax-Free Step-Up in Basis

It's possible to pass investments to your heirs without ever having paid a capital-gains tax bill on them. At the time of death, the value of a deceased person's securities can be written up for the benefit of beneficiaries, if the assets are held in ordinary taxable accounts. Suppose a person has a $175,000 stake in an S&P 500 index fund with a cost basis of $100,000 at the time of death. The heirs would be entitled to "step up" or increase the basis to $175,000, thereby sidestepping any taxes on the $75,000 in unrealized appreciation.

Obviously, this basis step-up can be of great value. For tax purposes, heirs can choose to use the basis as of the date of death or six months later. It usually makes the most sense to choose whichever date has the higher account value. The most tax-efficient funds are the best kinds to hold with this

---

Reducing a Losing Position

The wash-sale rule doesn't apply if you sell a part of your investment at a loss within 30 days of purchase for the primary purpose of cutting back your exposure. Suppose you bought 1,000 shares of a volatile sector fund at $10 apiece and a week later the price tumbles to $8. You decide to cut your allocation to this fund by half and sell 500 shares at $8. Your $1,000 loss will not be disallowed by the IRS under the wash-sale rule if you don't repurchase those 500 shares within the next 30 days. In this case, your objective was simply to reduce the size of your position.

objective in mind. Our top choice would be index funds because they ordinarily don't sell securities and realize gains. Vanguard and Schwab even offer some index funds that try extra hard to be tax-efficient.

If you should change your mind and decide not to bequeath an appreciated investment, you still benefit by deferring taxes over the years. When you sell, the gain would be considered long-term and taxed at the favored rate. Or, if you need some money temporarily yet don't want to sell, you could take out a margin loan against the value of your mutual-fund holdings as explained in Chapter 21, assuming you utilize a brokerage account.

It's important to realize that a tax-free step-up in basis can't be claimed for assets in tax-sheltered retirement plans or variable annuities. This is a significant drawback of these accounts. In addition, when you withdraw money from tax-sheltered vehicles, everything is taxed at your ordinary rate. The inability to apply preferential long-term capital-gains rates represents another shortcoming.

DEALING WITH THE "KIDDIE TAX"

Custodial accounts for children—available under what are known as the Uniform Gifts to Minors Act or the Uniform Transfers to Minors Act—offer a relatively easy way to get a child started in a mutual fund. You can establish either a UGMA or UTMA account, depending on the state in which you reside. Such accounts are funded with a gift, typically from a parent, who usually serves as custodian. The account title includes the child's name, with his or her Social Security number, as well as the custodian's name. The adult maintains control of the assets until the child reaches the age of majority and must make sure that investments are made prudently.

Getting More Help

An in-depth discussion of tax rules is beyond the scope of this book. And, of course, these rules are subject to change. For further information, see IRS Publication 564, "Mutual Fund Distributions;" Publication 550, "Investment Income and Expenses;" and Publication 514, "Foreign Tax Credit for Individuals." You may order these free IRS guides by calling 1-800-TAX-FORM (1-800-829-3676). The IRS Web site (http://www.irs.ustreas.gov.) also is helpful. Many mutual-fund companies offer tax pamphlets you may find helpful. And you should discuss the topic with your tax preparer or financial adviser, especially if you have a large nest egg or your situation is fairly complicated.

Tax considerations play an important role here so you need to plan your investment strategy carefully. For a child under age 14, the first $650 of "passive income" from the investments skirts taxation, and the second $650 is taxed at the minor's rate. Above that level, income would be taxed at the parents' rate, which may be as high as 39.6 percent. These thresholds are revised from time to time.

It's wise to plan a child's investments so that your own higher rate won't kick in. As a rule, opt for growth-oriented funds that don't generate much in terms of income. Tax-efficient index funds can serve well for your equity allocation. If you desire some fixed-income stability on a large-dollar account, you could shift a part of your child's portfolio to a tax-exempt bond fund.

Beginning at age 14, the tax situation gets better because all income and gains above $650 would be taxed at the child's rate, usually 15 percent. This is fortunate because you might want to transfer most of the assets into bond funds and other conservative investments as the college-enrollment date nears. Remember that any gift you make in a custodial account would be irrevocable. That means the child will have full control over the money when he or she reaches the age of majority, and can spend it as desired.

TAX EFFICIENCY

Unlike people who invest directly in stocks, mutual-fund shareholders have virtually no control over the timing and amount of gains realized. Managers are ranked and rewarded based on their pretax results, not on their ability to help investors minimize tax bills. In light of this predicament, how do you pick funds and divvy up investments among taxable and tax-deferred accounts so as to minimize your obligations to Uncle Sam? The answer seems straightforward enough: Hold tax-efficient funds in taxable accounts and inefficient portfolios in sheltered retirement plans.

Tax efficiency refers to the proportion of a fund's pretax return that you pocket, after paying all applicable taxes on any distributions. A fund's *tax-adjusted return* is its pretax return reduced by the bite on income and capital-gains payouts. Fund A would have a tax efficiency of 80 percent if it had tax-adjusted and nominal returns of 8 and 10 percent, respectively. Single-state municipal funds tend to sport the highest efficiency ratings, although the figure would fall short of 100 percent if a fund has paid out any capital gains. National muni-bond portfolios rate almost as high. Conversely, a high-yield corporate bond fund may have a tax efficiency of only 50 percent because of its large income dividends.

Researchers Morningstar and Value Line provide historic tax-efficiency numbers for the portfolios they follow. Morningstar, for instance, calculates 3-, 5-, and 10-year tax-adjusted returns by assuming that a fund's income dividends are taxed at the highest federal rate, and that long-term capital gains are subjected to a favored rate. All after-tax distributions are assumed to be reinvested. Morningstar ignores the impact of state and local taxes and assumes that the shares have not been sold by the hypothetical investor at the end of the measurement period. As these assumptions and conditions imply, tax efficiency differs from person to person, depending on each investor's federal and state tax brackets and the amount of profit, if any, realized on the ultimate sale.

A simple way to gauge a fund's tax efficiency is to see how its NAV has grown over the years. Index funds featuring a portfolio turnover of just 5 percent or so would have a large amount of unrealized appreciation, so you could expect to see a distinct buildup in the NAV. For example, the Vanguard Index Trust 500 was launched August 31, 1976, at a price of $14.15 and had grown to $85 by mid-1997. Conversely, portfolios that make large distributions regularly may exhibit little or no change in NAV over the years.

What Makes Tax Efficiency?

Several factors may affect a portfolio's ability to keep the IRS at bay. They include:

1. *The size of income distributions.* Funds that spin off relatively high dividends tend to be less tax-efficient than those that don't, other things being equal. These include all nonmunicipal funds on the bond side as well as equity-income, real estate, and utility stock products, with some exceptions.

2. *A fund's portfolio turnover.* Funds with low turnover rates tend to be more tax efficient than those that trade actively. This is a tricky point, however. For instance, a portfolio with a historically low turnover likely will have large amounts of embedded capital gains that could be triggered by future sales. Morningstar shows each fund's potential capital-gains exposure, as a percent of its assets. Some high-turnover funds have been found to be more tax-efficient than their passive counterparts because they seek to offset their capital gains with losses where possible.

3. *A fund's total return.* Recent research indicates that funds generating lofty total returns—typically stock portfolios—are less efficient because they have more gains that are spun off. Even though these profits may be taxed at the lower capital-gains rate, the total tax liability can be greater.

4. *A fund's cash flow.* Top-performing portfolios may be more efficient than their lackluster siblings if they're flooded with new cash. An influx of money allows the manager to add new positions without having to sell existing ones and realize gains. In addition, the new

cash reduces per-share distributions, benefiting older investors but not new ones.

The Bottom Line

While tax efficiency is something to pay attention to, it shouldn't be a primary factor in the selection of mutual funds. That's partly because a fund's past tax efficiency might not continue in the future. More to the point, a greater consideration is the ability of management to perform well relative to the competition. It's also important to select funds that have reasonable expenses. But you can use tax efficiency as a tie-breaking selection criterion if you're on the fence about a particular portfolio.

Probably the most important thing to remember about tax efficiency is that index funds normally are the most efficient stock funds of all. By infrequently selling their holdings, and with only a small amount of capital gains to distribute, these products work well in taxable accounts.

As alluded to earlier, some passive funds offered by Vanguard and Charles Schwab are designed to be even more tax-efficient than the garden-variety index fund. They do this by holding on to their winners, while taking losses on stocks that have slipped below cost. They sometimes buy back the losers after waiting at least 31 days, skirting the wash-sale rule. In addition, these funds might delay selling issues that have been dropped from the index that they're tracking.

AT THE CLOSE

Good tax planning is an important part of investment success. Although you should never let taxes dominate your decisions, you can improve your results by using smart strategies. Keep all the money you can in sheltered retirement accounts. This not only will help you build a larger nest egg by deferring taxes but it also will simplify the annual hassle of figuring out your gains and losses. In fact, if you want to do some trading with a portion of your nest egg, it makes sense from a tax standpoint to do it within an IRA or 401(k) umbrella.

For investments not held within retirement accounts, lean toward tax-efficient stock funds. Several factors affect efficiency, including trading activity and cash flow. In general, low-turnover index portfolios make the best choices in this regard.

CHAPTER 24

Using Your Computer

The popularity of mutual funds has paralleled the expansion of microcomputer usage. So it's not surprising that electronic investing has gained a wide following among people from all walks of life. Millions of Americans do at least some investment research or trading in cyberspace, and the numbers surely will expand in the future.

If you have access to the Internet, you can visit a fund group's Web site and download prospectuses, shareholder reports, and investor application forms. You can hunt for articles on a subject that interests you, maybe a particular fund or portfolio manager. You can post questions to a mutual-fund "message board" and receive responses from others. You can estimate future retirement or college needs by inputting your financial numbers to an online calculator or worksheet.

Perhaps you would like to sort through thousands of mutual funds to find just the kind of international portfolio you're looking for. Popular software packages can help you rapidly screen dozens of fields of data on thousands of funds to find those that meet your personal selection criteria.

Retirement-planning software can help you determine how much to save each year to meet your long-term goals. Or you might like to use your microcomputer to track your holdings and asset allocation.

Because our focus is on mutual funds rather than on computers, we assume you already have sufficient familiarity with computers and the kinds of software available. Suffice to say that products and services have been changing so quickly in the world of electronic investing that you will need to keep abreast of upgrades.

If you are not running your portfolio with help from a computer, don't worry. Computer users are not necessarily going to become richer than those who grow their nest eggs the old-fashioned way. Many of today's biggest names in investing—Warren Buffett and Peter Lynch among them—built their fortunes without knowing the difference between a mouse and a modem.

That said, there are many ways a computer can help with your investments. These processes are worth learning about because they will only become more widespread in the future. Generally speaking, a distinction can be made between (1) mining data contained on software that you load onto your computer's hard drive or CD-ROM and (2) going online into the world of cyberspace to access information or execute mutual-fund trades.

Our analysis of computerization focuses on the following areas:

- Using software to help plan how much to set aside each year to meet your retirement goals.

- Screening large databases to find a selected group of funds that meet your criteria.

- Comparing a fund's past performance with that of its peers and relevant benchmarks.

- Obtaining prospectuses, shareholder reports, and other information online from fund-company Web sites.

- Participating in online "message boards" and "chat" groups to ask questions and contribute your thoughts.

- Trading online and accessing information about your account.

- Tracking your investment holdings and monitoring your asset allocation.

SAVING FOR RETIREMENT

Retirement-planning software is offered by several fund companies and discount brokerages, including Fidelity, Scudder, Vanguard, and Charles

Schwab. These programs can help you decide how much to set aside annually at various rates of return to reach your goals. Saving for retirement is a top financial priority, and computers—with their high-powered number-crunching capabilities—can provide valuable assistance.

If you're familiar with computerized spreadsheets such as Microsoft Excel or Lotus 1-2-3, you can develop your own customized worksheet. Table 24-1 contains an example for Tony, a middle-aged executive who has neglected retirement planning in the past and needs to play catch up. Tony earns a good salary and is able to make fairly large contributions to his employer's 401(k) plan.

Table 24-1   Tony's Retirement-Planning Spreadsheet

Age	Yearly Investment*	Nominal Future Value @ 8%	Real Future Value @ 4%
45	$9,500	$9,500	$9,500
46	9,500	19,760	19,380
47	9,500	30,841	29,655
48	9,500	42,808	40,341
49	9,500	55,733	51,455
50	10,000	70,191	63,513
51	10,000	85,807	76,054
52	10,000	102,671	89,096
53	10,000	120,885	102,660
54	10,000	140,556	116,766
55	11,000	162,800	132,437
56	11,000	186,824	148,734
57	11,000	212,770	165,684
58	11,000	240,792	183,311
59	11,000	271,055	201,643
60	11,000	303,739	220,709
61	11,000	339,039	240,538
62	11,000	377,162	261,159
63	11,000	418,335	282,605
64	11,000	462,801	304,910
65	11,000	510,825	328,106
66	11,000	562,691	352,230
67	11,000	618,707	377,319
68	11,000	679,203	403,412
69	11,000	744,540	430,549
70	11,000	815,103	458,771

*Assumes end-of-year investments.

For the sake of simplicity, we assume Tony has no retirement nest egg now, although existing funds could easily be built into the worksheet. Tony has just turned 45 and we assume that his pension-plan contributions are made at the end of each year, even though he will make them monthly. Incidentally, there's no need to refine your spreadsheet to deal with monthly investments because your projections never will be perfect anyway. The rates of return you will earn on your investments and inflation are major uncertainties. The future will not necessarily be like the past; in fact, it probably will be different. Because of the unknowables, it's best to make conservative projections.

As seen in the worksheet, Tony plans to increase his yearly contributions when he turns 50 and again at 55. He estimates that he can earn a nominal 8 percent yearly on his balanced portfolio of mutual funds. But he also wants to build inflation into his projections, so he assumes a 4-percent inflation rate. That implies his assets will grow at a real rate of 4 percent.

Tony is not sure when he will retire, but he can see how much he would have in both nominal and inflation-adjusted amounts at various ages. Different annual investment amounts and rates of return can be entered into your spreadsheet, and their impact on the future values of your nest egg will be apparent immediately. If a portion of your assets is held in a taxable account, you can easily reduce your compounding rates to after-tax values based on your federal and state tax brackets.

A retirement-planning spreadsheet allows you to think about the future in quantitative terms. That makes it easier to determine how much you should be socking away each year and the kinds of returns you will need to earn. This exercise also can help you plan on a tentative retirement age.

SCREENING FOR WINNERS

With thousands of mutual funds available, you would be in for some serious work if you wanted to dig through all of these portfolios and compare their performances over various periods. But that's not all. A lot of data that you might want for making a selection, such as risk measures, are not available in most newspapers, magazines, or published sources. There simply isn't enough space to list it all. And, even if there was room, most people wouldn't want to wade through all the detail.

Screening Data Fields

Enter computerized mutual-fund software. Research firms such as Morningstar, Alexander Steele, and Value Line provide comprehensive packages for filtering through the fund universe in ways limited only by your imagination. Much of this data is contained in diskette and CD-ROM packs,

Measuring Risk-Adjusted Performance

Modern portfolio theory statistics are among the data fields included in the more comprehensive mutual-fund software packages. Risk measures such as standard deviation, beta, and R-squared were discussed in Chapter 6. Here's a look at three gauges of risk-adjusted performance.

Alpha compares the actual results of a portfolio with what would have been expected given the fund's beta and the market's behavior. If the fund fares better than predicted, it has a positive alpha. Below-par performance results in a negative alpha. Ideally, investors want managers who consistently can add value and generate high, positive alphas.

The Sharpe and Treynor ratios both use what's known as a "risk premium," or the difference between a fund's average return and the average return on a riskless Treasury bill over the same period. This premium can be positive or negative depending on how the fund performed. The *Sharpe ratio*, developed by Nobel Laureate William Sharpe, divides the risk premium by the fund's standard deviation. The *Treynor ratio* divides the same risk premium by beta. In either case, higher values are favorable as they indicate more return per unit of risk.

While logical and useful, risk-adjusted measures are not perfect. For one thing, the relevance of both the alpha and the Treynor measures depends on the accuracy of beta, as measured by R-squared. The closer R-squared is to 100 percent, the more useful the beta. And, as we've said before, historic data often don't predict anything.

but it also can be found online. Updates typically are available quarterly or monthly, depending on your needs. You can screen dozens of variables such as assets, turnover, expenses, 12b-1 fees, weighted-average maturity, returns for various periods, and assorted risk measures. You will come across some rather arcane statistics such as alphas, Sharpe ratios, and Treynor ratios.

For example, you could use Morningstar's software to filter for small-company value funds that fit the following seven criteria:

1. No front-end load.

2. Average annual return of at least 12 percent over the past 5 years.

3. An expense ratio of less than 1.5 percent.

4. Average annual portfolio turnover below 60 percent.

5. A median market cap for stocks held in the portfolio of less than $200 million.

6. Total assets of less than $300 million.

7. Average portfolio P/E ratio below 17.

If your criteria are too stringent, you may not find any small-company value funds that satisfy all, or even most, of them. Conversely, if your standards are lax, you may end up with far more choices than you want. Screening is something that's best learned by experience. When a program produces a manageable list of funds that satisfy your criteria, you can analyze each candidate more carefully to arrive at your final choices.

Evaluating Performance

You also can do a detailed analysis of a fund's performance over many years. Then, you could look at its return over various sub periods. This kind of data mining easily can become a waste of time, however. Your research would be of questionable value if the fund manager changed a number of times over this lengthy period or the portfolio's objective shifted. In addition, a portfolio that has experienced excessively fast growth in assets due to stellar results may have set itself up for more modest returns. It may no longer be nimble, and its assets perhaps have grown to the point where the manager's top picks have far less impact on performance.

On the other hand, a good use of historic performance is for monitoring the past results of funds you have owned for some time. Suppose you haven't been particularly pleased with your small-cap fund's performance over the last few years, and are looking for a reason to dump it. You could tap into your software to find out what the returns of its closest competitors were. You also could compare the results with alternative indexes. Perhaps the performance looks better than you thought when it's put into perspective.

The better software packages offer sophisticated graphics that facilitate a visually attractive comparison of your fund's performance with similar portfolios, group averages, and indexes, for whatever time frame you desire. All this can be shown in color on a line graph or bar chart.

Portfolio Information

The kinds of coverage provided by the different mutual-fund packages can vary widely. Also, most providers offer different versions of their software, depending on how much data you want. Some software packages, particularly those from Morningstar and Value Line, provide the sort of details you would get in a fund's annual report, with plenty of additional data and analysis. For example, *Morningstar Principia Plus* offers 130 data fields of information on about 8,000 funds, plus a page similar to what you would find in the bound *Morningstar Mutual Funds*. You can determine a stock fund's average P/E, median market capitalization, top holdings, a breakdown by industry, and the stock/bond/cash allocation. You also will find a narrative analysis like that in the hardcopy Morningstar publication. Incidentally, Morningstar also provides comparable software products for closed-end funds and variable annuities.

Mutual-fund software can be costly and might not be worth the price unless you are sure to get a lot of mileage from it. How much you pay depends in part on the quantity and frequency of the updates. A CD-ROM typically contains more data than a diskette and it may be easier to use. Online versions of fund data usually provide much less information and a more limited capacity for screening. If you need to download a lot of online data, the process might require considerable time.

GOING ONLINE

Vast amounts of mutual-fund and related investment information can be found in cyberspace with a few clicks of a computer mouse. If you want to go online, you will need a modem for your machine and a home base from which to enter the Internet. Your modem will interface with the access provider's computer, which will connect you to the desired information sites. Internet-access systems can be classified as either closed or open.

Commercial online services such as America Online, CompuServe, or Prodigy are considered closed because they can be reached only by people who sign up for them. Customers have access to special features offered by the online service in addition to an Internet connection. For example, AOL provides Morningstar data and reports, recent articles on mutual funds from various periodicals, and fund message boards.

Conversely, the Internet is an open system, so anyone who obtains a connection through a flat-rate access provider can utilize it. Check your yellow pages for smaller Internet-access providers in your area. Such local providers, however, may be more complicated for first-time Internet users to deal with. The commercial online services such as AOL provide an extremely user-friendly interface.

Cost is another factor to consider. Some Internet-access providers may charge a flat fee, while others bill you for the number of hours used. How you reach cyberspace depends on several factors such as your computer, online using patterns, research needs, prior experience, and how much money you want to spend. You need to do a careful cost-benefit analysis to reach the optimal decision.

The "Web" Versus the "Net"

The terms Internet and World Wide Web often are used interchangeably, but there is a difference. The Internet is a far-reaching, decentralized global network of computers linked primarily by modems and telephone lines. These computers are found at businesses, private residences, universities, government offices, and so on. You can locate information on virtually any subject somewhere on the Net.

Conversely, the World Wide Web provides a visually attractive connection with the Internet that allows you to browse easily for what you need. You call up a Web "home page" to find out what's available at a particular site. A Uniform Resource Locator or URL can be used to reach a Web site. This is nothing more than an Internet address. For example, Vanguard's Internet address is http://www.vanguard.com. Once you reach a home page, you click your mouse on a key word or phrase to move to the area of interest. Many Web pages have links that can take you directly to related sites. New Web sites are being added at a rapid pace.

There are several reasons for investors to go online. They include:

- Visiting a fund company's Web site to obtain news, share prices, returns, prospectuses, application forms, or other information.

- Participating in fund "chat groups," asking questions on "message boards," or corresponding with others by "e-mail."

- Obtaining magazine articles, reports, or other information on a particular subject.

- Buying or selling fund shares and keeping tabs on your account.

Visiting Web Sites

What do fund companies offer at their Web sites? The selection varies from firm to firm, but some sites contain an amazing amount of depth and breadth. Much of the information is sales and marketing literature, but you also might find educational material and interactive investment tools such as quizzes and worksheets. A big plus is that you can gain access to the information almost immediately, rather than having to wait for it to arrive in the mail. You can scan fund profiles, prospectuses, educational brochures, daily prices, news, research reports, and perhaps even profiles of fund managers. You can read these items while you're online, print them out, or download data to your computer's hard drive. You may be able to ask questions by e-mail to fund-company reps and get a personalized response.

Vanguard offers "courses" at its Web site covering various aspects of mutual-fund investing. Vanguard, Fidelity, and various other firms also have interactive "calculators" to help you figure how much you need to invest each month to attain a goal such as college for a child or your retirement. You simply supply some basic information and the calculator does the rest. You also can find interactive questionnaires to determine your risk tolerance or to allocate assets.

Some groups allow investors to view their accounts whenever they wish after providing appropriate identification for security purposes. Certain companies are upgrading their Web sites so you need to log on to find out what's currently being offered. You can find a fund company's Internet address by calling its toll-free 800 number. Appendix 2 contains the toll-free numbers for the major groups.

Other Web sites of possible interest to mutual-fund investors are listed in Figure 24-1.

Message Boards and Chat Rooms

If you have questions about mutual funds or investing in general, look for answers on a message board. On America Online, you can post questions on message boards operated by the American Association of Individual Investors, *BusinessWeek*, Morningstar, and Vanguard. Write your query, post it, and check back in a day or two for an answer. By posing a question in such a public forum, you can get the viewpoints of different people. Respondents might post replies or e-mail you directly.

Chat rooms allow for faster responses. Entering one is like being in a large room with others who are talking about, say, mutual funds or investing. There might be 50 people in the room and a dozen or more conversations going on simultaneously. Discussions change as people enter or leave. You can sit in and simply observe, or you could join in a conversation. Once you

Figure 24-1   Selected Web Sites of Possible Interest

Web Site	Internet Address
American Association of Individual Investors (AAII)	http://www.aaii.org
Bloomberg (financial and market news)	http://www.bloomberg.com
IBC (an excellent source of money-fund data)	http://www.ibcdata.com
The Internet Closed-End Investor	http://www.icefi.com
Investment Company Institute	http://www.ici.org
Mutual Fund Education Alliance	http://www.mfea.com
Mutual Funds Interactive	http://www.brill.com
Mutual Funds Magazine Online	http://www.mfmag.com
NETworth (a good starting point for fund surfing)	http://networth.galt.com
The No-Load Fund Investor	http://www.adpad.com/noload
U.S. Securities and Exchange Commission	http://www.sec.gov
WEBS (exchange-traded country index funds)	http://www.websontheweb.com

have joined, whatever you type is visible to all participants. And you can see all the messages that everyone else has typed in.

The benefit of a chat room is to get quick responses from different people on subjects that interest you. Just don't believe everything that you read. The information could be misleading because anyone can post messages or respond to yours. The same advice may apply to message boards—depending on who's answering.

Trading Online

You can buy and sell funds at certain Web sites or with special computer software provided by a discount brokerage such as Charles Schwab or Fidelity. Online transactions offer a few advantages for some people. For starters, you can enter an order at any time. Or perhaps you simply do a lot of work in cyberspace and feel most comfortable that way. You can see the order as you enter it, which may be an advantage for you. In addition, you may get a discount for doing certain trades online, depending on your brokerage's policy. Various no-load companies let investors exchange funds via their Web sites. However, most won't allow you to redeem shares directly, for security reasons.

Online investing has special advantages for people dealing in exchange-traded funds. With closed-end portfolios, Spiders, and WEBS, you can view the bid and asked prices, the quantity of shares bid for and offered (known as the "size"), and the number of shares traded throughout the day. This can help you keep tabs on intraday price fluctuations and changes in liquidity. Remember that limit orders with exchange-traded funds grant you more control over prices.

TRACKING YOUR HOLDINGS

Computers can help organize your investments so you can see the big picture more clearly. For instance, you can keep track of the percentages of your portfolio that are invested in various funds and your allocation amounts in stocks, bonds, and cash. Focusing on the big picture also can help you spot other problems such as portfolio clutter, or excessive duplication within a particular investment category. In addition, by viewing your portfolio as a whole, you are less likely to be disturbed by a sharp decline in a single holding.

You can set up a computerized spreadsheet using software such as Microsoft Excel or Lotus 1-2-3 that will keep track of what you own and your current asset allocation. Table 24-2 contains an example using generic fund categories. Many variations are possible. Once you have built the spreadsheet, you easily can update the NAVs and number of shares for each fund. You also can easily add new funds and delete former holdings. The far right-hand col-

Table 24-2   Portfolio Allocation Worksheet

Date:

Investment Positions	Share Price	Shares Owned	Dollar Value	Current Weight	Target Weight
Stock funds:					
Large-cap growth	18.37	1,951.232	$35,844.13	17.8%	
Large-cap value	6.61	8,981.451	59,367.39	29.5	
Total large cap			**95,211.52**	**47.3%**	**50%**
Small-cap growth	17.73	1,032.149	18,300.00	9.1	
Small-cap value	20.67	617.821	12,770.36	6.3	
Total small cap			**31,070.36**	**15.4%**	**15%**
International developed market	14.53	1,893.175	27,507.83	13.7	
International emerging market	8.89	1,793.932	15,948.06	7.9	
Total international			**43,455.89**	**21.6%**	**20%**
TOTAL STOCK ALLOCATION			**169,737.77**	**84.4%**	**85%**
Bond funds:					
Intermediate-term municipal	12.17	782.139	9,518.63	4.7	
Short-term corporate	14.11	391.982	5,530.87	2.8	
TOTAL BOND ALLOCATION			**15,049.50**	**7.5%**	**10%**
Cash:					
Tax-free money fund	1	16,332.373	16,332.37	8.1	
TOTAL CASH ALLOCATION			**16,332.37**	**8.1%**	**5%**
TOTAL PORTFOLIO VALUE			**201,119.64**	**100.0%**	

umn in our worksheet contains our target weights, making it easy to see how the current allocations match up with the long-run benchmarks. When you see significant deviations, it may be time to rebalance.

It's particularly useful to build a spreadsheet if you hold funds with several companies. That way, you can have an overall snapshot of your holdings. Conversely, if you hold all your funds at one family or with a single brokerage, you may not need to do this.

It's also useful to maintain additional spreadsheets for tax purposes. You can track all the details on your purchases and dividends. When it comes time to sell, it will be easy to determine your cost basis because everything you need will be in one place.

AT THE CLOSE

Electronic investing is in vogue. You can use a personal computer to figure out how much you need to save for retirement, screen through thousands of mutual funds, keep track of your asset allocation, and more. Also, the Web sites operated by fund families provide a handy way to access current information and download prospectuses and other material.

But while computers are wonderful tools, their widespread use to pick mutual-fund winners and execute profitable trades can be questioned for several reasons. In particular, mutual funds should be viewed as long-term investments. The ability to access tons of information online and buy and sell with several keystrokes and a few clicks of the mouse can cause a person to become a frenzied trader. "Switch and get rich" doesn't work. Also, there's a lot of hype and useless information on the Internet. Surfing the Web can become addictive and use up too much valuable time. It's often best to put your money into a good assortment of stock funds and simply let it grow.

CHAPTER 25

The Mutual-Fund Phenomenon

A generation ago, mutual funds were like the earliest mammals—small, vulnerable creatures that scurried about the undergrowth of the investment landscape. Since then, of course, funds have evolved into financial giants, with heavy footsteps that reverberate throughout the stock and bond jungles.

The mutual-fund industry has grown so much over the past several decades that it now ranks as the second-largest financial intermediary behind only commercial banks—and the gap in assets between the two continues to narrow. Funds are not just an American phenomenon, either. They also are popular in more than two dozen foreign nations, ranging from sophisticated financial centers like Britain and Japan to up-and-comers such as Greece, India, Portugal, and Taiwan.

Worldwide, mutual funds have captured close to $6 trillion in assets, with a significant slice of that residing in funds beyond our borders. This ever-increasing demand can be attributed in large part to the world's growing middle class. People around the globe have the same basic financial needs and goals. The fund phenomenon is truly universal!

WHY THE LOVE AFFAIR?

There are several reasons why mutual funds have become so popular since 1970. These factors include:

- *The introduction of money-market funds.* Many people were exposed to stock and bond funds by way of the money products. These portfolios also played a crucial role in popularizing telephone switching.

- *The trend toward voluntary retirement plans.* Mutual funds are ideal vehicles for self-directed programs such as IRAs and 401(k)s. Employees now assume more responsibility for their retirement planning.

- *The great bull market of the 1980s and 1990s.* The Federal Reserve gradually brought inflation under control during the 1980s, and the resulting robust stock and bond returns attracted legions of investors.

- *Appealing new products and services.* The increasing number of fund categories reflects a far higher degree of choice than ever before. The Investment Company Institute, for instance, now classifies funds into 21 different objectives compared with just eight groups in 1976.

- *A growing interest in international diversification.* With 60 percent of the world's total stock value outside the U.S., people have turned increasingly to foreign markets. Mutual funds, with their professional management and broad diversification, make obscure foreign stocks and bonds readily accessible.

- *Greater sophistication among investors.* The fact is that individuals are becoming much more financially literate. More people recognize the importance of diversification and asset allocation, and the inherent advantages of mutual funds. The old adage "a fool and his money are soon parted" seems to be less true than it once was.

In short, mutual funds have blossomed as more people came to understand their many advantages over holding stocks and bonds directly.

OBSERVATIONS AND CAUTIONS

Although mutual funds as a group perform their jobs well, this does not mean investors can afford to get careless. In particular, shareholders need to realize that the overly generous returns stocks delivered during the great bull market of the 1980s and 1990s will not last forever. "Regression to the mean"

Superior Performers May Revert to Average

The idea of "regression to the mean" also applies to individual funds, not just asset categories. After a hot spell, most portfolios can be expected to perform more in line with the competition. One reason is that as a fund grows larger due to its success, it becomes more difficult to run. The manager's one or two dozen favorite companies no longer will exert as much weight in the portfolio. Scores of additional choices may be needed to fill out the portfolio.

In addition, trading costs can take a big bite out of the returns of large portfolios. These costs include brokerage commissions, the bid-asked spread, and the unfavorable price impacts of large trades. Giant funds may need to buy blocks of shares worth tens of millions of dollars so that they can become a meaningful part of the portfolio. Consequently, the purchasing power of a large fund could push the price of a stock above the manager's target, while the downward price pressure on sales also can hurt returns.

---

describes the idea that extended periods of superior performance eventually will be followed by lengthy stretches of subpar returns. The reverse also holds true when markets have languished for a long spell.

Over many decades, U.S. stocks have returned a bit more than 10 percent yearly. But gains in the bull market that began in August 1982 have been far higher. It's still smart to invest all you can in equity funds because stocks are likely to be the best long-run performers over time. But you should remain cognizant of the risks and limit your allocation to a suitable amount.

One trend worth watching in the future is the ability of fund supermarkets at discount brokerages and full-service firms to attract large numbers of investors seeking the convenience of one-stop shopping. People want to pick and choose the best of what different families have to offer. They want to move their money quickly from funds at one family to another. Family loyalties have been weakened.

Critics of fund supermarkets hold that they lead to higher costs for all investors—those who don't participate in the supermarket as well as those who do. The higher costs result because fund companies are charged 25 to 35 basis points yearly for the privilege of being included in a superstore. In addition, these programs tend to foster a casino atmosphere by making it easy for individuals to hop from fund to fund, thereby perhaps saddling remaining shareholders with higher expenses. To get more bang for the buck, investors also may be tempted to margin their purchases, a risky practice.

One of our concerns is that the increasing number of choices, the ability to tap into more performance data quickly, and the ease with which people can shuttle their money around can lead to excessive short-term trading. It's best to buy an assortment of solid funds and stick with them for the long haul. Predicting near-term performance is very difficult, so it doesn't make sense to jump around often.

MAKING MUTUAL FUNDS WORK

Mutual funds generally don't make people wealthy in a short time. But if you're patient, they're the best, most convenient way to build up assets over the years. In that regard, here are our "24 steps to successful investing" that nearly everyone can apply.

1. *Learn the investment essentials.* Knowledge is the key component in the wealth-building equation. You simply need to understand how the stock and bond markets work, including the kinds of risks you face and the intricacies of mutual funds.

2. *Build up your emergency reserves.* Financial advisers recommend that you keep at least three months' living expenses in cash-equivalent accounts such as money-market funds and short-term bond portfolios. You can meet unexpected needs by drawing a check on a money-market fund rather than redeeming a portion of your stock holdings at what could be a bad time. In addition, money that you will need for planned big-ticket expenditures over the next five years should be kept in a safe harbor. You also can use extra cash to go bargain hunting when especially good values appear.

3. *Don't roll the dice.* Too many people seek instant financial gratification. High-risk speculations in options, futures, and individual small stocks generally aren't worth the potential losses. If a security declines 50 percent, it will have to double just to get back to its former price. If it tumbles 75 percent, it needs to soar 300 percent. Money surrendered on highly risky gambles disappears forever. Maintaining emotional discipline at all times is a hard but critical part of investment success.

4. *Take the time to do your homework.* There's rarely a big rush to put money into a mutual fund. Because of their built-in diversification, most funds move up and down more slowly than individual stocks do. Take time to familiarize yourself with the prospectus and learn about the investment so that you're not unpleasantly surprised later on. With more than 6,000 portfolios available, you have plenty of choices and don't need to worry about a high-flyer slipping away.

5. *Let time work for you.* The slow, sure route works best. The longer money stays put, the more opportunity it has to compound exponentially. The truly big gains materialize after a decade or more. Investing $100 a month at 10 percent for 10 years grows to $20,655; but in 20 years it rises to $76,570; and in 40 years it swells to an eye-popping $637,678. In addition, the risk of holding stock funds decreases as your holding period increases. That's because the good years far outweigh the bad when you practice "time diversification" over the decades.

6. *Stick with dollar-cost averaging through thick and thin.* The idea of investing small amounts regularly, such as $100 monthly, is a great way to build wealth and cope with market gyrations. You'll buy more shares when prices are down and fewer when they're high. This type of program also can help you become more disciplined because it encourages investing at market nadirs when people otherwise might be too fearful. If possible, double up on your purchases when prices are depressed. If you're able to spend more time monitoring your holdings, consider value averaging, a souped-up approach.

7. *Consider putting a large lump sum to work all at once.* Despite the emotional benefits of an averaging strategy, academic research indicates that it's often better to invest a large sum of money in the stock market in one fell swoop. The stock market has a bullish bias, rising in about seven out of every ten years. Thus, the expected return over any given period is higher for stocks than it is for cash. You always can reduce your risk by dividing a large investment among different stock-fund categories, such as foreign and small-company. A lump-sum approach can be particularly wise for younger investors with a long time horizon, assuming they have ample cash.

8. *Set aside all you can.* The simplest, surest way to build wealth is to invest meaningful sums. Regardless of when you start, your results will be better if you sock away more. Most people should try to save at least 10 percent of their gross earnings. Young adults who are just starting out and facing big-ticket purchases may not be able to achieve that. But as you grow older, you may be able to save substantially more.

9. *Invest as much in stock funds as you can.* Stocks provide the best long-term protection against inflation or purchasing-power risk. Even at 3 percent a year, inflation will gradually take its toll on a nest egg that's too heavily composed of cash and bond investments. Since retirees are living longer, stock products deserve a place in their portfolios, too. The key is to choose funds that suit your temperament for volatil-

ity. At a minimum, strive to invest a percentage equal to "100 minus your age" in stocks. More aggressive people with a long time horizon can increase this percentage to perhaps 120 minus their age.

10. *Avoid hard-core market-timing.* It's not uncommon for timers to move between the extremes of 100 percent in stock funds and 100 percent in cash. While there certainly are times to be more heavily invested than others, jumping in and out greatly increases your risk of under-performance. Participating in the best up months is far more important than avoiding the worst down months. The really dramatic stock-price surges are unpredictable, of short duration, and few and far between. Market-timers risk being in cash when the bull stampedes.

11. *Use tax-smart strategies.* While taxes should not take precedence over other investment considerations, they still are best minimized where possible. Here are four tips for managing investments in taxable accounts: 1) Use the most advantageous cost basis when selling only a part of your fund holdings; 2) buy stock funds after the end-of-year "ex-distribution" date, particularly when a large payout is likely; 3) sell losers to take advantage of write offs; and 4) invest in tax-efficient funds such as index portfolios. Refer to Chapter 23 for details.

12. *Take maximum advantage of tax-deferred compounding.* The main reason most people invest is to provide for a comfortable, secure retirement. You can build more wealth if you postpone paying taxes on the gains. IRAs, Keoghs, 401(k)s, and the like are great savings vehicles. Deductible plans offer an immediate tax saving in the year you invest, as well as tax-deferred compounding. In addition, retirement accounts impose a kind of discipline because you normally can't take out money before age 59½ without paying a 10-percent premature-withdrawal penalty.

13. *Be cost conscious.* There are three important variables to consider when analyzing any investment: costs, probable performance, and risk. Of the three, pay particular attention to costs, because they are the most predictable. Management fees, administrative costs, and 12b-1 outlays are only part of the burden on returns. Trading costs may be even more important for funds that do a lot of buying and selling. A fund's large purchases or sales can drive stock prices up or down in the process. A fund's brokerage commissions and bid-asked spreads also can weigh heavily.

14. *Include index portfolios in your investment mix.* These funds have a lot going for them. Low costs, the assurance of beating most active man-

agers over time, and tax efficiency are big plusses. Investors are learning that it's difficult to select long-run winners because a manager's past performance is often a poor guide to future results. Because of their tax efficiency, index funds are ideally suited for ordinary accounts. Indexing a portion of your portfolio—say, 30 to 50 percent—still gives you the chance to pick actively managed funds that you think can do well.

15. *Think globally.* About 60 percent of the market value of all publicly traded companies lies beyond our borders. Adding an international fund to your portfolio can pay off in terms of better risk-adjusted performance. A globally diversified portfolio tends to have less volatility than either a pure U.S. stake or a pure foreign one.

16. *Don't overlook emerging markets.* Up-and-coming nations in Eastern Europe, Southeast Asia, and Latin America offer an additional layer of diversification. That's because stock prices in these places are affected by unique circumstances at different times yet in general offer some of the greatest growth prospects. Consider placing 10 to 40 percent of your total foreign-stock holdings in emerging-markets funds, depending on personal factors such as your age and risk tolerance.

17. *Keep your assets in balance.* Based on your age, time horizon, and risk tolerance, determine what percentages of your nest egg you want invested in stocks, bonds, and cash. Your stock allocation can be subdivided into, say, funds that target large, small, and foreign companies. You also can subdivide your bond allocation. Review these weightings at least annually to make sure the percentages haven't drifted too far out of line. That way you avoid "risk creep," which can occur when your stock allocation rises well above your target due to superior equity performance.

18. *Mix dissimilar funds.* Don't view the riskiness of a single fund in isolation. Rather, determine how each investment meshes with others. A mix of various stock and bond funds can stabilize your overall portfolio. Volatile funds may not be that risky when used as a modest part of a well-diversified plan. This is especially true of international funds, because some foreign bourses may be charging ahead when the U.S. market is merely treading water or heading lower.

19. *Use real estate rather than gold funds for inflation protection.* Some advisers recommend keeping 5 or 10 percent of your nest egg in a gold fund, but gold has been a poor long-term performer. Consider opting instead for a real-estate portfolio because it should offer higher appre-

ciation potential. A 5 or 10 percent stake in a real-estate fund adds an important dimension of diversification, giving you exposure to tangible assets.

20. *Use appropriate benchmarks to measure performance.* If you mostly hold foreign, small-stock, or bond funds, it won't do you much good to track popular market yardsticks like the S&P 500 or the Dow Jones Industrial Average. If in doubt, use the indexes listed in the annual reports of each fund that you own, then weight your portfolio accordingly.

21. *Get rid of any duds.* Don't be too patient with laggards. Underperforming market benchmarks is a big risk to which some people are oblivious. Weed out funds that have trailed their peers over the past 18 to 24 months. Selling often involves admitting that you made a mistake. Humility is another key to financial success.

22. *Take maximum advantage of fund services.* Automatic investment plans, for example, are a great way to build wealth through a dollar-cost averaging strategy. Withdrawal plans can be helpful for retirees. If you have questions about your fund or its services, call the company. Most telephone reps are glad to be of assistance. If they don't know an answer, they can find out quickly from someone who does.

23. *Don't overlook systematic withdrawal programs.* Retirees who must tap their nest eggs can use dollar-cost averaging in reverse. A withdrawal plan established with a mutual-fund company can provide regular monthly or quarterly checks to help meet living expenses. By taking money out of stock funds in small increments, you don't expose yourself to the danger of selling a big chunk of shares when the market happens to be depressed.

24. *Consider closed-end funds.* If you're inclined to stray from the beaten path, these investments can offer special advantages when they trade at sizable discounts, as is commonly the case. Buying a closed-end fund at, say, a 15-percent markdown is like paying 85 cents for a dollar's worth of assets. Discounts deepen in market setbacks and during the end-of-year tax-selling season. Adding a closed-end fund or two is easy to do, especially if you already are buying mutual funds through a brokerage supermarket. Then again, closed-end funds are more complicated than their open-end relatives and demand extra sophistication.

AT THE CLOSE

The modern mutual fund is a far cry from its 19th century closed-end ancestors. The investment industry in general also is a fairer, safer one to deal with than it was in the freewheeling '20s. You don't have to worry about a crash and bear market of the same magnitude as the 1929-1932 fiasco, thanks to stringent federal regulations with plenty of safeguards in place.

Now the ball is in your court. You can deal directly with a fund family, go through a fund supermarket, or use both avenues. You can plug into your computer for information or merely dial an 800 number. And you can deal with a broker or financial planner, or do it yourself. The keys to investment success include knowledge, persistence, emotional discipline, and plain common sense.

Although the number of funds and fund categories probably will not expand at the torrid pace they have since 1970, the assets of the industry certainly will grow. The mutual-fund phenomenon is alive and well. It's an idea whose time has come.

CHAPTER 26

Mutual Fund Q & A

You've got to ask the right questions to get the real story.

Here is an assortment of questions and answers, organized into the following topic groups:

- Getting the facts
- Sizing up a fund
- Understanding the market
- Stock funds
- Foreign-stock funds
- Exchange-traded funds
- Bond and money-market funds
- Managing your mutual-fund portfolio
- Tax considerations
- Behind the scenes
- Computerized investing
- Fund supermarkets

GETTING THE FACTS

What are the essential things to look for in a prospectus?

Key things contained in each disclosure pamphlet include the following: A portfolio's objectives, policies, risks, sales charges, expenses, turnover, performance, asset growth (or decline), and shareholder services. Also check the minimum investment amounts and procedures for redeeming shares.

The financial-highlights table contains the most important summary of numbers in the prospectus. In it, you will find key per-share values and ratios for the past 10 years or the life of the fund, whichever is shorter. The fund-expenses table also is crucial. Among other things, it breaks out 12b-1 fees (if any), management fees, and other expenses, so you can see their relative contributions to a portfolio's total expense ratio.

What kinds of mutual-fund advisory services are available? Should I subscribe?

There are dozens. Some focus on market-timing and switching, others have a more general orientation and simply help you select good funds. A few services focus on just one fund family, namely Fidelity or Vanguard.

An advisory service costs money, so you have to determine whether it's worth the expense. You also may find that some newsletters promote switching more frequently than you might like. Remember that you can learn a lot about investments just by reading standard business publications. The quarterly mutual-fund surveys contained in *Barron's* and *The Wall Street Journal*, along with *Forbes'* annual fund edition, are good sources of performance data and commentary. Appendix 1 lists other worthwhile guides.

I want a benchmark against which I can measure the daily percent changes of my fund's NAV. I know stock-market indexes are available, but are there any daily fund indexes?

Yes. Lipper Analytical Services publishes daily indexes for 21 fund categories: 10 equity and 11 bond. The benchmarks are based on the largest funds within each objective. They appear in Part C of *The Wall Street Journal* with daily fund-price listings. Expanded coverage is available on Fridays in the "Performance Yardsticks" table, which is also a part of the fund listings. The indexes in Friday's Yardsticks table are based on all funds within each objective and show performance over longer periods.

What is the so-called "survivorship bias" that I sometimes hear about when fund performance is being discussed?

This statistical quirk in performance measurement occurs because portfolios with poor performance records often leave the mutual-fund databases. Even though the fund industry has enjoyed phenomenal growth, many weak sisters have disappeared. The duds are frequently merged into siblings with more respectable performances, thereby erasing their unflattering records. As the unsuccessful portfolios get weeded out, the average returns for broad fund categories during past years become artificially inflated. Thus, the past record of the industry gradually grows better.

Survivorship bias is probably more of an academic issue, however. The performance record of a specific fund stays the same—it's the averages that are inflated. In any event, past performance is an imperfect guide to the future.

SIZING UP A FUND

How does a fund's NAV differ from a stock's price?

Since a fund is diversified, its NAV normally will be more stable than a stock's price. That's because some of the fund's stock holdings will zig while others zag, producing an overall smoother ride.

Another difference is that each fund is required by law to distribute annually at least 98 percent of its realized capital gains to shareholders. Thus, the NAV usually does not grow over the years as much as a stock's price does.

The most tax-efficient stock funds can see their NAVs grow significantly over the years, however. That's because their prices appreciate along with the increasing amount of unrealized gains embedded in their portfolios. This is particularly true of index funds with minuscule turnover rates such as Vanguard's Index Trust 500 Portfolio.

Can a new fund be a good investment?

Yes, but there are several reasons not to buy one. New funds commonly debut in the advanced stages of bull markets, when investor interest is at its peak. Portfolios often are trotted out in areas that have been hot, such as global health care.

Also, new funds have no track record. If they stay small, they won't enjoy the same economies of scale that larger, established funds do, and thus will have relatively high expense ratios. This is particularly true of new stand-alone funds that may never attract sufficient money.

Why select a newcomer when there are always many proven portfolios to choose from? The biggest argument in favor of new funds is that small portfolios are more nimble. This is especially important for funds that invest in smaller stocks. If the cash-flow theory discussed in Chapter 4 is correct, a small portfolio could do very well if it experiences large cash inflows over several years. In addition, a new fund focusing on an area in which its family has unquestioned expertise may be a good choice. That's because families often nurture their newest members by stuffing them with their choicest stock picks.

Should large stock funds perform better than small ones because they benefit more from economies of scale?

In theory, a large fund should have a lower expense ratio. That's because the fixed costs of managing the portfolio can be spread over a larger asset base. But fund companies don't always lower their percentage management fee as they grow in size. In addition, 12b-1 fees may remain at the same percentage. Thus, a large stock fund doesn't always pass along its economies of scale to shareholders in the form of a lower expense ratio.

Even though many large funds do have lower expense ratios, they can incur higher trading costs, which eat into the bottom line. True, their commissions per share can be lower because they deal in larger quantities. But trading costs also include the bid-asked spread and possible adverse price impacts of large trades. The latter are unmeasurable but highly significant. Large portfolios obviously need to take bigger positions in many of the stocks they acquire. For this reason, the average costs of stocks a manager purchases often are far above the target price. Conversely, when a big fund wants to sell a large position it could easily push the price down. These adverse price impacts hurt the performance of large funds.

Not all mutual funds appear in the daily newspaper listings. Why not?

Requirements to be listed in newspapers are set by the National Association of Securities Dealers or NASD, a self-regulating industry group. Initially, a fund must have either 1,000 shareholders or $25 million in assets. To maintain a listing, 750 shareholders or $15 million is needed. Most newspapers trim the list even further, excluding smaller portfolios and out-of-state muni-bond funds, among others. Typically, more than 1,000 portfolios get left out of daily fund tables. Additional portfolios may be left out in the future due to the shortage of space resulting from the significant growth in the number of funds and the escalating cost of newsprint. The proliferation of share classes on broker-sold funds has contributed to the space problem since each class receives its own price. If your fund does not appear in your local newspaper, call the newspaper and request that it be included.

In plain English, what is the standard deviation, and why is it important to me?

Simply put, it's a yardstick of risk. It measures the fluctuations of a fund's monthly returns around their average. The higher the number, the greater the volatility.

If the monthly returns were always the same, the standard deviation would be zero. This never happens. When returns bounce up and down like a yo-yo, the standard deviation would be relatively high. You might see this with an aggressive-growth or gold portfolio.

The standard deviation is the best measure of volatility and can be used to make volatility comparisons among all types of funds—stock, bond, gold, and so on. We much prefer it to beta, which has been the subject of increased criticism.

Is it important to know whether my fund manager hedges with futures and options?

Yes. Hedging is done to reduce a portfolio's volatility. Options and futures can be used to lessen market risk, interest-rate risk, and currency risk.

Many funds are allowed by their prospectuses to hedge. The question is to what extent a manager actually does so.

Hedging should be viewed as insurance. Too much can prove costly and might reduce returns. That's why we prefer funds that don't do much hedging. Long-term investors need not be concerned about a portfolio's near-term ups and downs.

How can I tell if an expense ratio is too high?

Compare a fund's expense ratio with that of its peers. Remember that smaller funds tend to have higher ratios, as do international and global portfolios because of the greater costs of investing overseas. Expenses are especially important for bond and money-market funds, which earn lower returns than stock portfolios and thus need every bit of economizing.

Of the major expense components, look at the management fee. This outlay should be declining in percentage terms as total assets increase. So-called 12b-1 fees also constitute part of the expense ratio, making it important to avoid funds with high 12b-1 charges.

UNDERSTANDING THE MARKET

How can I tell if the stock market is cheap or "dicey"?

No single indicator works all the time, but some fairly simple benchmarks are pretty reliable at market extremes. For example, if the price-earnings ratios of the Standard & Poor's 500 or Dow Jones Industrial Average approach 20 and their dividend yields drop near 2 percent, you can be fairly sure the market is pricey. Conversely, P/Es around 10 or yields near 6 percent point to bargain-basement values. *Barron's* publishes both indicators on a weekly basis.

What are the differences and similarities between the market crashes of October 1929 and October 1987? Is it likely that we will again have such a crash?

On October 28 and 29, 1929, the Dow Jones Industrial Average tumbled about 23 percent cumulatively. The indicator also plunged about 23 percent on October 19, 1987. But that's where the similarity ends. The aftermath of the 1929 crash was much more severe, dragging the Dow down more than 80 percent by the time stocks hit bottom in 1932. The economy was in shambles during the Great Depression of the 1930s. Conversely, the crash of 1987 was very short lived and the market enjoyed a substantial recovery after a few months. The economy remained fundamentally sound.

Market crashes of this magnitude are few and far between. It's unlikely that one will occur anytime soon but if it does the main thing to remember is not to panic, sell, and lock in a loss. You must be patient and ride out the tumultuous times. Remember, stocks are a long-term investment.

What is the difference between growth and value investing?

These are the two primary stock-investment styles. Growth managers seek companies exhibiting dramatic revenue or earning increases—typically smaller to medium-sized firms. For the most part, they don't mind paying high prices to get the right stocks.

Conversely, value investors search for firms that can be bought cheaply. These outfits may sell at low ratios of price to earnings or book value, or they may have high dividend yields or "hidden" assets. As contrarians, value managers are more patient, longer-term buyers than growth investors. It often takes time for the market to recognize the value in a particular situation. Thus, a value portfolio would tend to have lower turnover and assume less risk than a growth fund would.

What is meant by the term "efficient market?" What are the implications?

An efficient market is simply one where stocks sell for what they truly are worth. You can't realize above-average performance since there are no significant mispricings of which to take advantage. If you are a firm believer in efficient markets, you would want to invest in index funds.The efficient-market theory, however, remains a controversial one.

STOCK FUNDS

How exactly do index funds work? What are their advantages and disadvantages?

These portfolios track a particular market index such as the S&P 500, Russell 2000, Wilshire 5000, or Morgan Stanley Capital International Pacific Index. The idea is to match the index's performance, not beat it. The funds hold stocks in proportion to their weight in a particular index. Usually, shares are simply bought and held, to minimize transaction costs and management fees. Index funds remain fully invested, with hardly anything in cash. This gives them an edge during market rallies.

Index funds appeal to people who believe in market efficiency and want to follow a low-cost, long-term, buy-and-hold strategy. This approach assures that you won't significantly underperform—not a trivial concern since a large proportion of equity funds end up doing worse than the popular averages. Tax efficiency is an additional plus. Since they may have turnover ratios of just 5 percent or so, the amount of capital gains distributed to shareholders is very modest.

Nevertheless, index products do have potential drawbacks. Although they have fared well with domestic blue chips, their record has been less stellar with small companies and foreign stocks. In these less efficiently priced arenas, skilled managers have more opportunities to add value. And active international managers aren't bound by the country weightings in a multi-nation index such as the EAFE.

Finally, because they're fully invested, indexed portfolios could be hit harder in a severe bear market than managed funds if investors cash out en masse. That would force the funds to realize and distribute large gains on low-cost positions that have been held for years.

Is there any way fund managers can beat the market?

Yes. Some managers undoubtedly possess rare stock-picking talent. Also, studies have shown that you can achieve superior long-term performance by investing in certain groups of stocks. These include companies that sell at low P/E and price-book value ratios. Also, a smaller portfolio that limits its holdings to a few dozen of the manager's choice picks may offer above-average potential. In addition, a well-chosen group of micro-cap stocks—which are so small that they're typically overlooked by Wall Street—may do well for patient investors.

That said, it is still virtually impossible to identify with any degree of certainty those managers who will beat the indexes in the future.

What is so-called "style drift" and is it a problem for investors?

Mutual funds are increasingly being labeled by their investment style—such as "small-cap growth" or "large-cap value." This tells you what kind of stocks they supposedly target. Managers, however, may not always stick to their knitting. They may stray from their style in an effort to improve performance if their group is lagging behind others. In another case, a small-stock fund may drift from its style because it has received so much new money that the manager decides to invest in some bigger companies. Still another example is a growth fund that moves heavily into cash and bonds because the manager fears a downturn in stocks.

Style drift can lead to unexpectedly good or bad performance of a fund relative to its peers. Suppose a small-stock fund invests a portion of its assets in blue chips. If those corporate titans roar ahead of their smaller siblings, the manager looks brilliant; if not, investors will be upset.

It's usually better if a fund sticks to its style so investors won't be surprised. Style drift can be a problem if you're trying to maintain a predetermined mix of funds in your portfolio. Suppose you have 20 percent of your equity allocation in a small-stock growth fund. If the manager shifts half of the fund's assets into blue chips, your small-cap weighting would decline to 10 percent.

FOREIGN-STOCK FUNDS

Why is it important to have exposure to foreign stocks?

About 60 percent of the world's total stock-market value exists outside the United States. By investing internationally, you're exposed to greater growth opportunities, particularly in emerging markets in Eastern Europe, Latin America, and Southeast Asia.

In addition, international diversification can reduce volatility, since stock markets in different countries generally don't move in lock-step. True, individual nations often exhibit greater economic, political, and stock-market risks, but these dangers are reduced through diversification.

I want to give international investing a try. What's a good way to get started?

The first thing to remember is that the more countries represented in a portfolio, the greater the diversification. A fund consisting only of Japanese stocks would be riskier than another that invests in perhaps a dozen markets. Also, big blue-chip foreign companies would be less volatile than smaller overseas stocks, especially those in emerging economies. So the riskiest type of foreign-stock fund would be a closed-end, single-country portfolio that owns the small stocks of an emerging market.

Most beginners should stick with an established global or international fund investing in good-quality companies in a variety of countries. Global funds differ from international portfolios in that they hold both U.S. and foreign stocks. International funds are generally a better choice because of their pure non-U.S. exposure.

What are regional portfolios and how are they used?

These are more specialized international funds that usually focus on one of the three major overseas regions: Europe, Asia, or Latin America. You also can find African and Eastern European portfolios. Regional funds invest in a group of countries within their target area. It's important to know what nations a regional portfolio invests in and how they are weighted. For instance, some Asian funds include Japan in their mix and others don't.

Regional portfolios appeal to moderately aggressive investors who want more focused holdings. For example, you might want all your international exposure in Europe if you feel it offers the best value. But since regional funds are less diversified than their global or international counterparts, they generally carry more risk.

Why do currency exchange rates fluctuate? How do these fluctuations affect investors in foreign-stock funds?

Currency rates move up and down like the prices of bananas, oil, or any other commodity. Rates vary because of shifts in demand and supply. An increase in demand, holding supply constant, will lead to a higher price. The supply and demand for a country's currency are closely related to its balance of trade (the difference between the value of its exports and imports), net foreign investment, and other factors. Major banks, multinational corporations, money managers, speculators, and tourists buy and sell currencies on a daily basis.

Suppose Country A has a healthy balance of trade surplus (exporting more than it imports) and offers relatively high interest rates, thereby attracting foreign investment. Country A's currency would be in strong demand since foreigners would need it to pay for their purchases and investments. The nation's currency also might be bid higher by speculators, if they think it will continue to appreciate.

Long-term investors in international funds shouldn't worry much about currency fluctuations. Gains and losses tend to balance out. Besides, changes in exchange rates are difficult to predict, so we don't recommend buying a foreign fund as a short-term currency speculation.

EXCHANGE-TRADED FUNDS

I'm confused by closed-end funds. In plain language, how do they work and how do they differ from open-end funds?

Closed-end funds are part stock and part investment company. They are professionally managed just as open-end funds are, but they have two prices: a share price that fluctuates throughout the day and an NAV. When the share price is less than NAV, a discount exists. There is a premium when the price exceeds NAV. Because their share prices fluctuate more than their NAVs, closed-end funds carry an added dimension of risk and return.

You normally don't buy closed-end shares directly from the fund company and you can't redeem them at NAV. You simply buy and sell through a broker like you would Wal-Mart or any other publicly traded stock. Most closed-end portfolios trade on the New York Stock Exchange. Because they are less liquid than their open-end relatives, you need to know how to place orders so as to minimize transaction costs. Seasoned investors always use limit orders to get a better price.

Closed-end funds require greater sophistication. The best time to buy them is when they're selling at big discounts, which typically occur during bear markets and at year-end, for reasons attributable to tax-related selling. A well-managed stock fund may be a genuine bargain if you can buy it at a discount of 15 percent or more. That's like purchasing a dollar's worth of assets for 85 cents or less.

Why are closed-end funds less popular than open-end funds?

Most people don't understand them. The name "closed-end" may even turn people off if they erroneously believe that it's difficult or impossible to make an investment. People who bought closed-end portfolios as initial public offerings, then watched their funds slip to discounts also may be disenchanted. Rights offerings also may have taken a toll, because investors who fail to exercise their rights will suffer dilution as a consequence. In general, closed-end funds are not as user-friendly as mutual funds, and they're not available to participants in 401(k) and 403(b) pension plans.

Why do closed-end funds occasionally have rights offerings and how do they work?

With an open-end fund, good performance attracts new investors who increase the fund's asset base and the total management fees that are earned. Not so with closed-end portfolios, which don't issue new shares to incoming investors.

Instead, management occasionally may issue rights, which can be used by shareholders to buy more shares at a predetermined price that's below the market price. You then have a few weeks to exercise your option. *Transferable* rights can be sold if you choose not to exercise them; *nontransferable* rights cannot. But you can exercise the latter and simultaneously sell the number of shares you purchased, locking in an arbitrage profit.

Rights offerings dilute the positions of shareholders who don't participate, assuming the fund trades at a discount. The size of the pie grows as the fund increases its assets, but investors' slices shrink because there are more shares.

Suppose Discount Fund has 10 million shares and wants to add 2 million more through a rights offering. Discount trades at $8.50, 15 percent below its $10 NAV. The subscription price is $8. The offering is fully subscribed and Discount raises $16 million (2 million shares *times* $8). Its net assets increase to $116 million and it now has 12 million shares. The NAV falls from $10 to $9.67 ($116 million/12 million), a 3.3-percent dilution. The market price also declines, as is typical when a distribution is made.

What are Spiders and WEBs, and how do they differ from closed-end funds?

Essentially, they are exchange-traded index portfolios designed to sell very close to their NAVs. In that sense, they are less risky than closed-end funds, although they don't offer the opportunity to buy at a discount. Spiders trade on the American Stock Exchange and target the S&P 500. World Equity Benchmark Shares, which also trade on the Amex, are available for 17 different nations—primarily developed stock markets. That distinguishes them from most single-country closed-end portfolios, which focus on emerging economies. Because Spiders and WEBS are index products, you are assured of not significantly underperforming the target benchmark. They also are tax-efficient and Spiders have a low expense ratio.

What is "liquidity" and how can it affect an investor?

Investors in any exchange-traded stock or fund need to be concerned about liquidity, or the ease and speed with which a security can be bought or sold. It essentially depends on the size of your trading order. A relatively large order to buy or sell a fund that trades, say, 5,000 shares or fewer per day can push its price up or down. In such a case, it would be important to be volume conscious when placing orders of more than several hundred shares. With a limit order to buy or sell at your price or better, you know in advance what price you will pay or receive. If the fund is relatively illiquid, only a part of your order may be filled, or none at all. Patience is needed when buying or selling illiquid investments.

BOND AND MONEY-MARKET FUNDS

Do index funds make as much sense for bonds as they do for equities?

Yes. It's axiomatic that lower expenses translate into better results. It's even more crucial to cut costs to the bone in the bond market because bond returns are lower than stock returns, on average. In addition, there's less opportunity for fund managers to add value since bonds are more homogeneous than stocks.

But passive fixed-income products work differently from their equity relatives. For one thing, these portfolios have higher turnover rates than you might expect. That's because an index will change as bonds mature or are dropped and new ones included in their place. In addition, a bond-index portfolio doesn't replicate the weightings of the securities in the benchmark like, say, an S&P 500 fund. It's simply too difficult to do that because many bonds in a typical benchmark are not easily marketable. For this reason, fund managers use their best judgment in selecting a meaningful sample of IOUs.

My bond fund just cut its monthly distribution. Does this mean trouble?

Probably not. This happens during periods of declining interest rates. Suppose you own a long-term, high-grade corporate fund and rates are falling. Two things may be happening:

1. New cash could be moving into the portfolio, assuming bank and money-fund yields are low. Unless the manager wants to invest the new proceeds in riskier debt, he or she will have to buy bonds paying lower yields, which reduces the fund's yield also.

2. Some bonds in the portfolio likely will be called, allowing the issuers to replace these securities with lower-coupon debt. Again, the manager will have to reinvest the proceeds in bonds with smaller yields.

Under these scenarios, the manager's best alternative is to reduce the dividend. Otherwise, he or she would have to pay dividends out of principal, which reduces the portfolio's long-term earnings potential. On the plus side, falling interest rates lead to rising bond prices, so even though the fund's yield drops, its total return may increase greatly.

What are the most important things to look for when shopping for a money-market fund?

First, determine whether you'd be better off with a taxable or tax-free product. Consider a single-state portfolio if you're in a fairly high federal bracket and live in a high-tax state like California or New York. Compare returns to determine whether you would be further ahead *after taxes* on the taxable fund or the muni portfolio. (Chapter 15 explains how to do the calculations.)

After you have decided on the money-fund category, take a close look at expense ratios. Costs are often the deciding factor because money funds are a fairly homogeneous group and there isn't much opportunity for a manager to add value. Returns aren't that high in the first place so it's crucial to have low overhead. In addition, check to see if any temporary fee waivers or expense reimbursements exist to entice unwary investors. At certain times, more than half of all money funds use "teaser" yields. They're nice as long as they last, but expenses can shoot up once the subsidy ends. It's best to have a money fund with everyday low costs—those with expense ratios below 0.50 percent.

MANAGING YOUR MUTUAL-FUND PORTFOLIO

Is it appropriate to dip into my long-term investment portfolio to help cover emergencies and big-ticket expenditures?

It's not wise to unless you have no other choice. Keep your emergency reserves and big-ticket reserves separate from your long-term portfolio. You don't want to disturb your nest egg because doing so might throw it out of balance, adversely affecting your long-term results. In addition, some of your money likely is stashed in tax-deferred retirement plans, which means you could face premature withdrawal penalties.

How many funds should I own?

There's no magic number. A new investor might start with just two: a money fund and either an S&P 500 index portfolio or a balanced product. A growth-oriented individual might do well focusing on just four or five. The mix might include a large-cap, small-cap, foreign-stock, and money-market fund. On the other hand, if you have a $1-million portfolio and enjoy keeping track of your investments, you easily could own 16 or more.

But too many funds is not good, particularly if the portfolio becomes a cluttered maze. Look to streamline duplicative holdings and to sell off laggards.

Are some fund categories best avoided?

If you own several funds, you might steer clear of all-in-one-products, such as balanced, asset-allocation, and multifund portfolios. You can control your asset mix better by avoiding these one-size-fits-all products. Certain "funds of funds" can be particularly costly because of a layering of fees.

You might want to avoid global funds for the same reason. These portfolios typically hold both U.S. and foreign stocks, and the manager can vary the mix without your knowledge. International funds—which stay totally in foreign markets—are the better way to go.

Finally, stay away from volatile, highly focused portfolios including single-country and industry funds, unless you're sophisticated in these areas and have a large nest egg. Even then, keep your collective allocation to these products to perhaps 10 percent of your assets.

I'm 62 and recently retired. I'd like to set up a systematic withdrawal plan, taking money out gradually from several of my conservative stock funds. How much can I safely withdraw each year so I won't run out of money, assuming I will live another 30 years or so?

Make some projections, as discussed in Chapter 22. For instance, you might assume that your equity funds will return 9 percent yearly and that inflation will average 4 percent. Taking your 9-percent projected return and subtracting the 4 percent results in a 5-percent "real" return, which can be viewed as a "safe" initial withdrawal rate. Thereafter, the amount you withdraw could be increased by, say, 4 percent yearly. For this plan to work over the long haul, it's important to keep the major portion of your nest egg in equities.

Of course, you still could experience rough sledding if inflation gets out of control and the stock market produces lackluster results. During adverse periods, you may need to tighten your belt.

TAX CONSIDERATIONS

How should I divvy up my fund holdings between taxable and tax-deferred accounts?

Conventional wisdom suggests that you hold your least tax-efficient funds in tax-deferred accounts such as IRAs and 401(k) plans. These can include big income producers such as high-yield bond funds and income-oriented stock portfolios. An opposing school of thought recommends that you hold growth-oriented investments in tax-sheltered accounts, so that you can defer taxes on the substantial appreciation that these funds may generate. Even though capital gains are taxed at a lower rate than income for assets held more than 18 months, the total tax bite can be substantial if a fund kicks off large distributions or if you incur sizable profits by switching your holdings.

Index funds are suitable for taxable accounts because their minuscule turnover rates make them highly tax efficient. Certain index and quasi-index funds are designed to minimize the tax impact. Of course, you need to be a buy-and-hold investor to minimize taxes because trading will trigger taxable events.

What is meant by a "wash sale"?

The IRS disallows a tax deduction for losses sustained in these transactions. A wash sale occurs when a fund is sold at a loss, then repurchased within 30 days. It also is triggered if shares were purchased within 30 days prior to the sale. You can avoid this problem simply by purchasing another fund within the 61-day window.

If a mutual fund has a net realized loss during a year, does it distribute that loss to shareholders just like it distributes net realized gains?

No. Losses are never distributed. The fund simply carries the amount forward to future periods to offset any gains. When the loss is totally used up, gains again will be distributed to investors. In the meantime, a loss carryforward can benefit new investors who want to buy the tax advantage of losses suffered by past shareholders. That's because a loss carryforward can temporarily reduce or even eliminate a fund's taxable gains. Of course, you don't want to invest in a dud just to get this possible tax break.

My 1099-DIV statement indicates that my fund paid a nontaxable distribution. What should I do?

Nontaxable distributions represent a return of your capital. Don't confuse them with the tax-exempt dividends paid by municipal bond funds. As the name implies, you don't pay any tax on this amount, but you should remember to make a corresponding reduction in your cost basis if the fund is held outside of a retirement account. Suppose Fund A paid a $1-per-share nontaxable distribution and you hold it in a taxable account. You need to reduce your cost basis by $1 per share, which will increase the size of your gain or lessen your loss when you ultimately sell.

I have lost some of my past mutual-fund statements and I need them to determine my cost basis. What should I do?

Call the fund company and explain your problem. Most families keep records on accounts going back at least 10 years. It may take some time for them to retrieve the information, however, so don't wait until the last minute.

BEHIND THE SCENES

Is it important for me to know who manages my fund? How can I find out about a manager's background?

You want a portfolio that will fare better than the market; otherwise, you might as well invest in a low-cost index fund. You pay a fee for professional management, so you want to get the most for your money.

Well-known, successful managers are written up in the financial press, profiled in books, and interviewed on television programs such as "Wall

Street Week." Lesser-known managers still draw media attention, but not nearly so extensively. It can be difficult to learn much about a particular person. *Morningstar Mutual Funds* provides a very basic biography on the managers of the portfolios it covers. In addition, the prospectus names the manager and indicates how long he or she has been at the helm. You also can call the fund company to find out more. For instance, the firm may be able to tell you if the manager has been written up or has received other special recognition.

Do mutual-fund managers have a team of analysts working for them?

Generally, yes. There simply are not enough hours in the day for managers to do everything themselves. They need help crunching numbers, digging up facts, and so on. But even with some assistance from analysts, managers have the final say about their portfolio.

Is personal trading by fund managers a problem?

It can be for several reasons. First, it may take that individual's mind off the portfolio he or she is being paid to run. Excessive trading can be highly nerve-racking. More important, it gives rise to possible conflicts of interest in a freewheeling environment. For instance, a manager may dump a personal position in a stock before it's sold by the fund, or vice versa on a purchase. Options trading and short selling also can pose conflict-of-interest problems.

Fund companies may not totally ban their managers from personal trading, but most monitor it closely. What a manager can and cannot do should be spelled out in the group's "code of ethics." Fidelity Investments recently took steps to toughen its policy on employees' trading. Fidelity's strict code is significant because of the company's high visibility in the industry.

Some critics think fund managers simply should not be allowed to trade at all for their personal accounts, reasoning that running a fund is a full-time occupation. If a manager's loyalties are divided, they say, the job may not be done as well.

Do fund companies and brokerages ever make mistakes on their statements?

Yes, but rarely. Even though the possibility of an error is remote, you should always check your statements carefully. A few complexes, including Fidelity, have committed some embarrassing mistakes that subsequently were corrected. Occasionally an item such as a distribution doesn't get reported on one statement because it occurs late in the period, but it's usually corrected by the company on the next one.

Who are the directors of a fund and what are their duties?

Directors or trustees tend to be experienced, prominent people in fields of business, government, or academia. Some are household names. The same group of perhaps five to 12 individuals may oversee all the funds in a family. But some directors oversee just one portfolio. Certain directors work for the fund's adviser, but at least 40 percent must be independent. Shareholders vote for directors on their proxy cards.

Directors play an important role in monitoring the fund's operations and policing potential conflicts of interest, particularly in the area of fees. Directors concern themselves with the big picture, not the day-to-day operations. They are responsible for hiring the fund's adviser and renewing the firm's contract.

Critics question how effective most directors really are, however. They point to rising fund expenses over the years, even though you might expect more economies of scale as mutual funds grew in size. Morningstar did a study relating directors' fees at 82 large fund groups to expenses charged by the funds and found that a relationship existed. Thus, if your funds have above-average expenses, it could be that the directors are well paid. You can find the outside directors' fees in the "Statement of Additional Information," or Part B of the prospectus. But just because the directors appear to be well paid is not necessarily cause for concern. Fees are a function of several factors such as the number of portfolios the directors oversee and the number of meetings they attend.

In plain English, what are derivatives, and how do fund managers use them?

Derivatives are financial contracts whose value is "derived" from some underlying asset, which could be a stock, bond, commodity, currency, or price index. Most common are standardized derivatives such as options and futures. More exotic fare are customized to suit the needs of professional investors.

Virtually all categories of funds employ derivatives. They traditionally are used to reduce risk by hedging against, say, adverse currency or interest-rate movements. Funds typically hedge against just a modest portion of their risk exposure.

Derivatives provide plenty of bang for the buck because usually they are leveraged to magnify the effect of price movements in the underlying asset or index. Speculators may use various contracts such as "inverse floaters" or "structured notes" in an attempt to juice up returns. That's why derivatives made the headlines in 1994, when massive losses were sustained by certain professional investors who had placed bets that interest rates would continue to trend downward. They were caught flat-footed when rates pulled a surprise and ratcheted upward early in 1994. The losers included some corporate pension funds, municipalities such as Orange County, California, and a few bond and money-market funds.

Derivatives are not something to be concerned about if used prudently and in moderation. They are a well-established part of the financial landscape. If you deal with a respected fund group that has built a good track record, there is no need to worry about their misuse. Good funds may use them a little as a hedge, or not at all. If you have any questions, call the company and ask about its policy regarding derivatives.

Why do funds and fund companies merge?

Asset building is the name of the game today. A fund company with $40 billion under management is generally better off than one with $2 billion. That's because more assets mean greater economies of scale, a wider range of portfolios and services, better managers, and more marketing muscle. Thus, mergers and consolidations often make economic sense. Funds with poor past performances are frequently merged into those with better histories, thereby erasing their unsuccessful pasts.

COMPUTERIZED INVESTING

Is it important for me to have my computer hooked up to the Internet to be a successful fund investor?

No. You can do very well with mutual funds even if you don't use a computer at all. It's easy enough to keep up with the financial papers on a daily basis. Getting prospectuses and other literature from fund companies by "snail mail" shouldn't pose a problem, either. And you always can find out information quickly by calling the shareholder reps at your fund company. Computers are not that important to long-term, buy-and-hold fund investors, which is what most people should be. In fact, using a computer can be counterproductive if it encourages a short-term mentality. In addition, information overload can prompt you to keep up with more than you really need.

What are the most important ways in which a computer could be used by fund investors?

The answer depends a lot on whom you ask, but we think computers can be useful for monitoring investments. A spreadsheet can help keep track of your individual holdings and asset allocation and can assist in long-range planning. For instance, you could see how much you need to sock away each year at various rates of return to reach your retirement goal. Or, if you are retired, you can determine how long your capital will last when making periodic withdrawals from a nest egg.

In addition, mutual-fund Web sites can provide useful information such as recent news, descriptions of portfolios, prospectuses, pamphlets, and application forms.

FUND SUPERMARKETS

What are the pros and cons of using a discount brokerage's mutual-fund supermarket?

These programs make sense for investors who want to build a portfolio of funds from different families and move easily among them. The no-transaction-fee funds included in a discounter's program usually have the most appeal. In addition, a brokerage's program can simplify your recordkeeping because all of your funds and other investments appear on one account statement. A discounter also can offer an economical alternative with a self-directed IRA or Keogh, since all your funds can be consolidated in one account.

Naturally, you face trading costs on certain no-load funds that aren't included in a discounter's no-transaction-fee program. But the costs tend to be relatively low percentagewise if your trades are fairly large. One disadvantage of brokerage programs is that they cater to investors' impulses. People may be tempted to hop from fund to fund because it's so easy to do.

How can discounters offer their no-transaction-fee programs for free? Is there any catch?

The programs aren't free. The discounters charge each participating fund company 25 to 35 basis points per year for the amount of money the group has with the brokerage. Fund companies are willing to pay because of the visibility and exposure that they gain. Being included in a supermarket can help a small, obscure company grow substantially. However, these charges lead to higher expense ratios for funds, and all shareholders bear the burden, even if they deal directly with the family. In addition, the kind of fund hopping that these supermarkets induce can result in higher portfolio trading costs, which can adversely affect all of a fund's shareholders.

I placed an order to trade a fund through my discount brokerage earlier today but now want to cancel. Is that possible?

Yes, provided you notify your brokerage prior to the cut-off time. Different funds have different deadlines for placing and canceling orders. For many funds, it's 3 P.M. Eastern Time.

I just opened an account with a discount brokerage. Can I move existing funds into this account?

Yes. Most discounters will provide this transfer service at no cost on funds they deal in. The advantage of making a transfer is that you can simplify your recordkeeping by bringing all holdings under one roof. Of course, you would incur a commission when you subsequently sell funds that are not in the discounter's no-transaction-fee program.

Why do full-service brokerages such as Merrill Lynch, Prudential, and Smith Barney offer no-load funds and how are investors charged for the service?

Wall Street giants are offering funds from no-load families to satisfy customer demand for these popular products. But fund supermarkets at full-service firms work differently than at a discounter because the portfolios are generally put into a "wrap" account, on which customers normally are charged from 1 to 2 percent annually. In return, the brokerage determines an appropriate asset-class mix for the customer, selects the funds, and monitors the mix.

I've built up a seven-figure portfolio of mutual funds over many years and keep most of my positions with just one large family. Should I go to a supermarket instead?

Not necessarily. If you're pleased with the offerings and services of your family, there is no need to change. Supermarkets are more useful for people who have positions with, say, four or more families, maybe including some closed-end funds and individual stocks, and want to consolidate everything onto one statement.

Glossary

Adviser   Also known as "investment adviser," this is the organization that serves as money manager for a mutual fund. The adviser is paid a fee based on the percentage of assets under management. *See* Management fee.

Agency securities   Bonds issued by U.S. government agencies and organizations, such as the Government National Mortgage Association and the Tennessee Valley Authority. Mortgage-backed bonds are a popular type of agency security. *See* Mortgage-backed securities.

Aggressive-growth fund   *See* Capital-appreciation fund.

Alpha   The amount by which a portfolio's actual return exceeds or falls short of its expected return. High positive alphas reflect extraordinary performance by the manager; negative numbers show underperformance.

Annuitization   A plan for taking a periodic distribution of money during an annuity's payout period.

Annuity   A series of periodic payments for a stipulated time frame. *See* Fixed annuity and Variable annuity.

Asked price   The price at which a security is offered for sale by a dealer. For a mutual fund, the asked or offering price equals net asset value plus any front-end load. *See* Bid price and Dealer spread.

Asset allocation   A systematic approach for divvying up your portfolio into stocks, bonds, and cash, including appropriate subcategories. Factors such as age, time horizon, risk tolerance, and portfolio size are determinants of an individual's asset allocation. This strategy is designed to minimize the danger of asset-class risk.

Asset-allocation fund   An all-in-one portfolio that varies its holdings of stocks, bonds, and cash within predetermined ranges as the manager's outlook changes. Many of these funds move their money among foreign as well as domestic stock and bond markets. The idea is to be in the right kinds of securities at the right time.

Asset-class risk   The dangers associated with having an excessive amount of your nest egg allocated to stocks, bonds, or cash or to a subclass such as foreign stocks. You can minimize this risk by sticking with a sensible asset-allocation plan and periodically rebalancing your portfolio to your target asset-class weights.

Automatic-investment plan   A service enabling you to have a designated sum of money transferred regularly from your bank account or paycheck to your fund account.

Automatic reinvestment   A service available from virtually all funds, whereby your dividend and capital-gains distributions can be reinvested into full and fractional shares at the prevailing NAV. A reinvestment program might offer several options. For example, you may choose to reinvest only capital-gains distributions and take income dividends in cash, or you may reinvest distributions from one fund into another within the same family.

Back-end load   A sales charge paid when an investor sells a fund. *See* Contingent deferred sales charge and Redemption fee.

Balance of payments   A summary number that tracks all money flowing into and out of a country over a specific period. A nation's currency fluctuations are related to changes in its balance of payments.

Balanced fund   A hybrid portfolio of stocks and bonds.

Bear market   A prolonged period of falling prices. Major indexes such as the S&P 500 decline 20 percent or more in a bear market.

Beta   A measure of the volatility of a portfolio relative to an underlying index, such as the S&P 500. Beta values above 1.0 indicate a volatile or aggressive portfolio, those below 1.0 show a more stable or defensive fund. For example, a portfolio with a beta of 1.25 would be expected to be 25 percent more volatile than the index.

Bid price   The current price a dealer is willing to pay for a security. For a mutual fund the bid is usually called the redemption price and equals the NAV less any redemption charge. *See* Asked price and Dealer spread.

Blue-chip stock   The stock of a large, well-established, high-quality firm.

Blue-sky laws   State securities laws to which mutual funds are subject in addition to federal regulations.

Board of directors The group of officials who exercise ultimate control over a mutual fund. Elected by the shareholders, board members are responsible for overseeing fund operations. The board is charged with looking out for shareholder interests. Among other duties, board members are expected to make sure fund fees are not unreasonable and that the adviser is doing a good job.

Bond A debt instrument that promises to pay interest (or coupon) payments and a fixed amount of principal at maturity. *See* Zero-coupon bond.

Book value The net assets of a corporation, typically expressed as a per-share number.

Breakpoint Investment thresholds at which any front-end load drops in increments. Eventually, the load levels out at a low percentage or is phased out entirely. Breakpoint amounts are listed in a table in the prospectus.

Bull market A prolonged period of rising prices.

Call option A contract granting its buyer the right to buy a specific asset, such as a stock, at a fixed price within a limited time. *See* Put option.

Call risk The danger that a bond carrying a relatively high coupon will be forcibly redeemed by the issuer prior to the maturity date. Calls hurt bondholders during times of falling interest rates because the redemption proceeds must be reinvested at lower rates.

Capital-appreciation fund Also known as "aggressive-growth funds," these volatile stock portfolios seek maximum gains. They may employ speculative strategies in an effort to enhance results.

Capital-gains distributions The paying out of net realized capital gains to fund shareholders. Gains are typically declared annually in December and payable in January.

Capitalization The total market value of a corporation, used as a measure of size. It is determined by multiplying the company's current stock price by the number of shares outstanding. A firm with 15 million shares trading at $10 each would have a $150 million market cap and thus would be considered a micro-cap company.

Cash flow Net, new shareholder money going into a fund. Some observers feel that portfolios enjoying consistent cash inflows have a performance edge.

Check-writing privilege A service enabling investors to write checks against their mutual-fund account balances. Checks usually must meet a certain minimum, commonly $250 or $500, and the service is restricted to money-market and bond funds.

Classes of shares An arrangement used with broker-sold funds giving investors a choice as to how they pay their fees. There is one underlying portfolio but several share-class options. "Class A" shares normally have a front-end load and often a modest 12b-1 charge. "Class B" shares generally have no front-end load but carry 12b-1 fees and a contingent deferred sales charge. "Class C" shares have a level load in the form of a high 12b-1 fee. Other share classes may exist for institutional investors and employees of the brokerage or fund company. *See* Contingent deferred sales charge, Front-end load, and 12b-1 fee.

Clone fund   A portfolio established to mirror another, which may have been closed to new money because of size.

Closed-end fund   An exchange-traded portfolio featuring a relatively stable amount of shares. Unlike open-end funds, they generally do not issue new shares to investors, nor do they redeem shares from sellers. Rather, you buy and sell them through a broker like any stock. Many closed-ends trade at discounts to NAV. Others change hands at premiums. This introduces an additional dimension of risk—and return.

Closed fund   A mutual fund that has shut its doors to new investors. This commonly happens when a portfolio has grown so large that it can't effectively achieve its objectives. Sometimes the management company starts up a clone with similar goals.

Commercial paper   A staple of money-market portfolios, these short-term IOUs are issued by large, creditworthy corporations.

Company risk   The danger that some misfortune—such as a lawsuit, poor earnings, or the loss of a key market—will befall a firm. Mutual-fund investors don't have to worry about this danger because it is largely eliminated by diversification. Also known as diversifiable risk or random risk.

Compounding   Earnings on an investment's reinvested earnings. Given sufficient time, compounding can result in exponential growth of money.

Contingent deferred sales charge (or CDSC)   A back-end load accompanying a 12b-1 plan on a broker-sold fund. The CDSC is highest if shares are redeemed in the first year. It might start out at, say, 5 percent and decline by one percentage point annually, usually phasing out after five or six years.

Convertible-bond fund   A hybrid portfolio focusing primarily on convertible bonds and convertible preferred stock. Convertibles have characteristics of both bonds and stock.

Corporate-bond fund   A portfolio that holds investment-grade corporate debt, or that rated triple-B or higher. The high-quality corporate funds generally restrict their holdings to issues rated single-A or better. Those in both groups also may own Treasury securities.

Correlation coefficient   A statistical measure of the degree of association between any two numerical series, such as returns on two different assets. The returns between most pairs of investments are positively correlated although the association may be low so that one may occasionally zig when another zags. The closer this coefficient is to +1.0, the greater the tendency for returns to move in tandem.

Country risk The danger international investors face that a nation will suffer severe economic or political problems, or even a natural disaster. This peril is greatest with a single-country fund that invests in a smaller emerging economy.

Credit risk The danger that the issuer of a corporate or municipal bond will experience financial difficulties causing a deterioration in creditworthiness, perhaps even a default. Treasury securities are considered free of this risk.

Currency risk The risk, faced by investors in foreign bond and stock funds, that the dollar will appreciate relative to the currencies in which the securities are denominated. When that happens, the fund will realize a currency loss.

Custodian The independent organization, usually a bank, that is responsible for the handling and safekeeping of a fund's cash and securities.

Daily dividend fund A portfolio that calculates dividends daily and pays out or reinvests dividends monthly. The term applies to money-market and bond funds.

Dealer spread The difference between the bid and asked prices on a security. For example, a stock quoted at 40 bid to $40\frac{1}{16}$ asked has a $\frac{1}{16}$-point spread. Highly active stocks have narrower spreads than inactive ones do. In addition to the broker commission, the spread is a part of the transaction costs.

Derivatives Financial instruments based on some primary underlying asset or index such as a stock, bond, commodity, or a benchmark of stock prices. Derivative securities fluctuate up and down in tandem with the primary security. Derivatives often are leveraged, making them more volatile. They can be used to speculate as well as to reduce or control an unwanted risk. Options and futures are standardized derivatives. Others are customized to meet specific needs.

Discount 1. Refers to a closed-end fund trading in the market at a price below the NAV of its portfolio. 2. Refers to a bond priced below its par (or face) value.

Discount brokerage A brokerage that offers reduced commissions on investor transactions but does not provide the kind of advice and research information that you would expect from a full-service firm. Many discounters also have mutual-fund supermarkets.

Distributor The organization that supplies mutual-fund shares to brokerages and investors. Also known as the underwriter, the distributor may sell shares to securities dealers, who then sell them to investors, or it might deal directly with the public.

Diversification The strategy of spreading money among different securities to reduce or eliminate company or asset-class risk.

Diversified fund A portfolio with many stock or bond holdings. For a fund to be considered diversified, the Investment Company Act of 1940 requires that it invest at least 75 percent of its assets in accordance with the following rules: no more that 5 percent can be placed in any one company, and not more than 10 percent of any company's outstanding shares can be purchased. The vast majority of mutual funds meet this definition. *See* Nondiversified fund.

Dividend yield The indicated annual dividend divided by the current price of an investment.

Dollar-cost averaging A widely used strategy that entails investing a fixed-dollar amount at regular intervals, such as $200 monthly, regardless of market conditions. More shares are purchased at lower prices and fewer at higher prices.

Duration A measure of the interest-rate sensitivity of a bond (or fixed-income portfolio) incorporating time to maturity and coupon size. Durations for bond funds holding coupon-paying securities are no higher than about 12 or 13, even though the bonds in the portfolio may have an average maturity of 25 or 30 years. The bigger the duration number, the greater the interest-rate risk. For example, a bond with a duration of 5 could be expected to decline 5 percent if interest rates rose by one percentage point. *See* Interest-rate risk.

EAFE index A popular indicator of foreign-stock prices tabulated by Morgan Stanley Capital International. The EAFE or Europe, Australia, and Far East index includes about 1,100 major companies.

Efficient market A market where assets sell for what they're worth. The efficient-market theory holds that since mispriced securities do not exist, you can't expect professional money managers or anyone else to beat the market indexes. The efficient-market concept remains a controversial one, but academic studies supporting the notion resulted in a proliferation of passive portfolios, or index funds.

Emerging-markets fund A portfolio that targets companies trading on stock exchanges in a variety of developing nations including those in Southeast Asia, Eastern Europe, and Latin America.

Equity A synonym for stock, the term refers to an ownership interest in a corporation.

Equity-income fund A portfolio that focuses on stocks with high-dividend yields, such as utilities, real-estate securities, and financial companies.

Ex-distribution date Normally one business day after the "record date." Investors purchasing shares on or after the "ex-distribution" date are not entitled to the payout of realized capital gains. The NAV falls by the amount of the distribution on the "ex" date. Newspaper tables place an "e" following the fund's name on its ex-distribution date. The terms ex-distribution and ex-dividend often are used synonymously. *See* Record date.

Ex-dividend date Normally one business day after the "record date." Investors purchasing shares on or after the "ex-dividend" date are not entitled to the payout of dividends from net investment income. The NAV falls by the amount of the dividend on the "ex" date. Newspaper tables place an "x" following the fund's name on its ex-dividend date. The terms ex-dividend and ex-distribution often are used synonymously. *See* Record date.

Exchange privilege A service that enables investors in a fund family to move money from one portfolio to another by calling a toll-free 800 number and giving their instruction. There is usually little or no cost for exchanges, although some fund families limit the number of switches an investor can make.

Exchange-traded funds Portfolios that typically trade on the NYSE or Amex like any other stock. In addition to closed-end funds, the group includes Spiders and WEBS. These portfolios must be bought through a brokerage firm. *See* Closed-end fund, Spiders, and WEBS.

Expense ratio The annual expenses of a fund, including the management fee, administrative costs, and any 12b-1 charge, divided by average net assets. Past ratios can be found in the financial-highlights table of the prospectus.

Family A group of funds under one umbrella. The most basic family would include a stock, bond, and money market-portfolio, although many outfits are much larger, and growing.

Fee table A table near the front of the prospectus that explains in detail the various kinds of fees charged to the shareholder and the impact of these charges over time.

Financial-highlights table A table, contained in the prospectus, that presents a concise financial analysis of a fund over the past 10 years or its life, whichever is shorter. Among other information, the table lists investment income, realized and unrealized gains and losses, distributions, total returns, and key ratios such as the expense ratio and portfolio turnover.

Fixed annuity A contract that generates guaranteed returns during its accumulation period and level payments during its payout period.

Flexible-bond fund A portfolio that can invest in a variety of bonds and alter the mix. The manager does not face restrictions on quality or maturity.

Foreign-bond fund A portfolio that invests in government and corporate debt denominated in non-U.S. currencies.

401(k) plan A popular defined-contribution program available through many employers. Within these tax-sheltered plans, participants often can choose mutual funds as one or more of the investment choices.

403(b) plan   A defined-contribution plan available to employees of certain charitable organizations and public school systems. Mutual funds often are an investment choice here.

Front-end load   A sales fee charged at the time of purchase. The maximum legal front-end load is 8.5 percent, although most funds today charge 6 percent or less.

Funds of funds   These are all-in-one portfolios that invest in other mutual funds.

Futures (or futures contract)   An exchange-traded contract calling for settlement on a specific asset (such as the S&P 500) at a predetermined price and time. Fund managers may hedge with futures.

Geometric mean return   A compound average rate of return. The geometric mean return for a mutual fund is usually an average of total annual returns over several years.

Global fund   A portfolio that invests in companies headquartered or traded in a variety of countries, including the United States.

Growth-and-income fund   A portfolio holding large, established companies offering the potential for both appreciation and dividend income.

Growth fund   A portfolio holding firms with good or improving profit prospects. The primary emphasis is on appreciation.

Growth investing   A popular investment style whereby analysts or fund managers search for firms showing promise of above-average earnings. Stocks are held primarily for price appreciation as opposed to dividend income. Growth investors often are willing to pay high multiples of earnings or book value for companies with exciting potential.

Hedge fund   A private investment partnership for wealthy individuals or institutions. In contrast to mutual funds, the minimum investment can be as high as $1 million or more. Hedge funds are typically unregulated and often maintain short as well as long positions in an attempt to do well in bear as well as bull markets. Many are global in orientation and deal in currencies and foreign securities as well as various domestic issues.

Hedging   A general term used to describe any of several risk-reduction strategies. A fund manager might partially hedge against a market decline simply by moving a larger fraction of the portfolio into cash. Alternatively, the manager could sell stock-index futures contracts. If the market falls, the gains on the shorted futures would more or less offset the decline in the portfolio's value.

High-yield bond   *See* Junk bond.

Hybrid fund   A category of funds that hold both stocks and bonds. Examples are asset-allocation and balanced portfolios.

Income dividends   Payments to shareholders made from the dividends and interest earned on the securities held by a fund, net of expenses. Bond funds often pay monthly income dividends. Stock funds distribute income less frequently. Income dividends are distinct from capital-gains distributions.

Income ratio The ratio of a fund's net investment income to average net assets. A kind of yield, it measures the extent to which a portfolio generates income. This number, which can be found in the financial-highlights table of the prospectus, should be examined in light of the fund's objectives.

Index fund A portfolio that replicates a particular market index such as the Standard & Poor's 500 by holding many if not all of the same stocks. With low-cost, passively managed index funds, you're assured of doing about as well as the target index.

Individual Retirement Account (or IRA) A tax-deferred retirement plan available to all wage earners under age 70½, as well as nonworking spouses. Contributions may or may not be tax-deductible, but earnings on IRA assets grow tax-deferred. Mutual funds are a common investment choice for IRAs.

Inefficient market A market where mispriced securities can be found. Fund managers seek inefficiencies so as to boost shareholder returns. An example of an inefficiency could be a small, neglected firm not researched by Wall Street analysts. Another example might be an obscure, nonrated junk bond.

Inflation-indexed Treasury bonds U.S. Treasury securities introduced in 1997 that are designed to protect investors against unanticipated surges in inflation. An increase in the consumer price level boosts the yields earned on these bonds.

Inflation risk The danger that the returns from one's investments will fail to keep pace with increases in the general price level. This is a major problem with secure investments such as Treasury bills. Common stock portfolios offer the best long-term inflation protection.

Initial public offering (IPO) The sale of a company's shares of stock to investors for the first time.

Interest-rate risk The danger that the price of a bond will fall as interest rates rise. Portfolio managers gauge a fund's interest-rate risk by calculating its duration. *See* Duration.

International-stock fund A portfolio that invests in the stocks of foreign companies. Unlike global funds, international portfolios generally do not have U.S. holdings.

Internet (or "Net") A huge, decentralized, worldwide network of computers. Information can be found at a vast number of different sites. In one sense it's like a giant research library where you can locate information on virtually any topic. You also can communicate with others on a wide range of subjects. Many mutual-fund companies now can be reached via their Internet addresses. *See* World Wide Web.

Investment adviser *See* Adviser.

Investment company   A highly regulated organization that pools money from many people into a portfolio structured to achieve certain objectives. An investment company can be established as a corporation, trust, or partnership. Open-end funds, closed-end funds, and unit investment trusts are all investment companies, but the open-end structure is the most popular.

Investment Company Act of 1940   Detailed federal legislation governing the activities of investment companies. It requires all funds to register with the SEC and to provide a prospectus to potential investors. Among other things, the prospectus must clearly indicate the fund's investment policies and risk factors. The Act also requires a minimum number of outsiders to sit on the board of every fund.

Investment Company Institute (or ICI)   The national trade association of the mutual-fund industry. The ICI serves its many member companies as well as government agencies, the news media, and the investing public.

Investment-grade bonds   Corporate and municipal bonds given one of the top four ratings by independent agencies. Issues rated triple-B or better are considered investment grade.

IPO   *See* Initial public offering.

Junk bond   Issues rated below investment grade—that is, below triple-B— by the major rating agencies. Although they often promise high income, junk bonds carry high credit risk and might be near or in default. Also known as high-yield bonds, junk securities are particularly sensitive to changes in economic conditions.

Keogh plan   A tax-qualified retirement plan available to self-employed individuals such as sole proprietors, business partners, and consultants. Mutual funds are a common investment choice with Keogh plans.

Leverage   The use of borrowed money to try to enhance returns. Leverage is a double-edged sword, however, because it also can compound investment losses.

Limit order   An order placed with a broker to buy or sell a stock or exchange-traded fund at a specified price or better. Limit orders can be *day orders,* in which case they expire at the end of the day if unexecuted, or orders that are *good-till-canceled* by the customer.

Liquidity   The ease with which an investment can be bought or sold. A person should be able to buy or sell a liquid asset quickly with virtually no adverse price impact.

Liquidity risk   A danger faced by holders of thinly traded or illiquid securities who are forced to sell a relatively large number of shares in a short period. When the selling pressure is too great, dealers quickly lower their bid prices. Junk bonds, small stocks, and stocks traded in thin foreign markets carry this risk.

Low-load fund A fund charging a front-end load ranging up to 3 percent.

Management company The firm that handles the daily administration of a fund's activities and usually serves as investment adviser. Typically it is also the company that organized the fund.

Management fee The percentage charge for portfolio management. The annual fee typically ranges from 0.4 percent to more than 1.0 percent of average net assets. This expense, which is stated in the fund's prospectus, may decline proportionately as the fund's asset base increases.

Management risk The possibility that a manager's hot hands may turn icy. In addition, there is always a chance that a celebrity manager could leave for better opportunities elsewhere. Index-fund investors avoid this risk.

Margin purchase The use of borrowed funds to finance a portion of the total cost of an investment. Margin can increase returns but it also can magnify losses if an investment sours. Mutual funds can be margined through brokerage firms.

Market capitalization *See* Capitalization.

Market order An order to buy or sell a stock or exchange-traded fund at the best price available. Those using market orders do not have control over the price paid or received as they would with a limit order. *See* Limit order.

Market risk The danger that the overall stock market could fall. Fund managers may try to deal with this risk by moving a larger percent of their portfolios into cash or by hedging with futures and options. However, market risk is not a one-way street; it's also the peril of being on the sidelines when stock prices surge.

Market timing The shifting of assets between stocks and a money fund in an effort to avoid or minimize losses when prices are expected to fall. At any moment timers might be as much as 100 percent in stocks or 100 percent in a money fund. When they're out of the market, they risk missing a big bull move. Thus, timers frequently underperform during uptrends.

Micro-cap fund A portfolio that targets the tiniest companies within the small-stock arena.

Money-market fund A mutual fund that invests in short-term debt securities such as Treasury bills and commercial paper. As the safest of all funds, these portfolios have a stable NAV of $1 and are available in both taxable and tax-free varieties. Dividends are calculated daily and paid or reinvested monthly.

Morningstar risk measure A yardstick, published by Morningstar Inc. of Chicago, that focuses only on a fund's potential for losses. The more frequently a fund's monthly returns fall short of the T-bill return, and the greater the underperformance, the higher its risk, according to this statistic.

Mortgage-backed securities   Bonds, such as Ginnie Maes, collateralized by a pool of insured home mortgages. Sometimes referred to as "pass-through" securities. The principal is paid back gradually, along with interest, rather than at maturity, as with an ordinary bond.

Mortgage-backed securities fund   A portfolio that invests primarily in various mortgage-backed bonds such as Ginnie Maes.

Municipal-bond fund   A portfolio that invests at least 80 percent of its assets in federally tax-exempt bonds. *National funds* invest in bonds from a number of different states. *Single-state funds* hold the bonds of one state so as to provide its residents with income exempt from both state and federal taxes. *Insured funds* hold bonds guaranteed by an independent insurance consortium. *High-yield funds* hold munis of lower grades.

Mutual fund   By far the most popular type of investment company. A diversified and professionally managed portfolio, the mutual (or open-end) fund stands ready to issue shares to incoming investors at net asset value plus any applicable sales charge, and it redeems shares at NAV from sellers, less any redemption fee.

Mutual-fund supermarket   A popular program offered by various brokerages that allows investors to buy and sell no-load and low-load funds from dozens of families in a single account, often without paying transaction fees.

Mutual-fund ticker symbol   The five-letter designation, frequently ending in an "X," that's assigned to each fund by Nasdaq. For example, the ticker symbol for Fidelity Magellan is FMAGX. The symbol is used for obtaining quotes or trading funds online or with a touchtone phone.

NASD (National Association of Securities Dealers)   A Washington-based self-regulatory organization for the investment business, including brokerages and other companies that distribute mutual funds. Among its responsibilities, the NASD regulates fees for selling fund shares and mutual-fund advertising.

Nasdaq   A computer-based communications network for trading stocks through hundreds of market makers or dealers. Many technology stocks trade in the Nasdaq market.

Net asset value (NAV)   The price or value of one share of a fund. It is calculated by summing the current market values of all securities held by the fund, adding in cash and any accrued income, then subtracting liabilities and dividing the result by the number of shares outstanding. Fund companies compute the NAV once a day based on closing market prices.

Net assets   The total value of a fund's cash and securities less its liabilities or obligations.

Nikkei index   The most widely reported stock-market index in Japan. The Nikkei tracks 225 large, popular stocks traded on the Tokyo Stock Exchange. Like the Dow Jones Industrial Average, it is a price-weighted number. It's also known as the "Nikkei Dow."

No-load fund   A fund with no front-end or contingent deferred sales charge. In addition, the 12b-1 fee, if any, must not exceed 0.25 percent per year. If the portfolio has no 12b-1 fee, it is often referred to as a "pure" no-load.

Nominal return   **1.** The stated, contractual rate of interest on a fixed-income security. **2.** The total return on an investment ignoring inflation. *See* Real return.

Nondiversified fund   One of a small number of funds that have elected not to meet the "diversification" definition of the Investment Company Act of 1940. However, nondiversified portfolios still must invest at least 50 percent of their assets in accordance with the same guidelines to which diversified funds must adhere for 75 percent of their assets. *See* Diversified fund.

Offering price   *See* Asked price.

Open-end fund   The more formal term for a mutual fund. *See* Mutual fund and Closed-end fund.

Option   *See* Call option and Put option.

Payable date   The date when shareholders will receive dividends and capital-gains distributions, assuming they have elected not to reinvest those payments in additional shares. The payable date follows the "record date" by anywhere from a few days to several weeks. *See* Record date.

Portfolio   A group of securities in a common account. The term is used as a synonym for mutual fund in this book.

Portfolio rebalancing   The process of periodically revising a portfolio to restore the asset-class weights for stocks, bonds, and cash to their long-run target values. You do this by selling shares in appreciated asset classes and buying shares in underrepresented categories.

Portfolio turnover   A measure of the amount of buying and selling activity at a fund. Turnover is defined as the lesser of securities sold or purchased during a year divided by the average of monthly net assets. A turnover of 100 percent, for example, implies positions are held on average for about a year. Past annual turnover ratios can be found in the financial-highlights table of the prospectus.

Premium   **1.** Refers to a closed-end fund trading at a price above NAV. **2.** Refers to a bond priced above its par (or face) value.

Prepayment risk   A danger faced by holders of mortgage-backed securities that the issuer will pay back principal early during a period of declining interest rates. This results from an increase in the number of homeowners refinancing their mortgages at lower rates.

Price earnings ratio (or P/E)   The price of a stock divided by its earnings per share. P/Es also are computed for individual funds, based on their portfolio holdings, as well as for market indexes like the S&P 500.

Profile prospectus   An easy-to-read summary of key information about a mutual fund presented in a standardized format. Profiles do not replace the full prospectus, however.

Prospectus A type of owner's manual for fund shareholders. The prospectus provides essential information about a fund's investment policies, objectives, risks, and services, and it provides information on fees and important financial data including past performance.

Put option A contract granting the buyer the right to *sell* a specific asset, such as a stock, at a fixed price during a limited time. *See* Call option.

Real return The amount by which a security's nominal return exceeds inflation. If inflation turns out to be much higher than investors had predicted, the real return can be negative. Obviously, the higher your real return, the better. *See* Nominal return.

Record date The date on which a fund determines its "shareholders of record" who are entitled to an upcoming dividend or capital-gains distribution. The record date is normally the business day prior to the ex-dividend or ex-distribution date.

Redemption fee A type of charge paid when selling a fund. Unlike the contingent deferred sales charge, redemption fees usually are fixed at a low number such as 1 percent and may be ongoing.

Redemption price The price you receive when you sell fund shares. It equals NAV less any contingent deferred sales charge or redemption fee.

Regional fund A type of foreign-stock portfolio that invests within a defined geographic area, such as Europe or Southeast Asia.

Regression to the mean An important law of financial markets holding that returns that have been well above their historical average for some time will diminish in the future, and if returns have been subpar they are likely to be above average in the future. Mutual funds as well as stock markets tend to regress to the mean over time. Funds that have delivered stellar returns for some time often falter for various reasons such as size.

Reinvestment date The date on which a dividend or capital-gains distribution will be reinvested in additional full and fractional fund shares. This is normally on the business day following the record date. *See* Record date.

Reinvestment privilege *See* Automatic reinvestment.

Reinvestment risk A danger, faced by bond and bond-fund investors, that coupon payments must be reinvested at successively lower rates. Zero-coupon bonds and target-maturity funds avoid this risk, which is most prevalent when interest rates are declining.

Repurchase agreements ("Repos") Short-term arrangements, often overnight, between a borrower such as a government securities dealer and a lender such as a money-market fund. The dealer sells the securities, frequently Treasuries, and agrees to buy them back at a slightly higher price.

Rights offering A technique used by closed-end funds to raise money. Subscription rights are issued to shareholders, giving them the option to buy a given number of new shares at a specified price, usually at a discount from the market price. Participating shareholders maintain their proportional ownership interest.

Rollover The process of moving assets from one tax-sheltered retirement plan to another without a tax penalty. Rollovers may be "direct" where the assets pass from one custodian to another or "indirect" where the plan owner receives a check from a former custodian and deposits it with the new firm. The direct, custodian-to-custodian transfer is generally recommended.

R-squared A statistical measure for determining how well diversified a given portfolio is. R-squared values close to 100 percent indicate a high degree of diversification, while numbers near 0 percent reflect the opposite. A high R-squared also tells you that you can have more confidence in a portfolio's beta coefficient.

SEC annualized 30-day yield A standardized yield reported by all fund companies on their fixed-income portfolios. It is computed daily according to a complex formula provided by the SEC. The objective is to make yields on different bond funds comparable.

Sector fund Any of various portfolios that invest exclusively in a specific industry or stock group. Often categorized as a "specialty" fund.

Sector risk The danger that a particular industry such as biotechnology will plunge.

Securities and Exchange Commission (SEC) A federal agency created by the Securities Exchange Act of 1934 that governs the investment industry, including mutual funds and their sibling portfolios.

Sharpe ratio A measure of risk-adjusted performance calculated by dividing a fund's excess return above a "risk-free" rate by its standard deviation. Treasury-bill returns are a common risk-free rate.

Short sale The sale of a stock or mutual fund today in hopes of buying it later at a lower price, thereby closing out the position with a gain. Short sales are the reverse of normal "long" investment transactions, and they require that you borrow the shorted shares from a brokerage. Short selling is a risky strategy since rising prices would result in losses.

Single-country fund A portfolio that targets a particular stock market. Typically, these funds are much riskier than more broadly based portfolios.

Small-company fund A portfolio that invests in corporations with relatively low market worth or capitalization. Such funds may have either a growth or value orientation.

Specialty fund Portfolios that pursue a narrow and sometimes unusual investment orientation. Examples include funds that avoid certain objectionable types of companies or industries such as tobacco and portfolios that invest in certain regions of the United States. Sector products are a subset of the specialty-portfolio universe. *See* Sector fund.

Spiders (SPDRs or Standard & Poor's Depositary Receipts) These are index funds that trade on the American Stock Exchange. One portfolio targets the S&P 500 (trading symbol SPY); the other tracks the S&P MidCap 400 (MDY).

Spread *See* Dealer spread and Yield spread.

Standard & Poor's 500 A value-weighted price index comprised of 500 big-capitalization U.S. stocks.

Standard deviation A statistical measure of the month-to-month ups and downs of a fund's returns. Higher numbers indicate greater fluctuations and thus heightened volatility.

Statement of Additional Information (or SAI) A more comprehensive mutual-fund disclosure statement, also called Part B of the prospectus. The SAI goes into considerable detail on a fund's investment policies, risks, and other matters. In addition, it lists the names of officers and directors and identifies major shareholders. Unlike the prospectus, the SAI is not required to be sent to investors, but fund companies will provide it on request, without charge.

Stock A security that represents an equity or ownership interest in a corporation. Changes in a firm's earnings and financial condition have a major effect on its stock price. A portion of the firm's profits may be paid as dividends to shareholders.

Strips Separate Trading of Registered Interest and Principal of Securities. These are zero-coupon Treasury bonds that have been created by separating regular Treasuries into interest and principal components.

Style An investment philosophy or approach pursued by a fund manager as seen by the types of stocks held, such as large-cap value or small-cap growth companies.

Style drift The tendency of some fund managers to stray from their usual types of investments. For instance, a large-cap value fund might move a major slice of its assets into small growth stocks, causing the portfolio to perform unexpectedly better or worse than its peers. Style drift makes it difficult to stick with an asset-allocation plan because it introduces unpredictable shifts in your mix.

Sweep account A type of investment account that features the automatic transfer of unreinvested dividends from stock and bond funds into a money-market portfolio. Individuals who don't want to receive checks for these payments use the sweep-account option.

Switching privilege *See* Exchange privilege.

Target-maturity fund A portfolio that invests mainly in zero-coupon bonds, especially "strips," which mature in a specific year. Like bonds, these funds promise to pay a predetermined value at a specific future date because that's when they liquidate.

Tax efficiency   The degree to which a fund exposes its shareholders to taxable distributions. Funds that make large shareholder payments are less tax efficient than others that don't, such as index portfolios. Municipal-bond funds also are highly tax efficient due to their tax-free income.

Tax-free bond fund   *See* Municipal-bond fund.

Time diversification   The concept of reducing risk by adding more years to a person's investment horizon. Time diversification is most important for stock investors, since the market is highly volatile in the short run yet has a strong tendency to rise over lengthier periods.

Total return   The most complete measure of investment performance. Total return considers the price increase or decrease of an asset, along with its income or yield.

Transaction by phone   A service allowing you to purchase or redeem fund shares over the telephone. The fund company debits or credits your bank account according to your instructions.

Transfer agent   The organization, usually a bank or trust company, that handles sales and redemptions of fund shares, maintains shareholder records, computes the fund's NAV each day, and pays dividend and capital-gains distributions. Some fund families perform the transfer-agent functions for themselves.

Treasury securities   Debt obligations of the U.S. government. The Treasury issues bills (maturities of one year or less), notes (2 to 10-year maturities), and bonds (maturities of 30 years). They all are considered to be free of default risk but may carry interest-rate risk.

Treynor ratio   A gauge of risk-adjusted performance calculated by dividing the excess return of a portfolio above a "risk-free" rate by its beta coefficient. Treasury-bill yields often are used as the risk-free rate.

Turnover   *See* Portfolio turnover.

12b-1 fee   A fee, authorized by the SEC in 1980, that lets funds charge shareholders for various distribution costs, including marketing expenses and commissions to salespersons. The rationale is that the fee will help a portfolio increase its assets and thereby benefit from economies of scale. The fees are part of the expense ratio and can amount to as much as 1 percent yearly. More than half of all funds today have 12b-1s.

Underwriter   *See* Distributor.

Uniform Gifts to Minors Act (UGMA)   Legislation containing rules for the administration of an investment account established in a minor's name. A gift, typically from a parent who usually serves as custodian, is needed to establish the account. Such gifts are irrevocable. Upon reaching the age of majority (18 or 21, depending on state law), the child acquires control of the account and its assets. In some states, this legislation is known as the Uniform Transfers to Minors Act.

Unit investment trust (UIT)   An unmanaged stock or bond portfolio with a fixed maturity. Most hold bonds, especially municipal bonds and Ginnie Maes.

U.S. Government bond fund   Portfolios that invest primarily in U.S. Treasury and agency securities. Such funds may emphasize short-, intermediate-, or long-term issues.

Value averaging   A long-term plan for purchasing fund shares that's similar to, but more sophisticated than, dollar-cost averaging. Value averaging requires that you coordinate transactions so that your account grows by a fixed amount each period, such as $200 monthly. That means you buy more shares of a mutual fund when its price is down and fewer shares when it's up. You might even sell some shares when the NAV is particularly high.

Value investing   A popular investment style that focuses on finding underpriced securities. In contrast to growth investors, value investors try to buy stocks selling for low multiples of earnings, book value, or other yardsticks.

Variable annuity   A mutual fund within an insurance wrapper. Variable annuities offer tax-deferred growth through various portfolio choices with different investment objectives.

Wash sale   The sale of securities at a loss and the repurchase of substantially identical investments within a 31-day period. A wash sale also occurs if the securities were purchased within 30 days prior to their sale. The IRS disallows capital-loss deductions in wash sales.

WEBS (World Equity Benchmark Shares)   These portfolios are country-specific index funds that trade on the American Stock Exchange. There are 17 WEBS that track individual foreign stock markets.

Wilshire 5000   The most comprehensive index of the U.S. stock market. The Wilshire includes all companies traded on the New York and American stock exchanges and many Nasdaq issues. All told, it tracks more than 7,000 stocks.

Wire transfer   The movement of money electronically between a bank and mutual-fund account. The method generally is used by individuals who want to transfer a large sum of money in a hurry—for example, to pay for the purchase of shares at today's closing NAV. Wire transfers usually are inexpensive.

Withdrawal plan   A service offered by many mutual-fund companies that allows you to receive checks from your mutual-fund account on a regular basis.

World Wide Web (or "Web")   A graphical system linked to the Internet, on which many mutual-fund companies offer information sites. These sites typically contain literature such as fund descriptions and prospectuses along with news about the mutual-fund family. Basically, the Web facilitates finding information on the Internet by letting you view pictures and key words and then move deeper into the Web site by clicking a computer mouse. *See* Internet.

Wrap account   A tailor-made, professionally managed portfolio of securities or mutual funds. Brokerage firms and some fund companies offer this service for larger investors who pay an asset-based fee of perhaps 1.5 percent yearly.

Yield   The income received from an investment—generally over the past 12 months—expressed as a percentage of its current price. *See* Dividend yield and SEC annualized 30-day yield.

Yield curve   The relationship at a given point in time between yields on fixed-income securities with varying maturities—commonly, Treasury bills, notes, and bonds. The curve typically slopes upward because longer maturities normally have higher yields, although it can be flat or even "inverted" or downward sloping.

Yield spread   The difference in yields between two fixed-income groups such as high-grade corporate bonds and junk issues. Astute fund managers often take advantage of unusually large spreads when they materialize.

Yield to maturity   The compound annual total return expected on a bond investment if it is held to maturity and the issuer makes all promised payments on time and in full. To realize this return, you must be able to reinvest each interest payment at a rate equal to the yield to maturity.

Zero-coupon bond   A bond that makes no periodic interest payments. The final maturity payment includes accrued interest as well as principal. Zero-coupon bonds are sold at a discount to their maturity values.

Resources for Mutual-Fund Investors

This appendix lists popular research tools that will help you find funds in different categories and access the data needed to make an evaluation. The more expensive publications may be available in larger libraries or through your broker or financial planner. You also may find other resources that you like—it's virtually impossible to cover everything.

In addition to using the resources covered here, you can keep up with recent developments and performance numbers by reading the mutual-funds sections in publications such as *Barron's, BusinessWeek, Financial World, Forbes, Investor's Business Daily, Kiplinger's Personal Finance Magazine, Money, The Wall Street Journal, Worth,* and the business sections of major metropolitan newspapers. A good way to keep abreast of mutual-fund news is by reading the daily "Fund Track" column in *The Wall Street Journal*. The monthly *Mutual Funds Magazine* is a useful publication for keeping up on the industry and individual portfolios.

The sources are grouped by category. Unless otherwise noted, the cost is quoted as an annual rate. Of course, rates and other information are subject to change.

MUTUAL-FUND DIRECTORY

The Directory of Mutual Funds and Other Investment Companies (annual, $8.50) published by the Investment Company Institute (1400 H Street, NW, Suite 1200, Washington, DC 20005-2148) contains more than 5,900 mutual funds and more than 400 closed-end funds. For those interested in industry data, the ICI's *Mutual Fund Fact Book* (annual, $15) offers a wealth of statistics and other information. The industry association also publishes other useful materials, which are listed in its directory. Internet users can visit http://www.ici.org, the ICI's Web site.

ANNUAL AND QUARTERLY BOOKS

A diverse assortment of mutual-fund guidebooks can be found. They vary widely in breadth and depth of coverage, and in cost. *Investor's Guide to Low-Cost Mutual Funds* (annual $15; MO residents $16.04) is published by the Mutual Fund Education Alliance (Department 0148, P.O. Box 419263, Kansas City, MO 64193-0148; phone 816-454-9422). This mini-guide contains descriptions of 42 mutual-fund families and data on more than 1,000 no-load and low-load portfolios, grouped into 12 investment categories. Each profile lists a statement of the fund's objectives and several statistics.

The Individual Investor's Guide to Low-Load Mutual Funds (annual, AAII members $19; nonmembers $24.95) is published by the American Association of Individual Investors in Chicago (800-428-2244 or 312-280-0170). The group's *Quarterly Low-Load Mutual Fund Update* (quarterly, AAII members $24; nonmembers $30) supplements the annual book. Both publications cover more than 860 no-load and low-load funds. The annual guide contains fund profiles, per-share data, performance and risk statistics, and other useful information. The quarterly publication reports recent return and risk information, as well as fund developments. Both sources list top-performing funds and show how relevant indexes have fared. The American Association of Individual Investors also publishes the *AAII Journal* (10 times a year, included in $49 annual AAII membership dues). It includes articles and columns on investing, including mutual-fund topics and fund-manager interviews.

The comprehensive *Handbook for No-Load Fund Investors* (annual, $45) is published by longtime mutual-fund analyst Sheldon Jacobs in Irvington-on-Hudson, New York (914-693-7420). Jacobs' book contains profiles of more than 2,200 no-load funds, including 10 years of annual performance data.

Jacobs also publishes *The No-Load Fund Investor* (monthly, $135), which includes his recommendations, model portfolios, and general commentary. Jacobs' annual book also features selected reprints of articles from his monthly newsletter and a complete directory of no-load funds.

Standard & Poor's/Lipper Mutual Fund Profiles (quarterly, $164) is published by Standard & Poor's Corp. in New York (800-221-5277). This reference features more than 800 load and no-load stock and bond portfolios using data provided by Lipper Analytical Services. Each presentation includes total returns, a risk indicator, and per-share data. An additional 2,700 taxable funds and 800 tax-free portfolios are profiled in the back of the book. You also will find lists of top and bottom performers, leaders and laggards grouped by investment objective, and other useful information.

IN-DEPTH BIWEEKLY SERVICES

The comprehensive *Morningstar Mutual Funds* (every other week, $425) is published by Morningstar in Chicago (800-735-0700 or 312-696-6000). The service comes in two sections—a summary report and a collection of fund profiles—and provides all-inclusive reports on 1,700 funds, including about 200 closed-end portfolios. Each profile is updated every 20 weeks. Each profile features an analyst's review that focuses on performance, risk, portfolio holdings, and recent developments. Funds are rated on both return and risk. Profiles contain modern portfolio statistics—alpha, beta, R-squared, and standard deviation. The reports include quarterly as well as annual total returns. Year-to-date returns on all funds are updated regularly. If you're looking for something that's less comprehensive, *Morningstar Investor* (monthly, $79) is a newsletter that covers 500 funds and includes articles and interviews with fund managers.

In-depth coverage in a similar format is provided by *The Value Line Mutual Fund Survey* (every other week, $295), published by Value Line in New York (800-634-3583 or 212-907-1500). This publication reports on 1,500 funds. It is supplemented twice yearly with reports on 490 smaller portfolios and descriptions of 100 fund families.

COMPUTER RESOURCES

If you have Internet access, you may want to visit a fund-company Web site to view or download a mutual-fund prospectus or other useful information, as described in Chapter 24. Simply phone the fund company and ask for the Internet address or Uniform Resource Locator (URL). However, virtually all information available on fund-company Web sites also can be obtained elsewhere. Other Web sites of potential interest such as Networth and Mutual Funds Interactive were referred to in Chapter 24 (see Figure 24-1).

Mutual-fund software is generally most appropriate for investment advisers, although some people with large portfolios may find it of interest. *Morningstar Ascent* (quarterly updates, $95; monthly updates, $195), Morningstar's more inclusive *Principia* (quarterly updates, $195; monthly updates, $395) and *Principia Plus* (quarterly updates, $495; monthly updates, $795) allow you to screen, rank, and graph fund data. Both floppy and CD-ROM versions are available for *Ascent* and *Principia*; *Principia Plus* comes on CD-ROM. If you're in the market for software, also check out *Value Line Mutual Fund Survey for Windows* and *Alexander Steele's Mutual Fund Expert*. The latter is published by Steele Systems in Los Angeles (800-237-8400 or 310-478-4213). The Value Line and Steele software generally are comparable to Morningstar's and are available in different versions.

An in-depth study of variable annuities is possible with Morningstar's *Variable Annuity Principia Plus* (quarterly updates, $495; monthly updates, $795), which covers more than 5,400 subaccounts. It includes editorials, analyses of policies, and the capability to screen, rank, and graph.

CLOSED-END FUND RESOURCES

Morningstar Mutual Funds, referred to above, includes standard Morningstar profiles for about 200 closed-end funds. *Standard & Poor's Stock Reports* (updated quarterly; available at major libraries) profiles virtually all closed-end funds in customary S&P format. *The Value Line Investment Survey*, another popular resource for stock investors, covers about 50 closed-end portfolios in the usual Value Line format.

Closed-end advisory letters include *The Investor's Guide to Closed-End Funds* (monthly, $365) published by longtime closed-end observer Thomas J. Herzfeld in Miami (800-TJH-FUND or 305-271-1900). Herzfeld's newsletter follows nearly 500 closed-end funds. The *Closed-End Fund Digest* (monthly, $199) is published by Patrick Winton in Santa Barbara (805-565-5651) and covers all closed-end funds. *Libera's Closed End Country Fund Report* (monthly, $190) is published by Washington, D.C.-based Washington International Advisors (202-783-7051). This thorough publication covers more than 90 closed-end foreign-stock funds and the 17 exchange-traded WEBS, or single-country index funds that are discussed in Chapter 11.

The Internet Closed-End Fund Investor (http://www.icefi.com) tracks roughly 500 closed-end funds using CDA/Wiesenberger data. Morningstar's *Principia for Closed-End Funds* (quarterly updates, $195; monthly updates, $395) is a comprehensive software package carrying nearly 500 funds on a computer diskette. It includes editorials, analyses of portfolios, and the ability to screen, rank, and graph.

Mutual-Fund
Telephone Directories

Directory A: Selected No-Load and Low-Load Fund Families*

AARP	800-322-2282	Bull & Bear	800-847-4200
Acorn	800-922-6769	Caldwell & Orkin	800-237-7073
American Century	800-345-2021	Capstone	800-262-6631
AmSouth	800-451-8382	Century Shares	800-321-1928
Analytic	800-374-2633	CGM	800-345-4048
API	800-544-6060	Clipper	800-420-7556
Aquinas	800-423-6369	Clover	800-932-7781
Ariel	800-292-7435	Cohen & Steers	800-437-9912
Artisan	800-344-1770	Columbia	800-547-1707
Babson	800-422-2766	Copley	508-674-8459
Baron	800-992-2766	Crabbe Huson	800-541-9732
Bartlett	800-800-3609	Dodge & Cox	800-621-3979
BB&K	800-882-8383	Domini	800-762-6814
Berger	800-333-1001	Dreyfus	800-782-6620
Berwyn	800-992-6757	Dupree	800-866-0614
Blanchard	800-333-7384	Eclipse	800-872-2710
Brandywine	800-656-3017	Fairmont	800-262-9936
Brundage Story & Rose	800-320-2212	FAM	800-453-4392
Buffalo	800-492-8332	Fidelity	800-544-6666

First Eagle	800-451-3623	L. Roy Papp	800-421-4004
Flex	800-325-3539	Payden & Rygel	800-572-9336
Founders	800-525-2440	Pax	800-767-1729
Fremont	800-548-4539	PBHG	800-433-0051
Gabelli	800-422-3554	Permanent	800-531-5142
Galaxy	800-628-0414	Philadelphia	800-749-9933
Gateway	800-354-6339	Preferred	800-662-4769
Gintel	800-243-5808	T. Rowe Price	800-225-5132
GIT	800-368-3195	Rainier	800-248-6314
Gradison-McDonald	800-869-5999	Reich & Tang	800-221-3079
Greenspring	800-366-3863	Reynolds	800-773-9665
Harbor	800-422-1050	Rightime	800-242-1421
Heartland	800-432-7856	Robertson Stephens	800-766-3863
Homestead	800-258-3030	Royce	800-221-4268
Hotchkis & Wiley	800-346-7301	Rushmore	800-621-7874
IAI	800-945-3863	Safeco	800-624-5711
Invesco	800-525-8085	Schroder	800-963-6786
Janus	800-525-3713	Schwab	800-266-5623
Jurika & Voyles	800-584-6878	Scout	800-996-2862
Kaufmann	800-666-9181	Scudder	800-225-2470
Key	800-422-7273	Selected	800-243-1575
Legg Mason	800-822-5544	Sentry	800-533-7827
Lexington	800-526-0056	Sequoia	800-686-6884
Lindner	800-995-7777	1784	800-252-1784
Longleaf	800-445-9469	Sit	800-332-5580
Loomis Sayles	800-633-3330	Skyline	800-458-5222
Mairs & Power	800-304-7404	Smith Breeden	800-221-3138
Markman	800-707-2771	Sound Shore	800-953-6786
Marshall	800-236-8560	SSgA	800-647-7327
Mathers	800-962-3863	SteinRoe	800-338-2550
Maxus	800-446-2987	Stonebridge	800-367-7814
Merger	800-343-8959	Stratton	800-441-6580
Meridian	800-446-6662	Strong	800-368-1030
Monetta	800-666-3882	Third Avenue	800-443-1021
Montgomery	800-572-3863	Turner	800-224-6312
MSB	800-661-3938	Tweedy Browne	800-432-4789
Neuberger & Berman	800-877-9700	US Global Investors	800-873-8637
Nicholas	800-227-5987	USAA	800-531-8722
Nomura	800-833-0018	Value Line	800-223-0818
Northeast Investors	800-225-6704	Van Wagoner	800-228-2121
Northern	800-595-9111	Vanguard	800-635-1511
Oakmark	800-625-6275	Vontobel	800-527-9500
Oberweis	800-323-6166	Warburg Pincus	800-257-5614

Wasatch	800-551-1700	William Blair	800-742-7272
Wayne Hummer	800-621-4477	WPG	800-223-3332
Weitz	800-232-4161	Yacktman	800-525-8258
Weston New Century	617-239-0445		

Directory B: Selected Load Fund Families**

AIM	800-347-1919	Nuveen	800-252-4630
Alliance	800-227-4618	One Group	800-338-4345
American	800-421-4120	Oppenheimer	800-525-7048
American Express	800-328-8300	PaineWebber	800-647-1568
Colonial	800-426-3750	Phoenix Duff & Phelps	800-243-4361
Dean Witter	800-869-3863	PIMCO	800-227-7337
Delaware	800-523-4640	Pioneer	800-225-6292
Eaton Vance	800-225-6265	Prudential	800-225-1852
Evergreen/Keystone	800-235-0064	Putnam	800-225-1581
Franklin Templeton	800-342-5236	Seligman	800-221-7844
Goldman Sachs	800-526-7384	Smith Barney	800-327-6748
GT Global	800-824-1580	Stagecoach	800-222-8222
John Hancock	800-257-3336	State Street Research	800-562-0032
Kemper	800-621-1048	SunAmerica	800-858-8850
Lord Abbett	800-426-1130	United Group	800-366-5465
MainStay	800-522-4202	Van Kampen	
MFS	800-637-2929	American Capital	800-421-5666
Merrill Lynch	800-995-6526	Vista	800-348-4782
New England	800-225-5478	Waddell & Reed/United	800-366-5465
Norwest	800-338-1348		

*The no-load and low-load directory is based upon the fund families included in *The Individual Investor's Guide to Low-Load Mutual Funds* (16th edition 1997), published by the American Association of Individual Investors in Chicago.

**Each of the load-fund groups had total assets of at least $9 billion as of 12/31/96.

Toll-free phone numbers of funds not listed in these directories can be obtained by calling 800-555-1212.

Total Return with Reinvestment

To calculate returns in situations involving reinvested dividends, you need to know the amount of each distribution and the NAV on the reinvestment date. Essentially, an investor is buying more shares at the reinvestment price.

Suppose a small-company growth fund starts the year at an NAV of $20 and finishes at a price of $21.50. Assume further that the fund made a $4 per-share distribution in December that was reinvested at an NAV of $21.

If the investor held one share at the start of the year, he or she accumulated 0.19 share (the distribution of 4 divided by the 21 reinvestment price) in December. Thus, our investor held 1.19 shares at year end.

The following steps are used to calculate total returns with reinvestment:

Step 1. Determine the investor's total account value at the end of the period:
(End of period NAV) x (Shares held at end) = 21.50 x 1.19 = 25.59

Step 2. Determine total value at the start of the period:
(Beginning of period NAV) x (Shares held at beginning) = 20 x 1 = 20

Step 3. Subtract the value obtained in *Step 2* from the one in *Step 1*:
   = 25.59 – 20 = 5.59
Step 4. Divide the result in *Step 3* by the result in *Step 2*:
   = 5.59/20 = 27.95 percent

The 27.95-percent return with reinvestment contrasts with a 27.50-percent number without [(4 + 21.50 – 20)/20].

As seen in this illustration, the difference between return with reinvestment and return without is often small for a single year. But these differences add up over time, particularly if a large sum of money is compounding.

Finding the Geometric Average Total Return

The geometric average annual return and the compound annual return are the same thing. Basically, we're taking results for individual periods and averaging them using a special formula. Suppose a fund had total returns of 15 percent, –20 percent, and 40 percent over three consecutive years. The geometric average easily can be found with a finance calculator.

The steps are as follows:

Step 1. Express each return as a decimal. Converting the preceding percentage values to decimals, we have 0.15, –0.20, and 0.40.

Step 2. Add 1.0 to each decimal value. Adding 1.0 to the numbers found in *Step 1* gives us 1.15, 0.80, and 1.40.

Step 3. Multiply together the values found in *Step 2*: 1.15 x 0.80 x 1.40 = 1.288.

Step 4. Raise the value found in *Step 3* to the 1/x power, where x equals the number of items being averaged. Since we are dealing with three periods, we have $1.288^{1/3} = 1.088$.

Step 5. Subtract 1.0 from the result in *Step 4* and express as a percent. Concluding the example, $1.088 - 1.000 = .088$, or 8.8 percent.

Thus, our hypothetical fund produced an 8.8 percent geometric average annual return.

Total Returns Can Be Shown in Three Different Ways

There are three standard methods of portraying performance over periods longer than one year: cumulative total return, compound sum of a specific initial investment (typically $10,000), and compound annual return. The following numbers illustrate the differences between the three over a 15-year period.

Cumulative Total Return	Result of $10,000 Initial Investment	Compound Annual Total Return
1,500%	$160,000	20.30%
1,000	110,000	17.34
800	90,000	15.78
500	60,000	12.69
300	40,000	9.68

With a finance calculator you can convert the larger percentage or dollar values to more meaningful compound average annual returns, if they're not also reported. Suppose you know a fund has produced a cumulative total return of 1,500 percent over 15 years. What does that equal on an annual basis?

Step 1. Take your percentage cumulative total return and express it as an ordinary number by moving the decimal point two places to the left, that is, 1,500 percent becomes 15.00.

Step 2. Add 1.0 to your result in *Step 1*. In the example, 15.0 + 1.0 = 16.0.

Step 3. Determine how many years (x) are involved. Then, using a finance calculator, raise the number obtained in *Step 2* to the 1/x power.
In the example, 16 raised to the 1/15 power equals 1.2030. (Note, this is the same as taking the 15th root of 16.)

Step 4. Subtract 1.0 from your result in *Step 3* and express it as a percentage. Concluding the example, 1.2030 − 1.0 = 0.2030, or 20.30 percent.

It's even easier to convert an accumulated sum of money based on an initial investment into a compound annual return. Suppose an initial $10,000 resulted in $160,000 after 15 years. Different calculators require different keystrokes, but in general the $10,000 is the initial (or present) value, $160,000 is the final (or future) value, and 15 is the number of periods. Given these three inputs, a finance calculator would generate a 20.30 percent compound annual return.

Index

A

AAII Journal, 16
Account-activity statements, 275-76
Account registration, 268-69
    corporations/partnerships/ other entities, 269
    gift or transfer to a minor, 269
    individual account, 268
    joint tenants with right of survivorship, 268-69
    tenants in common, 269
    titling accounts, 268-69
    trusts, 269
Administrative costs, 46, 330
Advisory services, mutual funds, 335
Africa, investment opportunities in, 129
Age, and risk tolerance, 9
Aggressive investors, 14
All-or-none restrictions, 285
Alternative minimum tax (AMT), 201-2
America Online, 319
Annual returns, 74
Arizona Republic, The, 16, 51
Asset allocation, 86, 253-66
    asset classes, 255-56, 260
    benefits of, 254-55
    bonds:
        avoiding, 263-64
        divvying up, 260
    college portfolio, 264-65
    diversification, 254
    flexibility, 262-63
    life-cycle approach, 257-60
    nest egg, managing in retirement, 265-66
    portfolio kickers, 259-60
    rebalancing plans, 260-62
    stocks, divvying up, 258-59
Asset-allocation funds, 23, 150-52
Asset building, 350
Asset-class risk, 73
Automated Clearing House (ACH) network, 273
Automatic-investment plans, 272
Automatic reinvestment, 272-73

B

Balanced funds, 23, 149, 331
Bankers' acceptances, 216
Barron's, 51, 74, 146, 220, 251
Bear-market funds, 158
Bear markets, effect on investors, 4
Beta, 76-77

shortcomings of, 77-78
Bid-asked spread, 285, 330
Board of directors, mutual funds, 20
Bond funds, 344-45
    advantages of, 177-78
    disadvantages of, 177
    and diversification, 179
    individual bonds vs., 176-79
Bond market, 163
Bond market indicators, 64-65
Bond ratings, 171
Bonds:
    callable feature, 165
    call risk, 167
    characteristics of, 164-65
    credit risk, 167, 171-72
    defined, 164
    inflation risk, 167
    interest-rate forecasts, 173
    interest-rate risk, 167, 168-70
        and bond duration, 168-69
    junk, 171, 186-90, 260
    liquidity risk, 167-68
    maturity spreads, 176
    prices, 165
    quality categories, 171
    quality spreads, 176
    reinvestment risk, 167
    risk, 165, 167-68
    segment spreads, 176
    total return, 172-73
    yield, 165
    yield curve, 166-67
    yield spreads, 175-76
    yield to maturity, 165
Brokerage commissions, 330
Bull markets, 3-4
Business Week, 51

C

Call risk, bonds, 167
Capital appreciation funds, 23
Capital preservation, fixed-income securities, 163-64
Cash flow, 53-54
Cash position, altering, 92
Cash reserves, 8
Central Registration Depository (CRD) report, 287
Certified Financial Planners (CFPs), 288
Chartered Life Underwriters (CLUs)/Charted
        Financial Consultants (ChFCs), 288

Chat rooms, 321-22
Closed-end funds, 27, 108-23, 332, 342-43
  and cash inflow/outflow, 111
  choice of, 112
  conversion to open-end status, 122
  defined, 109
  discounts/premiums, 109-10, 115-20
  initial public offerings (IPOs) of, 110-11
  investing in, 114-15
  investment blunders, 122-23
  leveraging, 112
  liquidations, 122
  merger of, 122
  NAV of, 109-10
  open-end funds vs., 113-14
  rights offerings, 112
  secondary stock offerings, 112
  in the 1920s, 109
  volatile, trading, 142
  WEBS (World Equity Benchmark Shares) com-
    pared to, 143-44
Closed-end muni funds, 207-8
  leverage, 207-8
Closet indexing, 107
Commercial paper, 216
Community property, advantages of, 270
Community property with right of survivorship, 270
Company size, screening companies by, 32-34
Company-specific risk, 131
Compound interest, 6-7
CompuServe, 319
Computerized investing, 313-24, 350
  chat rooms, 321-22
  going online, 319-22
  holdings, tracking, 322-24
  Internet, 319-22
    World Wide Web (WWW) vs., 320
  message boards, 321-22
  mutual-fund software, 316-19
    performance evaluation, 318
    portfolio information, 318-19
  online services, 319
  retirement-planning software, 314-16
  trading online, 322
  Web sites, visiting, 320-21, 350
Confirmation statements, 275
Conservative investors, 14
Contingent deferred sales charges (CDSCs), 25
Continuous professional management, and mutual
    funds, 29
Convertible funds, 150
Corporate bond funds, 181, 186
Corporate bonds, 164
  default danger, 171
  gilt edge, 171
Correlation coefficient, 126
Country holdings, rotating, 93
Country risk, 131-32
Country-specific index funds, 142-44

Coupon rate, bonds, 164
Credit quality, municipal-bond funds, 204
Credit risk:
  bonds, 167, 171-72
  junk bonds, 188
Currency exchange rates, fluctuations in, 341-42
Currency fluctuations, and single-country funds, 141
Currency risk, 132-35
Custodian-to-custodian transfer, 238
Customer's Afternoon Letter (Dow), 58

D

Daily fund indexes, 335
Dealer spreads, and transaction costs, 50
Derivatives, 196-97, 213, 349-50
Developing markets, opportunities in, 128-31
Directors, funds, 348-49
*Directory of Mutual Funds and Other Investment
    Companies*, 17
Disciplined investors, characteristics of, 7-8
Discount-premium fluctuations, and single-country
    funds, 141
Discounts, 108-23
Dissimilar funds, mixing, 331
Diversification:
    and bond funds, 179
    and global investing, 124-25
    international, 40-41
    and mutual funds, 23-24, 28-29
Dividend yield, 34
Dollar-cost averaging, 86-89, 329
Domestic equity funds, 23
Dow, Charles, 58
Dow Jones Industrial Average, short history of, 60-61
Downside risk, gauging, 79
Duration, 169

E

Early retirement, 265
Earnings multiple, 82
Economies of scale, and mutual funds, 29
Economist, The, 146
Educational literature/newsletters, 277
Education IRAs, 229-30
Efficient-market hypothesis, 98-99
Emergency reserves, building, 328
Emerging market funds, 23
Emerging markets, 331
    characteristics of, 129
    opportunities in, 128-31
Emerging Markets Database (International Finance
    Corp.), 128-29
Emerging-markets funds, 139
Emerging Stock Markets Factbook (IFC), 64
Emotions, dealing with, 4-6
Employer's stock, investing in, 231
Equity-income funds, 23, 37
Equity investing, 2

Eurodollar CDs, 216
Exchange-traded funds, 285, 342-44
    liquidity, 343-44
Ex-distribution date, 44
Ex-dividend date, 44
Expense ratios, 45-48, 338
    of large portfolios, 53
    tracking, 192-93
Expenses, and discounts/premiums, 117

F

Face amount, bonds, 164
Fear, 82-83, 117
Federal agency notes, 215-16
Federal Reserve ("Fed"), 173-75
    and inflation, 174-75
    monetary tools, 174
    and recessions, 175
    and Treasury Direct system, 178
Fee tables, 48
Financial supermarkets, 279-82, 327-28, 351-52
Financial Times, The, 146
Fixed annuities, 242-43
Fixed-income securities, 162-79
    bond characteristics, 164-65
    capital preservation, 163-64
    classification of, 180-81
        by quality, 180
        by taxability, 181
        by term to maturity, 180
        by type, 180
    income, 164
    inflation risk, 170
    liquidity, 163
    money and capital markets, 163
    real returns, 170
    reasons for investing in, 163-64
    segments, 163
Flexible bond funds, 181, 192
Flexible funds, 23
Flipping, 38
Focus, of small portfolios, 53
Forbes magazine, 17, 51
Foreign & Colonial Investment Trust, 109
Foreign-bond funds, 181, 191-92, 260
Foreign equity funds, 23
Foreign small-stock funds, 138-39
Foreign-stock funds, 340-42
Form 1099-B, 276
Form 1099-DIV, 276, 347
Form 1099-R, 276
401(k)/403(b) plans, 231-32
Front-end loads, 25
Fund distributor, mutual funds, 21
Fund families, 267-78
    account registration, 268-69
        corporations/partnerships/ other entities, 269
        gift or transfer to a minor, 269

individual account, 268
        joint tenants with right of survivorship, 268-69
        tenants in common, 269
    titling accounts, 268-69
    trusts, 269
    joint tenancy, perils of, 269-70
    shareholder services, 271-77, 332
        account-activity statements, 275-76
        automatic-investment plans, 272
        automatic reinvestment, 272-73
        check writing, 274-75
        confirmation statements, 275
        educational literature/newsletters, 277
        Form 1099-B, 276
        Form 1099-DIV, 276
        Form 1099-R, 276
        information by phone/computer, 276-77
        retirement plans, 272
        shareholder reports, 276
        transactions by phone/computer, 273-74
        withdrawal plans, 275
Fund management, 347-49
Fund matters, voting on, 26-27
Fund services, See Shareholder services
Funds of funds, 152-53, 345
    and layer fees, 47, 152

G

Gambling, 5
Gambling addiction, spotting, 5
General obligation (GO) securities, 202
Ghana, investment opportunities in, 129
Gift or transfer to a minor, 269
Gilt edge corporate bonds, 171
Global funds, 23, 346
Global investing, 124-35, 331
    Africa, investment opportunities in, 129
    company-specific risk, 131
    country risk, 131-32
    currencies, understanding, 132-35
    currency risk, 132-35
        coping with, 134-35
        hedging, 134
    discipline in, 146
    and diversification/growth, 124-25
    diversification, 145
    emerging markets, opportunities in, 128-31
    inefficiencies, profiting from, 127-28
    long-run allocations, determining, 145
    low correlations, reducing risk with, 126-27
    and mutual funds, 125
    opportunities in, 125-30
    overpaying for international funds, 145-46
    overseas markets, volatility of, 125
    patience in, 146
    purchasing-power parity, 133-34
    risk, 131-32

Global investing (cont'd)
    spreading, 146
    state-run enterprises, 130
    staying up to date, 146
    See also World-stock portfolios
Gold funds, 157-58, 331-32
Greed, 82-83, 117
Growth, and global investing, 124-25
Growth at a reasonable rate (GARP), 36
Growth funds, 23
Growth and income funds, 23
Growth investing vs. value investing, 339
Growth stocks, 34-35
Guarded investing, 6

H

Health-care portfolios, 259
Hedge funds, 27
Hedging, 337-38
    with futures/options, 92
High-grade issues, 171
High-yield bond funds, 186-90
    credit risk, 188
    investment considerations, 190
    junk bonds vs. stock, 187-88
    liquidity risk, 189
    reasons for investing in, 187
High-yield corporate bond funds, 181
High-yield municipal bond funds, 181
High-yield municipal-bond funds, 206
Humility, need for, 8
Hybrid funds, 148-53
    asset-allocation funds, 150-52
    balanced funds, 149
    convertible funds, 150
    defined, 148-49
    funds of funds, 152-53

I

Income:
    bond funds, 178
    fixed-income securities, 164
Income ratio, 48-49
Income risk, money-market funds, 219-20
Independence, need for, 8
Independent custodian, mutual funds, 20
Index funds, 23
    birth of, 99-100
    closet indexing, 107
    enhanced products, 107
    expense ratios, 106
    redemption fees/switching limitations, 106
    for taxable accounts, 106
    turnover, 106
Indexing, 41, 95-107
    checklist for, 106-7
    closet, 107
    efficient-market hypothesis, 98-99

investment choices, 102-4
    market anomalies, 101-2
    market efficiency, 101
    passive investing, resistance to, 100-101
    portfolio, building, 104-5
    regression to the mean, 96-97
    Standard & Poor's Depository Receipts
        (SPDRs/"spiders"), 105-6
    underperformance, 97-98
Indirect rollover, 238
Inflation:
    accounting for, 226
    and Federal Reserve ("Fed"), 174-75
    and nest-egg management, 232
Inflation-proof bond funds, 183
Inflation risk, 71-72
    bonds, 167
    fixed-income securities, 170
    money-market funds, 219-20
In-state taxable-equivalent yield, 200-201
Institutional funds, 20, 217-18
Insured bonds, 206
Insured municipal bond funds, 181
Interest-rate risk:
    bonds, 167, 168-70
    stocks, 169
International diversification, 40-41
International Finance Corporation, emerging-market
        indexes, 64
International funds, 23
International investing, getting started in, 341
Internet, 313, 319-22
    World Wide Web (WWW) vs., 320
Investing, speculation vs., 4-5
Investment advisors, 285-91
    benefits of using, 291
    Certified Financial Planners (CFPs), 288
    Chartered Life Underwriters (CLUs)/Charted
        Financial
            Consultants (ChFCs), 288
    credentials, checking, 287-89
    interviewing candidates, checklist for, 289-90
    mutual funds, 20
    Personal Financial Specialists (PFSs), 288-89
Investment Company Act (1940), 17
Investment Company Institute (ICI), 93
Investment-grade securities, 171
Investment risk, defined, 67-68
Investor questionnaire, 9-14
Investors:
    aggressive, 14
    conservative, 14
    disciplined, characteristics of, 7-8
    moderate, 14
Investor's Business Daily, 16, 220
Investor's Guide to Low-Cost Mutual Funds, 17
IRAs (Individual Retirement Accounts), 229-32
    changing IRA custodians, 238
    education IRAs, 229-30

Roth IRAs, 229-30
SEP-IRAs, 230
IRS publications, 309
IRS Website, 309

J

Japan:
Nikkei index, drop in, 131
OTC market, 63
stock market, and U.S. investors, 131
Joint tenants with right of survivorship, 268-69
perils of, 269-70
Jumbo certificates of deposit (jumbo CDs), 216
Junk bonds, 171, 186-90, 260
angles, 187
categories of, 187
credit risk, 188
investment considerations, 190
liquidity risk, 189
original-issue junk, 187
reasons for investing in, 187
stock vs., 187-88
Junk tax-exempt portfolios, 206

K

Kenya, investment opportunities in, 129
Keogh plans, 230-31
Kiddie tax, 309-10
Kiplinger's Personal Finance Magazine, 51

L

Labeling stocks, 35
Large lump sums, investing, 91-92
Large portfolios, 53
Leverage, closed-end muni funds, 207-8
Leveraging, 112
Limit orders, 285
Liquidity:
bond funds, 177
and discounts/premiums, 117, 118
exchange-traded funds, 285, 343-44
fixed-income securities, 163
and mutual funds, 30
Liquidity risk:
bonds, 167-68
high-yield bond funds, 189
junk bonds, 189
Lump-sum distributions, 237

M

Management, analyzing, 54-55
Management company, mutual funds, 20
Management fees, 46, 330
bond funds, 193
Management reputation, and
discounts/premiums, 117

Manager:
funds, 347-49
keeping tabs on, 92-93
Maneuverability, of small portfolios, 52-53
Margin, 283-84
Market indicators, 57-66
bond market indicators, 64-65
Dow Jones Industrial Average, short history of, 60-61
index illustration, 59-60
International Finance Corp's emerging-market indexes, 64
Morgan Stanley Capital International's EAFE, 63
and mutual funds, 65
Nasdaq indicators, 63
Russell indicators, 62-63
Standard & Poor's indexes, 61-62
stock exchange indicators, 63
Value Line Composite Index, 62
weighting methods, 58-59
equally weighted, 59
price weighted, 58
value weighted, 58-59
Wilshire 5000, 62
Market price, NAV returns vs., 120-21
Market risk, 69-71
Market-timing, 83-85, 330
Mature firms, getting income from, 37
Maturity, municipal-bond funds, 204
Maturity amount, bonds, 164
Maturity spreads, 176
Medium-grade issues, 171
Medium-sized companies, getting growth from, 37-38
Mergers, closed-end funds, 122
Message boards, 321-22
Micro cap funds, 23
Milken, Michael, 187
Mistakes, learning from, 8
Moderate investors, 14
Monetary tools, Federal Reserve ("Fed"), 174
Money magazine, 17, 51
Money-market funds, 163, 212-24, 344-45
expense ratios, 220-21
fee waivers/teasers, 223
income risk, 219-20
inflation risk, 219-20
money-fund applications, 214-15
portfolio building blocks, 215-17
portfolio choices, categories of, 217-18
portfolio turnover rates, 223
retail portfolios vs. institutional funds, 217-18
return, 220
risk, 218-20
tax-free products, 221-22
yield, 220
Moody's Bond Record, 203
Moody's Investors Service, 171
Morgan Stanley Capital International's EAFE, 63
Morningstar Mutual Funds, 34, 74, 319

Morningstar Principia Plus, 319
Morocco, investment opportunities in, 129
Mortgage-backed bonds, 181, 185-86
    pass-through concept, 185-86
    prepayment risk, 186
Mortgage-backed securities, 164-65
Municipal-bond funds:
    classification of, 204-6
        national funds, 204-5
    closed-end portfolios, 207-8
    credit quality, 204
    high-yield funds, 206
    insured funds, 206
    maturity, 204
    selecting, 210-11
    single-state funds, 205-6
Municipal bonds, 164, 198-211
    alternative minimum tax (AMT), 201-2
    capital gains/losses, 201
    characteristics of, 202-3
    default danger, 171
    general obligation (GO) securities, 202
    gilt edge, 171
    revenue bonds, 202-3
    risk factors, 203-4
Mutual-fund message boards, 313
Mutual-fund portfolio:
    managing, 345-46
    size of, 345
Mutual funds, 16-31
    advantages of, 28-30
    advisory services, 335
    analyzing, 42-56
    board of directors, 20
    building assets with, 328-32
    cash flow, 53-54
    categories of, 22-23
    cautions about, 326-28
    characteristics of, 17-21
    closed funds, 24
    daily fund indexes, 335
    disadvantages of, 30-31
    diversification, 23-24, 28-29
    domestic equity funds, 23
    expenses, tracking, 45-48
    families of, 19
    foreign equity funds, 23
    fund distributor, 21
    fund matters, voting on, 26-27
    income ratio, 48-49
    independent custodian, 20
    investment adviser, 20
    investment minimums, 19-20
    large vs. small stock funds, 336-37
    liquidity, 30
    management, analyzing, 54-55
    management company, 20
    and market indicators, 65

net asset value (NAV), 18-19, 44, 336
    newspaper listings, 337
    objectives of, 22
    payout, 195
    performance ratings, 55
    popularity of, 2, 313, 325-33
    portfolio size, 52-53
    portfolio-turnover rate, 49-50
    principal underwriter, 21
    prospectus, 21-22, 334-35
    published performance data, 51-52
    Q&A, 334-51
    risk, 67-80
    sales charges, 25-26
    shareholder distributions, 42-44
    shareholder ownership, 20
    sizing up, 336-37
    small-stock funds, 38-40
    standard fee table, 48
    steps to investing in, 328-32
    structural safeguards, 20-21
    survivorship bias, 335-36
    taxes, 302-12
    total returns, 44-45, 52
    tracking positions, 93
    transaction costs, 50-51
    transfer agent, 20-21
    and unethical practices, loss from, 30
Mutual funds industry, growth of, 325-33
Mutual Funds Magazine, 16
Mutual-fund supermarkets, 279-82, 327-28, 351-52
    pitfalls for investors, 282
    pros/cons for investors, 281-82
    transaction fees, 280-81

N

Nasdaq indicators, 63
Nasdaq stock market, 38
National Association of Securities Dealers
        (NASD), 38
National funds, 204-5
National municipal bond funds, 181
Natural-resource funds, 158-59
Nest egg:
    building, 244-45
    divvying up, 238-39
    managing, 232
        in retirement, 265-66
Net asset value (NAV), 18-19, 44
Net investment income, shareholder
        distributions from, 43
Net realized gain on investments,
        shareholder distributions from, 43-44
Nigeria, investment opportunities in, 129
Nominal fixed-income yields, 170
Nontransferable rights, 121-22, 343
No-transaction fee (FTF) funds, 280

O

Objectives, mutual funds, 22
Online investing, 322
Open-end funds, closed-end funds vs., 113-14
Organizational talent, and large portfolios, 53
Over the counter (OTC) market, 38
    Japan, 63
Overseas markets, volatility of, 125

P

Par value, bonds, 164
Patience, need for, 8
Payable date, 44
Performance, and discounts/premiums, 117
Performance ratings, mutual funds, 55
Periodic interest, bonds, 164
Personal Financial Specialists (PFSs), 288-89
Portfolio, building, 104-5
Portfolio composition, and discounts/premiums, 117
Portfolio size, 52-53
    large, 53
    small, 52-53
Portfolio-turnover rate, 49-50
Post-War Golden Era, 3
Precious metals, 157-58
Price-earnings (P/E) ratio, 34
Price-to-book ratio, 82-83
Price-to-book-value ratio, 34
Principal underwriter, mutual funds, 21
Principal for Variable Annuities/Life (Morningstar), 251
Private-activity bonds, 203, 221
Probable return, estimating, 83
Prodigy, 319
Professional management, bond funds, 179
Prospectus, 21-22, 334-35
Published performance data, 51-52
Purchasing power, increasing, 234-37
Put bonds, 221

Q

Quality spreads, 176

R

Real-estate funds, 156, 331-32
Real rate of return, fixed-income securities, 170
Rebalancing plans, 260-62
Record date, 44
Redemption, bonds, 164
Regional funds, 23
regional portfolios, 34
Registered investment advisers, 288
Regression to the mean, 96-97, 327
Regular retirement, 265-66
Reinvestment date, 44
Reinvestment ease, bond funds, 178

Reinvestment risk:
    bonds, 167
    reinvestment, 167
Relative performance, of small portfolios, 53
Repurchase agreements (repos), 216
Retail portfolios, 217-18
Retirement-planning software, 314-16
Retirement strategy, 225-39
    defined-contribution plans, 227
    direct rollover, 237-38
    estimating need, 227-28
    401(k)/403(b) plans, 231-32
    inflation, accounting for, 226
    IRAs (Individual Retirement Accounts), 229-32
        education IRAs, 229-30
        Roth IRAs, 229-30
        SEP-IRAs, 230
    Keogh plans, 230-31
    lump-sum distributions, 237
    nest egg:
        divvying up, 238-39
        managing, 232
    nest egg sources, 226
    purchasing power, increasing, 234-37
    Social Security benefits, 226-27
    starting early, advantage of, 234
    tax-deferred compounding, 232-33, 330
    voluntary retirement plans, 229-32
Revenue bonds, 202-3
Rights offerings, 112, 121-22, 343
    and discounts/premiums, 117
    nontransferable rights, 121-22
    transferable rights, 121
Risk, 67-80
    asset-class, 73
    bonds, 165, 167-68
    company-specific, 131
    country, 131-32
    currency, 132-35
    downside, 79
    gauging, 73-76
    global investing, 131-32
    income, and money-market funds, 219-20
    inflation, 71-72
        bonds, 167
        money-market funds, 219-20
    investment, 67-68
    liquidity, 167-68, 189
        high-yield bond funds, 189
    market, 69-71
    money-market funds, 218-20
    municipal bonds, 203-4
    pointers for handling, 79-80
    and price-earnings ratio (P/E), 74-76
    sector, 71
    and time diversification, 70
Risk tolerance, 9
Roaring Eighties and Nineties, 3

Roaring Twenties, 3
Roth IRAs, 229-30
R-squared, 78
Russell indicators, 62-63

S

Savings plan, 8
Screening companies:
  by company size, 32-34
  by degree of management activity, 33
  by national orientation, 33
  by stock-picking style, 33
  Sector funds, 23-24, 153-56
  drawbacks of, 159
  gold funds, 157-58
  natural-resource funds, 158-59
  precious metals, 157-58
  real-estate funds, 156
  reason to invest in, 155-56
  sector choices, 153-54
  sector-fund performance, 154-55
  utility funds, 156-57
Sector risk, 71
Sectors, rotating, 93
Securities and Exchange Commission (SEC), 17
  SEC 30-day yield, 195
Segment spreads, 176
Self-directed annuities, 242
Sell decision, 293-301
  appropriate funds, choosing, 299
  bailing out, 293-94
  clutter, eliminating, 295
  fund-specific motivations, 294
  personal reasons, 294-95
  staying put, arguments for, 296
  withdrawal plans, 296-301
    adjusting withdrawals for inflation, 297-99
    alternatives to, 301
    factors affecting success/failure of, 297
    setting up, 300-301
Selling shares, 305-9
Selling short, 284
SEP-IRAs, 230
Shareholder distributions, 42-44
  from net investment income, 43
  from net realized gain on investments, 43-44
Shareholder ownership, mutual funds, 20
Shareholder reports, 276
Shareholder services, 271-77, 332
  account-activity statements, 275-76
  automatic-investment plans, 272
  automatic reinvestment, 272-73
  check writing, 274-75
  confirmation statements, 275
  educational literature/newsletters, 277
  Form 1099-B, 276
  Form 1099-DIV, 276

Form 1099-R, 276
information by phone/computer, 276-77
and mutual funds, 29-30
retirement plans, 272
shareholder reports, 276
transactions by phone/computer, 273-74
withdrawal plans, 275
Short selling, 284
Simplified Employee Pension-Individual Retirement
    Accounts (SEP-IRAs), 230
Single-country funds, 23, 140-42
  caution about, 140-41
  closed-end, 259
Single-state funds, 205-6
Single-state municipal bond funds, 181
Small company funds, 23
Small portfolios, 52-53
Small-stock funds, 38-40
  asset base of, 39
  foreign, 138-39
  range of companies, 39
  relative P/E, sizing up, 39-40
Socially responsible investing, 160-61
Social Security benefits, 226-27
Specialized products, 153-61
  sector funds, 23-24, 153-56
  drawbacks of, 159
  See also Sector funds
Speculation, investing vs., 4-5
Speculative issues, 171
Spiders, 105-6, 284, 343
Standard & Poor's Bond Guide, 203
Standard & Poor's Corp., 171
Standard & Poor's Depository Receipts (SPDRs/"spi-
    ders"), 105-6, 284, 343
Standard & Poor's indexes, 61-62
Standard deviation, 76, 78-79, 337
Standard fee table, 48
Steep premiums, caution about, 119-20
Stock exchange indicators, 63
Stock funds, 329-30, 339-40
  advantages/disadvantages of, 339-40
  expense ratios, 47
  style drift, 340
  styles, 36-38
Stock investments, 2-3
  how much to invest, 14
  and risk, 9, 15
Stock market:
  benchmarks, 338
  efficient market, use of term, 339
  market crashes, 338-39
Stocks, 259
  growth, 34-35
  and interest-rate risk, 169
  labeling, 35
  valuing, 34
Strips, 183

Structural safeguards, mutual funds, 20-21
Style drift, 37
Survivorship bias, 335-36

T

Tactical asset allocation, 86
Target-maturity bond funds, 181, 184-85
Taxable bond funds, 180-97
    corporate bond funds, 186
    derivatives, 196-97
    expense ratios, tracking, 192-93
    flexible bond funds, 192
    foreign bond funds, 191-92
    grouping by maturity, 182
    high-yield bond funds, 186-90
    management fee, 193
    mortgage-backed bonds, 185-86
    target-maturity bond funds, 184-85
    U.S. government bond funds, 182-84
    yields, 194-95
Taxable-equivalent yield, 199-200
    alternative minimum tax (AMT), 201-2
    capital gains/losses, 201
    in-state, 200-201
Tax-adjusted return, 310
Tax anticipation notes, 221
Tax-deferred compounding, 232-33, 330
Tax efficiency, 310-12
    factors affecting, 311-12
    and selection of mutual funds, 312
Taxes, 302-12, 346-47
    distributions:
        capital-gains distributions, 303
        dividends on non-U.S. securities, 304-5
        nontaxable distributions, 303
        ordinary dividends, 303
        sorting out, 303-5
        upcoming, 303-4
    IRS publications, 309
    IRS Website, 309
    kiddie tax, 309-10
    selling shares, 305-9
        average cost-double category, 307
        average cost-single category, 307
        first-in, first-out (FIFO) approach, 306
        locking in losses, 307-8
        specific identification, 306
        in stages, 305-7
        tax-free step-up in basis, 308-9
    tax efficiency, 310-12
Tax-free income:
    shopping for, 198-211
    taxable-equivalent yield, 199-200
    unit investment trusts (UITs), 208-9
Tax-free money-market funds, 221-22
Tax-smart strategies, 330
Tenants in common, 269
Third-World bonds, 191

Time diversification, and risk, 70
Time horizon, and risk tolerance, 9
Timers, 330
Total return, bonds, 172-73
Total returns, 44-45, 52
Trading edges, and large portfolios, 53
Transaction costs, 50-51
Transaction-size effects, on transaction costs, 50-51
Transferable rights, 121, 343
Transfer agent, mutual funds, 20-21
Treasuries, 64
Treasury bills, 215
Treasury Direct system, 178
Trustees, funds, 348-49
Trusts, 269
12b-1 fees, 25, 46, 330

U

Underlying stock market fluctuations, and single-country funds, 141
Underperformance, 97-98
Understanding, need for, 8
Unethical practices, and mutual funds, safety from loss due to, 30
Uniform Gifts to Minors Act (UGMA), 309-10
Unit investment trusts (UITs), 28, 208-9
Unrealized appreciation, and discounts/premiums, 117
U.S. government bond funds, 181, 182-84
U.S. Treasuries, 64
U.S. Treasury bills, 215
Utility funds, 156-57

V

Valuation indicators, 82-83
    earnings multiple, 82
    price-to-book ratio, 82-83
    yield, 83
Value averaging, 89-90
Value investors, 35-36
Value Line Composite Index, 62
Value Line Mutual Fund Survey, The, 34, 74
Value strategy, pursuing, 92
Variable annuities, 240-52
    accumulation phase, 243
    annuitant, 241
    annuitization perils, 246
    beneficiary, 241
    contract owner, 241
    costs, 246-48
    criticisms, weighing, 248-51
    distribution phase, 244
    fixed vs., 242-43
    fund expenses, 247-48
    getting information on, 251
    how they work, 241-43
    insurance-related charges, 247

Variable annuities (cont'd)
    nest egg, building, 244-45
    options, 242
    subaccounts, 242, 243
    surrender charges, 246-47
    1035 exchange, 248
Volatile closed-end funds, trading, 142
Volatility:
    beta, 76-77
        shortcomings of, 77-78
    causes of, 68
    dollar-cost averaging, 86-89, 329
    gauges, 76-79
    large lump sums, investing, 91-92
    profiting from, 81-94
    R-squared, 78
    standard deviation, 76, 78-79
    value averaging, 89-90
Voting on fund matters, 26-27

W

Wall Street Journal, The, 17, 51, 146, 220, 251
    "Credit Markets" column, 187
    "Money Rates" box, 283
"Wall Street Week," 17
Wash sale, 347
Web sites, visiting, 320-21
WEBS (World Equity Benchmark Shares), 142-44, 284,
    343
    annual costs for, 144
    closed-end funds compared to, 143-44
    creation units, 143
    directory of, 142
Wilshire 5000, 62
Withdrawal plans, 275, 296-301, 332
    adjusting withdrawals for inflation, 297-99

    alternatives to, 301
    factors affecting success/failure of, 297
    setting up, 300-301
World economies and stock markets, classification of,
    128
World-stock portfolios, 136-47
    broad-based packages, 137-38
    country-specific index funds, 142-44
    emerging-markets funds, 139
    geographic focus, narrowing, 139-42
    single-country funds, 140-42
        caution about, 140-41
    small-stock funds, 138-39
World Wide Web (WWW):
    Internet vs., 320
    Web sites, visiting, 320-21
Worth magazine, 51
Wrap accounts, 291-92

Y

Yankee CDs, 216
Yield, 83, 194-95
    bonds, 165
    determinants of, 194-95
    payout, 195
    SEC 30-day yield, 195
Yield curve, 166-67
Yield spreads, 175-76
Yield to maturity, bonds, 165

Z

Zero-coupon bonds, 184-85
Zimbabwe, investment opportunities in, 129